James Brown started his working life as an apprentice electrician in steelworks after qualifying at Newcastle University, he worked as an Area Electrical Engineer for ICI. He then joined a large American/Saudi petrochemical company where he was again employed as an engineer responsible for the maintenance of a large crude oil unit. He also worked in Korea on the design of semi-submersible drilling platforms and lectured in Kuwait and Abu Dhabi. Afterwards, he was employed by a university Open Learning Unit where he edited and tutored several courses and authored a variety of course books.

For my family.

James Brown

A View from the Gods

AUSTIN MACAULEY PUBLISHERS™

LONDON * CAMBRIDGE * NEW YORK * SHARJAH

A CIP catalogue record for this title is available from the British Library.

ISBN 9781398457850 (Paperback)
ISBN 9781398457867 (ePub e-book)

www.austinmacauley.com

First Published 2023
Austin Macauley Publishers Ltd®
1 Canada Square
Canary Wharf
London
E14 5AA

Definitions:

Diviocracy – A system of celestial organisation wherein decisions are arrived at by a consensus of the gods, (male and female), on matters affecting their own wellbeing and that of their temporal subjects. A celestial prototype of government by temporal democracy.

Heliopianism – A form of religious culture consisting of a polytheistic pantheon in which the Sun God was held as the chief executive. The position was held on occasions, by the elder or father god of the pantheon and on others by the son of the father of the pantheon.

Chapter 1
The Ancient Egyptians: Myths and Culture
The Sun God and His Adversary

The earliest of the Egyptian Gods arose, according to the writing of the Egyptians[1] in prehistoric times, at a time when neither heaven nor earth existed and when there was nothing, but a boundless primeval water, shrouded in thick darkness; whence at some point, the spirit of the primeval water felt the desire to create. 'The spirit uttered the word, and the world sprang into being in the form envisaged in the mind of the spirit before it uttered the word.'

In this myth, we see the appearance of two ancient archetypal symbols, water of a divine spirit, prevalent in Near Eastern religions as celestial water of fertility. Often, this is depicted as being dispensed by the King, which accorded with the natural order in so far as the king was the fittest, i.e., most fertile, dominant, etc., to lead the tribe or nation and whose seed was often most proliferated.

The archetypal water of a Holy Spirit is still evoked in the ritual of Christian baptism. The other archetype is the 'word', an important symbol in Egyptian cultural and eschatological ritual. Such an archetype was thought to be the source of great magic and the use of such archetypes was the domain of the God of Wisdom—Thoth. The word was an integral part of the ceremony of the 'opening of the mouth' by which the deceased was able to live again in an afterlife.[2]

The archetypal 'word' is still retained in the Gospel of John ('In the beginning was the word') in the same context as the ancient Egyptian myth, a perhaps not surprising fact when considering the cultural origins of Christianity.

The myth, in explaining the origin of life, describes what is in effect, in a sense, the beginning of human psychological life, the dawn of human consciousness.

The primeval water, prior to the uttering of the word, depicts the human collective subconscious undifferentiated by consciousness from the rest of

Nature. The next act in the creation myth was the formation of a germ or egg, from which sprang the Sun god 'within whose shining form was embodied the almighty power of the divine spirit'. This may be compared with the Greek creation myth and others; for example, Tibetan and Polynesian, which feature the creation of an egg.

In the Greek, Eros is born from a silver egg and had golden wings. The egg is the symbolic birth mechanism of the conscious and corresponds to the transition or development of man from a being governed entirely by natural (subconscious) forces of fertility and survival, to one separated from the darkness of the natural world by a facility of conscious enlightenment. (Here, we may note that the spirit in ancient cultures was often depicted as a bird; this inferred an association with the primeval egg of creation.) Thoth, the Egyptian God of Word and Wisdom, is depicted 'opening the mouth of the deceased' from which emerges a bird. Here then is 'the Word' (cf. John) associated with the spirit.

This notion, the awareness of the powerful external forces of Nature controlling survival, is reflected in the inception of the need by man for Gods (and the need to remember stories of survival against such forces which in fact are what myths are).

In their earliest form, gods or powerful external forces were depicted as animals; for example, at Lascaux circa 22000-15000 BC, or the Protosyrian (Anatolian) lion or leopard god circa 8000-6000 BC. Later, and in harmony with man's cultural (psychological) development, the Gods gradually mutated into first, human-animal composites of the Egyptian Ptah cycle circa 3000 BC, and latterly, into an almost totally human pantheon of the Greek Classical Heliopianism.

One might pose the question, 'how was the notion of immortality of Godhood so robust in the face of primitive man hunting and killing his gods, the antelope or bison?' The reason can be found in the myth. Primitive man with little or no individuation was unaware, motivated as the rest of nature, by the collective subconscious, his comprehension of the antelope god was not on an individual antelope basis, but of collective antelope. Man found it a task to kill even a few antelope for survival, let alone conceive of killing all antelope, i.e., the god. Ironically, such a prospect only became a reality with the development of Homo sapiens and the dawn of human (collective) consciousness and individuation.

The latter description of the birth of Ra is attributed to Dr H. Brugsh[3] and closely coincides with the account of the creation in a chapter of the papyrus of Nesi Amsu, part of which was written with the sole purpose of overthrowing the serpent Apep, the great enemy of Ra.

The myths concerning the battles between Ra and Apep (or the Sun god and his adversaries who appear in many forms) can be interpreted on two levels equally validly. On one, the celestial (psychological) level between the forces of enlightenment and primitive fertility, and on a temporal level as the battle between two cultures representing those celestial forces; the latter as we shall see, corroborated by archaeological, mythological and historical evidence.

Apep, also known as Apophis and Nak or Seback, was often depicted as a huge snake that inhabited the primeval waters, there can be little doubt that the snake represents the ancient phallic serpent symbol of fertility in its basic form, though many other symbols were afterwards employed for the same purpose, such as the (serpent) rod of Moses and the Pillar. Ostensibly, the myth enjoins being interpreted on a macrocosmic scale, though its pertinence to the individual psyche of man will not be lost on some readers where the primeval waters represent the unconscious and the serpent, the Eros instinct of fertility and procreation. (The association of serpent and water occurs in many cultures notably in the Sumerian as described in the Epic of Gilgamesh and in the Scandinavian with the Midgarde Serpent.)

In this sense, the myth is applicable on a microcosmic scale, and in this respect, aligns with one of the fundamental concepts of Qaballism. Qaballism is thought to have originated in Judaism, though it will be demonstrated that, not surprisingly, Qaballism, like Judaic monotheism, had its origins in the Egyptian and probably Chaldean or Sumerian Cultures.

In passing, we note that the symbolism of the egg was a central concept of Mediaeval Alchemism and represented the sun and rebirth, a philosophy which contributed greatly to the Renaissance and which embraced much of Qaballistic philosophy, amongst others.

According to the 'Theban Recension', which is more widely known by the misnomer of 'The Book of the Dead', as the collection of papyri gave detailed forms of ritual and preparation for life after death; the deceased is instructed to say:

'My head shall not be separated from my neck, my hair shall not be cut off, my eyebrows shall not be shaved off', which seems to indicate that the deceased wished to keep his body whole.[4] The reason for this is apparent in Chapter XLII of the Book of the Dead whence the deceased says:

'My hair is the hair of Nu
My face is the face of the Disk
My eyes are the eyes of Hathor
My ears are the ears of Apuat
My nose is the nose of Kheuti-Khas
My lips are the lips of Anpu
My teeth are the teeth of Serqet
My neck is the neck of the divine goddess Isis
My hands are the hands of Ba-neb-Tattu
My forearms are the forearms of Neith the Lady of Sais
My backbone is the backbone of Suti
My phallus is the phallus of Osiris
My veins are the veins of the hands of Kher-aba
My chest is the chest of the Mighty one of terror
My belly and back are the belly and back of Sekhet
My buttocks are the buttocks of the eye of Horus
My hips and legs are the hips and legs of Nut
My feet are the feet of Ptah
My fingers and my leg bones are the finger and leg bones of the living gods.
There is no member of my body which is not the member of a god, the god Thoth sheildeth my body altogether, and I am Ra day by day.'

In Judaic Monotheism, this was modified to man being in the likeness of (one) God.

In the above Recension, we have the precise microcosmic man that is the microcosmic replica of the macrocosmic Egyptian culture with its family of Gods. There are two versions of the chapter formed by Nesi Amsu, but both versions have that men and women come into being from tears that fell from the 'Eye' of Kepera (another form of the Sun God). In these versions, the God says, "I made take it up its place in my face and afterwards it rules the whole earth."

Here then is the concept of macrocosmic Gods in the form of the body of a man. The same image of the sun god comprising many limbs, which is an allegory for the cultural unity of the nation, appears in the myth of Osiris who was a later evolvement of Ra.

In the myth, which is recounted later, the body of Osiris is dismembered by Seth (or Set) which therefore is a mythological record of cultural fractionalising or civil/religious strife often resulting in an exodus.

This was a not uncommon occurrence in recorded Egyptian history and can also be seen as involving cultural forces opposed to such a concept of a body or family of gods.

In another papyrus of Hunefer (circa 1350 BC)[5], Ra is identified with Temu:

"Homage to thee O Thou who art Ra when thou risest and Temu when thou settest, thou are the god who came into being in the beginning of time…thou didst create the earth…and thou dost give life into all that therein is."

In the papyrus of Ani (circa 1550 BC)[6], Osiris is identified with Khepera:

"The self-generated one; thou risest on the horizon and sheddest thy beams of light upon the lands of the North and South", and also:

"I am the god of Temu in his rising I am the only one, I came into being in Nu. I am Ra who rose in the beginning."[7]

It is clear from such writings that Ra, Nu, Khepera and Temu were closely identified with each other and, as being the Sun god. From the funeral texts inscribed on the monuments of the Kings of the V and VI dynasties[8] it is apparent that Temu was the great god of Heliopolis, one of the great theological centres of Ancient Egypt.

It was also known as Atmu, the setting sun. Khepera (Kheper-ra = divine beetle) was the 'sun at night' signified by a black scarab beetle. The priests at Heliopolis in setting Temu at the head of their company of gods acknowledged high honour for Ra, Nu and Khepera, hence they succeeded in electing their own god chief of the company whilst attaching the same importance to the older Gods.

"In this way," as Budge states, "the worshippers of Ra who had regarded their god as the oldest of Gods (established as far back as the V dynasty circa 3700 BC as the great god of heaven)[9] would have little cause to complain of the introduction of Temu into the company of the Gods and local vanity of Heliopolis would be gratified."

This mechanism of cosmological accommodation, a sort of 'democratic' polytheism ('diviocracy'), arose naturally in the course of time, for a multiplicity of gods of differing stations and type, similar to the Hellenistic polytheistic culture which itself drew heavily on Ancient Egyptian cultural ideas.

Ra, the meaning of whose name is lost in antiquity, was supposed to sail over heaven in two boats the ATET and MATET boat until noon, then in the SEKET boat from noon until sunset. Such symbolism is not far removed from the Greek chariot of Apollo, though with significantly different cultural ramifications.

The chariot was unknown to the Egyptians at the time of early Ra worship and the boat would reflect the culture's main mode of communication and hence indicate some maritime nature of the culture. (Subsequent to completing the draft manuscript, a boat was found buried next to the great pyramid, a possible indication of its importance in Egyptian eschatology.)

Ra at his rising (inception of the cult) was attacked by Apep, a mighty dragon or serpent of evil and darkness, whom he dispatched with fiery darts, destroying the monster by fire and his attendant fiends whose bodies were hacked to pieces.

The myth refers on one level to the emergence of man from the dark state of fertility and phallicism to the state of awareness and enlightenment as symbolised by the god Ra. On a temporal level, it describes an adversary culture opposed to Heliopianism. The fiery darts is a symbolism used throughout history to represent divine spirit and knowledge (c.f. tongues of flame) and enlightenment (arrow) both symbols (knowledge and enlightenment are attributes associated with Osiris as we shall see presently) can be often found in Renaissance Philosophical Alchemy.

The 'hacking to pieces' is an allegorical allusion to the actual military battle or battles which resulted from the cultural conflict.

The battle however was not conclusive, for Osiris, a later embodiment of the Sun god, is destroyed by Set his brother (c.f. Cane and Abel) but is restored by his wife Isis and son, Horus. Reflections of the same myth were incorporated in Christian Theology in the myth of Lucifer and the celestial battle of angels. The fact that the battle was inconclusive is an accurate description because the myths show time and again that no one culture completely vanquishes the other.

Ancient Egyptian history is a long story of bi-cultural internecine warfare of which more will be said later. The eternal struggle between the adversaries of this dual culture is a central theme of this book.

The concept of Celestial Union was conceived in the Egyptian culture, as all the gods joining one body. An inscription in the tomb of Seti I (1370 BC) has all the principal gods forming Ra's body[10] though as a concept it was much older, for the myth of Osiris has his body as representing the gods. The Greeks broadened this concept of a body of Gods to the concept of a family. It will become apparent that myths are pictorial histories of single or recurring real temporal events and the characters or symbols contained therein, whether human, animal, vegetable or mineral can represent:

- a single person
- a collective group often represented as a King
- a tribe or nation
- a culture

In the struggle of Set versus Osiris or Apep versus Ra, we see in the oldest of myths, an attempt at usurpation of the Sun God, the chief executive of the celestial pantheon or body of gods. This attempted usurpation appears in all Near Eastern heliopian cultures. On a temporal plane, the king, regarded as divine, was held to be the representative incarnate of the Sun God.

Traditionally, in the early dynasties of Egypt, the King adopted the Horus name, the victorious son of Osiris. At the beginning of the Second Dynasty (c 2770-2649 BC.) Peribsen, the only one to do so, changed his name from a Horus name Sekhemmib to Seth (Typhon the serpent, in Greek) which would indicate a shift in cultural emphasis. It may represent the ascendancy of the serpent culture of the Delta, a culture that figured largely in the bicultural struggle existing in Ancient Egypt.

The next king (or two kings) was called Khasekhem, meaning power of Horus and Khasekhemwy, which refers to the two powers of Horus and Seth. On objects from that period, figures of both gods can be seen and the sentence 'the two lords are at rest in him'[11], indicating an end to some period of cultural strife and the coexistence of two cultures. It is not until the 4th dynasty (c 2575-2465 BC) that the titles of Ra and Son of Ra reappear, coinciding with the building of the true pyramids and the prevalence of the solar religions.

We shall see that these names probably indicate the precedence obtained by a culture where Seth is the chief deity associated with the Delta and the infusion of an alien culture. The Hyksos manifested a later wave of the culture. The Hyksos were invaders who established the 15th Dynasty in the 2nd Intermediate Period (c 1640-1532 BC).

The infusion during the Fourth Dynasty probably corresponds with those referred to in Greek mythology dealt with in a later chapter.

It is in the reign of Radjedef that the name Ra is reintroduced as appropriate title for the king. The first appearance however was with Raneb of the 2nd dynasty, the predecessor of Peribsen. We see therefore the incidence of a real temporal cultural struggle at the very boarders of Egyptian prehistory, reflected allegorically in the myth as a record of history, though more often they record pre-history events.

The cultural struggle between Ra and Seth in later myths becomes the struggle between Osiris and Seth and Seth and Horus indicating that the conflict between the heliopian culture and its opponent was not an isolated incident, but a continuous conflict throughout Ancient Egyptian history. Nor was it confined to only that culture, but can be seen in all the Near Eastern heliopian cultures with remarkably similar symbolism.

Seth is more often described as being contemporary with Osiris, a later form of the Sun God, and Apep the serpent therefore is an earlier manifestation of the forces of Seth the adversary. Later we see a reappearance of Apophis or Apep as the name of a Hyksos King. Such a title indicates a change in cultural ascendancy to the culture of phallicism, which serves as a clue to the origins of the Hyksos, that being Crete, whence from prehistory, a fertility cult had predominated.

It is likely therefore that the earliest myths of Ra and Apophis referred to much earlier cultural incursions into Egyptian Heliopianism by the alien culture, almost certainly from Crete or and emergent Mycenean-Cretan Dominion.

Apep, symbolising phallicism of the dark waters in conflict with Ra, the symbol of life and enlightenment are macroscopic manifestations of collective unconscious and collective consciousness (i.e., the culture) which on the microscopic level represent the struggle between the subliminal and supraliminal selves.

In the papyrus of Ani can be seen the company of the gods seated above the Judgement proceedings, such a group was termed a Paut, which is interpreted as meaning 'original stuff'[12] out of which everything was made. A paut contained usually nine gods, but on occasions, ten or eleven and in the papyrus of Ani, twelve gods are shown though only ten thrones. Later, we shall see the paut in another culture, the Sumerian, from which the Egyptian culture was in large part derived.

The gods are shown appropriately above the proceedings, and hold the sceptre of authority to reinforce the visually conveyed concept of celestial power and authority. Osiris, larger to represent the executive of celestial power, holds three sceptres, besides the divine sceptre, he also holds the crook representing caring and welfare, and the flail representing authority to punish. It is of note that temporal kings were preserved and represented in life as having the two sceptres, crook and flail.

If Osiris represented the sun, and Isis the moon, it would be reasonable to assume that the Paut represented the planets, or more likely the stars. It was not unusual for the celestial executive to hold the title 'Lord of the Stars'; this was the title of Dagan, the celestial executive and chief God of the Protosyrian heliopian Pantheon, a contemporary cosmogony with the Egyptian[13].

Joseph's Dreams

In the Biblical story of Joseph, reference is also made to the celestial cosmogeny of stars in his dream (Gen XXXVII-9) and also in the Koran.[14]

In the biblical version, "and he dreamed yet another dream…and behold, the Sun and the Moon and the eleven stars made obeisance to me." We shall see later that a similar experience occurs to Gilgamesh, the hero of Sumerian heliopian mythology. The eleven stars are easily identified as the Celestial Paut.

In order to understand the symbolism and cultural forces at work, it is necessary to understand the cultural conflict that existed in Egypt. These cultures were to become known or identified as the cultures of 'the North and South' The Southern or Upper Egyptian culture was heliopian and the North or Delta culture who at one time, conquered enough of the Delta (not for the first time) to establish Hyksos dynasties. The cultural link is the ancient fertility cult, which in ancient Crete (see chapter 8) was characterised by a sacred pillar and a fertility goddess. We read in Genesis regarding Jacob's vow (Gen XXIX-22):

"And this stone which I have set for a pillar, shall be God's house."

It is known that the Hyksos also settled in Palestine and that Jacob's migration may have been to Egypt and may have fallen somewhere in the eighteenth or more likely the seventeenth century BC in connection with the Hyksos migration.[15]

Joseph, it is related in the Bible, married the daughter of Poti-Pherah priest of ON (Gen XLII-45). It is likely that the Pharaoh, who gave the woman to Joseph, was possibly even a Hyksos Pharaoh and that Poti-Pherah was, or was related to, the Pharaoh, as Pherah has similar etymological derivation to pharaoh, from 'PER' meaning 'house of' (cf. Peribsen).

On was the Biblical name for Anu or Iunu which, in Ancient Egypt, was a pillar or Obelisk. Heliopolis was the centre of the Anu cult, in the apex of the Delta, the area occupied by the Hyksos. The ramifications of connections between the tribe of Abraham and the Hyksos is interesting in many aspects but primarily in relation to the cultural conflict that existed and continued to exist throughout Ancient Egyptian history.

We are not told why Abraham left what was at Ur, a Heliopian culture, but indications are that Abraham, if not of royal birth, was certainly of some worthy or noble birth. In Genesis (XIII-2) when expelled from Egypt, 'Abraham was very rich in cattle, silver and in gold'. His forces in the battle of four kings against five (Gen XIV) are decisive and he is referred to as 'Lord' by the Hittite (Gen XXIV-II).

The special status afforded to Isaac and Jacob by the God Yahweh and the elevation of Joseph and Moses, is in keeping with the existing concept of the divine association of King's, right through to Christ, and his association with the royal house. Circumstances surrounding Joseph indicate nobility; that he and Benjamin were favourites of Jacob is the Biblical expression for heirs and hostility from his siblings and his near assassination, would not be an uncommon circumstance (cf. Jacob and Esau) surrounding dynastic power struggles.

In the Koran, Joseph is referred to as a 'man of learning'[16] a privilege afforded only to nobility. Joseph comes, like Moses, to reside in the house of the Royal Family who talks of adopting him as a son[17]. The prince's name was Potiphar, of similar construction to Poti-Pherah, his father-in-law. In this respect it is interesting to note that Moses is akin to Remeses (or Ramesses), without the acknowledgement of the Sun god Ra.

Whilst in prison, allegedly for seducing the wife of Potophar, Joseph is asked to interpret two dreams of the biblical royal chief butler and royal chief baker who according to the Koran, are referred to as two young men sent to jail with him. It is here (Gen XL) we see one of the earliest accounts of oneiromancy or dream interpretation, prevalent in the Bible, being used to promote a particular cultural cause, with Joseph as the Hierophant.

The butler dreamt of a three-branched vine which blossoms and fruits, from which he presses grapes into the Pharaoh's cup and offers it to Pharaoh. The baker dreams the Pharaoh is wearing a stack of three white baskets on his head containing all manner of bakemeats from which the birds of the air feed. Joseph gives a favourable interpretation to the latter dream rendering simplistically the common symbol of three being three days whence they would meet their respective fates. However on closer examination we see the grapes represent fertility, filling the cup or spirit of the pharaoh whilst the triple baskets alludes to the Triple Crown of Egypt and its bounties. (See chapter 2) Prior to bicultural Egypt, there were, according to an ancient chronicler, three kingdoms, the Hawk, the Reed and the Bee Kingdoms.

This appears to place Joseph in Egyptian history at a time when the Kingdoms were still extant. This could be relevant, as later on in the Bible, we see that Moses uses knowledge of the former three kingdoms to perform what appears to be a miraculous parting of the waters to effect an escape and ensure survival (See Chapter 8). This is an interesting example of the importance of the cultural mythological repository utilised for survival.

Such knowledge would have been handed down in the culture which has become for that ability, pre-eminent in preserving traditions of which the Qaballah was one such aural tradition.

Such a long tradition of scholarship must afford some insights of the human psychological condition.

The pharaoh is spiritual and temporal provider to the subjects of his realm (i.e., the birds, being a common Heliopian symbol for the spirit). The king is spiritual and temporal leader. Joseph then, is promoting the cult of fertility, the 'ON' cult, which we shall see was associated with the God Amen, the 'Hidden One'[18] which, in Phallic display, was the god Min. One of the symbols of the God was the ram.

Symbolic ram sphinxes can be seen at Karnak (modern Thebes) which was the main centre of worship of the God Amen for many centuries.

The cult of the sacred ram existed in Ur in Sumeria, the reputed birthplace of Abraham, excavated by Wooley[19]. Ultimately, Joseph, the patriarch's descendant, under the protection of the cult of the 'Pillar of On' is influential enough to bring his tribe safely into Egypt, probably the Delta, where subsequent Hyksos power was to be manifested. The fertility cult of Joseph's time seems to suggest that even in the time of Joseph, there was in the Delta, a (Cretan?) settlement of some proportions.

"'Welcome to Egypt safe if Allah Wills' Whence this said Joseph to his father (Jacob) is the meaning of my vision; My lord has fulfilled it."[20]

It is quite possible that Joseph's royal connections formed the basis of Moses' 'claim to challenge Pharaoh'. Moses' use of the serpent rod (Exodus VII-

19

10) is compatible with fertility cult symbolism, being also a symbol of the Delta Lower Egyptian Kingdom and Amen's daughter[21].

In another part of the story of Joseph, we see the appearance of the often-used archetypal cloak or robe in Judaic-Christian symbolism, still extant in Christian coronation ritual. Joseph's multicoloured robe would be symbolic of chieftain authority, the variegated colours representing the tribes, symbolised by his brothers, the Biblical progenitors, Joseph therefore would be an obvious candidate for removal in a dynastic struggle; a modus operandi being the rule rather than the exception in archaic politics of succession.

Towards the end of the saga of Joseph, we see an instance where Joseph removes Jacob's blindness by casting his coat over Jacob's face. In the intrinsic symbolic communication of the time, this can be interpreted as Jacob ultimately appreciating the dynastic strategy of Joseph, and in this vein, may be compared with the scales dropping from Paul's eyes on the road to Damascus.

Pre-Christian heliopian cosmogonies were not without their share of dynastic strife ostensibly, at the lowest level, involving blood lineage, but on examination, it becomes clear that at a higher level, these struggles were between cultural adversaries or opposites. These were characterised by, on the one hand, reaction and autocracy, with the persistent use of primitive animal archetypes, examples of which still characterise contemporary religious symbolism in such phrases as 'Lamb of God', and on the other, progress, changing symbolism and diviocracy (celestial pluralism or 'democracy').

The Heliopolis company of Gods was a development of an older company of gods of the Memphite family, most of whom, if not all, were represented as some form of animal. This was an indication that they reflected a pre-human or part human collective concept of man, not necessarily in the biological sense, but in the psycho-cultural developmental sense. Gods, representing human creatures of antiquity, consisted almost entirely of animal nature oriented. They acted on the unconscious, inducing the individual (as current gods must still do), to behave in concert, like a herd, motivated by survival, and ergo, fertility.

Thus is formed a sea of collective controllable unconsciousness (a part of the human condition that changes immeasurably slowly, if at all and susceptible, all the while, to ancient motivating archetypal symbols).

The creator god of this cycle was Ptah (the only god to appear in human form) who was a form of Ra, the Sun god. He was represented in the heliopian cycle in human form and, as such, represented a raising of a cultural level of consciousness, the inference being, human nature was divine by comparison with man's animal nature.

In the 'Book of the Dead' (more correctly called 'Going Forth By Day'), Ptah is alluded to as having 'opened the mouth' of the gods, a ritual that persisted through the ages as forming part of the funerary rites. This involved giving eternal life to the deceased, and hence marks the beginning of a new cosmological epoch. Many dual-natured gods were retained in the later pantheon, possibly to accommodate the cultural requirements of the least enlightened of the populace.

Ptah in his earthly manifestation, was the Apis Bull, a potent fertility symbol, still present in the Christian and formally pre-Christian celebration of birth and renewal in the Christmas crib.

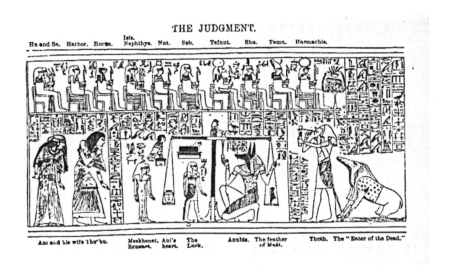

The Judgement in the Maati Hall showing the Paut of Gods
With Kind Acknowledgements to Sir A.E. Wallis Budge and Routledge and
Kegan Paul

The Sun God Usurped

Such then are only some of the principal gods in the Egyptian cosmogony which, because of its exoteric nature, embraced hundreds of deities. Such a pantheon was not without its usurpers, indeed, in all the contemporary heliopian cosmogonies of the Near East, usurpation of the ancient order is a common feature.

In the myth of Osiris, one of the oldest Egyptian myths, we see the vanquishing and the restoration of the cosmogony. As we said, the myth has its roots in pre-recorded history of real cultural events. In the accounts taken from Squires translation of Plutarch[22] Osiris is depicted as a wise and benevolent King:

"Osiris being now become King of Egypt, applied himself towards civilising his countrymen, by turning them from their former indigent and barbarous course of life, he moreover taught them how to cultivate and improve the fruits of the earth. He gave them a body of laws to regulate their conduct by and instructed them in reverence and worship which they were to pay the gods. With the same disposition he afterwards travelled over the rest of the world inducing people everywhere to submit to his discipline, not induced by compelling them by force or arms, but persuading them to yield to the strength of his reasons which were conveyed to them in the most agreeable manner, in hymns and songs accompanied by instruments of music."

Typically the modus operandi of the Sun god is enlightenment and education applied to civilised ends, and here he represents the Ancient Egyptian heliopian culture in its unifying infancy.

The myth has clearly a literal and an allegorical interpretation. The literal has a real king representing the culture, in the mould of Hammurabi or the unifier Narmer (through without the military dimensions), but clearly, from the point of view of some of the bizarrely absurd features that become apparent subsequently in the myth, the literal interpretation becomes inadequate.

Its allegory on the other hand, of Osiris representing the heliopian culture as being established in Egypt, is on the cultural level. The myth is the glass slipper that fits the foot, for it becomes a coherent story of the introduction of a Heliopian culture in Egypt, not by conquest, but by reason, i.e., tolerant enlightened incorporation of other cultures, which at some point is usurped by another culture. The usurping culture is a fertility cult represented by Seth (or the Greek Typhon, the Serpent). This destroys the unity of heliopianism, allegorised by the dismembering of the body of Osiris.

The myth, as representing the machro-cultural aspect of history, is not constrained in its validity, as would be the literal interpretation by the necessity of complying with historical chronological time. On the contrary it effects the allegory by intimating epochs, thereby elevating the sense from the individual historical chronology to the cultural epochal, where, for example, a king represents a nation, a cultural dynasty, an epoch.

In the Osiris myth, Osiris is enticed into a beautiful chest by Seth and seventy-two other guests at a banquet, including a certain queen of Ethiopia, Aso. In a manner reminiscent of the fairy tale, he is promptly nailed and sealed in lead and the chest is thrown into the Nile.

The chest drifts to the sea, where the waves carry it to the coast of Byblos, and becomes gently lodged in the branches of a tamarisk bush. In a short time, the bush grows into a large and beautiful tree embracing the chest, enclosing it on every side. The king of the land cuts the tree down and makes the trunk, where the chest is concealed, into a pillar to support the roof of his house.

In this part of the myth we see, veiled by literal absurdity, the continuation of the allegory where the heliopian culture symbolised by the chest containing the sun god, is embraced by a tree. The tree is an important central archetype typical of kindred heliopian cultures and represents the Tree of life of Mesopotamian and derived cultures, which is often depicted with a winged sun.

The tree is felled and incorporated as a pillar. The pillar was a typical and central archetypal symbol of ancient Cretan culture that was predominantly, a fertility culture and which, expanded prior to and during, the early second millennium BC into Egypt, the Southern Mediterranean, Anatolian and Levant coasts (e.g. as Hyksos in Egypt). The pillar therefore represents the containment or ascendancy over Egyptian heliopianism by the fertility culture.

The myth continues with Isis, the wife of Osiris, after a long and anguished search, locating the chest and is granted it by Astarte the Queen of Byblos (Astarte-a Canaanite fertility goddess, being a corresponding goddess to Isis in Canaanite and kindred cosmologies).

Isis opens it and 'takes out what she wanted'. This according to another version[23] is the essence of Osiris who, although dead, by the power of Thoth comes alive briefly and enables Isis to conceive of a son Horus. Isis replaces the chest in a secure place, only for it to be found by Seth, who proceeds to dismember the body of Osiris.

Here the regeneration of the heliopian culture proceeds. Thoth the keeper of words or more accurately, ideas or thought causes the resurrection of the culture and its continuity, symbolised by the Son Horus. It is appropriate that a renaissance takes place through learning after a Dark Age but this was simply one of the typically underlying enlightened philosophical basis of heliopianism.

This cultural mechanism, that is, the idea of resurrection of the culture by the birth of a son of the God, was later adopted by Christian mythology.

Horus, with the help of Thoth, would defeat Seth in (cultural) battle and re-establish the heliopian cosmology. However, for the moment Seth decimates the culture, symbolised by the mutilation of the body of Osiris. All the parts, with (naturally) the exception of the penis, representative of the usurping fertility cult, and one time member of the integrated cosmogeny, are recovered by Isis and buried in separate sepulchres.

This is 'so that Seth may despair at finding the true one' and so the culture begins to consolidate.

Seth flings the penis of Osiris into the Nile, which is entirely compatible with the instrument of regeneration being associated symbolically with water, representing fertility (shown often being dispensed by the Goddess Ishtar or the king, as a fountain of life or water from a jar).

The theme of consolidation prior to the decisive battle, proceeds in the myth with Osiris returning from the dead to train his son Horus in the battles against Seth, a literal absurdity, but perfectly tenable in the machro-cultural context. This is akin to the return to Greco-Roman classicism of the Renaissance and indeed, indicative of the same cultural mechanism.

The final part of the myth is concerned with the struggles between Seth and Horus in which the latter ultimately proves victorious and Seth is taken prisoner.

At this point a curious episode is recounted concerning uncharacteristic treachery of Isis, but which has its parallel in the Biblical story of Adam and Eve.

Isis 'far from putting Seth to death, even loosened his bonds and set him at liberty, which action so incensed Horus, that he laid his hands upon her and pulled off the ensign of royalty which she wore on her head and instead thereof Thoth (Greek Hermes) clapped on a helmet made in the shape of an ox's head.

Some sources claim Horus actually decapitated Isis; her head being replaced by that of an ox by Thoth; from this Isis and Hathor (A fertility goddess with bull's horns) became one and the same.

It is in the same context that Eve in the biblical creation myth is punished, in the sense that she ate of the tree of life, i.e., is necessarily associated with fertility.

In the Osiris myth the ox head identifies Isis with fertility, at the same time reducing her to something less that total god (a concept to be found in Sumerian mythology) for her consorting with Seth.

As the cosmogeny, developed Isis as goddess was re-established and Hathor became a separate goddess. This was in keeping with the development from the

Ptah cycle to the Osirian Company of Gods, hence the helmet and the head versions of the myth.

With the ascendancy of Horus, Seth, in what would seem a last-ditch effort, publicly accuses Horus of bastardy. This is possibly an allusion to Nephthys progeny by Osiris, but more realistically an attempt by the usurper to destroy the concept of a re-established heliopianism in the imagery of Osiris returning from the dead.

The ability of a hero to return from a journey to Hades in the heliopian cosmogonies, particularly the Greek and Roman, became almost a standard requisite for godhood, and features in Christian mythology. It is Thoth who assists Horus to obtain the judgement of the gods themselves, establishing the legitimacy of Horus.

A similar ambiguity regarding the fatherhood and Son of God exists in Christian mythology.

Seth was clearly identified by the Greeks, as being identical with Typho, the serpent. An incident in the myth described by Plutarch, relates how, among the great numbers who were continually deserting from Typho's party, was his concubine Thueris.

A serpent pursuing her as she was coming over to Orus (Horus), was slain by her soldiers, the memory of which action say they, is still preserved in the cord which is thrown into the midst of their assemblies and then chopped into pieces.

This episode has echoes in Exodus (VII 12) when Moses and Aaron throw down their rods which turn into serpents.

Seth is also represented in mythology as a hippopotamus or water horse and as an Ass[24], archetypes of religious power. Water horses in Greek Mythology were associated with Poseidon, originally a Cretan God. In some versions of the myth, at the victory by Horus, Seth is said to have been deprived of his testicle, mythological language for his phallic fertility cult being emasculated or defeated.

Seth is described in Egyptian texts as possessing of strong, if somewhat perverse sexual powers[25] and was indeed a fertility god. He is often alluded to in the ritual of the 'Baptism of Pharaoh' in which, together with Horus, he pours water over the Kings head, the water, a recognisable archetype especially to Freudians, is the celestial water of fertility or procreative power.

In the battles that took place between Horus and Seth, one is described in which Horus harpoons Seth in his guise as a hippopotamus. The story, which relates to the history of the Hyksos occupation of Egypt, is called the 'story of Apophis and Sequenenre'. It describes how the Hyksos king Apophis sends a message to the Theban king Sequenenre to stop molesting the hippopotami in the palace pools there because the noise of their roars kept him awake at night 'undoubtedly an allegorical reference to the old religious struggle'[26].

Here then, a fertility cult in the form of Seth or the serpent Typho, is associated with the Hyksos, who occupied the Egyptian Delta circa 1440-1500 BC, and probably not for the first time. The Hyksos were also to be found in Palestine during the same period and were known to worship a serpent goddess[27].

Apophis was the name of the great serpent and enemy of Ra the Sun God.

Within a few years of Ta'o II or Sequenenre, the Hyksos were driven out of Egypt by the Pharaoh Amose who reigned after Sequenenre's successor Kamose.

Here then are mythological clues to a cultural struggle whose culmination is possibly described in the Bible as the Exodus.

It stands also as mythological evidence for cultural struggle between the heliopian diviocracy and monotheistic autocracy, which was a continuing feature of the Egyptian culture. Egypt it is well documented was perennially attempting to unite the two 'Kingdoms of the North and South', Upper Egypt being largely Heliopian and the Delta the stronghold of the fertility culture.

Nor was the struggle confined to Egyptian heliopianism, but was a feature of all contemporary solar cultures. This may seem surprising but is to be expected if one considers that cultures are simply collective man or macrocosmic man. What happens in one heliopian culture will happen in others, as such cultures are simply collectives of the human condition with the same cultural mores. As one can see with the Egyptian, Greek and Roman each of these cultures grew from the previous culture to form a heliopian cultural continuum. This had lasted for five millennia but the cultural battle was about to be lost to autocratic monotheism which eventually overtook the Roman culture in the form of Christianity.

Such cultural conflicts in the human condition arising from man's dual nature (animal/human and consciousness/unconsciousness) ultimately are part of the driving mechanism for survival. At the cultural level the same competitive struggle is present but the psychological forces when harnessed as they were early on in man's development and are still today in the form of mega-religious affiliations, have a sea scale potency and tidal nature.

In the Aztec tradition 'three times the human race destroyed itself through pride and a new sun was made by the gods'[28]. That must be about every two millennia. Clearly in this eternal? Celestial battle victory has shifted sides on several occasions in ancient times. In the first millennia we saw victory pass to the dark forces of monotheistic tyranny. As the victor writing history, we can look upon the myth of Lucifer losing his battle with the forces of the monotheistic god as the heliopian forces of light fighting against the total power of a despot losing that particular round of the eternal battle.

References Chapter 1

[1] Sir A.E. Wallis Budge, Egyptian Religion, page 22

[2] M. Baines and J. Malek, The Atlas of Ancient Egypt, page 219

[3] Sir A.E. Wallis Budge, Egyptian Religion, page 23

[4] ibid, page 76/77

[5] ibid, page 31

[6] ibid, page 33

[7] Sir A.E. Wallis Budge, Book of the Dead, page 93

[8] Sir A.E. Wallis Budge, Egyptian Religion, page 89

[9] ibid, page 28

[10] ibid, page 101

[11] M. Baines and J. Malek, The Atlas of Ancient Egypt, page 32

[12] ibid, page 28

[13] P. Matthiae EBLA, An Empire Rediscovered, page 187

[14] Koran Trans, N. J. Dawood, page 38

[15] W.F. Albright, The Archaeology of Palestine, page 83

[16] Koran 12-32 Trans N. J. Dawood, page 41

[17] ibid12-21, page 40

[18] Christiane Desroches, Noblecourt Tutankhamen, page 15

[19] Sir Leonard Wooley, Ur of the Chaldees, page 47

[20] Koran 12-97 Trans, N. J. Dawood, page 46

[21] Christiane Desroches, Noblecourt Tutankhamen, page 188

[22] Greace et Anglica Squire from Plutarchi de Iside et Ostride Cambridge 1744, page 42

[23] Ibid, page 56

[24] The Encyclopaedia of World Mythology, Octopus Press, page 99

[25] ibid

[26] T.G.H. James, The Archaeology of Ancient Egypt, page 66

[27] W.F. Albright, The Archaeology of Palestine, page 97

[28] The Encyclopaedia of World Mythology, Octopus Press, page 71

Appendix 1. The Caballa (Qaballah)

The word caballa is Hebrew for 'Tradition' and describes an ancient esoteric Jewish mystical tradition of philosophy containing strong elements of pantheism, and yet is akin to Neo-Platonism. It was initially an aural tradition and Caballistic writing reached its peak between the 13th and 16th centuries AD. Caballism, it is claimed by many writers on subject, originated in Chaldea. Central to Caballism is a symbol system known as 'The Tree of Life' (a symbol found in many early Mediterranean cultures) which is an attempt to reduce to diagrammatic form every force and factor in the manifested universe and the soul of man, and to correlate them to each other and reveal them as a map.

The Tree of Life of the Caballa is a compendium of science, psychology, philosophy and theology intended as a means of or aid to enlightenment of students. The philosophy is concerned with the relationship between the microcosmic person and macrocosmic man. There is also the notion of spiritual progression through 'spheres' of knowledge, awareness and spirituality to higher planes. This is symbolised on the Tree of Life by 10 Sephira, each having several attributes such as a title, magical image often male or female and an associated archangel. Each Sephiroth has also and associated virtue and vice, a correspondence or position on the body of microcosmic man, a spiritual experience, representative symbols, corresponding relevant Tarot cards and associated colours.

The sephira are connected by paths along which the adept progresses and the sephira align into three pillars represented by Severity, Mercy and Mildness. The philosophy contains the concept of the recognition and reconciling of physical, psychological and spiritual opposites. Thus the opposite pillars of mercy and severity are reconciled in the central pillar of mildness. Each sephiroth corresponds to one of the planets of the ancient Zodiac as:

Malkuth – Earth
Yesod – Moon
Hod – Mercury
Netzach – Venus
Tipareth – Sun
Geburah – Mars
Chesed – Jupiter
Binah – Saturn

Chockmah – The Zodiac
Kether – The Crown

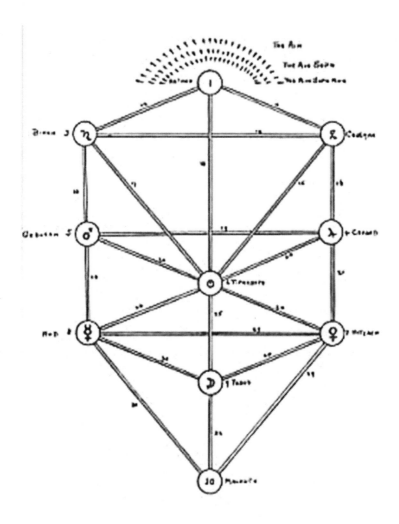

Tree of Life and the 32 paths
(With Kind Acknowledgement to Dion Fortune and Ernest Benn Ltd)

Chapter 2
Ancient Psychology and Ancient Struggles

According to Manetho[1] a third century BC Egyptian chronicler of Egyptian history, pre-dynastic Egypt was split into three kingdoms; the Hawk kingdom of Upper Egypt, the Reed kingdom or Middle kingdom and the Bee kingdom of the Delta. Circa 3200 BC, the Scorpion King of the Hawk kingdom, conquered first the Reed king then conquered the Bee kingdom. He became the first pharaoh of a united Egypt, his name was Menes. The symbol of the Bee King was, naturally, the bee, his crown, the red crown and he ruled from the Red House, the Ancient Egyptian for house, "Pero", being the root of the word pharaoh.

The bee symbol, often to be seen in king's titles, became a hieroglyph not only of the bee, but also meant "the North", i.e., the Delta[2].

The symbol of the Reed King was the papyrus reed, he wore a white crown and his palace was a white house. The symbol of a plant or reed was also the hieroglyphic symbol of "the South." (We shall recall this when Moses and the Exodus are examined later.)

The Hawk kingdom, whose symbol was the hawk or vulture, was in Upper Egypt located at the first cataract bordering Nubia. Throughout succeeding dynasties, the titles of the kings laid great stress on their being "Kings of the North and South", indicative of the long process of consolidation of the kingdoms in the face of internal political and culturally divisive forces, which are apparent in the long history of Egypt. To this end, the Pasekhemty crown of the pharaoh became a combination of the red and white crowns of the ancient kingdoms.

This symbolic fusion was not the only type of symbolic display to be employed by the rulers of Egypt.

Incorporated in the Nemset crown were the cobra and eagle, the latter was the symbol of the Upper kingdom, i.e., the south of Egypt, but in more general terms, represented from the earliest times and almost universally in heliopian cosmogonies, the spirit, and continued to do so throughout succeeding centuries.

The cobra or snake was representative of the Northern Kingdom or the Delta, and its display had a certain versatility of symbolism. At the primal level, it represented the phallus or fertility, which would be culturally appropriate for the Delta, especially with its Hyksos culture derived from Crete.

The mythology and archaeology of Crete abounds with goddesses, particularly fertility goddesses, associated with the snake. They are either holding a snake, or clothed in snake tasselled garments.

The snake, it is often postulated, represented rebirth, symbolised by the sloughing of its skin, which if true, such a concept would not be at odds with Egyptian eschatology. However, the cultural basis for the snake is to be found in Sumerian mythology from which culture, the Egyptian was, if not wholly, then at least in part, derived. The tree of life was a central symbol of the Sumerian culture as it was in many of the Middle Eastern cultures, including Egypt.

The Sumerian myth of "Etana and the Eagle"[3], concerns the re-establishment of Kingship on the earth after The Flood. If we discard the veil of literalism, which leads to the absurd, the flood can be viewed as the means by which kingship and hence heliopianism, by virtue of kingship representing the celestial executive, was re-established.

The Flood represents some cultural tide. Such tides were ever present and most often manifested themselves as struggles between the wielders of psychological power and those controlling temporal power in the monarchical framework, most usually as military conflicts.

In the primitive microcosm, this was Chief versus Medicine Man, and at the macrocosmic level, the religious establishment versus kingship. This cultural struggle forms one of the themes of this work.

In the myth of Etana at the "beginning of things", the eagle and the serpent had sworn a solemn oath of friendship. The eagle had its nest and its young at the top of the tree (of Life?) and the serpent and its young at the bottom. The eagle breaks the oath by devouring the young of the serpent (the invasion of one culture by another).

Shamash, the Sun God, shows the serpent how to ensnare the eagle and imprison it in a pit, which the serpent successfully implements. Ultimately, the eagle is released by Etana in return for which, the eagle promises to carry the king designate to the fertility goddess.

From the goddess, the king will receive the plant of birth (fertility) ensuring him a succession, the condition for receiving the kingship offered by the Gods.

The image of a tree with an eagle at the top and serpent at the bottom would in fact be representative of the state of Egypt, but undoubtedly referred to some similar ancient Mesopotamian cultural alignment or experience that shall be revealed later. Nonetheless, it is a measure of Mesopotamian cultural influence in Ancient Egypt that the eagle and cobra were so prominent, there were, as one would expect, other cultural influences in the formation of the Ancient Egyptian culture.

The Mesopotamian influence is further illustrated when the myth describes the insignia of kingship being laid before the head of the celestial pantheon, Anu.

This comprises the sceptre, crown, tiara and crook. The sceptres, in the form of a flail and the distinctive shepherd's crook are characteristic emblems of eternal kingship in Ancient Egyptian funerary rites. In such a cultural context, the sojourn of Abraham or indeed, the Israelites in Egypt and the serpent rods of Moses and Aaron, need not be viewed as being in such a culturally alien environment.

It is curious that in the Biblical myth in which the serpent, held by some traditions to represent wisdom[4] and therefore being naturally associated with the Tree of Knowledge, is cast as a bad lot, and there is in the Bible, a severe admonition against the desiring of knowledge to be found.

Another particular feature of Egyptian king's adornment was the peculiar proboscoid plaited beard, esoterically shaped as such, to resemble the proboscis of the bee. In the hieroglyphic of the bee, the proboscis is prominent, and its presence on the pharaoh, was the symbolic archetype of the head of the ancient Bee Kingdom.

Such a beard was also referred to as the "beard of the Gods"[5], that is, representing divinity. The bee was also used as part of the king's title "King of the North and South" wherein the bee was representative of half the kingdom, that being the North or the Delta. The wearing of the sacred beard postdates the unification of the country and would be compatible with a more advanced and sophisticated age of applied mass-psychology.

The Delta was the centre of various fertility cults, one of the major ones being the bovine cult of Hathor or Isis, so in the mists of the time, the Bee and Cow would be representative of a land of "Milk and Honey."

Perhaps the most major feature of the Nemset crown or headdress was the blue lapis lazuli and gold barred lapelled "wrutra", akin to the modern Arab headwear. It is this particular crown of headdress that characterises Egyptian mummified kings or indeed, Ancient Egyptians in the popular mind.

Because the Nemset was central to the funerary rites, it must have been associated with cultural religious significance rather different from the Pasekhemty Crown, which was often shown being worn by the pharaoh in battle. It is the Nemset that is most often associated with kingship and its authority, the crook and flail.

The lapis lazuli and gold lined Nemset, brings to mind the mane of a lion, which was precisely what it was intended to portray, for it was the animal archetype which completed the quartet of cultural archetypes consisting of the, the lion, Nekhabet, the eagle, Wadjet, the serpent and the bee. These were the most ancient cultural ingredients of the Ancient Egyptian culture.

The Nemset headdress is evidence of the highly sophisticated nature of the socio-psychological techniques employed by the ancient Egyptians. (A fact that one might argue is not at odds with the evolutionary theories of J B S Haldane and F C S Schiller.)[6]

The Nemset leonine headdress was perhaps the oldest of the archetypes, representing the archaic and widespread culture of the Levant and Proto-Syria, a heliopian pantheon whose existence has only recently become known and illuminated by excavations at Ebla[7]. Origins of the culture are dated to the early fourth millennium BC. The head of the pantheon was Dagan, almost certainly the same as Dagon of the Biblical Philistines and often represented by a statue of a lion.

The Protosyrian pantheon, in keeping with the heliopian cosmological philosophy of assimilation, consisted of in excess of five hundred deities of which Dagan, "The Lord of the Stars" was head.

If archaeological evidence had been lacking, the existence of a lion culture could have been deduced, as we shall see, when one of the oldest myths recorded, that of the Sumerian Gilgamesh, is examined.

The Nemset headdress represents the magnitude of the task of uniting the different cultural elements that made up the Ancient Egyptian nation from early immigration from the west and north, and perfectly corresponds to the historically recorded territorial struggles resulting in a unified realm.

Ultimately, the task was to unify two major cultural groupings corresponding to the north and south of the kingdom, which we shall see, were primordial cultural opposites. That it was successful for such a long period was due to the enlightened heliopian philosophy of cultural power sharing, rather than that of domination, the characteristic of cultural autocracies.

Such an enlightened philosophy was a feature of all Near Eastern heliopian cultures including those of Greek and Rome. A perennial adornment of the Egyptian kings would be some symbol of heliopianism and this was the broad circular breast plate with its variegated rings of precious stones, representing the Sun God Ra and equally, the god by his other designations of Osiris and Temu etc., from whom sprang the Egyptian culture.

As if to compliment the solar disk, the lines or bars of the Nemset crown rose like a staircase or ladder, an archetype of Egyptian origin referred to in the Bible in Jacob's dream. The ladder or steps was the ultimate symbol in Egyptian eschatology. It can be seen in the Egyptian illustrations of the Elysian Fields (see, for example, the Elysian Fields in the tomb of Seti I) where true hearted Egyptians went after death to labour for a time on the journey to where the waters divide and the stairs that lead to the home of the Gods. The stairs are shown on board the Tehetetfet boat with eight oars, which traditionally carried the righteous to the place of eternal dwelling.

A fuller interpretation of the symbolism of the Elysian Fields is left until later, for it embraces archetypes derived from other heliopian cultures. The enlightened philosophy of Heliopianism was not to go unchallenged, nor had it been uncontested in times previous, but a new god, imported into or conceived at Thebes, would, during the second millennia BC, rise in power to destroy almost totally, the heliopian cosmological influence. Thebes itself would become its almost unchallengeable cult centre of religious power, the name of its god was Amen (or Amun).

Amen represented the struggle of the forces of autocracy against the diviocratic forces of Heliopianism. Historical records show the struggles as being continuous throughout the evolution of Egyptian culture. Such conflicts between the two cultural ideologies were not confined to the Egyptian heliopian culture but were a feature of every surrounding kindred culture.

Such struggles were not new, but can be seen in an epoch, each epoch throughout history forming part of a macrocosmic cultural continuum of combat between the two adversaries.

The God Amen was originally the local god of Thebes, whose inception into the Egyptian culture was in the X11 dynasty[8] circa 2000 BC or about the time Abraham entered Egypt. We read in Genesis, how Abraham the Chaldean is exiled from Egypt after a sojourn for what amounted to bringing the monarchy into disrepute, insofar as he deliberately passed off his wife Sarai as his sister.

Sarai, being beautiful, was able to curry the king's favour which, for Abraham, meant wealth and influence. How Sarai achieved this is not stated explicitly, but indications are that she in fact became one of the king's concubines. We shall see that one of the temporal manifestations of the celestial struggle was the struggle for power between the monarch and the spiritual leaders, the priests.

The enormity of Abraham's transgression can be perceived when it is remembered that the monarch was regarded as a divinity, the temporal representative of the celestial pantheon, who, being deceived, would be perceived as being fallible as a consequence, the pantheon and its authority would be damaged.

We know from Sir Leonard Woolley's excavations at Ur[9] in the graves of the kings, were buried gold and lapis lazuli statues of a "ram of the goats" mistakenly thought to be the biblical "ram caught in the thicket", but which on inspection, clearly represented fertility.

The ram is standing with an erect penis, chained to a gold trefoil leafed tree, which was most likely meant to represent the archetypal tree of life. Such a statue would have some religious significance and its fabrication predates the era of Abraham.

One of the symbols of the god Amen, whose name meant "hidden"[10], was a ram, not of goats, but of sheep. In such a context, the followers of the god would regard a lamb as a "child of god" or "lamb of god." More often the god was represented as a man with a distinctive headdress conforming to the culture's mores of symmetry, that of two large plumes of feathers, reflecting the two horns of the Sumerian ram.

The feather, in the symbolic terminology of the time, represented "truth." It is against the feather of truth that the deceased's heart is weighed in the Hall of Judgement by Horus.

In the sophisticated use of visual archetypal symbols, we see in Amen, the proclamation of "the (one) true invisible god" who by the time of Tutankhamen of the XVIII Dynasty (reigned 1333-23 BC), was claiming to be the self-made God. This inferred no claim of allegiance to Ra and preceding all the Gods, and ultimate seniority, as the "Hymn to Amen" indicates[11].

Tutankhamen wearing the Nemset Crown
With Kind Acknowledgements to Cristiane Desroches-Noblecourt and Penguin Books

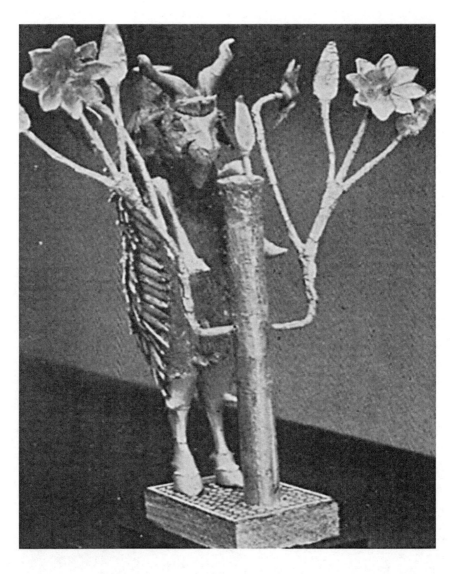

The Ram in the Thicket With Kind Acknowledgements to Sir Leonard Woolley and Pelican Books

"He had no mother for whom his name was made He had no father who begot him, saying, it is even myself. He shaped his own egg; the divine god, becoming of himself; all the gods were created after he came into being. One is Amen, he hides himself from them, he conceals himself from the gods. The man who utters his secret (or mystery) name, which cannot be known, falls down upon his face straightway and dies a violent death. No God knows how to call upon him."

That all the gods came after him is also the claim of the Cretan/Mycenean/ Greek Sea God.

According to Budge, "the existence of other gods is admitted, but they are merely forms of him, the great god whose three characters or persons were called Amen (of Thebes), Ra (of Heliopolis) and Ptah (of Memphis). His "oneness" of unity, was absolute."

Here we can see cultural traits that were carried into Judaic culture and through to post-Judaic Christianity in the "hidden God" whose name cannot be known or uttered, a characteristic of Yahweh and the idea of a trinity, central to Christian dogma. It is now well documented that this implied monotheistic god was engaged in, not for the first time, an internecine power struggle with the god Aten at the time of Tutankhamen, whose coronation name was Tutankhaten.

The cult of Aten was a vain attempt, as it turned out, to retain the predominance of the Sun god, but which fell to the "Lord of all things", "The creator of Creation" and the "Lord of truth."[12]

It is in the post-Hyksos period of Ancient Egypt that earlier machinations of the cult are described.

The Hyksos, who were estimated to have first occupied the Delta between 1640 and 1532 BC and of which little is known, are credited as having been responsible for the introduction of the horse into Egypt.

For reasons which will become apparent, it is proposed that the Hyksos were only, one and a late one, of early waves of invaders from Crete, who were at one time part of, or derived from mythical culture of Atlantis.

According to Plato, the god of Atlantis was Poseidon, the Greek God of the Sea. In ancient myth, Nereus, a previous title of the Sea God, was imputed to have created the horse[13], often seen as part sea creature, pulling the god's chariot. In this context, for the Cretans as a maritime nation, the horse may have symbolised a ship.

The horse was a divine symbol in ancient religions, integrated into the heavens as a constellation and must have represented power in one or more of its forms, especially due to its utility in war and agriculture.

The horse had a special religious significance in Islam. The prophet Mohammed is believed to have ascended to heaven on his horse. His general, Omar, gave an additional share of booty to the soldier with the best cared for horse[14] and he admonished the faithful to:

"love horses, tend them well, for they are worthy of your tenderness. Treat them like your own children, nourish them like friends of the family, clothe them with care, for the love of Allah do not neglect this or you will repent for it in this house and the next." The horse here is a symbol of the prophet's religious power and authority.

The ass form of the animal plays a similar role in the biblical story of Christ's entry into Jerusalem and students of Heraldry will recognise the horse as ecclesiastical authority which in the Judaic tradition represented the Law.

In the myth of Apophis and Sequenenre, the Hyksos king Apophis demands that Sequenenre stop molesting the hippopotami in the palace pools. It is suggested by James to have "more subtle religious reasons behind it."[15]

The water horses, possibly sacred to the Hyksos, echoes the religious power of the Cretan god. The Cretan culture as we shall see, contained a strong fertility cult. That dark ages seem to be associated with predominant fertility cults is evidenced by the fact that the Hyksos period is clothed in darkness until their expulsion from Egypt. Similar dark ages descended at the end of the XXth dynasty (Circa Twenty second century BC) coincident, in cultural time, with the total supremacy of Amenism, until the restoration of Greco-Persian heliopianism in the mid-sixth century BC.

A similar Dark Age was to descend with the eclipse of Greco-Roman heliopianism and the ascendancy of Judaic Christianism in Western culture which was to last until the revival of the Greco-Roman tradition in the Renaissance.

With the expulsion of the Hyksos from Egypt by Kamose, we see the beginning of the rolling back of the invading culture to its epicentre at Crete, shortly to be overcome in its Minoan form by Tuthmosis III (1479-1425 BC).

During the Hyksos occupation, it is possible, and even likely, that one of their adopted gods was Seth, as suggested by the water horses. Seth, the usurper of Osiris the Sun god and the celestial order, was also depicted as an ass[16] and there was a tendency to identify him with foreign invaders[17]. Indeed, he probably symbolised the Cretan derived culture of the Delta. He was certainly identified with sexuality, and hence, fertility.

He was also identified with the phallic Greek monster Typhon, the serpent, a central archetype of Cretan culture. In his fertility aspect, he could be regarded as an alternate form of the god Min, the manifestation of the god Amen's potency. Seth and Amen therefore, in the Delta, could be seen as having common cause in usurping the consensus power of the heliopian cosmogony.

At the beginning of the XVIIIth dynasty (circa 1550 BC), the god Amen's power was already considerable, for we see the second king of the dynasty, the successor to Amose "the Liberator" (from the Hyksos) take the god's name Amenhotep I (or Amenopsis I). The son of Amenhotep I, who did not see fit to include the god Amen in his title, instead, choosing Thoth, was to become one of Egypt's greatest kings, responsible for extending the empire and culture to Syria and the Euphrates.

Tuthmosis I, whose accomplishments during the thirteen years of rule, almost equalled those of Alexander the Great, died without legitimate male heir, a circumstance that presented a unique opportunity to the Amenite priesthood for furthering their design for cultural supremacy.

Tuthmosis I's only surviving child by his royal wife was Hatshepsut, who married her half-brother, a son of the king by a concubine. The son became Pharaoh Tuthmosis II with Hatshepsut as queen. The couple had no sons, but daughters, the eldest of whom, according to tradition, married the king's son by a concubine as his father had done.

This seems to indicate that bloodline filiation was paramount in succession at that time and that a woman could not be pharaoh.

Hatshepsut, who later claimed the throne, found it necessary to call herself "His Majesty Herself." The reasons for this legality are plain, arising from the cosmological pantheon, where the Celestial Executive was invariably king and male.

The pharaoh was a personification of, in the Egyptian case, Ra, and to establish a female pharaoh, would require a change of cultural mores.

A woman attempting to gain the throne would therefore require considerable cultural religious support from the populace.

The Amenite priesthood was not bound by such cosmological considerations and Hatshepsut, with their support, seized the throne, to become the first woman pharaoh.

Women, as History has shown, are never any match for monotheistic religious power, and have often been intermediaries for the conversion of kings.

Hatshepsut ruled for twenty-one years, the rightful heir, later to become Tuthmosis III, was locked away. During this time, the Amenite priesthood ruled through their surrogate, almost supremely. Hatshepsut had built, a magnificent temple at Deir el Bahri dedicated to Amen, but as her title indicated, the ancient heliopian tradition had still to be respected. Why Hatshepsut built her magnificent temple at Deir el Bahri has not been established, however, one reason may be that the site held a special significance for the Amen cult, a cache of whose priests were found there in 1891[18]; usually, such sites are shrines of former prophets.

In 1920, H. E. Winlock discovered there, the tomb of Meketre[19], a chancellor to the kings Nebhepetre, Mentuhotpe and Sankhare Mentuhotpe (circa 2000 BC). Meketre was a proud cattle owner and had a son Intef, so much can be ascertained from the tomb. The artefacts give clues to the daily life of the time and cattle modelled are the distinct black and white Friesian type. One is reminded that Jacob bred a special type of cattle "ring straked speckled and spotted" (Gen XXX-39).

Jacob also has a dream:

"the rams which leaped upon the cattle were ringstraked speckled and grizzled" (Gen XXXI-10).

In its symbolic form and stripped of its absurd literal interpretation, we see the ram as the symbol of the god Amen impregnating the cows of the Hathor of Isis cult prevalent in the Delta, primitive symbolism for the plebeians, of a union of the god Amen and Hathor/Isis. If this interpretation is accurate, then the cosmological imagery is typical of the mainly animal Ptah cycle of gods, where Ptah only was represented as a human and before Amen was imaged as a man.

This may be some indication as to the stage of development of the cosmogony at the time of Abraham, Isaac, Jacob and Joseph.

How then could Amen gain supreme power as long as the pharaoh represented Ra-Osiris, Ptah of the ancient cosmogony?

To support a woman as pharaoh would be to abrogate the ancient legal and religious laws, the divine link with Osiris would be broken, and the divinity of the king destroyed. The appointment of the ruler would become an Amenite religious sanction, a similar state of affairs to say the papal sanction in the Holy Roman Empire. The means whereby the legalisation of Hatshepsut was achieved was to identify Hatshepsut with Isis in the form of the goddess Hathor, so as the wife of Osiris, she would have popular and legitimate status.

The goddess can be seen represented on the capitals of the sanctuary at Deir el Bahri, with the face of a woman and the ears of a cow. The same capitals appear at Dendra, which have been defaced.

Dendra was the temple of Hathor in Ptolemaic times, though parts are much older. Cleopatra VII, the Cleopatra associated with Julius Caesar, is prominent on reliefs on the outer wall which show her headdress with the horns and disc of Hathor combined with the feathers of Amen. It will be remembered that Cleopatra either sought ultimate power in heliopian Rome or the secession of Egypt from Roman hegemony.

As a first step in the legitimisation of Hatshepsut, the story which was propagated and has now passed into myth, concerned her divine birth[20].

Paintings in her mortuary chapel depict a sacred wedding between the god Amen and a human woman who later became the mother of Hatshepsut. From the depiction of Hatshepsut having bovine ears, the inference is that the woman, her mother, was Hathor Isis. In this way, Hatshepsut "was of the god's seed and that his divine blood (and that of Isis), flowed in her veins."

Although she would not be the progeny of Osiris-Ra directly, as would a male pharaoh, she would be this indirectly, an incarnation of Isis and Osiris by association, as Amen was also called the "Son of Ra" that is, Osiris. In this way, the ancient order would be modified, her claim validated, the ascendancy of Amenism assured and heliopianism vanquished.

The symbol of Amen was the ram and of Isis-Hathor, the cow.

A marriage between Amen and Isis-Hathor was a union of the ram symbol of Amen, and the black and white (ringstraked) cow sacred to Hathor, the symbolic union of Jacob's dream. Here then in the Bible is the same cultural mechanism utilised by the "Hidden" god Amen to secure temporal power in Ancient Egypt. The cultural objective undoubtedly was the unification of the Amen fertility cult influence in the Delta and the very powerful Hathor-Isis cult that dominated the Delta.

This incident therefore places Jacob in the Ptah cycle epoch as one would expect, the archetypal ram being rightly derived from the Sumerian via the Chaldean Abraham, seeking unification with the "Flood" culture of the Delta originating from Crete. This was achieved with Joseph marrying into the "ON" priesthood. At this point, there appears possibly only strategic reasons for such a union, but it will become clear that there were common cultural heritage grounds for a union between Sumerian-Chaldean stock and Cretan cultural stock of the Delta. The Sumerian Ziggurat god, probably symbolised by the ram erectus, was also wont to visit young women in the sanctuary on top of the Ziggurat, hence a Sumerian-Chaldean influence may be detected in the myth.

Such an ingenious cultural ploy by the Amenites must have been conceived at the outset of Hatshepsut's reign and sealed with the building of Deir el Bahri. This re-arrangement of the cultural order must have seemed profane to the orthodox heliopian Egyptian. The supplanting by Amen of Osiris as the husband of Isis, inferred the bastardy of Horus (a myth formerly instigated by Sethites in their usurping of Osiris) making a mockery of Isis' travails upon which her legendary fidelity was based.

It is worth noting that the divinity of kings as a concept, had been established in the ancient empire about 2000 years prior to Hatshepsut by a similar device[21] in which myth the god Ra came to earth and, assuming the form of a priest of Ra, the husband of one, Ruttet, begot by her three sons.

Each of these would become king of all Egypt, a clue perhaps to the existence of the early three kingdoms. From that time, the legend has it every king prefixed the title "the son of Ra" to his personal name. It would seem therefore, the priests of Amen also lacked originality and were not above a little plagiarism of the methods of the ancient priesthood of Heliopolis. A small point perhaps, but at a macrocosmic level, this plagiarism indicated a cultural characteristic of the monotheistically driven Amenite culture that would be put to widespread use by the culture and its mutations throughout the ages. It is symptomatic of the lack of imagination and the immutable intellectual darkness that pervades monotheistic epochs.

It may have been that very plagiarism that betrayed the Amenite assault strategy to the ancient heliopian orthodoxy, for action was taken to secure the ancient order.

At a great festival of Amen at Karnak, at which Hatshepsut's court was present, priests appeared carrying a statue of Amen seated in the Sekhet boat, a symbol associated with the Creation (which perhaps became the ark of the Old Testament). Tuthmosis III describes the scene as a bystander:

"The god made the circuit of the hall on both sides of it searching for my majesty in every place, though the hearts of those who were in front did not comprehend his actions. On recognising me, he halted; I threw myself on the pavement, I prostrated myself in his presence…"

The barc was then bowed before Tuthmosis, clearly indicating his divine right, the god doing obeisance. This incident can be interpreted as a move by the heliopians or the orthodox caucus of the Amenites, or both, to re-establish the claim of Tuthmosis to the throne and hence the rehabilitation of heliopian orthodoxy. The fate of Hatshepsut has never been determined, nor has her mummy been found.[22]

Tuthmosis III became pharaoh and is thought by some to be history's first great general, extending the kingdom to include Syria, Phoenicia and Nubia.

Tuthmosis destroyed all trace of Hatshepsut's name late in his reign and images of her he ordered to be replaced by images of himself and his two predecessors[23]. The power of the Amen cult remained strong as is evidenced by Tuthmosis III's successor Amenhotep II (or Amenopsis II), whose name "Amen is satisfied" was adopted as part of the process of reconciliation whilst the heliopians consolidated their restoration.

On his return from Upper Rethennu (Egyptian Sudan), he came back:

"With a heart expanded with joy to Father Amen because he had overthrown all his enemies and enlarged the frontiers of Egypt..."[24]

The accession of his son Thothmosis IV (or Tuthmosis IV) circa 1450 BC seems to have been due not to the priests of Amen, but to the priests of Heliopolis[25], which may account for the choice of name.

A huge red granite stele between the paws of the sphinx at Giza, not now there, recounts the legend of Tuthmosis IV where it is written, whilst out hunting, the young Tuthmosis sat to rest himself under the shadow of the sphinx. There he fell asleep and dreamt that the four-fold Sun god Herakhuti-Khepera-Ra-Temu (or Tem, a typically heliopian syncretistic title) appeared to him and promised him the "crowns of Egypt if he would clear away from the sphinx and his temple, the desert sand which had swallowed them up."

The sphinx was believed to be the image and dwelling place of Temu Herakhuti the oldest god of Heliopolis, whose name was synonymous with Ra, Khepra and Osiris. The sphinx embodied the major archetypes of the culture, the head of a man, the body of a bull, the limbs of a lion with Dagon mane, and the wings of the eagle. These archetypes were later appropriated to symbolise the four evangelists of Christian ideology, indicative of the origins of the cult.

The answer to the riddle of the sphinx was "man" and the sphinx represented a symbolic archetypal macrocosm of the major elements of the contemporary culture, of which each individual was a microcosm, and a reflection of heliopian theological philosophy. The latter was concerned with endeavour into the nature of man from which the sociological and organisational structures of the society would have issued.

In clearing the "sands of the desert from the god's temple", that is, reversing the slow arid death of the heliopian culture, would revive the culture from the sands of time. Tuthmosis IV did ascend the throne with the assistance of the heliopian priesthood, despite the fact that his mother was not of royal rank, though according to Budge, her sympathies lay with the solar gods of Heliopolis.

Tuthmosis IV however, did nothing to alienate the Amenite priesthood and there are gifts listed to Amen from his campaign spoils in Syria and the Sudan[26]. He married a Mittannian princess from a culture adjacent to the Hittites and Syrians. Cuneiform tablets of the culture indicate that the Mittannian gods were heliopian in nature, bearing a close resemblance to the Indian gods Mithras, Varuna, Indra and Nasatiya.[27]

Ostensibly a political marriage, the infusion into the Egyptian culture of a kindred heliopianism could only strengthen the struggling ancient culture of the Egyptians and was instrumental in subsequent events. Tuthmosis IV was succeeded by his son by the Mittannian princess Mutemuaa, Amenhotep III (or Amenopsis III). The Amenite priesthood of Thebes countered by employing the well-tried cultural device of proclaiming the Pharaoh the Son of Amen and Mutamuaa, the god having assumed the form of Tuthmosis IV.

As we have seen, the device of the god impregnating mortal woman was not new to the Amenites and a similar idea surrounds the patrimony of Christ.

Amenhotep III, some of whose titles were "the chosen of Ra", "the chosen of Temu" as well as "the chosen of Amen"[28], married a formidable women called Ti (or Ty or Tei) whose influence over her husband and family was great, and, one can assume, ran counter to the overwhelming influence of the Amenite priesthood. It is in the reign of Amenhotep III, who also brought Mittannian blood into the culture, that attempts were made to re-establish an ancient form of the Sun god by the name of ATEN, the globe or face of the sun. A stele[29] erected during the reign of Amenhotep III is dedicated to Amen and Aten and the lavish praise to the former, reflects the power of the cult at the time.

It is held in many quarters that Amenhotep III was the instigator of the Aten cult and not his son Amenhotep IV.

Akhenaten, sometime co-regent[30] was driven to declare Atenism as the state religion in a desperate attempt to disenfranchise the Amenite power centre by reverting to an ancient cultural archetype. This alone is testament to the sophistication of the psychological expertise of the enlightened ancients.

Amenhotep III's son Akhenaten, took the unusual step of "concluding that the ancient solar gods, Tem, Ra and Horus of the two horizons only were worthy of veneration in the form of Aten"[31].

The solar globe or mandala, the abode of Tem, and later Ra of Heliopolis, reflects a measure of desperation on the part of the ancient priesthood of Heliopolis and a realisation that the Amen cult would not be satisfied with less than total cultural power.

This cultural intolerance was characteristic of early Christianity, Islam and all "youthful" modern monolithic ideologies as measured on the cultural millennia time scale. Atenism, in its attempt to establish a solar monolithic ideology based on a rationalisation of the ancient gods can be seen in this context as pre-empting what must have seemed as the inevitable approaching domination of the state by a monotheistic Armenite culture. This was a long running power struggle between the powerful priesthood whose objective would lead to the usurpation the king's (divine) authority by the Amenite priesthood. This did not represent any new cultural phenomenon but what must have represented a natural state of the human condition from the ancient times of the medicine man-tribal chief rivalry for power. The spiritual power of the medicine man wishing power of the chief who represented the animal alpha male temporal power. The supremacy of the priest power ultimately came to pass on a grand scale with the institution of the Holy Roman Empire.

Aten, the globe or sun, was associated with Tem, who dwelt in the solar globe. Aten was declared self-generated, one and alone[32].

This was not new, as the primary forms of the sun god Tem, who was also in the heliopian pantheon Ra, Khepera and Osiris, had always been regarded as such. The declaration restored the sun god's status, which had in latter centuries, been usurped by the younger god Amen who also claimed to be self-generated.

Tem or Temu, was depicted in the form of a man, a symbol which had become increasingly associated with Amen, but was originally associated with the older god. Sir A. E. Wallis Budge writes:

"Of the style and nature of the worship of Tem, we know nothing, but from the fact that he was depicted in the form of a man, we appear to be justified in assuming that it was of a character superior to that of the cults of sacred animals' birds and reptiles, which were general in Egypt under the earlier dynasties"[33].

It was clear then, when the rationalisation of the culture was being formulated, that the symbol of a man may have been unacceptable to all but the most enlightened of the heliopians for the following reasons:

Despite the fact that the figure of a man as representing god, was originally a heliopian advanced concept propagated early in the long development of the culture, it would be indistinguishable from the Amenite symbol, laying open the heliopian philosophers to the charge of plagiarism. (Plagiarism was more particularly an Amenite trait arising out of the closed mono-cultural mores.) Such a charge would be absurd as the heliopians had developed a pantheon over the epochs. It is probable the it may have been compiled according to a "celestial" plan, embodying principles of tolerance through plurality whose aim was nothing less than the raising of the cultural consciousness of mankind (an objective singularly absent in monolithic cultures).

At that time of crisis, possibly the only option would have been to instigate the conceptual foundation of the next stage of cultural development, that being the idea of an abstract conception of the gods, with an appropriate symbol. We know that the full development of the pantheon in terms of almost exclusive human imagery was not to come until the Greek Hellenistic pantheon, a millennium later.

The introduction of the central human archetype in the form of Temu and Ptah predated this by several millennia. The precedent therefore already existed.

The problem was of course to preserve the concept of plurality, just as with the ascendancy of monotheism, in the early centuries AD, the problem was to maintain the monotheistic concept.

The symbolism chosen was most apt, being the solar globe with many arms or members. Such a symbol preserved the ancient symbolism of Ra, Temu, Osiris and Khepera etc., and though ostensibly a monotheistic cultural symbol with its many arms of life-giving enlightenment, symbolised the plurality of the pantheon in the unity of the celestial executive.

In this manner, whilst preserving the concept of plurality, a certain strength due the rationalisation would result. The solar globe, which also symbolised the king or pharaoh presiding over a country of united cults, represented a cultural concept that could only reinforce the concept of kingship and royal authority in the face of burgeoning Amenite religious power. We see such a cultural conception in all Near Eastern cosmogonies from the earliest times, from the Greeks through to the Romans.

The concept represented by the globe Aten was abhorrent to the Amenites (and testifies to the vision of the heliopian ancients) which was demonstrated by the backlash provoked with reintroduction of Amenite power during the subsequent reign of the, significantly, young king Tutankhamen, originally named Tutankhaten.

Following the dark age that eclipsed Roman heliopianism, it was not for almost two millennia, that such a step from a paternal image of God to a conceptual idea of God was again mooted.

A natural consequence of the cultural innovation or rationalisation, was the action of Amenhotep IV who changed his name to Akhenaten (or Ikhnaton) meaning "all is well with the globe."

He moved the religious capital from Thebes, the cultural capital of Amenism, to Aketaten, "the city of Aten" in central Egypt. Such a move was clearly aimed at positioning the cultural capital at a symbolically unifying location in a country traditionally divided in two (the north and the south), for Aketaton lay approximately midway between Thebes and Heliopolis, centres of the opposing cosmogonies.

This action greatly diminished the influence of Thebes and it is probable that government support for the cult centres was terminated if not their being actively suppressed, for reports tell of Amen centres being neglected, the god's name erased on a wide scale and in some places, "gods" was obliterated.[34]

There was, in the wake of the cultural change, something of a renaissance in Egyptian art, with the abolition of conventionality and the introduction of new colours and designs. The Aten cult worshipped the triad of life, beauty and colour, and art was integral with the religion.[35] This had no place for guilt, sin and forgiveness by a deity, which were significant mores of Amenism[36]. The status of women seemed to be advanced in so far as Akhenaten's queen Nefertiti is seen wearing a new style crown. It is reminiscent of the king's crown of Lower Egypt. Only the king's daughters were shown on reliefs.[37]

Possibly the headdress of the queen,[38] crowns being potent symbols, was intended to signify the complement to the male crown, the union of the fertility goddess of the Delta with the north, in the wholeness of the family unit. Such a concept aligns with the Qaballistic concept of microcosmic man, a reflection of macrocosmic man, the culture, a philosophy extant in Ancient Egypt.

Amenhotep III and Akhenaten's cultural innovations were short lived, after Akhenaton's death. Nefertiti, who may have briefly reigned, was succeeded by

Amenhotep III's only surviving son Tutankhaten though Smenkhkare, Akhenaten's sometime co-regent, may have briefly reigned since their deaths were almost simultaneous. Tutankhaten was compelled at some time in his reign to adopt the name of Amen, and after a brief reign of nine years, was buried as Tutankhamen, evidence of the re-establishment of the influence of the cult.

In what can be viewed as an attempt at Amenite consolidation was the alliance proposed by Ankesenamen, Tutankhamen's widow, with the Hittites, enemies of the Mittanni, the allies of Egypt. The Hittites, an Anatolian culture, comparable in size to the Egyptian, had long contested Egyptian influence in the Near East. Ankesenamen wrote to the mighty Hittite king Suppiluliumas I requesting his son as spouse[39].

Suspicious of the offer of an alliance, after some procrastination, the king agreed and sent a son who was murdered on his arrival in Egypt. The murder of the Hittite prince thwarted the Amenite attempt at placing another woman on the throne in all but title. Tutankhamen's old vizier Ay became pharaoh and was in turn succeeded by the former's commander-in-chief Horemhab, whose sympathies lay with the heliopian priesthoods of Ptah of Memphis and Ra of Heliopolis.

For a short period therefore, in cultural terms, the Heliopian\Amenite balance was restored. One point of interest as to why the cult of Atenism did not succeed, notwithstanding the potency of the Amen cult, is proffered by Sir A E Wallis Budge in so far as the Hymns to Aten suggest that Amenhotep IV and his followers conceived an abstract image of the god and worshipped him inwardly.

As far as the general populace was concerned, this would have been unpopular for two reasons, firstly, the average Egyptian understood concrete images and was unable to assimilate a conceptual form of god and secondly, their admonishment, as is the case today, was towards the god without, which makes for controllable cults of common interest and perception rather than an individual perception of god.

In times of cultural upheaval, such as that of Atenism, an exodus may have followed. This may have been the Biblical Exodus, which casts a shade of Amenism over early Judaism. However, there were many such exoduses, the expulsion of Abraham and Lot being one of them.

Major cultural exoduses are comparatively rare. Another may have occurred with the expulsion of the Hyksos, who were also extant in Palestine during the same period. It can be deduced that Amenism and the Hyksos shared common cultural mores of fertility veneration.

The Bull cults of the Delta were associated with Amen. Tiye's father Yuya, was a "prophet of Min", Min being the ithyphallic form of Amen and "was in charge of the Oxen of Min", her mother Thuya, was "superior of Amen's harem".

The tradition of the god conceiving of mortal woman, as we have seen in the stories surrounding Hatshepsut, Mutummia and Tutankhamen, probably had its origin in Mesopotamian tradition. There it was held that on certain festivals, a young woman would stay in the temple on the top of the Ziggurat where the god would enter and procreate.

The architectural style of the Ziggurat is reflected to some extent in the Hatshepsut temple at Deir al Bahri with its prominent and extensive staircase into the Amenite temple, redolent of Jacob's Ladder in Genesis.

It was during the flood season of the Nile, the season that would renew the fertility to the land that the god Amen chose this festival to visit his harem. Water, not surprisingly, as Freud rediscovered, was a psychological archetype of sex and fertility as was the Ox. Oxen or bull cults were widespread in the Delta.

A particularly prevalent cult that we shall see, had links with the Greek culture, was the Apis Bull cult or the Seraphs (a derivation agreed to be from Osiris Apis). Part of the ritual of the cult was to bury sacred oxen.

A serapeum was discovered by August Mariette in 1850 and the discovery was later extended by W. B. Emery. The Apis was worshipped at Memphis from the time of the first dynasty, associated with Ra and Ptah. The cult was introduced into the restored heliopian cosmogony as the Seraphs possibly to mollify the Delta populace at a time when immigrant Greeks flooded into the Delta subsequent to the Conquest of Alexander.

The Ptolemaic form of the Apis had a human head wearing a modius (a corn measure, another symbol of fertility) representing, in religious terms, a development of the original archetype. The main centre of the cult was Saqqara near Memphis, the ancient Lower Egyptian cultural capital of Ptah. The god Amen had ensured that it was widely identified with the primitive Delta cults, for among the regional gods of the Delta, were Sekhmet, the lion headed goddess, Bastet, the cat goddess of Bubastis, Wepwawet, the wolf god of the Asyut region, Harsaphes, the ram headed god of Herakleopolis, Sokar, and the falcon headed god, Nefertum of human form and lotus headdress, the perfectly beautiful.

The chief god was Ptah. In the Theban Ritual of Amen, the god claims sovereignty over many of these:

"The Aten of heaven his (Amen's) rays are on thy face (i.e., Aten whose substance is Amen)...Hawk destroying his attacker straightaway. Hidden lion roaring loudly, driving his claws into what is under his paws, Bull for his town...lion for his people...Thou didst exist first in forms of the Eight Gods (of Hermopolis)...and then thou didst complete them and become one. Thy body is hidden in the chiefs, thou art hidden as Amen at the head of the Gods."

Indications exist which point to the fact that the Delta Bull Cult was a major political as well as cultural force in a region which still must have retained considerable Hyksos cultural mores. In 1852 Mariette found an intact tomb holding two Apis bulls whose distinctive black and white markings which accord with Jacob's dream where:

"Ring straked speckled and grisled rams (the symbol of Amen) leaped upon the cattle" (the Delta populace) (Gen XXX1-10).

Situated in the Delta also, is the ancient city of Anu or On of the Bible, later called Heliopolis by the Greek and Latin writers. Although it was the site of the ancient Sun cult of Ra, the cult of the standing stone was probably older.

Anu meant the 'city of the pillar'. The obelisk, or pillar, was originally not an emblem of the Sun God for its phallic nature associates it with a fertility cult and, as we shall see, was probably imported into Egypt by a Cretan or former Hyksos cultural incursion into the Delta.

Anu or On, was the cult into which Joseph married and it is not surprising to read in Genesis, Joseph's father Jacob, dreams Yahweh promises to: "bring thee again into this land." Upon waking, Jacob:

"took the stone that had put for his pillows, and set it up for a pillar and poured water on the top of it" (GenesisXX1X-15,18).

Here, not surprisingly, is the association of water and the phallic pillar, both ancient fertility archetypes that link the patriarch to such cults of phallicism.

The two buried bulls found by Mariette, were buried in the reign of Rameses II, the great king of the 19th Dynasty, only some thirty-three years after Tutankhamen to ascend the throne (circa 1290 BC). Much of the contents of the tomb was inscribed with the name Khaemwese, the eldest son of Rameses II. A large relief on the walls of Luxor shows the king hunting bulls in the reeds of the Delta, such scenes were meant to convey, in keeping with the mores of the mass cultural communication of the time, something more than the king doing a spot of hunting.

It is possible that they were meant to convey the routing of some alien culture in much the same way as depictions of Gilgamesh were intended (which appear in a later chapter). Pictures at that time were the major means of communication (as in medieval times) and were understood by the wholly uneducated and illiterate populace.

Valuable domesticated animals were unlikely to be found wild, but they did hold widespread religious symbolism.

Hitherto, by examining ancient Egyptian culture and mythology to what has to be a limited degree, indications of conflicting cultural traditions have emerged and to some extent, the use of cultural archetypes for mass cultural communication.

Other contemporary ancient Near Eastern cultures will subsequently be examined in order to ascertain if similar cultural conflicts existed.

References Chapter 2

[1] E. Payne, All about the Pharaohs, page 27

[2] Sir A. E. Wallis, Budge Egyptian Language, page 70

[3] S. H. Hooke, Middle Eastern Mythology, page 59

[4] E. Pagels, The Gnostics, page 70

[5] C. Desroches, Noblecourt Tutankhamen, page XX

[6] G. N. M. Tyrrel, The Personality of Man (for example), page 10

[7] P. Matthiae Ebla

[8] Sir A. E. Wallis, Budge Egyptian Religion, page 103

[9] Sir Leonard Woolley, Ur of the Chaldees, page 40

[10] Sir A. E. Wallis, Budge Egyptian Religion, page 103

[11] Sir A. E. Wallis, Budge Tutankhamen, page 42

[12] Ibid, page 43

[13] Encyclopaedia of World Mythology, ed R. Warner, page 216

[14] R. Trench, Arabian Travellers, The European

[15] Discovery of Arabia, page 122

[16] T. G. James, Archaeology of Ancient Egypt, page 124

[17] Encyclopaedia of World Mythology, ed R. Warner, page 99

[18] Ibid, page 99

[19] J. Baines and J. Malek, Atlas of Ancient Egypt, page 103

[20] T. G. James, Archaeology of Ancient Egypt, page 59

[21] Sir A. E. Wallis, Budge Tutankhamen, page 21

[22] C. Barocas, Monuments and Obelisks of Egypt, pages 81 and 21

[23] Elizabeth Payne, All about the Pharaohs, page 75

[24] J. Baines and J. Malek, Atlas of Ancient Egypt, page 44

[25] Sir A. E. Wallis, Budge Tutankhamen, page 18

[26] Ibid, page 18

[27] Ibid, page 69

[28] Ibid, page 21

[29] Ibid, page 65

[30] Ibid, page 33

[31] F. Giles, The Ikhnaton Legend and History

[32] Sir A. E. Wallis, Budge Tutankhamen, page 18

[33] Ibid, page 59

[34] Ibid, page 79

[35] J. Baines and J. Malek, Atlas of Ancient Egypt, page 45

[36] Sir A. E. Wallis, Budge Tutankhamen, page 96

[37] Cristiane Doreches Noblecourt 'Tutankhamen', page 109

[38] Ibid, page 80

[39] Ibid, page 154

Chapter 3
Aspects of the Hittite Culture

The Hittites were a race that emanated, it is thought, from Southern Europe or Russia, to settle in Asia Minor at about the time of the early Egyptian dynasties.

As early as 2200 BC, tradition has Naram Sin, the fourth king of the dynasty of Akkad (Sumeria), fighting against a coalition of seventeen kings, one of whom was a king Pamba of Hatti[1] or the Hittites. What was to become an empire to rival that of Ancient Egypt and its official language have become known as Hittite.

The language, an Indo-European derivative, was superimposed on the non-Indo-European Hattian, which originally was the language of the "Land of Hatti" and at one time, had a pre-cuneiform hieroglyphic form similar to the Ancient Egyptian.

If cultural incursion did occur in that area, as is likely, then the pre-existing culture would consist in part, if not wholly, of the Proto-Syrian, which was widespread in the west and south of Hatti (present day Anatolia), of which Dagan, the lion god, was the principal deity.

As a religious archetype, the lion is prominent in the Hittite pantheon. One great gate at the capital Hattusas is called the Lion Gate. There was also considerable common culture with the Mesopotamians, for the Hittites adopted many Mesopotamian deities such as Enlil, Ninlil, Ea etc from the Hurrians[2] in the east, who at one time formed part of the Empire.

This custom of adopting deities has been encountered with the heliopian Egyptian culture.

The Hittite pantheon, like the Egyptian cosmogony, consisted of many deities to reflect the diverse tribal and cultural entities that composed the Empire. The cultural link with the Mesopotamians is borne out by the Biblical narrative surrounding Abraham.

Reference to the Hittites as a tribe (which in those days almost equated to a nation), occurs in Genesis (XX111-10) when Ephron the Hittite son of Zohar, king of Bela, is approached by Abraham concerning the purchase of a cave or sepulchre for his wife Sarah. Ephron was a person of some wealth and dominion, having a "gate to his city", a possible reference to the capital Hattusas, which had particularly impressive gates. Abraham is referred to by the children of Heth, among whom Ephron the Hittite dwelt, as a "mighty prince among us" (Genesis XX111-6) who had a household army of three hundred and eighteen (Genesis X1V-14). It could be argued that, denied succession at Ur, Abraham had set out to find a kingdom of his own, engendering claim in the prophesies of Yahweh, a cultural trait which was to surface in the story of Moses.

Of Sarah, the Bible states:

"And she shall be a mother of nations, kings of people shall be of her" and of Ishmael "twelve princes shall he beget" (Genesis XV11-16, 20).

Although written centuries after the events, a claim of Abraham to royal birth seems to be implied and tacitly therefore, his lineage.

The Hittites eventually amassed an empire which, at its height (circa 1400bc), encompassed most of Asia Minor, embracing a quarter of a million square miles from, on the west, the Aegean Sea, to Hebron in the South, and Northern Iraq in the east.

The empire rivalled that of the Egyptians and (circa1600 BC), it had sacked Babylon. At the end of the 13th century BC, the empire came to an abrupt end and the capital Hattusas was burnt to the ground, the end, as some believe with good reason, of Troy.

Ninety years previously, Rameses II had fought against the Hittites at the battle of Kadesh, now regarded as resulting in no decisive victory for either of the combatants. Rameses II, who consequently married the daughter of the Hittite king Hattusili III, to forge a cultural alliance with the great heliopian culture, mitigated the cold war instigated by the Ankesenamen affair.

After its demise in the 13th century BC, the world did not suspect its existence until the late 19th century AD.

The Hittite cosmogeny was Sun based, whose member gods numbered in excess of eighty[3] in the reign of Mursili, the son of Supilluliuma, with major gods like the Egyptians and many minor cult deities representing local and tribal variations.

Some of the principal gods were, the Sun god, the Sun goddess, the Moon god, the goddess of War, the god of Water and Teshub, the Storm god.

The latter, like Zeus, became the head of the pantheon and was referred to as "King of Heaven, Lord of the Land of Hatti."

The treaty between Hattusilis III and Rameses II is said to be:

"For the purpose of making eternal, the relations, which the Sun God of Egypt and the Weather God of Hatti have established for the land of Egypt and the land of Hatti"[4].

Hittite mythology, of which only a small part survives, must have been extensive, and comparable with that of Ancient Egypt. That which does exist has, in some of the myths, a striking similarity with classical Greek myth. This is not as surprising as it first appears, for we shall see that there was a considerable cultural intercourse with the pre-classical Greeks.

One of the earliest Hittite myths corresponding to one of the earliest Greek myths, that of Hesiod's Ouranos, Kronos and Zeus, is the myth of Anu, Kumarbi and Teshub[5], as related in the "Song of Ullikummi." This is a long epic that describes the struggles surrounding celestial kingship, a not unknown theme encountered in the Ancient Egyptian mythology.

According to the myth, originally Alalu, a pre-Hesodian deity, was the king of Heaven who sat upon the throne. "Anu, the first among the gods (and he was also head of the Mesopotamian pantheon, and was known as On in Egypt) stood before him, bowed down at his feet and handed him the cup to drink."

This latter action, as well as denoting respect for seniority, embodied a central Middle Eastern archetype, the cup would contain the celestial waters of everlasting life. In many reliefs, the king as temporal reflection of the celestial order, is shown dispensing the life-giving waters from a cup. In the context of the myth then, Anu is cast as the celestial potentate in the heliopian tradition, ultimately to become king.

"Alalu reigned for nine years, and in the ninth year Anu made war on Alalu and conquered him and Alalu fled before him to earth"

To whence he fled is not stated but speculation suggests the Underworld. In this respect, it may not be far wide of the mark, for the defeat of Alalu begins to look like the defeat of Apophis by Ra. Alalu is probably the equivalent of a Titan in Greek mythology.

The Titans were incarcerated in Tartaros "deep below" the earth, as deep below the earth as the earth is below the sky[6].

Another clue is the magical number nine "An anvil dropped from the sky falls for nine nights and on the tenth, reaches the earth. Likewise it falls nine nights and days from the earth and on the tenth, it reaches Tartaros surrounded by an iron wall and three times encompassed by night."

"Anu then sat on the throne, while the mighty Kumarbi ministered to him and bowed down at his feet." Anu reigned for nine years and in the ninth year, Kumarbi made war on Anu.

The latter abandoned the struggle "and flew like a bird into the sky, but Kumarbi seized his feet and pulled him down. Kumarbi bit off Anu's member and laughed for joy."

One can compare this with the usurpation of Ouranos by Kronos, whence Gaia, the earth, who had made a mighty sickle with sharp teeth, induces Kronos to cut off his father's member whilst he lay with his mother.[7]

It can also be compared with the Seth-Osiris saga in which Seth dismembers the body of Osiris and flings his penis into the Nile. Here then, in the myth we see the struggle of the heavenly pantheon against the celestial usurpation powers represented in the Hittite, by Kumarbi in the Egyptian by Seth, and in the Greek by Kronos.

This is further illustrated as the Song of Ullikummi unfolds:

"Anu turned to Kumarbi and said, 'Do not rejoice over what thou hast swallowed. I have made thee pregnant with three mighty gods. First I have made thee pregnant with the mighty Weather God, secondly, I have made thee pregnant with the river Aranzakh (the Tigris) and thirdly, I have made thee pregnant with the Great God Tasmisu (a minion or vassal of the Weather God). Three terrible gods I have planted within thee as fruit of my body.'"

With this, Anu flew up to the sky and disappeared, but Kumarbi spat out the seeds and the earth in turn gave birth to the three "terrible Gods."

In this passage, comprising a fine literal absurdity, there lies an elegant symbolic sense to which a later reference shall be made.

The tablets at this point become largely unintelligible, but the story is later taken up when Kumarbi is seeking to defeat the king of the pantheon.

The defeat of Kumarbi by his son is the Hittite equivalent of Zeus defeating Kronos and the vanquishing of Seth by Horus, resulting in a victory for the heliopian pantheon. Such common themes suggest a common cultural source and repetitive struggles for celestial (i.e., cultural) ideology and psychology between heliopian pluralism and autocratic monotheism.

In the Greek cycles, the consequent battle of the Olympians against the "turbulent sons of heaven" the Titans, "who resembled their father more than Zeus did" finds its echoes in the revenge of Kumarbi, where the heliopians find themselves pitted against a gigantic adversary.

Kumarbi planned to create a mighty rebel who would defeat the Weather God. He gained the support of the Sea (God) and married the Sea's daughter, who in versions, is called "a great mountain peak"[8], and who bore him a monstrous creature made of diorite stone named Ullikummi.

Kumarbi summoned the Irshirra deities and they carried the child down to earth, and placed him on the shoulders of Uppelluri, an Atlas figure[9], where he grew to gigantic proportions. The sea reached only to the middle of his body "like a loin cloth" and he eventually grew 9000 leagues tall.

The Sun God, on seeing Ullikummi, was filled with anger and dismay and hastened to tell Teshub, who, with his sister Ishtar, climbed to the top of Mount Hazzi (Mons Cassius near Antioch)[10] where they could see the monstrous Ullikummi rising out of the sea.

Teshub ordered Tasmisu to bring his bulls Serisu and Tella and adorn them, to summon thunder and rain. A battle commenced, but nothing prevailed against the monster, which reached the gates of the Weather God's city Kummiya and forced him to abdicate.

Teshub then appeals to Ea "the all wise" whose home was the Nether Sea. Ea summoned the gods to a council where Kumarbi revealed his plot and the council broke up in dismay. Ea tells Enlil, a mighty god, what has happened (this is probably myth symbolism for the Proto-Hittites consulting Sumerian allies whose god Enlil is representative of the culture).

Ea then consults Uppelluri, who provides a revealing response:

"When heaven and earth were built upon me, I knew nothing of it and when they came and cut heaven and earth asunder with a copper tool, that also I knew not. Now something is hurting my right shoulder, but I know not who the god is."

When Ea heard this, he turned Upelluri's right shoulder round and there stood the Diorite Stone on Upelluri's right shoulder like a post(?).

This revealed to Ea the means of destroying the Stone God. He ordered the ancient storehouses to be opened and the ancient saw (in those days sickle shaped) with which heaven and earth were divided, to be brought to him. With this, he severed the Stone God at its feet, destroying its power, at the same time, he urged the gods to renew the battle.

The end of the story is lost, but it can be safely assumed that the heliopians triumphed, as we shall see. The sickle and the saw are easily identified in myth, as in dreams, with male power and the phallus.

In the case of Kronos and Ouranus, we see youth defeating age within an unchanged fertility culture. With Zeus and Kronos, and Teshub and Ullikumi, we see not only youth again defeating age, but also a battle of cultures (as also with Zeus and Typhon the serpent).

In the wider macrocosmic sense, we see Teshub as the Anatolian culture defeating the stone (phallic) culture that was also older.

In a celebrated case history of Jung's, the sickle appears in the dream of an incestuously abused girl who was suffering from a severe psychosis.

As an archetypal symbol, it demonstrates how the individual psyche is the repository of ancient cultural symbols and the contribution that myths play in fashioning the "collective unconscious", each member of the culture containing in his or her subconscious, central archetypes. The collective individuals' pool of archetypes form, as a group, a collective subconscious. As such, there is therefore, a collective archetypal memory, which perhaps is slightly misleading, since the unconscious does not seem to acknowledge the dimension of time, as do not the myths which fashion it.

In its literal form, the myth of Ullikummi appears absurd and the real meaning must be divined from translation of the cultural archetypal symbols which abound and from which a perfectly reasonable story emerges.

We see, as in Egyptian mythology, a heliopian company of gods being usurped by a would-be celestial autocrat.

In the Egyptian, the usurper was Seth, reflected in historical terms as a phallic cult, possibly the cult of Amen, connected in some way with the Hyksos, who were probably from Crete. Here the usurper is Kumarbi. What therefore, if any, was the culture associated with Kumarbi?

In order to determine the answer to that, it is necessary to investigate the ancient legend of Atlantis.

The legend of Atlantis was first attributed to Plato[11] who in his trilogy Timaeus, Critias, Hermocrates, relates how the Greek poet Solon (circa 600) brought the story back from Ancient Egypt, having been told it by the old priest of Neigh.

Atlantis, a great empire, had laid claim to most of the Mediterranean (and beyond), and Athens alone had stood against and defeated it.

According to Critias[12] the earth was divided among the gods. Poseidon the Sea God, received Atlantis, an island onto which he begot children by a mortal woman and settled them on the island.

In due course, a daughter Cleito, was born to Evenor and his wife Leucippe, primeval beings, who died shortly after Cleito reached womanhood.

Poseidon fell in love with Cleito and produced five pairs of twins, the first born becoming the first king. Poseidon prepared the island for habitation by producing alternate zones of land and water in a circular fashion with interlinking bridges, aqueducts, canals, fortification walls, temples, and houses, not unlike modern Venice.

There was abundant wood, animals and minerals for all the population's needs. In the temple, dedicated to Poseidon and Cleito. The god and his bride stood, in a chariot with six winged horses as high as the roof, around which were a hundred nereids on dolphins.

The god also instituted laws regulating status of the kings and justice. These laws were inscribed on a pillar of orichalcum (a mineral almost as precious as gold, abundant on the island) and determined for example, the meeting of the council of kings every fifth and sixth year, to give the odd and even numbers. Also, the king was not to have the power of life and death over any of his kinsmen, unless he had the assent of the majority of ten (twin kings).

Other laws related to obligations of mutual defence and precedence.

Sacrifices were made to the God to ensure that for the future, they would not, if they could help, offend against the "writing on the Pillar" (One is reminded of hieroglyphed obelisks).

These sacrifices took the form of sacrificing one of the sacred bulls, which were free to roam the temple.

We have encountered such sacred bulls in Hittite myth, and the Saqqara bull cult was prevalent in the once Hyksos occupied Nile Delta.

The bull, caught with only staves and nooses, was led to the sacred pillar and its throat cut, such that the blood flowed onto the sacred inscription.

This was no doubt to impart fertility or life to the sacred pillar and its inscriptions, which included admonishments in the form of curses for the disobedient.

This is possibly a reference to the earliest association of divine word and blood ritual.

Subsequent to slaughter, the carcass was burnt and into a bowl of wine was poured some of the bull's blood from which each present drew a potation in a golden cup.

A libation was poured onto the fire whilst swearing obedience to the laws of the pillar and praying for the God's help in upholding them.

For many generations, the Atlanteans thus enjoyed great power and "despised everything but virtue", being self-controlled, sober and indifferent to goods and luxury.

However, those vices that they eschewed, began to increase and "the divine portion fade slowly."

Zeus decided to inflict a punishment on them, "and in a single day and night of misfortune, the island of Atlantis disappeared in the depths of the sea. But afterwards, there occurred violent earthquakes and floods."[13]

What further punishment is not known, for Critias breaks off however, such a punishment by the Greek God of Thunder, the equivalent of the Hittite Weather God, might easily have translated into temporal terms as a catastrophic volcanic eruption as described by Plato.

Such a postulation is well supported by archaeological evidence by Professor Luce et al.

In their thesis, they argue that the volcanic island of Thera, 120km north of Knossos, the capital of ancient Crete, was in fact Atlantis, which disappeared abruptly sometime in the fifteenth century BC. due to a colossal eruption.

Before proceeding to show that there is some support for this in mythological interpretation, it is worth examining the inception of the land of Atlantis, which for reasons Professor Luce explains, was wrongly sited by Plato, due to the growing knowledge and awareness of the Greek culture, as being in the Atlantic Ocean, beyond Gibraltar, "the Pillars of Hercules."

One of the reasons for deducing this, was the fact that Plato misread its largeness and greatness as being in the literal sense when, in fact, such references alluded to the extent of its cultural influence in the sense of its being a "great power", a power or influence directly attributable to say the mastery of a form of communication such as maritime communications. This was perhaps similar to for example, the sea skills of the Phoenicians.

The unique shape of the islands forming the city of Atlantis, alternate rings of land and sea, is described by Critias in Plato's narration as being created by the God of the Sea, which, in mythological terms, probably meant that the islands arose out of the sea by some mighty power.

It would not be a great stretch of the imagination to suggest that the same mechanism which caused the destruction of the islands, though attributed to a different deity, was responsible for their inception, that is, volcanic activity.

Such activity, characteristic of that region, over aeons, would give rise to circular rings of land above sea level. There are prehistoric levels of volcanic layers beneath Minoan Thera[14].

Since writing this, the author has become aware that there is a better candidate for Atlantis being destroyed by volcanic action and that is the island of Santorini with its huge caldera.

Atlantis begins to appear then, as an integrated multi-ringed volcanic mountain, "the great mountain peak", the Hittite name of the Sea God's daughter, Kumarbi's bride.

The mountain was also probably visible from mainland Turkey.

Returning to the account of Critias, we see that the central symbol of Atlantean culture was the sacred pillar, a similar symbol to the Egyptian Anu cult or On of Genesis, the cult into which Joseph married, the sacred obelisk whereon kingly laws and panegyrics were inscribed.

K. T. Frost[15] as Professor Luce points out, was the first to suggest Crete as Plato's Atlantis. The island was "the way to other islands" as the Timaeus and Critias has it and Professor Andrew's[16] translation of Atlantis "being mid-way between Libya and Asia" lends credence to the now widely accepted assertion.

(Crete, being possibly only part of what was once a larger integrated commonwealth of landmasses).

Luce also corrects the widespread misconception concerning the origin of the word "Atlantis." He asserts that it is not derived from "Atlantic", though Atlantis and Atlantic are linguistically related.

They are, in the Greek, adjectival forms of Atlas, the former meaning the island of Atlas, and the latter, the sea of Atlas.[17]

Crete was the centre of the Minoan culture to which we shall refer again later.

Central symbols on Cretan-Minoan artefacts depict a pillar and a fertility goddess. It should now be clear in the persons of Kumarbi, Upelluri and Ullikummi, to which invading and usurping culture the Hittite myth is referring, can be no other than the manifestly phallic fertility cult of Atlantis.

In its symbolic interpretation, the Song of Ullikummi makes a lot of sense when viewed together with the legend of Atlantis.

Kumarbi represents the Hittite version of the celestial autocratic forces (of phallicism and fertility) attempting to usurp the diviocratic heliopian pantheon of Hittite Anatolia. The headdress of Kumarbi is reputed to be horned, an allusion to the strength and fertility of the bull, a symbol perennially associated with Minoan Crete (and the Hyksos infused Egyptian Delta).

In seeking support of the Sea, he is not seeking the help of Ea of the heliopian pantheon, the equivalent of Thoth of Egypt, but the ancient Sea God of Atlantis, who in the Greek pantheon, became the reconciled God Poseidon, one of the many names of the Sea God of Atlantis.

Kumarbi becomes in fact the Sea God by marrying the God's daughter.

This is a similar theme to the god Poseidon marrying mortal woman from which the sacred pillar culture of Atlantis issues, as featured in Minoan and Mycenean artefacts.

In the Hittite myth, the issue of the union is Ullikummi, a mountain, who appears in Mesopotamian myth as Humbaba, the mountain conquered by Gilgamesh (Mesopotamia) and Enkidu (possibly representing the Hittite and or Hurrian cultures).

If Plato is correct, and most of that which was Atlantis disappeared into the sea, what originally did it encompass?

Most probably Crete and surrounding islands, together with Rhodes, for Rhodes is also associated with a mythological colossus which was possibly visible from the Anatolian mainland. In the words of Upelluri, the Hittite Atlas, we detect a hint of the age of Atlantis relative to the mainland continents.

He "knew nothing", that is, did not exist in the beginning when the lands and seas were formed. He does not know "who that god is", a suggestion that the Sea God is a stranger to the heliopian family.

It turns out, the symbol of the God is a diorite post or pillar.

Stone, particularly diorite, held signal potency, for several statues of pharaohs of early Egyptian dynasties were sculpted in diorite.

Stone became a central archetype of the Judaic Biblical tradition (c.f. Jacob's altar stone) and of course was the material of the sacred pillars of On.

A pillar figures largely in later Cretan-Minoan culture in association with a fertility goddess who is often depicted grasping snakes, a common phallic symbol like the pillar.

In Ancient Egypt and surrounding cultures, Minoan Crete was known as Keftiu, the root Keft, being connected with Caput and the Biblical Kaphtor for Crete, the former meaning the capital of a pillar. It is probable that the Atlantean culture had extended influence onto the then Mycenean and Anatolian mainland and even beyond to for example, Egypt and the Levant. The culture, as legend relates, was a maritime culture, with, at its head, the Sea God, who would afford protection and encouragement to seafarers and explorers.

The Sea God is later depicted associated with a chariot driven by horses or sea horses, no doubt symbolic of his great power. In the celestial sense, the sea or waters represented to the psyche, psychological or waters of fertility, hence his power is both temporal and celestial (psychological).

The Hyksos therefore, with their introduction of the horse into Egypt could, as invaders from the north, i.e., the sea, become to look like possible invading Atlanteans introducing their sacred pillar culture to the Egyptian Delta.

We shall see more evidence linking Cretan culture to the lands of the Southern Mediterranean later, when the Minoan culture is examined.

With the demise of the Atlantean culture, its remnants would remain on the Greek and Anatolian mainlands and would become a source of conflict between the mainland cultures throughout the centuries and is evident at the present time.

The Hittites also believed in the divinity of kings. Labarna I (Hattusili), on discovering the treachery of a nephew, also named Labarna, apparently a possible successor, disowns him and proclaims Mursili, "In place of the Lion, the God will set up another Lion"[18]

The pre-Hittite Proto-Syrian (Anatolian) lion archetype can be seen as the god Dagan, the "Lord of the Stars" the celestial executive, the appointer of kings.

As a symbol of royal power, it can be seen to be very old and is still in use today in heraldry particularly evident on the British Royal coat of Arms.

The Hittites had over two hundred statutes of highly sophisticated laws governing social mores such as divorce, which was permitted, to Labour laws and pricing rules. Laws of compensation, as well as retributionary laws reflected a high degree of humanity, absent in contemporary codes of Hammurabi and the later Biblical codes.

Mandatory capital punishment reserved for the refusal to submit to the authority of the king and certain types of bestiality and rape "in the mountains." Unopposed rape in the victim's house however, was only classed as adultery and it seems "crime passionelle" was permitted should an injured third party discover the rape.

It may appear therefore that the attitude to women appeared a little severe. Curiously, the incident involving Labarna was to trigger a series of palace coups by other claimants to the throne and was contemporary (circa 1525 BC) with the Egyptian Hatshepsut episode (circa 1480 BC).

After seventy-five years, order returned with re-establishment of male succession[19] following the edict "let a prince the son of a wife of the first rank be king. If there is no prince of the first rank, let one who is a son of the second rank become king. If, however there is no prince, let them take a husband for a daughter of the first rank and let him become king." This circumstance was the one that Tuthmosis III of Egypt claimed succession over Hatshepsut and the assertion of the edict indicates the presence of similar cultural conflicts in the Hittite culture as were present in contemporary Egypt.

The Biblical Abraham was a cultural contact representing the Sumerian influence common to both cultures, his being also the patriarch of Hebrew monotheism.

The defeat of Kumarbi by Teshub also has its parallel in the sequel to the battle of the Titans.

Zeus does battle with the monster Typhon "whose head reached to heaven" and he was so tall, being man above the hips, that he overtopped the highest mountain and his head often knocked against the stars[20]

From his head grew a hundred heads of serpents and his body was covered in wings. Hissing, he flung fiery stones at Heaven and from his mouth spurted flames. Zeus pursued him, wielding a steel sickle, to Mount Kasion. Eventually, the monster is defeated.

It is clear that the story has many symbols in common with the legendary Atlantis culture such as (phallic) serpents of gigantic proportions spitting fire, corresponding to the pillar and volcanic eruptions.

The great power of the culture must have extended on to the Mycenean and Anatolian mainlands where many Cretan artefacts or similar have been found, as well as pillar altars at for example, Pylos and Tyrins.

The passage of time saw the demise of Atlantis, Kumarbi and the three heliopian cultures take its place, that of probably the Mycenaeans, the Hittites and the Egyptians. The three seeds spat from the pregnant Kumarbi became the flowering of three heliopian cultures.

Some of the oldest myths concerning the creation of the world, in the Egyptian cosmogony, describe Atum as the first god who created himself by masturbation (a phallic reference indicating the age of the culture; phallicism dominated the pre-heliopian age) and thence other gods. His offspring, the twins Shu and Tefnut, were respectively, born by spitting Shu out and vomiting Tefnut[21]

This similarity with the (Cretan) Kumarbi is another indication of early Cretan influence in Egypt. The twins Shu and Tefnut may have been an early heliopian device to explain the dual cultures of Upper and Lower Egypt. The abode of Atum was the same as the Cretan Sea God, the primeval of Nun (water).

The Theban, Memphite, Hermopolitan and Heliopian cosmogonies all held a central concept of a primeval hill rising out of Nun, each claiming that their cult centres stood on the site.[22] (How like modern times.)

Again, one can see a similarity with the myth of Ulikummi, the monstrous mountain god of Hittite myth. Thebes, the seat of Amen, claimed primacy of site. The headdress of Amen, feathers in a Lower Egyptian Delta Red Crown, is very similar to Pulisati (Cretan) invaders of the twelfth century BC. and early Minoan headdresses of deities.

The rivers mentioned in the Kumarbi-Anu myth, may also have been an allusion to Hittite, Babylonian and possibly Egyptian cultures which also, were to arise.

The "Slaying of the Dragon" also forms part of Hittite mythology, not surprisingly, and tells how Teshub, the Storm God, with the help of Anara, a woman, sets out a sumptuous meal for the dragon that is preying on the populace (Cretan invaders), and she is able to slay it.

This is an allusion to a battle in the distant past and represents the Hittite culture conquering the fertility dragon culture. In an alternative account of the myth[23], the dragon defeats the Weather God and gains possession of his heart and eyes, that is the Hittites are themselves conquered.

In order to recover them, the Weather God begat a son by the daughter of a poor man, a possible reference to a vassal kingdom or neighbouring culture.

When the son grew to manhood, he married the dragon's daughter, with instructions to demand the return of the heart and eyes. When restored, "the God went off the sea to do battle and when they came to do battle with him, he succeeded in defeating the dragon Illuyankas."

In this version, the culture is restored, it would seem, by cultural and dynastic alliances, culminating in a battle for ascendancy.

Also in this vein, another myth relates the absence of the ancient heliopian culture.

In the myth of "the God who disappeared"[24] several deities, including the Sun God, disappear. The main version concerns Telipinu, the God of Agriculture and son of the Storm God, who "goes off in a temper and in haste putting his right boot on his left foot and his left boot on his right foot."

Some of the words which form the description that follows are uncertain. The description could equally apply to a description of Thera or Pompey following the eruption of Vesuvius. In the literal sense, the myth describes famine and blight, but in mythological terms, describes a war, a cultural eclipse.

"Dust (?) clouds beset the window, smoke (?) besets the house, the embers on the hearth were choked (?), the Gods stifled (in the temple), the sheep stifled in the fold, the oxen stifled in the stall, the ewe spurned her lamb, the cow spurned her calf…Barley and emmer wheat throve no more. Oxen, sheep and humans ceased to conceive, and those who were pregnant could not bear; both men and Gods began to starve. The Gods great and small set out to search for Telipinu. The Sun God sent out the swift eagle… The eagle went forth but found him not."

On the advice of the Goddess Hannahannas, the Weather God sets out to search.

"He knocked at the gate of his town, but he could not get it open and (merely) broke the shaft of his hammer, so the Weather God…gave up and sat down (to rest)."

In mythological terms, this signifies a battle with the culture suffering defeat. Hannahannas then proposes to send a bee.

"The Gods, great and small, have sought him but not found him. Shall this bee now search and find him. His wings are small and he is small." The bee is sent however, and stings the god into action, but far from returning home with the bee, the god proceeds to destroy mankind, oxen and sheep, that is, the land remains at war.

The story becomes fragmentary at this point, but eventually, the god returns on the back of an eagle, which in many Near Eastern cultures, is the spirit and guardian of the Tree of Life (and Abundance).

The heliopian culture returns, symbolised by the celestial executive, reflecting temporal kingship. In a parallel myth[25] it is the Weather God himself who vanishes (i.e., kingship).

"Telipinu returned to his temple. He took thought for the land, he released the dust(?) cloud from the window, the smoke from the house (the land). The altars of the Gods were made ready…Telipinu (took thought for) the King and Queen, he took thought for them to grant them life and vigour for the future, Telipinu took thought for the King."

In the Weather God myth which is very similar, the villain is Hahhimas, who, "paralysed the whole earth, he has dried up the waters (of life). Hahhimas is mighty."

This description is redolent of Kumarbi. The curious symbolism of eagle and bee is evocative and is possibly an allusion to the Eagle and Bee kingdoms of early Egypt, maybe allies in the cultural struggle.

"Melissai" or bees were sacred to the Anatolian Mother Goddess Cybele, the Great Mother of Asia Minor, who may have been a derivative of Hannahannas or Grandmother[26]

It is however, not surprising, that similar cultural traits and therefore, cultural forces, should transcend national boundaries. This can be observed in the present century, as cultural tides are no respecters of national boundaries.

The cult of the sacred pillar is evidenced in Mycenae as testament to the Atlantean influence in the form of the lion gate. The pillar cult was also prevalent in the Egyptian Delta, the stronghold of Amenism.

Kumarbi, biting off the genitals of Anu (On of the Bible), has its echoes in Ouranos' severed manhood falling into the sea resulting in the birth of Venus[27] and Seth flinging the Osirian member into the Nile, to be eaten by the Lepidotus, Phagrus and the Oxyrynchus fish. These latter symbols in all likelihood representative of the indigenous inhabitants.

Here – Fish symbolism features largely in Cretan mythology whence the goddess is often depicted as half fish.

Early Hittite communications were hieroglyphs, very similar to those of Egypt. The prominent members of the Hittite pantheon can be seen at the sanctuary of Yazilakaya (meaning "hewn out of rock" which indeed it is).

The symbol of celestial life-giving power held by the celestial executive, is a slightly modified form of the Egyptian ansata cross, incorporating a lotus flower, the symbol of life, which signified the spiritual authority of the king.

Other prominent symbols are the double-headed eagle. This dual bird motif is common in Cretan artefacts, but usually, the birds are separated. The uni-horned sacred bulls, together with the celestial king astride what may be two priests, is a possible symbolic representation of kingship ascendancy over religious power.

The queen Habat is seen standing on the back of a winged lion. This is in all probability, a representation of the power of the god Dagan of Protosyrian origin whose influence permeated many of the Levant states that were later to succumb to Hittite hegemony. Certain deities can be seen holding a lion's tail, a common feature of the pantheon's authority and indicative of the multicultural nature of the cosmogony.

The Storm God of Hatussas can be seen astride two blocks of stone, which can be taken to be mountains. He carries, like the hieratic Storm God, a club, which later became a feature of the Greek hero Herakles.

The two mountains are almost certainly meant to represent the sacred "Mashu Mountains" which formed the portals of Heaven as related in the Mesopotamian "Epic of Gilgamesh."

71

In this ancient epic, the hero vanquishes lions that as we shall see, are clearly representative of a hostile culture.

Such common symbolism betrays a cultural affinity between the Hurrian Hittites and the Sumerians.

The senior Sumerian culture, it will be seen, influenced many of the later surrounding cultures.

Telipinu, giving "thought to the king", implies that kingship was in need of being repaired or restored. A similar restoration occurred aeons before in the Mesopotamian culture evident in the Flood Myth.

This is not surprising, for as we have seen in the heliopian culture of Egypt, the authority of temporal kingship as a reflection of the celestial order, was constantly being challenged by the exponents of religious power. It can be deduced therefore that the assailing of kingship was part of the mechanism of the perennial battle between the heliopian and autocratic monolithic cultures.

In the Epic of Gilgamesh, one of the oldest myths ever recorded, we encounter the hero battling against a monstrous rock or mountain.

This is probably the Sumerian culture's encounter with the same culture against which the Storm God in the Song of Ullikummi does battle, that is, the Cretan-Atlantean pillar culture.

The Gods "bellowing like cattle" in the Hittite myth, is a similar description to the Egyptian early dynastic or pre-dynastic style of describing of events when Near Eastern cosmogonies still had many animal deities.

Such deities must have reflected the level of the population's collective awareness. As collective awareness grew, so the pantheon changed to include more and more human formed gods, as is demonstrated by the development of the Ancient Egyptian pantheon.

The cosmogony changed from the Ptah cycle, which was predominantly animal, to the Ra-Osiris-Temu cycle, which contained animal and human or hybrid gods. The pantheons of the Greeks and Romans, a later heliopian development, consisted of deities who were overwhelmingly human in form.

The Egyptians realised, even in the earliest times with the symbolism of Nu, that the populace required some psychological symbol of safety and security in the psychological ocean (the collective unconscious). This was the ocean which formed part of Nature's "sea of life", whose immutable law was that of the jungle, the law of survival.

Such symbols, one could assay, would obtain a degree more potency with a population whose progress from Darwinian origins would be somewhat less than those of present-day populations albeit some would agree such progress being only marginal. The religious symbol that the Egyptians developed, was the Sekhet Boat, a potent and recognisable symbol of safety in an unfathomable sea. This symbol was one that was to be mythologised to good and powerful psychological effect in the Flood myths of Sumeria. The archetypal symbolism of the boat was put to powerful psychological effect in the story of Noah.

Another equally, if not more potent psychological symbol however, is the rock, which, as we have seen in Hittite mythology, was used to challenge the Gods. It is also in the Judaic Biblical narrative that the symbol is often to be found, in such instances as for example, the "rock that will become a mountain" or "the mountain of the lord's house shall be established in the top of the mountains" (Isiah 2-2) and "The mountain of the House of the Lord shall be established as the highest of mountains" (Micah IV I-3) etc.

In the translation of Judaism to Christianism, the symbol was invoked as the "rock" of the Church, all of which are distant cultural echoes of Atlantean-Hyksos archetypes.

The pyramids of Egypt embodied the concept corresponding to early phases of religious development owing in their architecture, some influence of the Mesopotamian Ziggurat with a consequence that, as religion became more pluralistic, the rock symbol devalued so pyramid building ceased, displacing associated concepts of immutability and immobility.

The Sekhet Boat, representative of safety, communication and mobility becomes central to the heliopian cosmogony, depicting the vessel of the Sun God Ra and a number of other deities and is the means of transport for the deceased for the final journey to heaven.

It was to this end that a large boat was buried beside the Great Pyramid, only lately discovered when the body of the pharaoh was interred. The Sekhet Boat itself may have been imported from the Mesopotamian culture where it was used as the symbol for, ostensibly, Man's deliverance from a Great Flood. It must also have had a sacred symbolism for the sea going Cretan derived Hyksos, as it had for the Vikings.

The Epic of Gilgamesh, which will be examined presently, sees the hero travelling in a boat over "nether" waters in which the serpent of death dwells.

In one of the oldest of Egyptian myths, the primeval waters is the abode of Apophis, the serpent enemy of Ra.

These mythological links casting the Cretan-Atlantean serpent pillar rock culture as the adversary of the heliopian cultures shall be further explored.

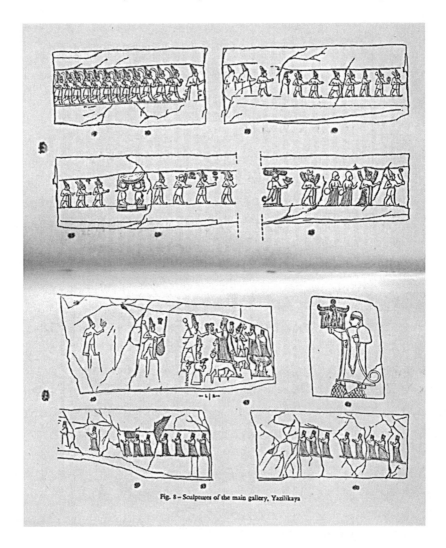

Fig. 8 – Sculptures of the main gallery, Yazilikaya

"The Hittite Gods"
With Kind Acknowledgements to O.R. Gurney and Pelican Books

74

References Chapter 3

[1] O. R. Gurney, The Hittites, page 18

[2] ibid, page 138

[3] J. Hicks, The Empire Builders, page 75

[4] O. R. Gurney, The Hittites, page 142

[5] ibid, page 193

[6] C. Kerenyi, The Gods of the Greeks, page 20

[7] ibid, page 18

[8] O. R. Gurney, The Hittites, page 194

[9] ibid, page 194

[10] ibid, page 195

[11] J. V. Luce, The End of Atlantis, page 23

[12] Plato Timaeus and Critias, 108c-109a,113-end

[13] J. V. Luce, The End of Atlantis, page 44

[14] ibid, page 96

[15] ibid, page 36

[16] ibid, page 32

[17] ibid, page 31

[18] J. Hicks, The Empire Builders, page 98

[19] ibid, page 99

[20] C. Kerenyi, The Gods of the Greeks, page 23

[21] Egyptian Mythology (based on text by D. Ames, page 30 from Mythologie General Larousse)

[22] ibid, page 36

[23] O. R. Gurney, The Hittites, page 184

[24] ibid, page 186

[25] ibid, page 187

[26] ibid, page 191

[27] C. Kerenyi, The Gods of the Greeks, page 18

*See Europe of the Ancient Regime by David Ogg for reference of origin of Turks (i.e., latter-day Hittites) Page 54 'The Ottoman Turks were probably descended from a nomadic Siberian tribe......' This confirms the opening statement of this chapter and indicates that the Turks were likely descendants of the Hittites.

As will be demonstrated at points throughout the book, cultural military invasions were not one-off events but often one of a series throughout a long period of history. In Anatolia there was the settlement of the Hittites followed in the 12th Century the invasion of the Mongols which can be regarded as a second wave of the same culture. Certain characteristics portray the Turks as from nomadic background in so far as in the 18th and 19th Centuries when other nations were industrialising, they 'had no manufacturers save those of brass ware, carpets and perfumery; nor (except among the upper classes) did they have any pride in household possessions'. (Ibid).

It is significant that in the 20th Century the Turkish State became a secular state. This must have been in part to the fact that unlike other Islamic states, being nomadic in origin and 'having no culture of their own they borrowed extensively, their Mohammedan faith from the Arabs, their arts from Persia and Byzantium. Their culturally different origin enabled their culture to break with the shackles of Islam.

See also BBC series *Lost Cities of the Ancient 'Hatti' (Hattusas).*

Latest archaeological research has shown that the Hittite Empire was brought down by the falling out of the Princely Brotherhood that strictly controlled the populace and was held together by sacred ancient oaths. After the battle of Kadesh, the victorious general returned and sent the reigning king into exile. Civil war broke out, lasting various generations. Ultimately the empire ended with a burning of the king's palace, most of the temples within the hugely fortified walls and a mass migration of the remaining population. These facts seem to corroborate Virgil's account of the Aeneid and Aeneas' migration. The defeat of the Trojans from within would equate to the wooden horse bringing to an end the ten-year siege, probably a much longer period than a cultural time of ten years. The Greks could have somehow entered the great city and sacked it probably after the migrants were given safe passage to leave.

Chapter 4
Mythology of the Sumerians, Mesopotamians, Akkadians and Canaanites

For the purposes of mythological culture, the Mesopotamians, Sumerians and Akkadians, occupants of central Mesopotamia prior to 2000 BC, will be treated as being part of the same cultural tradition; though from an archaeological view, this may not be regarded as being the case.

The Pantheon

It is from the Babylonian Creation Myth "Enuma Elish", recited during the Babylonian New Year Festival, that the creation of the Mesopotamian pantheon can be ascertained[1]. The festival was not only a celebration of the temporal renewal of life, but reflected, like the Hittite "Song of Ullikumi", the renaissance or regaining of celestial precedence by the post primordial members (i.e., younger deities) from the oligarchy of primordial gods. Similar events are also chronicled in Greek mythology, in the myths of Zeus and Kronos.

Some of the primordial gods were:

Apsu...the primordial begetter, the equivalent of the Hittite Kumarbi.

Tiamat the "Lady mountain", a similar title to the mate of Kumarbi and the mother of Ullikumi, called "a great mountain peak." Tiamat bore the new gods and appears in Mesopotamian mythology as attempting, in the manner of Ullikumi, to usurp the pantheon. Apsu and Tiamat begot Lahmu, Lahamu, Anshar and Kishar. Anshar's first born was Anu, whom we have encountered as head of the Hittite cosmogony and whose name was also given to the seat of the heliopian cosmology in Egypt.[2]

Anu was the supreme king, divine sovereign, the "heavenly repository of final authority" of the post-primordial deities.

According to Thomas Carlyle's etymology[3], the king's power was often described as "Enlilitu" or the "EnlilShip." Here then we see the symbol of the "ship" having precedence over the "rock" of Tiamat.

The Enlil ship features as the vessel of salvation in the Sumerian Flood myth.

Enlil was the Wind or Storm God. He was also a king and executive of Anu, the direct equivalent of Teshub of the Hittite pantheon.

As celestial executive, he was the patron of kings, the celestial image of temporal kingship. In a fragment of the Mesopotamian account of the Flood[4], it states:

"Ziusrudra, the king, prostrated himself before Anu (and) Enlil, Anu and Enlil cherished Ziusrudra."

It is Enlil to whom the "Enlilitu", the king's power is attributed and which was mainly invoked in the temporal struggle against suffering.

Ea Sumerian Enki, was the God of Sweet Waters, Wisdom and patron of the Arts, who lived "in the deep", a probable reference to the primeval waters (i.e., the collective unconscious of all life, that is Man's natural nature).

The same god was encountered in Hittite mythology, instrumental in saving the pantheon.

In the Mesopotamian Flood Myth, it is he who advised Ziusrudra, a king, the Akkadian Utnapishtim and Biblical Noah, how to survive the Flood.

Ninki was the mother of Enlil whose name was probably another form of Ninhursag.

Ninhursag, the Sumerian Mother Goddess was one of the four principal Sumerian gods with Anu, Enlil and Ea (Enki). Sometimes she is the wife of Enki. She created vegetation and was also known as Nintu "lady of birth" and Ki, the earth.

Ninlil was the wife of Enlil, the Goddess of Heaven and Mother of the Moon.

Sin, Sumerian "Nanna" was chief astral deity, father of the Sun God and Ishtar, the equivalent of Isis and Aphrodite. The "Sin" of Ur is reported by Wooley as being the Moon God, but in all heliopian pantheons, the Moon was regarded as a female deity.

Ningal was the wife of Sin and mother of the Sun God.

Shamash the Sun God, was principally the judge and lawgiver, with some fertility attributes. This god can often be seen in a similar role to Marduk, the city god of Babylon who became identified with Enlil as Marduk Enlil. In Syria and Palestine, Marduk was called Hadad, but more often, was known as the Canaanite Baal (the Lord).

Sun God titles were common to both Zeus and Apollo in the Greek pantheon. Shamash's celestial authority as judge, equates him with Osiris in the Egyptian pantheon. Osiris was chief executive in the Maati Hall of Judgement before the gods.

Shamash was the husband and brother of Ishtar, he and Ishtar being a direct correspondence to Osiris and Isis, who were also married siblings. Shamash is also depicted as having a consort Aya, the Dawn.

Ishtar, Sumerian Inarra, was the goddess of Love and fertility and Queen of Heaven. She is often depicted under the crescent moon and, in many ways, is identical to Isis. Such correspondences are indicative of the influence that the Sumerian culture had on the later Egyptian culture.

Ishtar was the daughter of Anu. She is also represented as having Tammuz (Sumerian Dumuzi) the dying God of Vegetation as consort.[5]

In an Akkadian poem, she descends to the underworld in search of her young husband. This has echoes of Isis' search for Osiris.

Ereshkigal and **Nergal** were deities who ruled the Underworld into which Ishtar descended through seven gates, at each, gradually being divested of all that symbolised her divine authority. In another version she sheds seven veils. A similar ritual is alluded to in the New Testament in the story of Salome.

There were many other deities in the vast Mesopotamian-Sumerian pantheon that, like the Egyptian, clearly practised the heliopian principle of religious toleration and cultural incorporation.

One more god is worthy of inclusion and that is:

Nebo, the son of Marduk the Sun God. He was intermediary of the gods and patron of Writing and Speech, a similar god to the Greek Hermes. In the "Enumu Elish" myth ("when on high"), written it is thought around 1700 BC, Marduk is temporarily confined in the "Mountain" and is eventually released by Nebo.

The mountain is most likely a reference to the Atlantean culture at some archaic point in the past, conquering Mesopotamia. This shall be shown later to be the case. This story has similarities to the myth of Zeus being confined in Cilicia (Anatolia) by Typhoeus, the serpent, a symbol of the Cretan culture, where Hermes and Aigipan restore Zeus' 'sinews'.[6] It is worth noting that Nectanebo was the last king of Egypt before the Ptolemys, his name betraying the influence of the Persian occupation of the land prior to Alexander's conquest.

Budge refers to him in his "Egyptian Magic" as leaving Egypt for the court of Philip of Macedon to become the Vizier of the court where he predicts the birth of a god (Alexander) to Olympias.

It has been stated previously that myths were propagated primarily for cultural purposes and as a means of preserving early history in communities without means of communication such as writing and literature and without the universal franchise of learning. This was probably as a result of the then prevailing requirements of subsistence in the absence of anything but the most primitive of technology.

The myths themselves were formulated in a symbolic way, readily understood by the collective unconscious and in accord with the then, generally low level of individual awareness. This is evident from the many instances where the literal interpretation lies in the realms of the absurd (though this has not prevented the myths from being promoted and accepted literally).

The myth of the Flood is a good example of literalism which, as we shall see, when interpreted in a cultural context, has been given by the propagators of literalism, a meaning quite the contrary of its originally intended admonishment. It has long been agreed that the story of the Flood, as told in Genesis, is based on the Sumerian legend, of which, the oldest written versions go back to before Abraham.[7]

In a comparison of myths by Professor Hooke[8] of Sumerian and Babylonian accounts, it is the Gods or Enlil, or in some cases, Ishtar who decree the Flood, and in the Biblical account, Yahweh. In the Sumerian and Babylonian accounts it is a king Ziusrudra (or Utnapishtim in the Babylonian) who is instructed to construct a ship as a defence against the flood from storm and rain and to take all kinds of animals on board. In the biblical version, Noah, not named as a king, is instructed to do the same.

The flood lasts longer in the biblical account. In the original versions, the flood subsides after Utnapishtim sends out a swallow, a dove, and a raven, the latter being in Greek mythology the symbol of the Sun God.

In the Sumerian, Ziusrudra offers sacrifice to the Sun God, in the Babylonian, to the gods on Mt Nisir. The biblical version has Noah making sacrifice to Yahweh, presumably at Mt Ararat in Turkey. This poetically conveys the transportation of the heliopian Mesopotamian culture to Anatolia.

It is known that a substantial component of Hittite culture of the second millennium BC consisted of Hurrian, a close derivative of the Mesopotamian culture.

Subsequently, immortality is given to Ziusrudra and Utnapishtim, symbolising the survival in the non-literal sense, of the spirit of the heliopian culture in man as represented by Ziusrudra.

In the biblical account, Yahweh promises not to destroy the earth again by flood, and provides the rainbow, a multicoloured (phallic) symbol, as a sign of remembrance. This corresponds, in the Babylonian account, significantly, to Ishtar's necklace of lapis lazuli, given as a sign of remembrance. Lapis Lazuli forms part of the pharaonic regalia, and represents the Sun.

It is apparent that the myth has been tailored to suit the particular culture's religious mores. The Babylonian and Sumerian versions are full of heliopian regal and solar symbolism, where the biblical account contains fertility symbolism, is prophet oriented and is lacking any reference to kingship. There are two versions in effect, the heliopian and the monotheistic versions of the myth.

On further examination, and abandoning the literal interpretation, we see the Flood as being a psychological cultural flood that would have eclipsed the heliopian cosmogonies of the time. The "Flood" clearly represents the forces of the primordial monotheistic Sea God of Water, i.e., the ancient archetype of procreation and fertility.

It is easy to perceive how Enlil became associated with the instigator, being the Storm God, however, in the symbol of the ship and animals, we see the preservation of the heliopian diviocracy. The boat or ark is similar to the Egyptian Sekhet Boat, the boat of Nu rising out of the primeval water, bearing in his hands, the boat of the Sun God Ra in the company of other deities.

Here is another example of the senior Mesopotamian culture influencing a subsequent culture.

But who were the deities represented in the Sekhet Boat if indeed the Ark was the forerunner?

The deities symbolised by the animals of which all kinds were taken in the Sumerian and Babylonian myths represent the plurality of the cosmogonies. This concept is also apparent in the biblical version for traditionally Noah selected the animals in twos, an allusion to the natural requirements of procreation (fertility).

This duality can later be seen in the Egyptian Maati Hall of the gods where the gods are seated in twos.

The animals also testify to the archaicness of the myth, for many of the deities in the pre-Osirian that is, Ptah cycle were represented as animals, and would be typical of contemporary Mesopotamian deities. The form of such deities suggests an early stage of man's conscious need and conception of divine beings and corresponds to the early stages of his conscious development.

It can be understood therefore why Anu and Enlil cherished Ziusrudra the king as saviour of the culture, preserving kingship from what can only be described as the opponent of temporal regal order.

During the Flood, kingship, representing the heliopian culture, had been vanquished (by the religious estate?) for in the accounts of Sumerian king lists, we read:

"Then came the Flood and after the Flood "kingship" again descended from Heaven."[9]

Ziusudra's reward from the gods was:

"Life like a God they give him, Breath eternal like a God they bring down for him. Then Ziusrudra the king, The preserver of the name of vegetation of the seed of mankind, In the Land of Dilmun, the place where the sun rises, they caused to dwell."[10]

We shall see that the concept and imagery embodied in this latter part of the myth, contributed greatly to subsequent Ancient Egyptian and Greco-Roman eschatology.

Finally, before leaving for the time being this myth, it is worth noting Ishtar's involvement. Ishtar, the fertility goddess was a precursor of Venus, and Aphrodite, the Cypriot goddess who had her prototype in Cleito.

Cleito as we have seen was the Cretan goddess and fabled daughter of the Sea God Poseidon, formerly known by several archaic names and Lord of Atlantis.

Poseidon reigned supreme as the (fertility) pillar god. In mythological historical terms then, the Flood myth can be seen as an account of the widespread conquest by the Atlantean culture of the known commonwealth of heliopian Near East.

In the Babylonian Creation Myth, we can read an account of a story in mythological terms, the same as the Hittite myth of Teshub and Ullikumi. This is possibly not surprising, considering the Hurrian (Mesopotamian) influence in the Hittite culture.

In it, the same god of wisdom Ea has overcome the primordial god Apsu and has begotten Marduk-Enlil. The primordial gods challenge the Celestial Court in the form of Tiamat, a female deity, the "Lady Mountain" (a possible allusion to Cleito) whose army is a "monstrous brood" spawned by a primordial mother, the goddess Hubur.

As in the Hittite pantheon, the celestial court is dismayed. Kingu, Tiamat's commander in chief, invested with the "tablets of Destiny", some form of sacred communication, and redolent of the tablets of Moses, threatens the destruction of the pantheon.

Eventually, Marduk-Enlil engages Tiamat in single combat riding in his chariot of four, the Killer, the Relentless, the Trampler and the Swift, and armed with bow, mace, lightning, net and winds, defeats Tiamat.

The allies of Tiamat are slain and captured; the Tablets of Destiny are taken from Kingu and fixed by Marduk on his own breast, establishing again the authority of the celestial executive.

"The Lord trod on the legs of Tiamat…He bade them not to allow her waters to escape (i.e., cultural military forces) He constructed stations for the great Gods Fixing their astral likenesses as constellations He determined the year by designating zones He set up three constellations for each of twelve months After defining the days of the year by means of heavenly figures He founded the station of Nebiru to determine their heavenly bands, that none might transgress of fall short…"[11]

Here can be seen evidence of early Mesopotamian-Chaldean religious astrology and astronomy. The Ras Shamra texts show the same myth in Canaanite mythology[12] with the story of Baal and Anat (the Canaanite Ishtar).

In the Baal (or Bel) cycle of myths, Baal is the Storm God and Anat his sister, a similar relationship to the Sun God Shamash and Ishtar and Osiris and Isis.

The Prince and Ruler of the Sea and Ocean Current, attempts to usurp the divine court under El (Anu). Baal enlists the help of the Skilful and Percipient One that is, Ea or Enki (in Egyptian mythology, Thoth) who fashions for Baal double mace or axe with which Baal vanquishes the usurper.

Such double-headed axes are to be seen in Roman reliefs and the same axe was given to Marduk-Enlil. It takes another mace,[13] the "Expeller" with which

Baal delivers the fatal blow between the eyes of his adversary to finish the job and deliver the pantheon.

In recognition of his valour, Baal, like Marduk-Enlil, has a house built for him by the "Skilful and Percipient One" after complaining that he has no house like the other gods. Presumably, the Canaanite culture was not considered at that point to be developed or powerful enough to be included in the heliopian pantheon.

Baal the mighty exulted "I have built my house of silver and my palace of gold" metals associated with the Moon and Sun.

In the Canaanite texts, there follows an account of a disputation between the "Skilful and Percipient One" and Baal, as to whether a roof-shuttered window should be installed in the house as desired by Baal.

"And cause the clouds to open when the Skilful One opens the window."

This is a clear reference to admitting the Sun God into the powerful house of Baal, and though seemingly trivial, provides a cultural link to the Mesopotamian mythological tradition and ancient urgency of the Flood myth, for in the account of Ziusrudra's (and the pantheon's) escape, it states:

"Utu came forth, who sheds light on heaven and earth Ziusrudra opened a window of the huge boat, The Hero brought his rays into the giant boat."

Thus the power of Baal is elegantly sanctioned by the eye of the Sun, for the requirement of celestial contact and the recognition by Baal of the supremacy of that body is a safeguard against the god being seduced by his own exploits.

In temporal terms this could mean that the Canaanite culture is not seduced with expansionary ambitions.

"Now that Baal returns to his house, shall any king make earth his dominion."

The myths surrounding Baal show marked similarities with Egyptian, Hittite, Mesopotamian and probably Babylonian mythology, testifying to their homogeneous heliopian essence. A common theme in all these cultures is the Celestial Executive's descent into the underworld and successful return symbolising the conquering of death. This was the test of godhood and immortality.

The myth of Baal's descent into the underworld translates into Hittite mythology as the Myth of the Missing God and in the Egyptian as the story of the disappearance of Osiris. In the Christian tradition, the decent was required as one of the divine credentials of Christ. The drama involving royal siblings, sister

84

desperately searching for her royal brother is common to many if not all of the Middle Eastern mythologies.

In the Baal myth Anat, his sister, in her search for Baal:

"Ranges every mountain to the heart of the earth, every hill to the midst of the fields."

This is the same story as Isis searching for Osiris, Ishtar searching for Tammuz, Demeter searching for Kore and Aphrodite for Adonis.

Baal is also admonished by Mot or Death:

"Thy face thou shalt surely set towards the Mountain of Concealment. Take the mountain on thy hands, the hill on the top of thy palms."

This enigmatic passage seems to portray Mot the god of the Underworld urging Baal to be suppliant to the archetypal Mountain, the personification of Death. Egyptian tomb paintings and manuscripts show the deceased holding two hill shaped objects on upturned palms in the presence of Osiris. Here it would seem the Egyptian culture shared or influenced the neighbouring Canaanite culture in matters of eschatology.

Mesopotamian seals and the stele of Naram Sin (circa 2159-2123 BC) show the same imagery representing mountains. This is another example indicating cultural incorporation of ancient mythological concepts from earlier heliopian cultures.

Ultimately, Anat, like Isis, destroys Mot (overcomes death).

"In the fields she scatters him, His remains, the birds eat, wild creatures consume his fragments."

In the hymn from Babylon, Ishtar, Anat's Babylonian equivalent, is addressed as "Mighty one, Lady of Battles who overturns mountains."[14] This may be contrasted with Isiah (Kings 2.2):

"And it shall come to pass in the latter days, that the mountain of the house of the Lord shall be established as the highest of Mountains."

Baal in some version of the myth, after ferocious and undecided battles with Mot, returns to ascend his mighty throne, signifying the survival of the culture.

In the Old Testament, where much use is made of the mountain archetype, Baal or Bel is cast as the devil. When surveying these similar myths of contemporary neighbouring heliopian cultures, we see events clothed in different symbols, but signifying the same challenge to the incumbent ancient diviocratic cultures.

But what of the seemingly disparate different symbols?

In Hittite mythology, the celestial challenger was the "Monstrous Mountain", Ullikiumi of Atlantean culture, whose central symbol was the Sea God's phallic pillar, the primordial symbol of sacred fertility.

In the Mesopotamian, Tiamat, the "Lady Mountain" is the probable precursor of the Hurrian Ullikumi. In Canaanite mythology, it is the "Prince of the Oceans", undoubtedly, another reference to the same ancient Sea God, a primordial God of Water, called by another name.

Apsu and Tiamat were gods of fresh underground and salt water respectively.[15] These names, arising in different but neighbouring cultures indicate the widespread influence of the "Flood" of the Atlantean conquest. The corresponding ancient Egyptian myth is that of Ra and Apophis the sea serpent.

Apophis, the adversary of Ra the Sun god, who had his abode in the Primordial Sea, has obvious fertility and phallic imagery.

These myths then, portray on the psycho-cultural and temporal levels, the celestial forces of enlightenment being challenged by the dark primordial subconscious forces of phallicism and fertility.

On the temporal plane it resolves into the heliopian cultures struggling against a powerful fertility cult of widespread influence around the eastern and southern Mediterranean.

A culture, maritime in nature, which enjoyed the support of a primitive but powerful Sea God. Indications are that the culture was possibly that of pre-Minoan Crete, Atlantis, as shall be indicated when that culture is examined later. Whether this was the case or not, is incidental to the mythological evidence and later historical-archaeological evidence testifying to the continuous cultural struggle between diviocratic heliopianism and autocratic monotheism which transcended national and cultural boundaries as we have seen.

Mesopotamian Influences in Other Cultures

It has previously been suggested that there are to be found Mesopotamian influences in the Ancient Egyptian culture. The Hittite culture was to a large extent, based on the Mesopotamian-Hurrian. Examining some of the central mythological symbols of these cultures, we can see major symbols common to all.

One of the most notable is the Ram of Amen, the invisible or Hidden God. The ram, via Judaic culture, found its way into the Christian Tradition as the lamb, representing the progeny, the son of the Judaic God.

There is to be found in the Mesopotamian culture, the famous golden erectile ram (circa 2700-2500 BC) found at Ur by Wooley and of obvious religious significance.

The ram, a fertility symbol, with penis erect, was at one time erroneously thought to be the "ram in the thicket" associated with the Biblical Abraham. It is seen standing in veneration of the Tree of Life, a central symbol of the story of creation in Genesis, and it is to be found in profusion on Mesopotamian and other seals.

The ram was also a symbol of the ancient Cretan-Mycenean Sea God, later personified as Poseidon and was probably imported into Mesopotamia at the time of the Flood (i.e., Cretan conquest discussed in the following chapter).

A ritual that was extant in Hittite culture involved a ram with a multicoloured wreath or crown of blue, red, yellow, white and black wool. The ram was driven into the hills with the incantation:

"Whatever god of the enemy land has caused this plague, see, we have now driven up this crowned ram to pacify thee, just as a city wall is strong but makes place with the battering ram, do thou the god who has caused this plague, make peace with Hatti" (the Hittites).

"Plagues" was often myth-speak for the austerity during or following a war, the adversary in this case possibly being a strongly Amenite Egypt.

A crowned Hittite ram rhyton was excavated at Karahuyuk in Anatolia.

In the Biblical tradition, Yahweh was a god who had the power to cause plagues and whom Moses invoked in Egypt. The Hebrew ritual of the Day of Atonement, originally part of the Autumn New Year Festival[16] has two goats, one of which was slain, whilst the other was driven into the desert a ritual almost identical with Hittite practice. This suggests a possible Hittite cultural influence on the Judaic. There are references in the Bible concerning Abraham's association with Hittites.

The multicoloured crown was possibly an allusion to an appeal to the Mesopotamian goddess of fertility, Ishtar, to overcome death resulting from the plague.

Ishtar, who, having unsuccessfully "culturally" flooded the world, offers her "multicoloured necklace of Lapis Lazuli" a symbol of the sun, to the Gods as a token of Remembrance[17] and as an act of homage to the authority of the pantheon.

In the Judaic version of the Flood, the necklace is the rainbow, a gift from Yahweh, and a symbol of obvious phallic significance. The allusion to multicolour and its association with fertility symbolism occurs in Genesis (XXXVII-7, 23). Joseph has a dream:

"For behold, we were binding sheaves in the field, and, to, my sheaf arose, and also stood upright; and, behold, your sheaves stood roundabout, and made obeisance to my sheaf."

Corn was naturally adopted in the earliest times as a symbol of fertility. It was sacred to Demeter, a later Western Mediterranean fertility goddess.

Shortly thereafter, Joseph is stripped of his coat of "many colours" but clearly, the coat represented strength and power, often attributed to kings as its source.

"And his brethren said to him 'shalt thou indeed reign over us?'" (Genesis XXXVII-8).

This is a cultural aspiration to kingship that was to be enacted by Moses.

The Tree of Life

The symbol of a tree depicting the Tree of Life was central to the Mesopotamian celestial cosmogony, representing fruit and abundance and hence the concept of fertility. The tree was often depicted associated with Ishtar, the fertility goddess and, under the aegis of a winged sun, which represented the ordinance of the heliopian cosmogony.

The tree, depending on the sun and weather for its life, is an analogy drawn from nature as a vehicle to explain how life, and in particular, human life, depended on the celestial gods, personified as the Sun, fertility, weather etc., for its existence.

The tree is preserved as a central symbol in the Qaballah which, many claim, had its origins in the Chaldean (i.e., Mesopotamian) culture and was preserved in the Judaic tradition. That the tree was central, is evident from the numerous depictions on Mesopotamian, Assyrian, Babylonian and even Hittite seals[18] which, like the Egyptian stone carvings, delineated religious as well as secular motifs.

Generally, the tree is shown in a symmetrical fashion, a common feature of Egyptian art and that of kindred cultures, reflecting the concept of symmetry of opposites, a feature of Qaballistic philosophy.

Often the tree can be seen with two eagle headed human figures similar to the Egyptian Horus, with wings, indicating a spiritual or celestial dimension.

These jins or genii in Arabic mean spirits. On some seals, the genii are holding a seed pouch with which they fertilise the tree. This same seed pouch can be seen on Hittite statuettes. One, carved on stone is still extant in the Roman fort within the confines of the mediaeval Brougham Castle in Westmoreland.

On other seals, the concept of fertility has taken other forms, such as symmetrical erectile rams or bulls with penises erect. (CF the ram and tree from Ur.) In some cases Ishtar represents the concept. On some seals, the tree becomes simply a pillar redolent of the Sea God culture, flanked by erect membered males.

Human headed lions are also evident, on some northern Mesopotamian seals, these (Protosyrian) lions, have the particular crook shaped tails and probably indicate Hittite-Cretan influences.

In some cases, the tree itself, though ostensibly covered in leaves and flowers, is in the shape of and erect male member. Not all seals carried the tree symbol; some were designed to carry mythological scenes.

An example is the "Gilgamesh Seal" in the Vorderascatisches Museum Berlin, which shows the Mesopotamian mythological hero Gilgamesh astride two crowned winged lions holding two fearsome lions by their tails. This refers to the vanquishing of Ishtar by the hero. In cultural terms, this translates as the Mesopotamian culture vanquishing some Istarian fertility culture as indeed was the case, as we shall see, when the Epic of Gilgamesh is explored.

Although not as prominent in the Egyptian culture as the Mesopotamian, the tree was associated with some of the earliest Egyptian myths[19], indicating cross-cultural influences.

In the myth of Osiris, Isis searching for him, receives news that the chest containing the body of Osiris, has been carried to the coast of Byblos in Egypt, and is lodged in the branches of a bush of tamarisk. In a short time, the bush had grown into a large and beautiful tree.

Here the Sun God is associated with a magically transformed tree of beauty, the inference being that the Sun God endows the tree (of Life) with vigour and vitality. (In the New Testament it is a fig tree that incurs the wrath of Christ.)

The goddess Nut, the mother of the gods, represented as a female along whose body the Sun travels and sometimes as a cow, had a sacred tree[20], the sycamore.

In the "Book of the Dead" she is seen residing in the "Tree of Heaven" with the incantation:

"Hail thou sycamore tree of the Goddess Nut, Grant thou to me of (the water and of) the air which dwell in thee. I embrace the throne which is in Unnu (Heliopolis) and I watch and guard, the egg of Neket-Ur the Great Cackler Khepera, It groweth, I grow, It liveth, I live."

The tree is symbolised as being able to endow eternal life to the deceased. A painting in the tomb of Pashedu and vignettes in the Book of the Dead, shows the deceased receiving the "Water of Regeneration" from the sycamore goddess, evocative of the goddess Ishtar, dispenser of "living water" from the never-failing jar.

Ishtar is also identified with Hathor (or Isis) in the Egyptian pantheon and Hathor is associated with the sycamore tree[21]. The deceased in the Book of the Dead, when asked what food he will eat in the Elysian Fields, says:

"I will reply, let me eat my food under the sycamore tree of my Lady the Goddess Hathor…"

Another reference is to be found in the litany[22] whence the deceased says:

"Homage to thee Lord of the Acacia tree, the Seker boat is set upon its sledge…"

This tree was in Heliopolis and the cat (the Sun) sat near it. A vignette depicting this can be seen in the Book of the Dead. The idea was extant in the twentieth dynasty (circa1200 BC).

The painting in the tomb of Inherkhani shows the cat striking Apep, the serpent god of the primeval waters and enemy of Ra. Apep was killed by Ra using fire, the symbol of the spirit and knowledge.

Enlightenment therefore triumphs over the darkness of blind phallicism. In the Mesopotamian influenced Judaic tradition, the tree, abode of the Sun and whose fruit was a source of life and enlightenment, is forbidden to man by Yahweh, though the serpent as adversary is retained.

Possible Origins of the God Amen

Evidence that the Egyptian god Amen was derived from the Sumerian Moon God can be deduced indirectly from the characteristics of the God and its associated symbols. The association of the God with Isis, often portrayed as the Moon Goddess, in the episode of Hatshepsut's claim to sovereignty by the marriage of Amen to Isis, was an ingenious attempt by the god and his collective following, to establish Hatshepsut's divine credentials. This was a prerequisite at that time for kingship.

This association by marriage can be traced back to the first and third dynasty culture of the Sumerians (circa 3000 BC and 2000 BC respectively). Artefacts uncovered by Sir Leonard Wooley during his excavations at Ur, between 1923 and 1929, predate the first dynasties of Egypt by almost a thousand years.

In the mosaic "Standard" of Ur, both sacred ritual rams and bulls are prominent. These symbols were, respectively, to become associated with Amen and Hathor-Isis in subsequent Egyptian culture. This is perhaps not surprising considering the influence the Mesopotamian-Sumerian culture had on the Egyptian culture and other surrounding subsequent heliopian cultures.

Under a house at Ur, attached to one of the temples, two limestone figures of rams were found[23], thought to be supports for a throne, the "seat of some god whose sacred emblem was the ram."

The famous fertility ram erect against the tree of life, one of a pair, was also found, perhaps not entirely erroneously thought at the time to be the biblical "ram caught in a thicket."

The ram subsequently was the symbol of the god Amen of Egypt. The Sumerian Standard shows at the top level, seated figures similar to the "paut" of the Maati Hall and already, suggestions of symmetry are apparent.

The spiral horns of the ram became a feature of one of the royal crowns of Egypt that also features the feathers of the god Amen.

The particular shape of the feathers of the headdress of Amen are reminiscent of the traditional shape of the sacred tablets of Moses.

Such shaped stones formed the headstone of Bur Sin's grave in the temple of the Moon Goddess at Ur. Sin was reputedly the Moon God of Ur. His association with the Moon Goddess as consort would seem natural; however, subsequently the heliopian consort of the Moon Goddess, in harmony with what was known about the universe and natural laws, was the Sun God the source of life and light.

This change of celestial deity reflected the natural progression of man as his dim consciousness moved out of the darkness of Nature's jungle laws, through the twilight, symbolised by the Moon, into the bright light of day. This would mean redundancy for the Moon God who to survive (as a collective human following) would have to mutate into a new god.

This coincides with the relative newness of the god Amen and his often-claimed relations with the Moon Goddess. As the accumulation of knowledge grew regarding the workings of nature and the influence of the heavenly bodies for example, the Moon and tides, the Sun and rain etc., sciences originating in Sumeria, so religious mores were modified to reflect what was felt to be a scientific truth, a cultural mechanism which history has demonstrated.

It perhaps comes as little surprise, that the Chaldeans were thought to be adept at astronomy and astrology. Since a cultural modification would have taken place over centuries if not millennia according the law of cultural change (whose clock appears to be stationary when viewed from the normal historical perspective), such a change would also reflect man's cultural development. This, being so slow, when viewed from a possible end point at infinity, explains the expanded time scale required when measuring cultural change.

Nonetheless, one of the consequences of such a change would be the deposition of an ancient god (of which there are many mythological examples) who would in a pantheon with no place for him be obliged to change and seek recognition perhaps as the "Hidden God."

Presumably, his aim would be to regain his standing as head of the Pantheon, using where possible, the influence of his one-time consort, the Moon goddess.

This is curiously parallel with the fortunes of Abraham, the founding father of Judaism.

It is possibly worth noting that from this thesis arises the possibility of the singularity of action of a group collective conscious or unconscious mind. The Mesopotamian Ziggurat at Ur, known to the nomads as the "mound of pitch" contained a brick, in the sacred area, on which Dungi, a third dynasty king, refers to earlier buildings as the "House of the Mountain."[24]

In a larger version of the temple at Al Ubaid, four miles from Ur, of plano-convex bricks, indicative of the earliest times, there is an inscription on the foundation stone by Annipadda king of Ur stating:

"…for his Lady NinKharsag"[25].

NinKharsag also known as Ninhursag, translates as "Lady Mountain."

This is also the title held by Tiamat, usurper of the pantheon, who was the wife of the Hittite usurper, Kumarbi.

It is probable that the archetypal "mountain", found often in the Judaic writings, originated with, or was derived from this deity.

The Sumerians carried their culture to the mountains of Anatolia[26], manifested as Hurrian culture, and to the shores of the Mediterranean. So much can be deduced from the comparative mythology of the Near East. NinKharsag represented the earth and hence fertility, and as such, was similar to Demeter, a precursor of Ishtar.

Another route by which the ram god entered Egyptian culture was via the Cretan infusion into the Delta by the Hyksos. A Hyksos sphinx from Tanis in the Delta where the invaders settled depicts the sphinx with a ram's head. The face is also bearded, a feature typical of early dynastic Egyptians as shown on the palette of Narmer. The ram was one of the symbols of the Cretan Sea God. (See Chapter 7)

The Canaanite Culture

In the Canaanite culture, Baal is the heroic king figure like Gilgamesh of Sumeria, who triumphs over the Prince of the Oceans, the would-be usurper of the pantheon. As the Canaanites probably post-dated the Sumerians, the "Prince of the Oceans" can be seen as a later personification of the Flood or fertility culture forces. This is another indication of the perennial struggle between the Heliopian culture and the monotheistic theocracy. This has its modern-day counterparts in the struggle between autocracy and democracy.

Most of the Sumerian gods have their equivalents in the Canaanite pantheon. Anu was known as El and Ishtar as Anat. In the Sumerian Epic of Gilgamesh, Ishtar is associated with the "Bull of Heaven" which:

"With his first snort, cracks opened in the earth and a hundred young men fell down to death, with his seconds. Two hundred young men fell down to death."

Anat is also cast in a ghastly light. She:

"Prepares seats for warriors, dressing tables for soldiers, footstools for heroes. Violently she smites and gloats, Anat cuts them down and gazes. Her liver exults in mirth, her heart is filled with joy. For in the hand of Anat is victory. For she plunges her knees in the blood of soldiers. Her loins in the gore of warriors till she has had her fill of slaughtering in the house of cleaving among the tables."[27]

Anat, like Ishtar, is received back into the pantheon represented by re-sanctifying of the temple and by washing away her own stains in the celestial waters (of fertility and renewal).

"She scoops up water and washes. Even dew of heaven, the fatness of the earth, the ram of him who mounts the clouds. The dew which the skies pour forth. The rain, which is poured forth by the stars, she sprays herself with perfumes of a thousand mountains. Her slops in the sea (are cast)."

The ram who mounts the clouds, is an allusion to Baal, the representative of kingship, the equivalent of Enlil[28] often referred to as "Him who mounts the clouds"[29].

With the help of the "percipient one" (presumably Ea in the Sumerian, and Thoth in the Egyptian), Baal is given lightning bolts to "Drive the Sea from his throne, even Ocean Current from the Seat of his Sovereignty"[30].

In the Sumerian epic, the hero Gilgamesh defeats the mountain Humbaba and in the Flood myth, Ziusrudra the king builds an ark in order to survive the deluge. This is reflected in the Canaanite myth called the "Building of the House." El allows Baal to build a house again with the help of the "percipient one."

"This house will preserve the manifestation of Baal (i.e., kingship), in the storms of winter"[31].

Moreover Baal appoints "the time for his rain, the time for his moisture with downpour."

"Hadad", who, as Adad in the Sumerian "Epic of Gilgamesh" in which the Flood is recounted, is referred to as the "Lord of the Storm"[32] and also appears in the Canaanite myth.

Baal, who has defeated the mighty Ocean cult forces, is then in a position to threaten the power of the gods, a conflict resolved by the fitting of a window to allow the entry of the Sun God.

Baal, representing the Canaanite culture, so becomes a member of the heliopian commonwealth of cultures, later to be represented as Aries (the zodiac Ram). (See chapter 6).

Another encounter of the Canaanite culture with the mighty maritime (Cretan) forces which rendered the culture doubly great, providing the foundation of its claim to election as a premier force among its neighbours constituting the cultural pantheon, is to be found in the myth of Baal and Lotan.

Baal defeats Lotan, the seven headed sea serpent which he accomplishes with the help of Anat. In Hebrew mythology, Lotan was the Leviathan[33] the giant invading culture. The Biblical Jonah enters the Whale that is the Assyrian Army or Empire, for 'three days' presumably to negotiate peace that is not secured as Jerusalem falls shortly after.

The serpent, the perennial adversary of the heliopian cultures was encountered in the Egyptian as Apophis or Apep, the adversary of Ra, who resided in the primeval waters (of fertility).

In the Sumerian, the serpent controlled the waters of Death over which Gilgamesh and Urshanabi sailed. (See chapter 5). Such waters were not literal waters but cultural, where primal fertility forces ruled without enlightenment, in other words, the natural animal world.

With the coming of the gods, that is, with homo sapiens, the evolvement and mutation from animal to man commenced or was reflected in the creation of the gods, coinciding with the development of man's consciousness.

Significantly, in the early bi-nature representations of the earliest cycles of gods. Such a spiritual evolvement may have post-dated physical development by several millennia for it is known that man's cultural progress is a much slower process than his physical, assuming of course, both had their inception at the same time.

The same adversary appears with reduced notoriety somewhat, in the Greek cultural myths, as the Hydra for example, in one of Herakles' labours.

Another important myth in the Baal cycle is the God's encounter with Mot (Death) and the hero's decent into the Underworld. Such a journey and return became, in later heliopian cultures, and from which the Christian culture borrowed, a necessary task to be undertaken by a human individual in order to establish divine credentials necessary for immortality.

The heroic individual, as we shall see, was the mythological embodiment of the culture (the Qaballistic Macro-man) whose successful accomplishment of the journey ensured immortality for the culture.

Before his descent, Baal mates with a heifer, taken by the purely literal interpreters to indicate bestiality in the culture, but which in mythological terms again alludes to assistance by Anat the counterpart of Hathor-Isis and Ishtar, one of whose symbols was the cow representing fertility and strength.

Baal allies himself with Anat and it is she who eventually rescues him from the Underworld. Baal, in returning from the underworld defeats Mot or death.

The dichotomous relationship that exists between Baal and Anat, sometimes allies, sometimes foes, is apparent in the Sumerian, existing in the relationship between Gilgamesh and Ishtar.

An archaic Egyptian myth of the Ra cycle runs very similar to the myth of Anat in the Canaanite and may have been its precursor.

In the latter, Anat "plunges her knees in the blood of soldiers" has very similar form to the Egyptian myth of "Ra in his old age."[34]

Ra, discovering that men were plotting against him is advised by Num, the eldest of the gods that the "eye of Ra" in the form of Isis, be sent against mankind. Isis began to slaughter and "waded in blood."

Not desiring total destruction, Ra produced 7000 jars of barley wine and red ochre that were mixed and poured into the fields to a depth of 9 inches (half a cubit). The Goddess, on seeing her reflection in the red waters, drank and forgot her rage so mankind was saved.

It is possible that this mythical archetype was employed by the compilers of the Bible when Moses used the threat "to turn the rivers to blood." Presumably, this was to unleash Isis in the form of a bloody battle, in order to pressure the Pharaoh.

The myth also has elements in common with the Sumerian, in so far as Ishtar threatens mankind with the horrors from the Underworld and indeed is held responsible for the Flood which, it will be shown, was an allegory for war (see chapter 6).

The myth of Baal and Mot relates Mot as summoning Baal to the Underworld saying "Thy face thou shalt surely set towards the Mountain of Concealment. Take the Mountain on thy hands; the hill on the top of thy hands."

This is evocative of funerary scenes in many Egyptian tombs where the deceased is shown holding two hill type objects in the palm of his hands. The Egyptian influence is also apparent when Anat, like Isis searching for Osiris, "ranges every mountain to the heart of the earth, every hill to the midst of the fields. She comes to the pleasant land of the back of beyond, the fair tracts of the strand of death, she comes upon Baal fallen to the ground."

Similar themes in Canaanite mythology also appear in the Hittite, indicative possibly cross-cultural intercourse.

The episode of Baal in the Underworld, apart from similarities with the Sumerian Gilgamesh in search of immortality, echoes the Hittite myth of the "Lost God" when, in the god's absence, drought and famine (allegorically) seize the land and heliopianism is eclipsed, presumably by another "darker" culture.

In the Canaanite myth of Krt or Keret, the king of Hubur, Krt falls ill after carrying out a quest for El because of his failure to fulfil a vow to Asherah "the

Lady of the Sea", a probable Cretan importation, being the consort of the Sea God.

Drought and famine (the wages of war) consume the land until El sends out a goddess of Healing "Shatagat" to fly over a hundred cities and towns to find a release for Krt from his sickness which she apparently does.

This Sibylline flavoured myth is reminiscent of the Hittite myth where the Goddess of healing, Kamrusepa finds Telipinu, the son of the Storm God and proffers him healing essences.

Krt is wretched because he has lost his wife, children and palace (presumably in battle with a sea people).

The heliopians in the form of El or Anu come to his aid and characteristically Sumerian, Krt is admonished to wash and anoint himself before making oblation, a recurring ritual in the Epic of Gilgamesh.

The Ras Shamra texts from which much of the Canaanite mythology was discerned, describes the seat of El "at the well-head of the two streams, in the midst of the source of the two deeps", an identical description of Dilmun, dwelling place of eternal man Utnapishtim and his wife in the Epic of Gilgamesh.

There are further echoes of the Sumerian influence in the Canaanite myth of Aqhat son of Danel or Daniel. In this myth, king Danel petitions the gods for a son. Baal intercedes with El and Danel's wife conceives a son. Danel is brought a bow and arrows by the craftsman god Kothar-U-Khasis that the king gives to his son Aqhat.

Anat (Ishtar) desires to possess the bow and promises Aqhat immortality if he will surrender it. The bow and arrows were, especially the latter, talismanic of Gilgamesh and more generally, a symbol of enlightenment.

Aqhat rejects the Goddess' request, like Gilgamesh, saying she cannot confer "immortality upon man whose destiny is to die."

Here, Anat is spurned as Ishtar was spurned by Gilgamesh (see chapter 5) and her reaction is the same. Anat flies to the Gods and, with threats addressed to the King of the Gods, obtains permission to carry out her scheme to obtain the bow.

Ishtar employs a similar strategy in the Sumerian, threatening unimaginable horrors to obtain her will, all indicative of the powerful cultural influence of the Fertility Goddess, represented in temporal terms as the Cretan-Atlantean culture.

Anat then goes to Yatpan, a warlike deity and proposes to change him into a vulture or eagle so that he may fly over Aqhat whilst he is eating and strike him down to obtain possession of the bow. Yatpan, in carrying out Anat's request, kills Aqhat but the bow is broken and lost.[35]

The consequences of Aqhat's death, like that of Baal and Telipinu et al, is that drought and failure of the crops ensues. When Pughat, Aqhat's sister, in an Isis role, brings news of his son's death to Danel, he vows vengeance and prays to Baal to enable him to ascertain which vulture devoured his son's remains so that he may recover them and acquit a proper burial.

Baal brings down the vultures one by one until Aqhat's remains are found in Sumul, the Mother of Vultures. Danel curses three cities which lie in the neighbourhood of Aqhat's murder, then returns to his palace and mourns for seven years. The mother of the vultures may be a reference to Anat or a surrogate. The symbol of a vulture certainly represents a spirit.

The myth continues with Pughat determining to employ Yatpan as her agent in her plan of vengeance, but the myth is not concluded.

In translating the myth into real terms, we see that, like the majority of myths, it concerns the pre-history recording of military conquests between cultures. Anat, the fertility goddess, whose cultural epicentre in antiquity was Atlantean-Crete, had vast influence due to the nature and point of development of the human condition. It is apparent that the culture spread into the Levant and points east (Anatolia), south (the Hyksos in the Egyptian Delta) and at some point into the Sumerian hinterlands.

Aqhat represents the "Repum" possibly, Canaanites or some vassal state and Yatpan, another young culture, possibly a pre-unified Upper Egypt whose emblem was the eagle or vulture. The myth therefore translates as the vulture of Egypt in alliance with some Cretan allied culture conquering the Canaanite or Canaanite vassal state, an event that occurred several times throughout Egyptian history, and the states recapture by the potent Baal culture.

An important characteristic of the myths of the heliopian cultural commonwealth, apart from serving as cultural strongboxes of pre-historical events, is that when viewed in hindsight of historical perspective, they display the ebbing and flowing of cultural boundaries in a continuum and not as singular events. A single event is often the impression obtained when cultural changes are viewed on a historical time scale.

This is because, due to the magnitude of cultural time-scales, historical time scales present only a snapshot of an instant of cultural change and millennia of hindsight are required to see trends. If there is any truth in this assertion, then the roles of the ancient seers in formulating myths for future generations becomes more comprehensible.

As was characteristic of Hittite myths, the aftermath of war is drought and infertility in the sense that the defeated culture's flower of manhood (and womanhood) had been destroyed, its resources ransacked and it had been reduced to servitude.

This is mitigated by the reconquering and re-establishment of the filial culture of Danel, the Repum, originally a Canaanite culture, and mythically described as the "return of fertility" to the land.

The myth leaves little doubt that Danel, like Baal, is attacking cult centres of the fertility goddess. "The king curses the source of water, out upon thee O source of water, For upon thee lies the guilt of the slaughter of Aqhat the hero."[36]

The hero as adversary of the fertility goddess recurs in several heliopian cultural myths instance Perseus and the Medusa in the Greek for example.

Ishtar is often depicted as a goddess dispensing the celestial waters of fertility "from a never-failing jar." The theme of Hero as her adversary is prominent in Sumerian mythology.

The goddess was not the only archetype depicted as the source of celestial fertility, often kings are shown dispensing the sacred waters in Egyptian and Assyrian art and the concept is not at odds with Darwinian law of natural selection and the natural law.

Dnil or Danel is similarly referred to "They shed tears for the offspring of Dnil, the Dispenser of Fertility"[37].

In this respect, he is associated with the Rpum or Repum, the dispensers of fertility, identified in the Bible as the Rephaim.

On the same tablets describing the coronation of Baal, the Repum are invited by El and eight in number are led by one Repu-Baal. They arrive on horses, asses or chariots[38], the horse being an ancient and religious archetype associated with the Hyksos of Egypt and the Cretan God of the Sea who is often to be seen in his sea borne chariot of four water horses often accompanied by his consort.

It is known that the Hebrews appropriated several Canaanite rituals and myths [39], as well as Sumerian, as indicated by the Flood and Creation myths, and re-tailored them in a monotheistic context.

Danel's petition to the pantheon is echoed in Genesis (XV-2-5) by Abraham who is promised and heir by Yahweh. It is in the early biblical chapters that the

Rephaim are mentioned (Genesis XIV-5, XV-20). They are drawn as distinct from the Canaanites (XV-21) and are grouped with the Hittites (XV-20).

The Canaanite culture, possibly because of its cultural position with respect to the great surrounding heliopian cultures, to the north Minoan and Mycenean, to the east, the Hittite and Protosyrian, to the south the Babylonian, and to the west the Egyptian, became something of a cultural confluence.

Many such influences can be detected in Canaanite art and ivory carvings. The ivory panels from the royal couch in the palace of Ras Shamra show various archetypes such as the Sumerian tree of life.

The panels are in the Egyptian style and the lion is prominent.

In the myth of the "Marriage of the Moon God and the Moon Goddess", the marriage of Nikkal (Sumerian Ningal) an Isis/Ishtar fertility goddess, to Yarikh the Moon God is described. Nikkal is referred to as the daughter of Baal[40], "the regent of high summer."

Athtar is referred to as the Lion and Son of Baal. The lion, as well as being associated with Ishtar, was, in the Canaanite, the archetype of Dagan, the Protosyrian "Lord of the Stars" that is, the Lord of the Gods.

Dagan was the principal deity of the Philistines, who occupied Canaan before the Hebrews.

"The Lion will give the daughter of his father in exchange."

The lion with a god on its back is shown on a Canaanite stele and is reminiscent of the depictions on the sanctuary of Hittite gods at Yasilikaya.

On the ivory couch panels is also to be seen, a male figure standing on the back of a deer or stag. Such figures have been found among Hittite steles and are thought to represent the Hittite "Protective Genius" or "Providence"[41].

The myth of Nikkal and Yarikh may therefore refer to some major ancient cultural alliance, for example, between the Sumerians and the Hittites, a connection we know existed in the Hurrian. The myth also describes the weighing of the bride price by her father, mother and siblings, a judgement of the bridegroom's suitability. Such a unique celestial ritual may have been derived from Egyptian eschatological tradition.

Its use as a ritual of judgement associated with an alliance can be seen in the Book of Daniel when Belshazzar is admonished by the writing:

"mene mene tekel upharsin", "thou have been weighed and found wanting."

Another ancient archetype to be seen on the ivory couch is a fertility goddess suckling two children. In the Egyptian tradition, this was Isis shown with hcaddress of horns with the Sun or Moon at centre, or as her earlier form as Hathor, a cow.

In the Canaanite myth of Krt, the goddess is Athirat or Anat, the Babylonian Ishtar.[42] The heir of Krt is described as he "who sucks the milk of Athirat who sucks the breasts of the Virgin."

The notion that the king and his heir are executives of the celestial pantheon was also extant in the Canaanite culture, indeed as it was in all heliopian cultures.

In Egypt, as we have seen, the Amenites used this particular cultural concept, that is, the ruler as child of the goddess Isis to, legitimise the claim of Hatshepsut.

Many of the Canaanite archetypes are to be found in the surrounding cultures.

The stag as Hittite can also be seen in what Professor Gurney, author of 'The Hittites', thought was a Mitannian seal impression.

Many symbols are common to the Akkadian or Sumerian, Ishtar flanked by two human figures, the tree of life flanked by winged stags, lions above the Istarian goats indicating a strong Sumerian influence.

The stag was also a Sumerian cultural symbol, described in the Hittite as a "child of the open country"[43], a description reminiscent of Enkidu in the Sumerian epic of Gilgamesh.

In second millennia Mesopotamia, a temple door capital shows a lion headed eagle flanked by stags. In later Greek mythology, the stag is associated with the Moon Goddess Artemis, which accords well with its presence in the Hittite and Mesopotamian cultures where the deity was prominent.

The stag's presence in the Greek culture is a possible indication of Anatolian influence on that culture, particularly by the Hittites.

The eagle features in Mesopotamian myth and can be linked to the Egyptian archetype of the Upper kingdom. It is also prominent in the Assyrian culture in association with the Mesopotamian Tree of Life. The eagle appears as a part-human, a spirit that fertilises the tree of fertility with a seed pod. The same pod is held by the king (as the most fertile) performing the same ritual.

The plunder from Damascus found in the Assyrian palace of Aslan Tas depicts ram-headed lion sphinxes flanking the tree of life and in Anatolia, the stag is to be found associated with the bull and the solar orb.

Many of these archetypes are to be found in the Zodiac which came to epitomise the central philosophy of ancient heliopianism, that was, cultural co-existence between people.

This was achieved by cultural incorporation in the celestial pantheon by means of shared common archetypes that arose via cultural intercourse.

This tradition, as we have seen, existed in heliopian Egypt from the time of the earliest cultural cycles of gods. The wisdom of such a cultural philosophy is evident in so far as such cultural arrangements must have led inevitably to the easing of cultural conflicts (though not eradication, for such is the nature of humankind) and the reduction of the possibility of catastrophic mega-cultural conflagrations.

Underpinning such a philosophy was the belief in the ultimate aspiration of a culture, that as macrocosmic man, it would be possible to achieve divinity. Such a philosophy was opposed (according to the law of cultural action and reaction, appreciated by the ancient Qaballists) by its opposite, that was, autocratic monotheism, imbued with, by its nature, cultural intolerance.

Heliopianism on the other hand, sought to incorporate new cultures; Ancient Sea God fertility monotheism sought their destruction or subjugation.

Where then was the fountainhead of such ancient heliopian wisdom? The answer must be sought in the most ancient of heliopian cultures, that of the Sumerians and Mesopotamians, for their influence, being the oldest, began the tradition and was most instrumental in the formation of later heliopian cultures.

References Chapter 4

[1] J. Gray, Near Eastern Mythology, page 26

[2] Sir A. E. Wallis, Budge Tutankhamen, page 60

[3] J. Gray, Near Eastern Mythology, page 14

[4] S. H. Hooke, Middle Eastern Mythology, page 31

[5] N. K. Sandars, The Epic of Gilgamesh, page 124

[6] C. Kerenyi, The Gods of the Greeks, page 24

[7] Sir Leonard Wooley, Ur of the Chaldees, page 15

[8] S. H. Hooke, Middle Eastern Mythology, page 133

[9] Sir Leonard Wooley, Ur of the Chaldees, page 151

[10] S. H. Hooke, Middle Eastern Mythology, page 3

[11] J. Gray, Near Eastern Mythology, page 35

[12] ibid, page 78

[13] S. H. Hooke, Middle Eastern Mythology, page 31

[14] N. K. Sandars, The Epic of Gilgamesh, page 26

[15] J. Gray, Near Eastern Mythology, page 33

[16] S. H. Hooke, Middle Eastern Mythology, page 125

[17] ibid

[18] O. R. Gurney, The Hittites, page 22

[19] Sir A. E. Wallis, Budge Tutankhamen, page 48

[20] ibid, page 95

[21] ibid, page 184

[22] ibid, page 67

[23] Sir Leonard Wooley, Ur of the Chaldees, page 58

[24] ibid, page 77

[25] ibid, page 51

[26] ibid, page 50

[27] J. Gray, Near Eastern Mythology, page 80

[28] ibid, page 77

[29] ibid, pages 77-78

[30] ibid, page 79

[31] ibid, page 83

[32] N. K. Sandars, The Epic of Gilgamesh, page 110

[33] S. H. Hooke, Middle Eastern Mythology, page 82

[34] ibid, page 74

[35] ibid, pages 90-91

[36] J. Gray, Near Eastern Mythology, page 99

[37] ibid, page 100

[38] S. H. Hooke, Middle Eastern Mythology, page 92

[39] ibid, page 104

[40] J. Gray, Near Eastern Mythology, page 91

[41] O. R. Gurney, The Hittites, page 139

[42] J. Gray, Near Eastern Mythology, page 101

[43] O. R. Gurney, The Hittites, page 139, Figure 7

Chapter 5
The Epic of Gilgamesh
The Concept of Kingship

Kingship existed before the "Flood" from the clues unearthed at Ur by Sir Leonard Wooley. After the Flood, as we have seen, kingship returned. In tribal societies prior to the introduction of kingship, the chief held temporal precedence.

What is special about the concept of kingship?

The answer is probably related to the fact that kingship was a more elevated status because it was state designated and was sanctioned by the celestial order. Kingship came about inextricably with the development of the culture, particularly the religious culture.

With kingship came the idea that there was a divine aspect about man.

The king in the heliopian order was, via his divine nature and sanction, the temporal reflection of the celestial order, the temporal executive of the will of the gods and the reflection on earth of the celestial executive of the heavenly company of gods.

In the Egyptian and other Middle Eastern cosmogonies, this heavenly executive was the celestial king, Osiris. In the Greek, it was Zeus, in the Mesopotamian, Enlil, in the Hittite, Teshub, and in the Canaanite, Baal.

This state of affairs would naturally give rise to the tradition of a royal bloodline as the ordered means of succession. In this way, the king became both head of the secular and religious spheres of the culture. This was a departure from the previous order of the dual estates of religion, represented by the medicine man and secular power, as represented by the chief. These also reflected the psychological (or spiritual) and physical attributes of man.

In effect, the concept of kingship was a culturally unifying concept, removing to a large extent, the need for separate intermediaries such as shamans and priests between gods and men.

To be able to communicate with the gods carried extremely esoteric status and considerable power over the populace.

Kingship or more precisely, divine kingship therefore represented a considerable shift in the control and application of power, for it combined celestial that is, psychological power and temporal power in one divinely appointed being, the king.

The king was both chief and priest. This meant that the power of the priests was severely diminished and, as has been demonstrated in Ancient Egypt, gave rise to perennial struggles between the religious and monarchical establishments.

The monarchical forces that included enlightened hierophants, due to, among other things the pressures of government and the need to divide the opposition, favoured diviocratic pantheons.

The more power motivated part of religious establishment, being versed in matters psychological, and manipulative of the human psyche, particularly of the subconscious, promoted widespread fertility cults, harnessing a common human motivating force, the sex drive. It tended therefore to monotheism, whose god was the god of the "nether" (psychological) waters of the id.

Despite such an evolvement in the cultural power structure, considerable power was retained by the religious acolytes and appointed servants of the celestial cosmogony under the heliopian culture.

Their roles became advisors to, rather than intermediaries between, the pantheon and the king. The aim was to arrange the temporal order as a reflection of the celestial, an order which embodied concepts of consensus, mutual dependence, tolerance etc., in short, to arrange the temporal social order like an extended family, in the same manner as the celestial order represented a family of gods.

This social engineering was an attempt by the ancients to preclude a state of affairs wherein the religious estate assumed total power using the vehicle of an autocratic god with attendant vices, the complements of those heliopian virtues.

Many of the religious struggles in Ancient Egypt can be understood as a struggle for power between the heliopians who supported divine kingship, and the Amenites, who wanted a monotheistic supremacy, that is, a supremacy of temporal religious power of the priests as opposed to the secular power of kingship.

Observing seals, it appears that kingship, as a concept, had its inception in the Near East at about or before 5000 BC if kingship "returned" after the flood.

Of the earliest myths to refer to the state is that of the Mesopotamian-Sumerian "Legend of Gilgamesh" and later, that of "Sargon of Akkad" (or Agade).

The myth of Gilgamesh introduces the concept of mortal kingship as distinct from "celestial" kingship, and marks a link between pure celestial mythology and the approaches to human recorded history.

The device used to forge the link was to make the hero two-thirds god and one third man[1] who is endowed with heavenly qualities of beauty, courage, knowledge and wisdom. This proportioning is a prototype concept for the later Christian concept of man and god combined and the Trinity.

The hero is also "as strong as a star from heaven." The star is a heavenly body and a symbol of a divinity, god or member of the celestial cosmogony (c.f. Anatolian Dagan, the lord of the stars).

Early in the epic, Gilgamesh is described as king of Uruk, who is derelict in his duty. "Yet the king should be Shepherd to his people." This ancient metaphor to describe his status is to be found again in the gospels and is recognisably apt in describing the state of solicitude and caring.

The epic is inscribed on tablets in Akkadian[2] (circa 1500 BC), in Hittite on tablets from Hattusa, on tablets from Palestine (circa 1200 BC), possibly Canaanite, and on Sumerian fragments. The epic relates the exploits of Gilgamesh, the king of the Sumerian city of Uruk during the period of approximately 3000 to 2750 BC. The fact that the epic is preserved in the major surrounding cultures is confirmation of the inter-cultural influences the Sumerian-Mesopotamian culture exerted on these sibling cultures.

In Gilgamesh's companion Enkidu, one could easily observe the embodiment of the Hittite culture on the same basis that Gilgamesh represents the Sumerian-Mesopotamian culture of the time. The vehicle of the king of a culture as representative of the culture was common in the myths of the time and is to be found in the Bible with such instances as Jacob representing Israel and so on.

The personification of a culture by a representative person is often found in dreams when for example, Nebuchadnezzar dreams of a huge figure of gold, silver and bronze.

This is not surprising as dreams with their bizarre imagery and lack of conventional time frames, have much in common with mythology.

The Coming of Enkidu

After a short prologue, the first chapter opens with Gilgamesh described as a powerful but arrogant king, and, being the son of a goddess, none can challenge him. In response to the requests of the citizens of Uruk, Anu, the chief deity (as he was to the Hittites), and god of Uruk, hears their laments and orders Aruru to create his equal:

"his second self, stormy heart for stormy heart...let them contend together and leave Uruk in quiet."

The Goddess of Creation, Aruru, conceives an image in her mind and.

"It was the stuff of Anu, of the firmament. She dipped her hands in water and pinched off clay, she let it fall in the wilderness and the Noble Enkidu was created."

This is similar to the biblical account of the Creation:

"Let the waters bring forth abundantly..." (Gen 1-20) and:

"The Lord God formed man of the dust of the ground" (Gen 11-17).

It is significant that the (nether) waters are associated with fertility in the Biblical version.

Enkidu is introduced on the literal plane and is described as a friend and companion of Gilgamesh, but symbolically, and, which is characteristic of myths, he represents a friendly and allied culture with whom it was necessary to forge an alliance in order for the two cultures to survive a powerful adversary.

This is later unfolded, as the epic describes in metaphor in the mythological tradition.

Enkidu was known as "the Mountain Man", probably meaning in the context, a mountain dweller possibly of mountainous Anatolia.

"He knew nothing of the cultivated land...His body was rough, he had long hair like a woman's, it was waved like the hair of Nisaba, the Goddess of Corn, his body was covered with matted hair like Samuquan's the God of Cattle."[3]

Here could be a description of contemporary Hittite mountain dwellers of Anatolia, who plaited their hair like a woman's after the fashion of ears of corn or wheat, a sibylline fertility totem. They also wore deerskins typical of hunters always following game.

"Enkidu ate grass in the hills with the gazelle and lurked with wild beasts at water holes, he had 'joy of the waters' with the herds of wild game."

This description is more apt of a culture than of an individual but this personification of a culture is common in myths. The epic goes on to describe how the two cultures encounter each other:

"But there was a trapper who met him one day face to face at the drinking hole for the wild game had entered his territory. On three days he met him face to face and the trapper was frozen with fear."

The trapper returns home "dumb benumbed with terror", informing his father of the wild man who comes down from the hills who: "fills in the pits I dig and tears up my traps."

The trapper is sent to Gilgamesh who formulates a plan to seduce and entrap Enkidu by cultural means. "When next he comes down to drink at the wells, she will there (a temple harlot), stripped and naked, and when he sees her beckoning, he will embrace her and then the wild beasts will reject him."

Enkidu is seduced and after six days and seven nights (of mythological time as for example in Genesis 1 and 11-2), his consort says "you are wise Enkidu and now become like a god, why do you want to run wild with the beasts of the hills? Come with me, I will take you to the strong walls of Uruk, to the blessed temple of Ishtar and Anu, of love and of heaven where Gilgamesh lives who is very strong and like a wild bull, lords it over man."

Ishtar is the patroness of the bull cult, a fertility cult that in part, had sensual rituals as part of the rites. If this description represents cultures, and cultural interaction, then here the pair are seen as the Sumerian culture civilising the 'mountain culture'.

"Enkidu was pleased, he longed for a comrade, for one who would understand his heart."

The alliance is not without a battle or challenge, as the gods intended.

"I will challenge him boldly" states Enkidu, "I have come to change the old order (Sumerian hegemony?) I am he who was born in the hills; I am he who is strongest of all."

Enkidu is warned by the temple maid that Gilgamesh, because of his gifts of understanding from Shamash, Enlil and Ea, that:

"Gilgamesh will know in his dreams that you are coming!"

There follows in the epic, an account of Gilgamesh's dream, possibly the earliest account of a dream as a source of prophesy, several instances of which appear in the Bible.

The dream of Gilgamesh is similar in many respects to one of Joseph's

(See Genesis XXXVII-9, and the Koran, Joseph 12-1).

Gilgamesh, in telling his dream to his mother, the goddess Ninsun, is echoed in Genesis (XXXV11-10):

"And he (Joseph) told it to his father."

Gilgamesh relates: "Mother, last night I had a dream, I was full of joy, the young heroes were around me and I walked through the night under the stars of the firmament and one, a meteor of the stuff of Anu, fell down from heaven. I tried to lift it but it proved too heavy; all the people of Uruk came to see it. The common people jostled and the nobles thronged to kiss its feet; and to see its attraction was like the love of a woman. They helped me, I braced my forehead and I raised it with thongs and brought it to you, and you yourself pronounced it my brother."

The meteor of course is Enkidu, or rather the culture that he represents. The meteor is the material of the stars from the heavens that also appear in Joseph's dream.

The attraction of Enkidu, described as "like that of a woman", makes sense when Enkidu is taken to represent some cultural complement, a Jungian collective cultural anima complementing the animus of the Sumerian culture.

In Qaballistic terms (a philosophy thought to have originated in Sumeria and can be seen manifested in symbolic terms in Ancient Egyptian tombs), microcosmic man (the individual) and macrocosmic man (the culture) were thought to have complementary male and female aspects, a theme common in medieval Philosophical Alchemy.

In global terms, this means mankind has two cultural male and female aspects. This aligns with biblical and other accounts of mankind being derived from male and female aspects of human nature, a condition mirrored in the (microscopic) individual. This is simply another manifestation of the many aspects of duality of the human condition.

An interesting manifestation of this is hinted at in the Korean national flag which is essentially a red and blue representation of the dual aspects of man as seen by the Chinese that is, the Yin and the Yang.

The flag represents a united whole yet consisting of two parts, the divided Korean nation.

It may be that the ancients intended Enkidu to represent some eastern culture or cultural incursion to the environs of Sumeria. Many aspects of the Hittites, the later adjacent culture suggest eastern origin.

Even as late as 1889, the constitution of Japan, based on those of Prussia and Austria Hungary, declared that the person of the Emperor was sacred and inviolable, being one of "a line of emperors unbroken for ages eternal." The emperor traced his descent back to the Sun Goddess whose divinity he personified.[4]

This insinuates, like Gilgamesh's dream, Enkidu is personified as a culture with feminine aspects. This cultural personification is the complement of early Western cultural representations where the king was the earthly representative of the Sun God, a symbol of masculinity.

Gilgamesh proceeds in his account to relate a second dream to his mother Ninsun:

"In the strong walls of Uruk, there lay an axe, the shape of which was very strange. I loved it like a woman and wore it at my side."

Ninsun explains:

"That axe…that is the comrade whom I gave you."

This description is evocative of the hieratically scaled warrior that guards the lion gate at Hattusa. The lion gate is flanked by two lions like the Mycenean lion gate, probably evocative of the Protosyrian god Dagan, a probable early deity of both cultures.

Oneiromancy was in those times a potent and widespread channel of communication with the gods and is found in the Bible. Interpretation of dreams could have broad cultural effects affording those with the gift of interpretation, unique influence. It was an art, as the Bible indicates, not always used honestly and was often tailored to the ends of the interpreter as we shall see with Daniel.

Enkidu is being tended by the temple maiden who upbraids him "when I look at you, you have become like a god. Why do you yearn to run wild again with the beasts of the hills? Get up from the ground (and take) the bed of a shepherd" (i.e., a king).

"She divided her clothing into two and with one half, she clothed him and with the other, herself; and holding his hand, she led him like a child to the sheepfolds, into the shepherd's tents. There, all crowded round to see him, they put bread in front of him, but Enkidu could only suck the milk of wild animals…The woman said, 'eat bread, it is the staff of life, drink wine, it is the custom of the land'…He rubbed down the matted hair of his body and anointed himself with oil; Enkidu had become a man; but he had put on man's clothing, he appeared like a bridegroom."

111

In this passage appear many archetypes that also occur in the Christian tradition. The image of a child only able to suck milk in the presence of shepherds or other kings is evocative of Bethlehem. The notion of maturity, which is associated with a bridegroom, is echoed in the Canaan marriage and the parable of the Ten Virgins, signifying the coming of Christ the Bridegroom.[5] The (ritual) donning of clothing often appears in the Biblical narrative as signifying the bestowal of God's authority. The rite is usually performed, as here, by some appointed temple functionary and prophet of Yahweh, as for example, in the case of Samuel and David. Often the ritual is the ceremony of coronation.

There is a significant difference in the epic in so far as Enkidu anoints himself. Enkidu, as bridegroom of the goddess Ishtar, presumably signifies the cultural marriage of the neighbouring culture with the Sumerian. His status as king puts him in a position to challenge Gilgamesh who:

"Is about to celebrate marriage with the queen of love" (Ishtar) and who "still demands to be first with the bride, the king to be first and the husband to follow, for that was ordained by the gods from his birth."

This ancient "droit de seigneur" was in keeping with the natural law and mores of the society whose king was the dispenser of celestial water (of fertility). If the husband is an allusion to the culture represented by Enkidu, then the conflict becomes one of precedence in the favour of the Gods.

A battle ensues between Gilgamesh and Enkidu, which ends in victory for Gilgamesh, the personification of the senior Sumerian culture, and a sealed friendship between the two. (Sumerian and Hurrian Hittite?)

In real terms, the battle is a mythical expression of some pre-history battle between the two cultures, which ends in an alliance against a third much larger and dangerous common foe that is described subsequently.

The Forest Journey

The epic continues with Gilgamesh and Enkidu setting forth to the mountainous "country of the living…because of the evil in the land…we shall go to the forest and destroy the evil; for in the forest lives Humbaba, whose name is "Hugeness", a ferocious giant…he is a great warrior, a "battering ram", the watchman of the forest who never sleeps" and whom Enkidu has seen before.

Enkidu also knows the place where Humbaba lives… "the mountain throne of Ishtar."[6]

Humbaba undoubtedly represents the culture occupying the Levant, the proverbial "Forests of Lebanon" Humbaba, "at whose voice (Mount) Hermon and Lebanon used to tremble."[7]

Associated with the fertility goddess Ishtar, Humbaba represents the Sumerian version of Ullikumi of Hittite mythology, the "monstrous rock", the Cretan-Atlantean Flood, that is, the Sea God (monotheistic) culture that would be supreme in the celestial order. This culture occupied the Eastern Mediterranean.

Gilgamesh is the hero of the Sun god Shamash, appointed, like Teshub, to vanquish Humbaba. Humbaba is also referred to as Huwawa, a possible Hurrian or Hittite variant and thought by some[8] to be an Anatolian god due to similar phonetic construction to Hittite names.

The mythical hero is a common archetype to many cultures and appears in the folk tales of many countries even today for example, in tales such as Jack the Giant Killer. The hero, representing the culture is a role model for members of a culture in the struggle for survival.

Mythology, extant before the written word, was the source of living history of the culture clothed in bizarre imagery for ease of remembering with awe and interest. In this way, the culture was always presented as having a way forward, a raison d'être, elicited from the past. This itself seemed essential for the survival of the culture.

The emergence of the written word made a culture's past easier to remember, provided records remained, and remembered in greater detail. It is significant that in the event of vanquishment, the history was usually obliterated by the conqueror and replaced by a version of events glorifying the conqueror and his or her culture. This provides the role model for future generations and as such an essential mechanism for survival. It is of course endemic throughout all cultures and humankind.

Exaggeration of gains and minimisation of losses during wartime are part of the same psychology. It is worth noting that Jung contended that "what myths are to race (or culture), dreams are to the individual."[9]

The individual, in dreams may act the role of hero. It is not surprising therefore that the hero communicates with the gods through dreams and dreams have their place in myths. This is because dreams are to do with the subconscious as are myths.

In relating a myth, neither the narrator nor the listener(s) may consciously be aware of the actual symbolic meaning, nonetheless the symbolism is immediately understood by the individuals' subconscious and the group or collective subconscious depositing the archetypal symbols necessary for future actions and communications for survival of the group.

Since most myths are, for the most part, heliopian "inventions" which serve as cultural repositories of man's prehistory, then dreams are, in some way, connected also with the conscious, a fact many would disclaim.

Dreams are constructive and purposive as described, directly affecting the conscious state, as for example, in the cure of neuroses, which reside in the subconscious. [10]This is affecting the conscious in a survival-assisting manner.

Mythical symbolism is the same as that appearing in dreams of the individual (the microcosm) and the interpretation of dreams is similar to that of interpretation of mythical symbolism since much of source of dream symbolism lies in the myths of a culture.

As Jung found, which was a spectacular discovery (but known to the ancient Qaballists) the individual subconscious is a repository of the total archetypal symbolism of the culture. Much of the symbolism, deriving from the universal condition of man on the planet, is common to many cultures.

For example, the sacred tree common to the Mediterranean cultures is also a central archetype in Norse mythology.

In the context of the ancient philosophical duality of opposites of Qaballism it becomes clear that diviocratic heliopianism was concerned with the development of the collective conscious of man and monotheism the manipulation of the collective unconscious, primarily via fertility cults.

The epic continues with Enkidu and the elders of Uruk trying to dissuade Gilgamesh in his quest:

"We have heard that Humbaba is not like men who die...(that is, he is a culture, a philosophical concept)...when he roars, it is like the torrent of a storm, his breath is like fire, and his jaws are like death itself...it is no equal struggle when one fights with Humbaba that battering ram."

This description is not unlike many describing dragons. Battering rams of antiquity were carved poles with a ram's head at one end. The ram was one of the symbols of the ancient Cretan Sea god Poseidon and has long been a symbol of fertility.

Gilgamesh's resolve is undiminished, the Sun God appoints him strong allies, the Great Winds; the North, the Whirlwind, the Storm, the Icy Wind, the Tempest and the Scorching Wind. These:

"Like vipers, like dragons, like scorching fire, like a serpent that freezes the heart, a destroying flood and the lightning fork", appear as attributes of a Storm God.

The account could be another description of the helpmate culture personified by Enkidu, an incipient Hittite Anatolian culture whose later pantheon was dominated by the Storm God Teshub.

The brothers set forth on the quest. During the quest, the pair have many misgivings but are further comforted by dreams, in the first of which, Gilgamesh dreams he seized hold of a wild bull in the wilderness:

"It bellowed and beat up the dust till the whole sky was dark, my arm was seized and my tongue bitter. I fell back on my knee, then someone refreshed me with water from his water skin."

Enkidu gives a rather contradictory interpretation of the dream to the hero:

"Dear friend, the god to whom we are travelling is no wild bull though his form is mysterious. The wild bull that you saw is Shamash the Protector; in our moment of peril he will take our hands. The one who gave water from his skin, that is your own god who cares for your name, your Lugulbanda."

Enkidu refers to Humbaba as a god, mythological symbolism for a culture (as for example the Christian God and Christendom). It is unusual to see the Sun god described as a bull, a symbol of fertility.

This symbolism was more descriptive of a manifestation of Ishtar.

In a later episode of the epic, the valiant pair fight the "Bull of Heaven" that is, Ishtar.

The dream symbolism would make sense if the bull was, in fact, Humbaba, the fertility cult of the Levant originating in Crete and enemy of the Heliopian cultures. The reviver would be the hero's patron, the Sun god Shamash who, administering water (of life), a common motif of that time, would be fulfilling his eternal duty especially to the hero, the embodiment of the culture.

This seems the more reasonable interpretation as can be seen in the following passage of the Epic. The bull also appears in the legend of Mithras that has similarities with the Epic. In the legend of Mithras, the bull is an embodiment of evil, the term used to describe Humbaba.

A second dream visits Gilgamesh presaging (again) their encounter with Humbaba:

"I dreamed again. We stood in the deep gorge of the mountain, and beside it we two were like the smallest of swamp flies; suddenly the mountain fell, it struck me and caught my feet from under me. Then came an intolerable light blazing out, and in it was one whose grace and whose beauty were greater than the beauty of this world. He pulled me out from under the mountain, he gave me water to drink and my heart was comforted, and he set my feet on the ground."

It is clear here that the hero's saviour is his patron, the Sun god (the blinding light of the Sun). The mountain, as one would deduce, is the Hero's and Sun god's adversary, the culture represented by Humbaba.

As Enkidu explains:

"He said to Gilgamesh the young God, 'Your dream is good, your dream is excellent, the mountain which you saw is Humbaba, now surely we will seize and kill him and throw his body as the mountain fell on the plain.'"

Gilgamesh, representing the Sumerian culture is described as a young god who defeats the "monstrous mountain", the older mythological Atlantean culture, the Ullikumi of the Hittite pantheon, which was defeated by Teshub, the Storm god. The enemy is depicted as a mountain, the symbol often used in the Bible to describe the power of Yahweh (c.f. Isaiah).

In the description of such a confrontation, one would expect to encounter some military allusions veiled in allegory, as is usual in myths. These are present, as we shall see shortly.

Before the battle presaged in the dream takes place, Gilgamesh has another dream that causes his resolve again to falter. This is a dream in which:

"The heavens roared and the earth roared again, daylight failed and darkness fell, lightnings flashed, fire blazed out, the clouds lowered, they rained down death. Then the brightness departed, the fire went out and all was turned to ashes fallen about us."

This looks like defeat by the dark forces. Gilgamesh suggests that the two return down the mountain to reconsider "what we should do."

The heroes, and the mountain Humbaba, as personifications of cultures, represent the opposing armies. The mythological device of a hero or god personifying an entire culture or army is used often in many mythologies. It is used several times in the epic as illustrated by subsequent events.

Gilgamesh, recovering his courage, decides his strategy, for when they come down from the mountain, Gilgamesh seizes the axe in his hand and "felled the cedar", that is, he attacks first. The attack signals engagement.

When Humbaba heard the noise "far off", he was enraged:

"Who is this that has violated my woods and cut down my cedar?"

The symbolism is similar to the incident of the Hyksos pharaoh and pharaoh Senqenrere where "noise" is used to describe what is seemingly a military venture. The fact that the attack is far off seems to suggest that it is some distance from the capital of the culture.

Gilgamesh is urged by Shamash to advance and "do not be afraid." He is seized by a profound sleep that may be intended to indicate that he is unapproachable as far as his strategy goes. Enkidu endeavours to rouse him:

"Oh Gilgamesh, Lord of the Plain of Kullab, the world grows dark, the shadows have spread over it, now is the glimmer of dusk, Shamash has departed."

This passage employs appropriate symbolism of light and darkness to indicate the cultures and the status of the battle. The battle is running adversely for the heroes. At length, Gilgamesh hears him and dons his breastplate, "the voice of Heroes" and with renewed resolve, recalling his undertaking, prepares for battle with Humbaba.

This is clearly the prelude to the decisive battle. Enkidu who knows the enemy to have powerful teeth (soldiers), which "are like dragon's fangs" has strong misgivings.

"His (Humbaba's) countenance is like a lion, his charge is the rushing of the flood, with his look, crushes alike the trees of the forest and the reeds of the swamp."

Teeth are found several times in myths as symbols of soldiers for example, in the myth of Jason who sprinkles teeth that spring up as soldiers.

The lion is the ancient symbol of earthly power and in those days the powerful and widespread god Dagan, the Lord of the Stars.

It is noticeable that the symbol of a flood (teeming life) is used to illustrate overwhelming military strength and fits the context of a battle nicely.

We have already proposed in an earlier chapter that the mythical "Flood" was in fact allegorical of a cataclysmic military event in the perennial struggle between the heliopian and monotheistic religious cultures.

The symbolism will again be seen in a similar context in a later chapter concerning the Judaic tradition and the Exodus from Egypt in which also, reeds represent militia (c.f. the parting of the Red (Reed) Sea in which the Pharaonic forces are "flooded." It is perhaps not surprising to see the same allegorical device in the Judaic tradition which is examined later, as Abraham, the patriarch of Judaism was traditionally a notable of Sumeria (Chaldea) who was an early initiator of the tradition of emigrating.

Gilgamesh dismisses Enkidu's pleadings with:

"Immolation and sacrifice are not yet for me, the boat of the dead (the Sekhet boat, in later Egyptian eschatology) shall not go down nor the three ply cloth be cut for my shrouding…All living creatures born of the flesh shall sit at last in the boat of the West (where the sun goes down) and when it sinks, when the boat of Magilum sinks, they are gone…"

Gilgamesh instructs Enkidu to take his axe in hand: "Humbaba came out of his strong house of cedar." Enkidu urges Gilgamesh to engage:

"…close in…if the watchman is there, do not allow him to escape into the woods (his Host?) where he will vanish."

"Humbaba fastens on Gilgamesh his eye, the eye of death, in the manner of a serpent."

This imagery uses the symbol of the serpent of death that appears as the serpent of the waters of death, later in the epic. The serpent is also a central archetypal symbol of the Sea god fertility cult and enemy of the Sun God.

In Ancient Egyptian mythology, this was Apophis who also inhabited the primeval waters (of the human psyche).

Gilgamesh, in tears, appeals to Shamash the Sun god, who sends the mighty eight winds, which beating against the monster's eyes, enable him to go neither forward nor back. The winds symbolism seems a mythological device to indicate some military surrounding manoeuvre. This seems to be the case as the battle starts to move in Gilgamesh's favour:

"He felled the first cedar…and they cut the branches and laid them at the foot of the mountain. At the first stroke, Humbaba blazed out, but they still advanced, they felled seven cedars and cut and bound the branches and laid them at the foot of the mountain and seven times Humbaba loosed his glory upon them. As the seventh blaze died out, they reached his lair. He slapped his thigh in scorn, like a noble wild bull roped on the mountain, a warrior whose elbows are bound together."

Here the sacred number seven abounds as it does throughout the epic and probably derives from the reputedly Sumerian Qaballistic concept of the union of male and female and spirit and body, the circle and triad three and the cross, four, which make up the ansata cross.

The binding of prisoners at the elbow is often to be seen on Ancient Egyptian stone carvings, celebrating victory over the Sea Peoples for example in Rameses III's reign. The archetypal symbols of blazing mountain and bull describing Humbaba are also to be found in Plato's description of Atlantis and the Atlantean Bull's blood ritual.

The Stele of Naram Sin (circa 2159–2123 BC) who was the grandson of Sargon of Akkad, a Sumerian presumably, shows the king winning a great victory over an enemy depicted as a mountain. Naram Sin is shown in identical dress and headdress to seal impressions of Gilgamesh.

The enemies are distinguished by their pigtails, a particularly Hittite characteristic, which may indicate that the Hittites were of Asian origin, at least in part.

A tree is shown at the bottom of the mountain and the Sun god emblem appears above the mountain maybe to signify the ascendancy of the god over the mountain.

Enkidu, meanwhile still has reservations about killing Humbaba, but Gilgamesh counters with a suggested military strategy which of course, is veiled in allegory:

"First entrap the bird and where shall the chicks run then? Afterwards we can search out the glory and the glamour when the chicks run distracted through the grass." (i.e., when the rout has begun)

Humbaba is put to death by Gilgamesh's and Enkidu's axes.

"At the third blow, Humbaba fell. Then there followed confusion for this was the Guardian of the Forest whom they had felled to the ground. For as far as two leagues, the cedars shivered when Enkidu felled the Watcher of the Forest, he at whose voice Herman and Lebanon used to tremble. Now the mountains were moved and all the hills, for the Guardian of the Forest was killed."

This passage illustrates the mythical imagery of battle, with the use of cedar trees to represent military contingents and allies of the mountain culture. Gilgamesh and Enkidu then uncover the "sacred dwellings of the Anunnaki." These were nameless "Great Ones"[11] who once lived above with the host of heaven but subsequently were the "Seven Judges of the Netherworld" (felt by some to be the "Repum" of the Ras Shamra, Canaanite texts, the Rephaim of the Bible) and direct equivalent of the Ancient Egyptian "paut" of gods.

The latter were judges of the Maati Hall of truth and judgement, seen on, for example, the Papyrus of Ani. The uncovering of the dwellings of the Anunnaki can be interpreted as the restoration of heliopianism from the domination of the monotheistic mountain culture.

Enlil, the Sumerian Storm God, disapproves of the killing of Humbaba for reasons not revealed, and despite intercession of the Sun God, decrees the death of Enkidu. If Enkidu represents the proto-Hittite or some allied culture, then his death possible alludes to the eclipse of that culture. This was an event with which the ancients were familiar, for the Sumerian culture was to ostensibly, disappear and mutate, manifested as numerous traits in subsequent cultural progeny, as was the Hittite culture (circa 1200 BC).

Cultures, like most living organisms, are not obliterated but mutate into some other form. The time scale on which they grow, mature and die, is best measured in millennia.

The Heroes' Battle with the Bull of Heaven

Subsequent to the defeat of Humbaba, the Epic goes on to relate how the Goddess Innana, the Babylonian Ishtar, seeing Gilgamesh in his glory (as representing the Sumerian heliopian religious culture), desires to marry the hero. This seems a natural consequence arising out of defeat in battle, a sort of cultural equivalent of the victor marrying the daughter of the defeated king, a marriage alliance (as for example that of Henry V).

In this case it is proposed marriage between heliopianism and the monotheistic fertility cult of Ishtar in order, probably, to sustain the survival of the fertility culture.

"Come to me Gilgamesh and be my bridegroom, grant me the seed of your body." Offering the while, gold, lapis lazuli, copper and the homage of kings, rulers and princes, in short, vast worldly power, the motivating desire of such phallic cults.

Here marriage is the means whereby the forces of cultural monotheism attempt to acquire collective religious power in a similar manner to the Ancient Egyptian Amenites in the era of Hatshepsut. It is apparent that such manoeuvres were common in the perennial struggle between heliopianism and cultural autocracy.

It comes as little surprise therefore that Gilgamesh rejects Ishtar's offer, she whose cultural "flood" had caused the eclipse of heliopianism and kingship.

In a long list of past suitors, beginning with Tammuz, Gilgamesh describes the fickleness of her love. The lovers, who are not always persons, are representatives of cultures embraced by the monotheistic fertility cults which at that time were widespread.

Gilgamesh describes:

The many-coloured roller, a bird whose wing Ishtar broke, and which, laments his broken wing in a grove. The Lion, "tremendous in strength…The magnificent Stallion, for him you decree whip, spur and thong, to gallop seven leagues by force and to muddy the water before he drinks, and for his mother Silili, lamentations. Ishullanu, the gardener of your father's palm grove…he was changed into a blind mole." So with the words "should not I be served in the same fashion as these others whom you loved once?"

Gilgamesh rejects the Queen of Heaven.

When Ishtar heard this, she fell into a bitter rage. She petitioned her father Anu, the head of the pantheon, to give her the "Bull of Heaven" with which to destroy Gilgamesh. Anu is unwilling to accommodate Ishtar, pointing out that what Gilgamesh had spoken of her "abominable behaviour", her "foul and hideous acts" was only the truth.

At this, Ishtar threatens "to break in the doors of Hell and smash the bolts…to bring up the hosts of dead to eat with the living."

This passage may be compared with Isaiah XIV-9

"Hell from beneath is moved for thee, even all the chief ones of the earth."

It is a tribute to the power of Ishtar that Anu succumbs to her request.

"If I do what you desire, there will be seven years of drought. Have you saved enough grain for the people and grass for the cattle?"

Replying that preparations had been made, Anu gave her the Bull of Heaven. The myth is describing in allegory, an impending cultural war between Ishtarian fertility forces and the Sumerian heliopians. There is an echo in Genesis (XLI, 17-20) with the Pharaoh's dream of seven fat and seven lean kine.

It is known that at the earliest times, as the Ptah cycle of gods indicates, such animal imagery resided in the Ancient Egyptian cultural psyche. An ancient bull cult was extant in the Delta, whose goddess was Isis, a more benign, but nonetheless, fertility goddess under her guise as Hathor.

Hathor could be regarded as a lower human animal composite of the goddess fashioned for the less sophisticated members of society. The sacred number seven occurs frequently throughout the epic of Osiris, which again, is possibly a further example of Sumerian influence in the Ancient Egyptian culture.

It is probable that the Pharaoh of Genesis was of early Cretan-Hyksos descent and the subsequent Exodus of the Bible describes the consequences of the perennial struggle between heliopianism and the monotheistic fertility culture of the Delta. This is investigated in a later chapter.

The battle that ensues between Gilgamesh and the Bull of Heaven has much in common with the myth of Mithras, the heroic champion of the Sun god who defeats Ahriman, the evil one. The allegory is similar, enlightenment versus darkness, consciousness versus the subconscious, human nature versus animal nature.

The Mithraic myth is possibly, a later version of this episode of the Epic but is, in any event, a description of the perennial conflict. It is of interest to note that there is a mithreum on the ancient site of Uruk in Mesopotamia.[12]

When Ishtar and the Bull reach the gates of Uruk, the Bull "went down to the river, with his first snort, cracks opened in the earth and a hundred young men (warriors) fell down to death, with his second snort, cracks opened and two hundred fell down to death." At the third snort however, Enkidu seizes the Bull by the horns and, in answer to Enkidu's urging to thrust his sword "between the nape and the horns", Gilgamesh seizes the Bull by the thick of its tail and slays it. Cutting out its heart, they give it to the Sun god, signifying victory for the heliopians.

The scene describes the counter attack of the "flood" or fertility forces. The Bull represents the Cretan-Atlantean culture trying to regain the Anatolian and Levant territory lost as described in the Humbaba saga. Cretan culture seems the likely candidate since in later times it is represented by the Minoan Bull and Minotaur in Greek myth which makes frequent reference to a snake bearing fertility goddess often seen on Minoan artefacts.

The culture referred to in the epic however would have to be some pre-Minoan culture. On the walls of the throne room at Knossos, the ancient Minoan capital of Crete, can be seen the famous "leaping the bull" fresco. Two male figures are shown ostensibly leaping over the bull. Is this an allusion to the epic brought by some past conquering culture, to become part of Minoan mythology?

The Bull of Heaven episode takes the advance from the shores of the Mediterranean into the epicentre, Crete, the ancient Atlantis (the "heart"?) which was made a gift to the Sun god.

Later, it will be shown that the island was associated with the Sea god from ancient times and several fertility goddesses, reincarnations of the original consort of the Sea God, Cleito.

From the Hittite myth of Ullikumi, the "monstrous mountain" which it is suggested was Atlantean Crete, the Sumerian epic leads back to the same culture which, at one time, must have been very powerful and extended. It is suggested also that this culture was the common adversary of the Sumerians and pre-Hittites, the brother cultures represented by Gilgamesh and Enkidu.

The Epic is testament to the power of the fertility culture and the importance of its defeat. In the Ancient Egyptian and later derived polytheistic cultures, there were always fertility cultures but never concentrated in one powerful deity strong enough to challenge the Sun god. The epic, of extraordinary strength and vigour, of similar stature to the vague but persistent legend of Atlantis, found wide currency in contemporary heliopian cultures which derived, in the main, from the Sumerian culture.

It is in all probability the prototype hero epic that is so characteristic of Greek mythology. One should bear in mind, myths, like dreams, have no temporal (chronological) time scale for several reasons and do not require one for their survival.

One reason is that myths existed long before writing or written records or calendars were instituted.

Myths however, are essential, like propaganda stories in war, to provide cultural adhesion and group pride, which provide a people with cultural role models and archetypes for emulation in times of threat. Equally important, they reveal military strategies and valorous deeds, without which, leave cultures naively vulnerable.

The markers on the temporal continuum of culture are the periods of cultural change and the trends, the flowing of cultural tides. The time scale, if it could be measured, would be calibrated on a scale of millennia.

Heliopianism, though not without its struggles against monotheistic atavistic fertility cults, spanned at least from the fourth millennium BC. to the middle of the first century AD in a succession of cultures from the Sumerian through

Egyptian, Hittite, Persian, and Greek to the Roman, just to name the major cultures.

Ostensibly, some of these cultures appear dead, but this is not the case, as they lived long enough to establish cultural archetypes within their nation's collective psyche. These live on (even today) and influence, or are absorbed, into later derived cultures, for this is the cultural means of survival which is mirrored in the reproduction of the individual.

It is easy to trace many archetypes and cultural traits that appear in the Ancient Egyptian which have their origin in the Sumerian culture. From the study of myths, we see as an ingenious but wholly natural, the use of human individuals, the hero, and less often, the heroine, as the representation of whole cultures so that each member of the culture can identify with him or her.

This is not surprising, as each individual is the microcosm of the culture as macrocosm, the individual's psychological life is the result of the culture and collectively, is the culture.

The unique relationship between Gilgamesh and Enkidu suggests an alliance between two cultures, perhaps the Sumerian and some more northerly pre-Hittite Hurrian. Many twin god idols have been found among pre-Hittite sculptures and artefacts. The ancients were aware of the ephemeral nature of empires or tribal societies in the "family" of heliopian cultures.

The death of Enkidu may have served the purpose of educating the populace to the transitoriness of human existence, and prepared them for the final chapter which describes the death of the hero Gilgamesh, presaging the passing of the culture.

This may also have been tacit recognition of the might of the dark forces of Sea god monotheism.

After the slaying of the Bull of Heaven, the "brothers" rested, but Ishtar rose up and mounted the great wall of Uruk; she sprang onto the tower and uttered a curse: "Woe to Gilgamesh, for he has scorned me in the killing of the Bull of Heaven (her fertility cult)…When Enkidu heard these words, he tore out the Bull's right thigh…Enkidu tossed the thigh in Ishtar's face saying, 'If I could lay my hands upon you, it is this I should do to you and lash the entrails to your side.'…Then Ishtar called together her people, the dancing and the singing girls, the prostitutes of the temple, the courtesans. Over the thigh of the Bull of Heaven, she set up lamentation."

The prostitutes of the temple were, in all probability, the priestesses of the cult rituals, of which similar can be seen on the walls of Minoan Crete administering the ritual of the sacred pillar as described in Plato's Atlantis.

There was also the Sumerian belief that the god (of fertility presumably) entered the sanctuary on top of the Ziggurats to lie with young women, hence possibly their description as divine prostitutes.

It is probable that the Minoan frescoes showing youths ostensibly leaping over a bull is in fact, a depiction of the Bull of Heaven episode of the Epic. Frescoes and stone carvings were, like gothic cathedral windows too valuable for mere ornamentation but were communications reinforcing cultural myths.

Atlantis was by tradition, like a bullring, a series of concentric canals.

Gilgamesh called the smiths and armorers, all of them together. They admired the immensity of the horns. They were plated with lapis lazuli two fingers thick, thirty pounds each and their capacity was six measures of oil. Gilgamesh made a gift of the horns to his guardian god Lugulbanda, washed his men, their hands in the Euphrates, embraced and parted, Gilgamesh returning in triumph to Uruk with Enkidu, and there was feasting and celebration.

When daylight came, Enkidu got up and cried to Gilgamesh, "Oh my brother, such a dream I had last night. Anu, Enlil, Ea and heavenly Shamash took council together and Anu said to Enlil, 'Because they have killed the Bull of Heaven and because they have killed Humbaba who guarded the Cedar Mountain, one of the two must die.'"

The glorious Shamash answered the hero Enlil "It was by your command they killed the Bull of Heaven and killed Humbaba, and must Enkidu die although innocent?"

Enlil, the warrior god, is particularly hostile to the heroes, Enlil, the executive of the head of the pantheon, is sometimes referred to as the "father of the gods" and is also known as "Enlil of the Mountain"[13], an allusion to his status as Hittite Storm God.

"Enlil flung round in a rage at glorious Shamash, 'You dare say this, you who went about with them every day like one of themselves'."

Enkidu is taken with sickness and, in what must be a eulogy to Gilgamesh, and the Sumerian culture, he bitterly regrets the outcome of the quest.

"While Enkidu lay alone in his sickness, he cursed the gate as though it was living flesh, 'You there, wood of the gate, dull and insensible, witless, I searched for you over twenty leagues until I saw the towering cedar. There is no wood like you in our land. Seventy-two cubits high and twenty-four wide, the pivot and the ferrule and the jambs are perfect. A master craftsman from Nippur has made you, but O, if I had known the conclusion, if I had known this was all the good that would come of it, I would have raised the axe and split you into little pieces and set up here a gate of wattle instead. Ah if only some future king had brought you here or some god had fashioned you. Let him obliterate my name and write his own and the curse fall on him instead of Enkidu'."

There is here a description of a hieratically scaled door some 110 feet high and 36 feet wide that is clearly symbolic of something or someone. The wood is cedar which is associated with Humbaba. The symbolism suggests that the door is symbolic of some contingent of the enemy having been incorporated into the fabric of Uruk. A not unlikely event to be seen in the Bible with such stories as Abraham being incorporated into the Pharaoh's retinue in Egypt followed later by Joseph in the same manner.

Both also were monotheists as, it has been suggested, was the culture represented by Humbaba. The passage is also redolent of Solomon and King Hirom (or Hiram) of Lebanon and the building of the Temple in Jerusalem whose porch had almost the same gigantic dimensions.

"Send me also cedar trees…for the house which I am about to build shall be wonderful great." (II Chronicles Ch II 8,9) "The porch that was in the front of the house, the length of it was according to the breadth of the house, twenty cubits and the height was an hundred and twenty." (II Chronicles Ch III, 4).

Enkidu curses the "Trapper" (death?) "that vile Trapper, the Trapper of Nothing because of whom I was to catch less than my comrade." Having assailed the trapper, Enkidu then brings down curses on the harlot priestess of Ishtar that civilised him. Shamash the Sun God upbraids him:

"Why are you cursing the woman, the mistress who taught you to eat bread fit for gods and drink the wine of kings?…She who put upon you a magnificent garment, did she not give you glorious Gilgamesh for your companion?…He has made the princes of the earth kiss your feet…When you are dead, he will let his hair grow long for your sake, he will wear lion's pelt and wander through the desert."

With this, Enkidu relents and blesses Gilgamesh, "kings, princes and nobles shall adore you", and prophesises great wealth, respect and his entrance into the presence of the Gods.

(Later Gilgamesh sets out on a journey for the plant of everlasting life. This is probably the prototype for cultural heroes to gain everlasting life by first making the journey to Hades and return, as did Hercules and Christ on the Cross.)

During his sickness, Enkidu has another dream that describes aspects of Sumerian eschatology. Similar aspects can be found in later Egyptian and Greek eschatology clearly derived from the Sumerian.

"The heavens roared and the earth rumbled back an answer, between them stood I before an awful being, the sombre faced man-bird (Pazuzu), he had directed on me his purpose. His was a vampire face, his foot was a lion's foot, his hand was an eagle's talon. He fell on me and his claws were in my hair, he held me fast and I smothered. He then transformed me so that my arms became wings covered with feathers. He turned his stare towards me and led me away to the palace of Irkalla, the Queen of Darkness, to the house from which none that enters ever returns, down the road from which there is no coming back.

This is the house whose people sit in darkness; dust is their food and clay their meat. They are clothed like birds with wings for covering, they see no light, and they sit in darkness. I entered the house of dust and saw the kings of the Earth, their crowns put away for ever, rulers and princes, all those who once wore kingly crowns and ruled the world in days of old. They who had stood in the place of the gods, like Anu and Enlil, stood now like servants to fetch baked meats in the house of dust, to carry cooked meats and cold water from the water skin.

In the house of dust that I entered, were high priests and acolytes, priests of the incantation and ecstasy. There were servers of the temple, and there was Etana, that king of Kish whom the eagle carried to heaven in the days of old. I saw also Samuquan, god of cattle and there was Ereshkigal the Queen of the Underworld, the Belit-Sheri squatted in front of her, she who is the recorder of the gods and keeps the book of death, she held a tablet from which she read…"

The dream starts with Enkidu standing between heaven and earth, echoing the previous passages of his initially, cursing, and then blessing Gilgamesh. Irkalla is then depicted as a place of darkness and dust, in contrast to the Egyptian concept of the Elysian Fields and the home of the gods.

This view is associated with the gods of fertility like Samuquan. There is also the hint that those who would seek worldly domination and power ended up there.

Ereshkigal seems to be a prototype Persephone, whose mother Demeter was the Anatolian fertility goddess, one of whose symbols was the ear of corn. The inhabitants of Irkalla have the form of birds that, presumably, depict spirits.

This is general to the Middle Eastern cosmologies where for example Thoth in the ceremony of the opening of the mouth lets out the spirit of the deceased shown as a bird.

Pazuzu has attributes similar to Horus in Ancient Egyptian eschatology who leads the deceased into the presence of Osiris. He also has many of the aspects of the sphinx. Belit-Shei has parallels with Thoth, the celestial recorder.

The Maati Hall of Truth, where Osiris and the "paut" of gods sit to observe the weighing of the heart of the deceased seems to have its opposite in Irkalla, part of the domain of fertility culture, and is ruled by a woman. This is not out of keeping with the cultural opposites that existed, that is, heliopianism and monotheism.

The traditionally Sumerian Qaballism would accommodate this concept of male and female opposites. The passage of the epic seems to confirm the findings of Wooley at Ur, that kingship existed before the flood, and that the Flood myth is an allegory of military conquest.

Also in the passage is a reference to the look or stare of death, the hypnotic effect of the (phallic) serpent. The look of death was previously encountered in the Epic during the episode of the battle with and death of Humbaba.

Similar instances of the power of the "death look" are to be found in Greek mythology with such myths as the Gorgon Medusa and Orpheus and Eurydice in Hades, a similar place to Irkalla.

Food and drink, albeit dust and clay are described as being eaten in Irkalla. This is in contrast to the Ancient Egyptian Heliopian concept of the deceased eating ordinary food. In Egypt, the deceased was buried with plentiful supplies of food and offerings of food were made to the gods. This clearly implied that the abode after death was a congenial place for those whose heart survived the weighing.

In contrast, there does not seem to be any corresponding place in the Sumerian. The representation of the human spirit by a bird was a custom later adopted by the Egyptians, Babylonians, Assyrians and subsequent heliopian cultures.

In the final passages of this part of the Epic, a sorrowful Enkidu dies, to the accompaniment of great mourning by Gilgamesh and the people of Uruk.

To commemorate his "brother", Gilgamesh has a great statue made of Enkidu. "With a great weight of lapis lazuli for the breast and gold for the body."

This description is evocative of the sarcophagi of the Egyptian Pharaohs with their circular breastplates of lapis lazuli representing the Sun.

It was a tradition in Sumerian culture that the king erect a great image of himself.[14]

In the Biblical account of the Book of Daniel reference is made to the erecting of a great statue of gold by the king (Daniel 11-31 et sub). In the Book of Daniel the culture is the Sumerian derived Babylonian and the king is the great Nebuchadnezzar who has a dream which Daniel interprets as:

"This great image, whose brightness was excellent...This image's head was of fine gold; his breast and arms of silver; his belly and thighs of brass, his feet, part of iron and part of clay. Thou sawest till that a stone cut out without hands which smote the image upon its feet...and break them into pieces...and the stone that smote the image became a great mountain and filled the whole earth...For as much as thou sawest that the stone was cut out of the mountain."

There are a few interesting things to note in this imagery. Here, the image of a man dreamt of by the king was probably Nebuchadnezzar himself but more importantly the image is a personification of the Babylonian culture, just as the mythical Gilgamesh represented a personification of the Sumerian culture, the forerunner of the Babylonian.

This also infers a similarity or correlation between myths and dreams as far as the human psyche goes, especially in relation to the subconscious.

The full interpretation of the dream of Nebuchadnezzar and Daniel's motives is left to a later chapter where it is dealt with in its proper context and time. It is, perhaps, not surprising to encounter the imagery of the mountain again destroying the image of a man, the Babylonian culture, in a similar manner to the "monstrous mountain" usurping the heliopian pantheon or the "mountain" Humbaba falling on Gilgamesh in his dream.

Two millennia after the Sumerian experience, the "mountain" fertility culture is still in conflict with the heliopian Babylonian culture, despite the Atlantean Cretan ascendancy having long since passed.

This perennial eternal struggle, as we shall see, did not ever abate, nor has it yet. The fertility culture, one of whose central archetypes is the rock or mountain, lived on in the cultural psyche of the Egyptians and other cultures. It had migrated to the southern shores of the Mediterranean as the Sumerian experience indicated.

It had waged incursions in archaic times into Egypt, chronicled in Greek mythology and later cultural infusions by it into the same culture took place later as represented by the Hyksos invasions of Ancient Egypt.

References Chapter 5

[1] N. K. Sandars', The Epic of Gilgamesh, page 61

[2] J. Gray, Near Eastern Mythology, page 39

[3] N. K. Sandars, The Epic of Gilgamesh, page 62

[4] Chamber's Encyclopaedia, Vol 8, page 57b

[5] Great Events of the Bible, Various Editors, page 149

[6] N. K. Sandars, The Epic of Gilgamesh, page 76

[7] ibid, page 83

[8] ibid, page 32

[9] J. A. Hadfield, Dreams and Nightmares, page 48

[10] ibid, page 50

[11] S. H. Hooke, Middle Eastern Mythology

[12] N. K. Sandars, The Epic of Gilgamesh, page 118

[13] Atlas of Ancient Archaeology, ed. Jacquetta Hawkes, page 172

[14] Sir L. Wooley, Ur of the Chaldees, page 104

Chapter 6
The Epic of Gilgamesh and
Its Influence on Ancient Eschatology

The chapter on the death of Enkidu ends with a ritual that is commonplace in Egyptian tomb paintings.

"A table of hardwood was set out and on it a bowl of carnelian filled with honey and a bowl of lapis lazuli filled with butter. These he exposed, and offered to the Sun; and weeping he went away."

Offerings of food often accompanied the deceased in Egyptian funerary rites. Butter and honey are evocative of the desirable qualities of the Judaic Promised Land, the land of milk and honey. It is however, in the concluding chapters of the Epic that the greatest contribution of the Sumerians to the culture of the Ancient Egyptians, and no doubt other heliopian cultures, was made in respect of their ideas on the afterlife.

Gilgamesh's Search for Everlasting Life

Gilgamesh is seized with unremitting sorrow at the death of Enkidu "weeping" bitterly for his lost brother and fraught with despair at the realisation that such an end awaits him. Such weeping was an integral part of ritual and signified a state of genuineness.

Incidents are found in Roman history[1] for example, among Celtic chieftains petitioning Caesar.

Gilgamesh resolves to go in search of Utnapishtim, "the Faraway" whom "the gods took after the deluge and they set him to live in the land of Dilmun in the garden of the Sun; and to him alone of men they gave everlasting life."

Gilgamesh refers to Utnapishtim as "my father"[2]. If the allegorical translation of the myth has Gilgamesh as representing the heliopian Sumerian culture, then Utnapishtim, who was the old Babylonian equivalent of the

Sumerian king Ziusrudra and the Old Testament Noah, represents a possible allusion to the parent culture.

This would indicate that of India from whom most of the Near-Eastern cultures were derived and remains today, the major polytheistic cosmogony.

Gilgamesh sets out for the Mashu Mountains, the legendary "twin" mountains[3], the gates to heaven. He travels through mountain passes and one night he awakes to find himself surrounded by "lions round him glorying in life." Taking his sword, he fell upon them "like an arrow from the string" and destroyed them.

It is in the imagery of this small episode that the heroic images of Gilgamesh were cast for posterity. He is often shown holding two lions by their tails, a symbolism evident in the Hittite pantheon where the major figures at Yasilikaya are to be seen holding lion's tails.

The lions are allegorically a culture and probably represent the god Dagan:

"Lord of the Stars" of Protosyrian origin, popular in the Levant, Anatolian and Syria. The cult must also have spread as early Protosyrian influence to the northern shores of the Mediterranean, for the lion is also prevalent as a symbol in Mycenae, the culture that would become the long-time adversary of the Anatolian Hittites.

Eventually, Gilgamesh arrives at the Mashu Mountains "Its twin peaks as high as the wall of heaven" to find the gate guarded by two men-scorpions who recognise him as being two thirds god "but one third man", an early reference to the concept of a trinity and celestial qualities associated with man.

The image of the scorpion men aligns with the pre-history images of Egyptian gods of the Ptah cycle who, with the exception of Ptah, were human-animal composites. The scorpion it should be remembered, became in the Egyptian and subsequent heliopian cultures, a celestial constellation, the scorpion men recognising their kin in Gilgamesh grant him admittance. (There is a reference in the literature to the Gutians, an obscure tribe in the environs of Sumeria who are described as "the snake, the scorpion of the mountain").[4]

Gilgamesh discloses the reasons for his quest, those being that his "life is nothing" since Enkidu, despite his weeping, had not returned and so his searching for Utnapishtim "to question him concerning the living and the dead."

The man-scorpion admonishes Gilgamesh with a warning:

"No man born of woman had done what you have asked, no mortal man has gone into the mountain; the length of it is twelve leagues of darkness; in it there is no light but the heart is oppressed with darkness."

Gilgamesh, undeterred, embarks on a long journey through the mountain consisting of "twelve leagues of darkness…giving a great cry. At the end of eight leagues of darkness, for the darkness was so thick, he could see nothing ahead and nothing behind him. At the end of twelve leagues, the sun streamed out and there was the garden of the gods."

This presumably, became the later Egyptian Elysian Fields.

Here is the prototype journey of the Hero into the after world, encountered in Greek mythology with the exploits of Herakles, Theseus and others. Such a journey became, in the Greco-Roman tradition, a qualification for godhood and immortality. In the epic it is the quest of Gilgamesh.

The garden of the gods contains bushes and vines, bearing gems, fruit of the carnelian, and lapis lazuli leaves thick with fruit. In place of thorns and thistles, there were rare stones, hematite, agate and pearls from out of the sea.

Shamash, the Sun God seeing Gilgamesh in the garden by the edge of the sea is distressed at his wild and emaciated appearance and advises him that he will never find the life for which he searches.

Beside the sea (presumably in the garden) lives the Woman of the Vine, Siduri, the maker of wine "with the golden bowl and golden vats that the gods gave her." Siduri, as the Woman of the vine, an ancient symbol of fruitfulness, fertility and life, is cast as an Ishtar type of figure who was also associated with fertility and the Tree of Life.

The imagery of the garden with the profusion of precious stones is echoed over two millennia later in the Judaic Book of Revelation's description of the city of God (Revelation chapter XX1), that "had no need of the Sun, neither of the Moon to shine in it."

It is perhaps not surprising that the Sun and Moon are disclaimed. This is typically predominantly symbolic language of Revelation, which use was a probable necessity arising out of the adversarial cultural environment existing when it was written, as could be said for much of the Bible narrative.

The Sun and Moon translate as representing the most powerful contemporary Roman cults, the Jupiter, Apollo, Mithraic cult of "Sol Invictus" and the Isis cult in their various manifestations. Babylon of Revelation is now widely acknowledged to signify the Roman Empire.

The Garden of the Sun was probably the mythical forerunner of the Garden of Eden with Siduri replaced be Eve and the proprietor by Yahweh. At first, Siduri is suspicious that Gilgamesh is truly he who killed the Bull of Heaven, overthrew Humbaba and killed the lions at the passes, but after hearing his lamentations, advises him to attend to the joys of living and forget his quest. Eventually, Siduri, in the face of Gilgamesh's resolve, tells him that he must cross the "Ocean of Death" which only Shamash alone in his glory has been able to do.

In the Ocean of Death lives the Serpent of Death, the same adversary of Ra, the Sun God of Egypt, Apophis, who lived in the primeval waters (of death). This again is another instance of Sumerian culture influencing later heliopian cultures.

Siduri directs Gilgamesh to the woods where lives Urshanabi, the ferryman of Utnapishtim. "With him are the holy things, the things of stone. He is fashioning the serpent prow of the boat."

The boat is another example of eschatological symbolism that found its way into subsequent heliopian cultures, notably, as the central archetypal Sekhet boat of the Egyptian deceased and the Ferry of Charon of Greek mythology.

The fashioning of the serpent prow is the charm to assuage the (phallic) serpent of the Ocean of Death. Similar prows arising most likely from related myth are to be seen on the prows of Saxon-Viking long boats. These probably had the same talismanic value of assuaging the Midgarde Serpent, the enemy of Odin the head of the Norse pantheon.

The holy things, the things of stone, or the sacred stones of Destiny, is a recurrent archetypal symbol in Mesopotamian-Sumerian mythology.

In the legend of Zu[5] Zu steals the tablets from Enlil, the celestial executive, "while he was washing." It is left to Lugalbanda the patron god of Gilgamesh, to recover them as the Sun God Marduk had done, from Kingu, the marshal of the celestial usurper, Tiamat.

Zu is represented on seals as a man bird and the "Bull of Heaven" is referred to the spawn of Zu. Zu's abode, not surprisingly, is a mountain, evoking shades of the Atlantean archetypes. The wresting of the stones of destiny again insinuates a struggle for celestial power, and the stones themselves may represent a mythological portrayal of the onset of written language and the power of the written word.

This was attributed to the God of Wisdom, Ea, and in Egypt to Thoth, whose sacred secret magic words were associated with everlasting life.

Certainly, the sacred tablets of Moses, also obtained from a mountain, suggest they were derived from the Sumerian tradition. This is perhaps not surprising, as tradition has Abraham born in Sumerian Chaldea. The mountain is also a prolific symbol in the Bible.

Gilgamesh is further advised by Siduri, "Look at him well, and if it is possible, perhaps you will cross the waters with him, but if it is not possible, then you must go back." On hearing this, Gilgamesh is seized with anger, and taking his axe and dagger, he "fell on them like a javelin."

Precisely what Gilgamesh has destroyed is not clear until Urshanabi explains:

"Those things you destroyed, their property is to carry me over the water to prevent the waters of death touching me. It was for this reason that I preserved them, but you have destroyed them and the Urnu snakes with them."

It seems therefore, that Gilgamesh has destroyed the talismanic images of the sea serpent, the totem poles, and the phalli that would, like the prows of Viking longboats, have satiated the serpent spirit of the primeval (psychological) waters, the waters of death and the domain of Apophis.

Gilgamesh's anger, on encountering totems of the sea serpent as a heliopian, is perhaps understandable. As a consequence of his actions, Urshanabi tells the hero to:

"Go into the forest, with your axe, cut poles, one hundred and twenty, cut them sixty cubits long, paint them with bitumen, set them on ferrules and bring them back." This Gilgamesh does and the pair embark.

"For three days they ran on as it were a journey of a month and fifteen days, until they reached the waters of death" whereupon, Gilgamesh is instructed to take a pole and thrust it into the waters. He throws a second and so on ensuring that "his hands do not touch the waters."

When all the poles are gone, the hero holds up his arms, and, using his covering skins as a sail, they are brought to Dilmun "at the mouth of the rivers", the home of Utnapishtim the Faraway.

This description of the location of the home of the gods is quite specific 'at the mouth of the (two) rivers. Later we shall see that Dilmun figures in the description of the Egyptian Elysian Fields.

Utnapishtim, the biblical Noah who with his (Sekhet) boat, the ark, had preserved the early heliopian culture. Urshanabi's serpent-prow boat with its many oars also features prominently in Egyptian depictions of the Elysian Fields, the abode of the blessed.

Gilgamesh, representing the Sumerian culture, is constantly being advised by the Gods that everlasting life is not possible, not even for cultures and that these must either mutate or die.

This is entirely in harmony with the natural law of survival. Utnapishtim may represent the antecedent of the Sumerian culture, possibly originating in India. The earliest artefacts of Indian culture bear a general resemblance to those found in Sumerian sites at Kish and Susa in Mesopotamia[6].

It is clear that the myth is a very potent form of pre-history, pre-writing form of cultural communication. According to Sir Leonard Wooley, it is to the Sumerians:

"We can trace much that is at the root of not only Egyptian, but also of Babylonian, Assyrian, Hebrew and Phoenician art and thought"[7], a conclusion that is evident from the examination of ancient Near Eastern mythology.

The first written history of Sumeria appears as a short symbolic inscription at Al'Ubaid at Ur[8] dated about 3500 BC.

"A-anni-pad-da King of Ur, son of Mes-ani-pad-da King of Ur, has built this for his lady Nin-Kharsag." There is here a succession inferring a time scale, necessary for historical accuracy.

Mythology on the other hand, devoid of historical time scale that would render myths difficult to propagate and survive, being primarily concerned with cultural change that evolves from the human psyche, by necessity, uses symbols with which to communicate with the human subconscious.

The subconscious has the extraordinary ability to remember indefinitely with its archetypal memory. It must have been realised aeons ago by the ancients that this facility was available. It must also have been realised that, as a necessary part of survival, man had a need to remember his cultural history, possibly as a method of learning the means of how to survive.

It is daunting to think that, as Jung realised, ancient potent symbols which translate into historical pageant, of which the subconscious is aware, still reside in all individual archetypal memories, though born of (a few) different cultures, for nearly all of the Near Eastern cultures were derivatives of those that had gone before.

It is thus an astonishing achievement of the ancients to have developed and propagated myths that eventually were almost superseded by the power of the written word.

In the epic, Utnapishtim is cast as the "ancient in wisdom." Gilgamesh addresses him with his question:

"O father Utnapishtim, you who have entered the assembly of the Gods. I wish to question you concerning the living and the dead, how shall I find the life for which I am searching?"

Utnapishtim is fatalistic:

"There is no permanence. Do we build a house to stand forever?...does the flood time of rivers endure? The sleeping and the dead, how alike they are, they are like a painted death...when the Anunnaki, the judges come together and Mammetun, the Mother of Destinies, together they decree the fates of men."

"Tell me truly, how was it you came to enter the company of the Gods and to possess everlasting life?" to which Utnapishtim replied, "I will reveal to you a mystery, I will tell you a secret of the Gods."

Here we note also a cultural trait, that of judgement after death, that was inherited by the later Ancient Egyptian Culture.

The Allegory of the Flood

Utnapishtim proceeds to tell Gilgamesh the story of the Flood and it becomes clear that the story is allegorical for the flood waters are in effect "nether" waters, the celestial waters of fertility forces[9].

The story opens with the scene set for a cultural revolution, for Shurrupak, the city on the banks of the Euphrates, "grew old and the gods that were in it were old."

We can assume some ancient heliopian culture prevailed and had existed for some considerable time.

"In those days, the world teemed, the people multiplied, the world bellowed like a wild bull."

It is Enlil, the Storm God, whose anger caused the demise of Enkidu, who is again angry and claims in celestial council that:

"The uproar of mankind is intolerable and sleep is no longer possible."

The Gods, yielding to the celestial executive, decide "to exterminate mankind, Enlil did this." It is Ea the God of Wisdom and Sweet (nether) Waters, who "because of his oath" warns Utnapishtim:

138

"He whispered their words to my house of reeds…Reed house, reed house! Wall, O Wall, hearken reed house, wall reflect, O man of Shurrupak, son of Ubara-Tutu, tear down your house and build a boat, abandon possessions and look for life, despise worldly goods and save your soul alive"

"Tear down your house and build a boat" translates as "gather your tribe and move, migrate, possibly using camels, boats of the desert. It is clear a migration is intended for Ea advises Utnapishtim to explain to the city elders (the city representing the culture) that his reason for building a boat is to 'go down to the Gulf (because of Enlil's wrath) to dwell with Ea where he will rain down abundance of rare fish, wild fowl and in the evening, the 'rider of the storm will bring you wheat in torrents."

After seven days (a prolific and sacred number in Sumerian mythology) the boat with punt holes, similar to Urshanabi's is complete and Utnapishtim loads it with "gold and of living things, my family, my kin, the beast of the field, both wild and tame and all the craftsmen."

The steersman across the nether waters this time is Puzur-Amurri "with the navigation and the care of the whole boat."

Allegorically, Puzur-Amurri probably represents the military commander, for the cultural flood would have in its wake, military conquest, and so it is described:[10].

"Then the Gods of the Abyss (death) rose up; Nergal pulled out the dams of the nether waters, Ninurta, the war lord threw down the dykes and the seven judges of Hell, the Anunnaki, raised their torches, lighting the land with their livid flame. A stupor of despair went up to Heaven when the God of the Storm turned daylight into darkness, when he smashed the land like a cup. One whole day, the tempest raged, gathering fury as it went, it poured over the people like the tides of battle."

Here, the flood is described as nether water, the cultural waters of the Gods of darkness and death and specifically in this case war, against the heliopian cosmogony.

The passage is strewn with military allegory, the cultural forces sweeping the land in a tide of battle, smashing it like a cup. Similar imagery is to be seen in an apocryphal story of Jesus.

The cup is also an ancient archetype for the spirit, as in the 23rd Psalm "my cup runneth over." The torches of the netherworld judges, the light of the culture has been turned to darkness.

"One day", if in a similar vein to the Biblical creation time scale, probably refers to a unit of cultural time, a considerable period in real time. As one would expect, in the face of such annihilation, the heliopian cosmogony would be endangered, and so it was for:

"Even the Gods were terrified at the flood, they fled to the highest heaven, the firmament of Anu, they crouched against the walls, cowering like curs."

Here is an early reference to the Qaballistic concept of the celestial architecture consisting of several mansions or spheres (to which reference is made in the New Testament). This concept of celestial spheres is claimed by some to have originated with the Chaldean Sumerians and depicted in the form of a tree (the tree of life).[11]

The highest sphere is associated with the planet Jupiter or Zeus, the Greek equivalent of Anu.

Although the marshalling of the flood forces is imputed to the Storm God, it is Ishtar, the fertility goddess, whose sister, Ereskigal is the Queen of Irkallah, who claims responsibility for the disaster and bringing war to the land.

"Alas the days of old are turned to dust because I commanded evil, why did I command this evil in the council of the Gods? I commanded **wars** to destroy people, but are they not my people, for I brought them forth? Now like the spawn of fish, they float in the ocean."[12]

"The Great Gods of Heaven and of Hell wept, they covered their mouths."

It is clear that the flood was indeed a cultural conflict with its concomitant battles.

This is confirmed by comparison with two dreams related in Herodotus "The Histories." They are dreamt by king Astyages, the son of Cyaxares who had united much of Asia under the Medes.

In the first dream Astyages dreamt that his daughter, Mandane made water in such enormous quantities that it filled his city and swamped the whole of Asia. Some years later he has a second dream in which a vine grew from the private parts of Mandane and spread over all of Asia.

The dreams, which are easy to interpret clearly employ fertility symbolism presage the destruction of Asyage's empire by the Persian Cyrus the Great and son of Mandane.[13]

It may be of interest to note that C. G. Jung, who did much work on the correlation of mythological allegory and dream symbolism, had an overpowering vision in 1913, during a period of critical self-analysis. He saw:

"A monstrous flood covering all the northern and low-lying lands between the North Sea and the Alps. When it came to Switzerland, I saw the mountains grew higher and higher to protect our country. I saw the mighty yellow waves, the floating rubble of civilisation and the drown bodies of uncounted thousands. The whole sea turned to blood…! I asked myself whether these visions pointed to a revolution, but could not really imagine anything of the sort and so I drew the conclusion that they had to do with me myself and decided I was menaced by a psychosis. The idea of war did not occur to me at all. Similar dreams repeatedly came in the summer of 1914, whence the land was turned to ice. In June 1914, the dream had an unexpected ending. There stood a leaf bearing tree but without fruit, whose leaves had been transformed by the effects of the frost, into sweet grapes, full of healing juices."

In December 1913, he had a dream involving Siegfried, the German mythological hero, on the crest of a mountain, on a chariot made of bones of the dead, driving at furious speed.

Jung concluded that Siegfried represented what the Germans wanted to achieve, to impose their will[14].

War broke out in Europe on the 1st of August 1914. There is an astonishing similarity between Jung's vision and the Sumerian epic, even in the use of descriptive archetypes such as the mountain and the tree (of life).

One could deduce that Jung had ancient Middle Eastern blood in his veins, vindicating his assertion that ancient archetypes reside in the human psyche.

In the vision of Jung, it is plain the flood represents cultural conflict, that is, war. Also, if Jung's analysis of the symbolism of Siegfried is correct, then, as has been postulated here, the individual cultural hero represents the culture or macrocosmic man.

The tree of life, as depicted in the dream, accords with many of the representations of it in ancient heliopian cultures and such dreams reveal the cultural influences and affiliations of Jung's forebears.

Moses (see chapter 8) uses similar flood allegory in the biblical Exodus.

Ishtar, in the epic, by threatening the pantheon, is cast in the same role as the usurpers Ullikumi, Tiamat and the "Prince of the Oceans."

Appropriately, the debris of the struggle is described as fish floating dead in the (cultural) sea. Fish are a particular feature of Cretan pottery and Ishtar is easily identifiable with Cleito, the consort of the God of the Sea and sacred (phallic) pillar, representing blind natural dark forces of man's animal nature.

The heliopian pantheon, as the opposite pole, represents man's human (i.e., divine by contrast) enlightened consciousness. It is perhaps not by chance, that the boat, the ark of Utnapishtim comes to rest on a mountain, the mountain of Nisur, for the image suggests the reassertion of the heliopian pantheon. This is represented by the ark and its human and animal occupants. Humans and animals constitute the earliest images of the gods.

The boat coming to rest on a mountain, possibly signifying the place of the (monotheistic) god, is appropriate symbolism to signify the pantheon's triumph over the usurper whose associated symbol is the mountain and its might.

This image is retained in ancient Egyptian eschatology, the mountain being encompassed by the boat, is invariably depicted in scenes of the Elysian Fields. (A large boat was buried at the side of the Great Pyramid at Giza.) The mountain in depictions of the Elysian Fields is shown as a step pyramid or a series of steps, probably derived from the architecture of the Ziggurat, at the top of which, was the sanctuary of the (monotheistic) God.

In the biblical version of the flood, the ark comes to rest on Mount Ararat in Anatolia which could be taken to mean the Sumerian heliopian culture being transported to Turkey possibly as the Hurrian.

The curious "covering of the mouths of the Gods" is evocative of the Egyptian ritual of "opening of the mouth" of the deceased, presumably in connection with the secret words of Thoth, for only Ea, the Sumerian precursor of Thoth, is credited as "alone who knows all things"[15] and is described as "opening his mouth" before he speaks, as does Ninurta, the god of wells and canals. Both are gods of nether waters.

Dilmun, the heavenly abode of Utnapishtim is described at the mouth of the (two) rivers.[16] As if to underline the destruction caused by the cultural inundation, it is the Storm God who is ostracised by the celestial council at the instigation of the self-confessed culprit Ishtar, in what seems an attempt to shift the blame:

"Let all the gods gather round the sacrifice (of Utnapishtim) except Enlil (the Storm God of War). He shall not approach this offering for without reflection he brought the flood; he consigned my people to destruction."

It can be seen that the myth portrays Ishtar as, at once, being a very powerful celestial force, and at the same time somewhat perfidious, reason enough for the gods to respect her wishes. Nonetheless, she swears allegiance to the gods, vowing a dubious constancy:

"O ye Gods here present, by the Lapis Lazuli around my neck, I shall remember these days as I remember the jewels of my throat, these last days I shall not forget."

The Lapis Lazuli necklace, representing an obeisance to the Sun, was also a ritual breast adornment of Egyptian pharaohs, the temporal embodiment of the Sun God.

The demonstration of allegiance by Ishtar, carries with it, the tacit admission of disloyalty and it is left to Enlil, the king and celestial executive to reward Utnapishtim.

In this confused situation, which possibly arose in the telling by the two factions, Ea the wise, asks Enlil "the wisest of Gods" why he instigated the flood.

Enlil, whilst conceding that mankind is subject to the celestial laws of justice, denies the savagery of the flood destruction:

"Lay upon the sinner his sin,
Lay upon the transgressor his transgression

Punish him a little too hard or he perishes;
Would that a lion had ravaged mankind
Rather than the flood,
Would that a wolf had ravaged mankind
Rather than the flood
Would that pestilence had wasted mankind?
Rather than the flood."

Interceding for Utnapishtim, who represents the heliopian culture still extant, Ea disclaims revealing the secret of the gods but that "the wise man learnt it in a dream", advising Enlil to "take your counsel what shall be done with him."

Utnapishtim continues: "Then Enlil went up into the boat, he took me by the hand and my wife and made us enter the boat and kneel down on either side, he standing between us. He touched our foreheads to bless us saying:

'In time past Utnapishtim was a mortal man: henceforth he and his wife shall live in the distance at the mouth of the rivers (Dilmun).'

Thus, it was that the gods took me and placed me here to live in the distance, at the mouth of the rivers."

The image evoked in the final passage of the flood chapter is the classic Qaballistic concept of the sacred triple combining the marriage of opposites, the celestial eternal deity, the king, representing immortality standing between the human opposites of man and woman.

Dilmun, between the mouths of the rivers, is a scene prevalent on Sumerian seals often depicting the Sun God seated or Ishtar between two celestial streams. The modern Qaballah, mainly based on Judaic tradition, has the same central concept of fertility, the tree of life combined as three pillars which define (celestial) spheres.[17]

The outer pillars are pillars of opposites, the pillar of severity and the pillar of mercy. The former is dominated by the female aspect of Binah, and the latter, by the male Chokmah. The central pillar links the earth of the temporal via the female Moon (Yesod) and the male Sun (Tipareth) to the celestial or supernatural Kether, the Crown or the celestial king corresponding the Sumerian Enlil.

Dilmun "between the two rivers", the place of everlasting life, is to be seen in the tableau as heaven, as represented by the celestial executive, between the two waters or rivers of the male and female of the species. In mythological terms, the pillar and the waters have the same meaning and compliment the motif of the Tree of Life.

The interpretation of the archaic symbolism makes sense when Utnapishtim and his wife are seen as representing collective man or mankind. They are rewarded by the gods with everlasting life that is, the ability to self-reproduce eternally.

On an individual level of course, life eternal, some would accept that this is not possible, and explains why Gilgamesh, as an individual or even as representing part collective man, a culture, cannot claim life eternal. This accounts for the remorse of Ishtar, bewailing the fact that she had almost destroyed "her people", she being the patroness of the mechanism which sustains man's immortality.

The point of departure between the Sumerian flood allegory and that of the Judaic Biblical version is that in the Sumerian, the gift of everlasting life is bestowed upon man by the heliopian pantheon of gods, whereas in the Biblical version, this is attributed to the monotheistic god (of the seas of fertility) Yahweh, who was "enthroned" during the flood, a later appropriation.

It would seem cultural tides, unlike temporal oceans, have different areas of influence and confluence. In North American Indian mythology, similar flood

144

myths are still currency. There still remain stories of Nisagalkuk collecting animals onto a raft in order to survive a great flood.[18] This is in a culture where animals carved on totem poles were venerated and still are, to a lesser extent, as gods.

Archetypes such as Stone Ribs, the son of Volcano woman, are reminiscent of Tiamat and Ullikumi. These are the same symbols as the monstrous mountain, the pillar and the Lady Mountain of the flood culture. Atlantis' demise was reputedly due to a volcanic eruption. Such may be clues to a possible ethno-cultural link between the Hittites and that large ethnic Sino-cultural group to which the American Indians belong.

Given the basic homogeneity of mankind, it would not be unexpected to encounter common pre-history myths, if Utnapishtim represented Homo sapiens emerging from the darkness of Darwinian origins.

What is curious is that the Flood Myth exists in all cultures from the Near East to South Pacific Cultures. This universality suggests a universally experienced cultural occurrence. The event which would explain the presence of such myths would be the melting of icecaps, the ending of the last ice age circa 16000 years ago. Universal flooding would have occurred in coastal locations where many early settlements would have existed. This was a momentous event in prehistory but recent enough to enter the story/myth culture of early man. It suggests the melting of the icecaps over a relatively short period where wholesale devastation occurred.

The Influence of the Epic on Ancient Eschatology

The Qaballistic symbols and philosophy arising from the epic of Gilgamesh are to be seen on many early Sumerian seals. The two streams of Dilmun, Ishtar between the celestial streams of fertility, the male and female motifs forming asymmetry, are all common.

Gilgamesh and Enkidu slaying the Bull of Heaven under the auspices of the Sun God represented as the Sun, and the hero slaying Humbaba, represented as a man inside a mountain, are also popular motifs. On the seal depicting the latter, a figure whose foot appears to be caught by the mountain corresponds with the description of Gilgamesh's dream where the mountain fell and struck his feet from under him.

The Sun God astride the Mashu Mountains, the portals of Heaven, and Gilgamesh and Urshanabi in the serpent-prow boat are clearly to be seen indicating the influence of the epic and its importance by its association with one of the communication mediums of the time.

The Scorpion-Man guardian of the portals of the Mashu Mountains is clearly to be seen on the exquisite harp found at Ur by Wooley.

Dilmun depicted in the Egyptian Elysian Fields

We have seen instances of how the Sumerian culture influenced contemporary and later heliopian cultures. This is most noticeable in the Epic's symbolism that appears in the scenes on Egyptian papyri depicting the deceased's journey to the Elysian fields, or the fields of Ialu.

The scenes comprise an easily intelligible sequence of events, in much the same manner as Christian gospel scenes were depicted in mediaeval church windows. The scenes are supplemented with hieroglyphics, the latter, according to classical authors, embodied abstract concepts in a symbolic universally intelligible form.[19]

With minor variations, the sequence of scenes describes:

1) Presentation of the deceased before a complement of gods, often a trinity.
2) A journey in a Sekhet boat bearing offerings.
3) Arrival and presentation of the deceased to Osiris, the God of eternal life or to Horus his son, or both, where offerings are represented.
4) The obtaining of sacred implements required for cultivating celestial fields and the cultivation of them.
5) The arrival of the deceased at Dilmun at the mouth of the two rivers where the serpent-prow boat waits to carry the deceased over the Waters of Death to the place of the Gods. A Company of gods shown seated signifies this.

These events are presumably, subsequent to the judgement of the deceased in the Maati Hall of the Gods. The papyrus of Ani, which depicts the famous Judgement before Osiris, with Horus and Thoth performing the rites, shows Thoth guiding the deceased before three gods, one of which, is Seth.

After a boat journey bearing offerings, the deceased arrives at the door of the temple of Osiris and Horus, who is shown as a hawk. From there, the deceased is shown with the mythical sickle harvesting giant corn, a symbol of fertility. The

146

giant corn has its origin in the Sumerian myth narrated by Ansurbanipal of Assyria in keeping with the assiduous Mesopotamian-Sumerian tradition of establishing kingship as a divine heliopian commission:[20]

"After Ashur, Sin, Shamash, Adad, Bel, Nabu, Ishtar of Nineveh, Queen of Kidmuri, Ishtar of Arbela, Urta, Nergal and Nusku, had caused me to take my seat joyfully upon the throne of my father who begot me, Adad sent his rains (Adad, the Sumerian Lord of the Storm[21]), Ea opened his fountains, the grain grew five cubits tall in the stalk, the ear was five-sixths of a cubit long…"

Corn associated with the Gods was thus about eight feet high. Another Labour in the Elysian Fields was ploughing, the plough being pulled by, usually, a pair of oxen, often piebald or "ring straked and speckled" similar to those described in Genesis XXX1-8, as belonging to Jacob.

These cattle, also archetypal symbols of strength and fertility, were sacred to Isis, the consort of Osiris, as they were with Ishtar, the Sumerian prototype of Isis.

Isis, in her associated form of Hathor, the oxen headed goddess, was the patroness of an extensive fertility bull-cult in the Egyptian Delta. It is these sacred cows that the Amenite ram fertilises in Jacob's dream, a proselytising allegory that accounts for the widespread Amenite support in the Delta, the one-time Hyksos territory.

Following the celestial cultivation, the deceased is then shown venerating the Bennu bird, the phoenix, and the symbol of rebirth. The Sun God visited the temple of the Sun in the form of a Bennu bird alighting on the Ben Stone "in the house of the Bennu in Anu", that is, Heliopolis[22], the city of the obelisk or pillar. The bird is shown perched upon the triangular temple.

In some scenes of the Elysian Fields, the ploughing is shown twice. After completing the ploughing in the "fields of peace", the deceased arrives at the meeting of the two rivers, Dilmun of the Gilgamesh Epic.

In the magnificent depiction of the Elysian Fields in the tomb of Sennedjem, belonging to the reign of Sethos 1 (circa1306-1290 BC), after the ploughing, the deceased, who are Sennedjem and his wife Lyneferti, the journey continues through a grove of trees by the sea. The trees are copiously laden with fruit and the place is undoubtedly the heavenly garden of the Sun God as described in the epic.

From this, the journey proceeds to the "place between the two rivers" where the serpent-prow boat of Urshanabi awaits them, to transport them over the Seas of Death to the place of immortality. Some depictions of the Elysian Fields show two boats, the papyrus of Ani shows two but only the first is serpent-prowed. It is also distinguished by the number of oars, the first having eight, an allusion possibly to Urshanabi's many-poled or oared boat. The second boat is a depiction of the ark or Utnapishtim's boat in which he survived the flood. This is a prototype of the biblical ark and symbol of the survival of the deceased according to the heliopian concept of the Elysian fields and the company of the Gods.

In the middle of the boat between the two rivers are some stone steps, a probable allusion to the Ziggurat temple and/or the early step pyramids that housed the remains of the king, possibly Ziusrudra.

In Sumerian tradition, it was at the top of the Ziggurat that the temple was situated which the gods visited. This tradition is reflected in the biblical Jacob's ladder. The stone steps may be an allusion to the "sacred stones" that Urshanabi stated "are with him" referring to Utnapishtim, the man blessed with immortality.

The pyramids of course, were sacred burial places of the divine king. The Sumerian tradition clearly provides the fabric of the Judaic tradition of the flood, probably via Abraham of Sumerian decent.

Yahweh, "enthroned" as a result of the flood, may be the link between the "hidden" (ram) god of the Ziggurat and the "hidden" god Amen.

Judaic links to the Sumerian are also linked to the Hittite, not surprisingly if Enkidu represents a brother culture, for besides associations of Laban and Abraham with the Hittites, Esau is involved in a dynastic marriage with "Judith, the daughter of Beeri, the Hittite and Bashemath, the daughter of Elon the Hittite" (Gen XXV1-34).

Jacob (Israel) whose descendants, via Joseph, married into Egyptian blood did not meet this with approval. The cultural division between Esau and Jacob, is reflected in the later territorial struggles between Egypt and the Hittites, culminating in the battle of Kadesh in the 13th century BC.

The archetype of sacred stones is (like its symbolism), remarkably durable. It was presumably chosen for this reason and is a central archetype of Christianity and Islam. Its potency was encountered in the Roman culture during Hannibal crisis of 204 BC.

Sibyl of Cumae advised the building of a temple to Ceres, the Goddess of Corn, during the famine of 493 BC. The Sibylline books predicted that Hannibal would be compelled to leave Rome if Cybele, the oriental equivalent of Ishtar was brought to Rome. Her sacred black stone was brought in 204 BC. and Hannibal left in the following year.

The altar of Cybele, made of stone, shows the sacred stone arriving in the midst of a ship, a scene not dissimilar to the boat scene of the Elysian Fields. The incident illustrates a singular piece of psychological warfare, for Carthage was reputed to have been founded by cultural inhabitants of the Levant, according to Roman tradition.

Cybele, the Great Mother of Asia Minor, was an alien oriental introduction into the predominantly Greek cosmogony of Rome.[23]

Hannibal, the Carthaginian being of such cultural allegiance would be deterred from sustaining war on such a holy centre, a fact, if true, vindicates the mythological "history" of the Aeneid.

In the tomb of Sennedjem, the scene of the Elysian Fields is crowned by the Sumerian Qaballistic sacred triple. In the centre, sitting in the Sekhet Boat is the son of the Sun God, Horus, above whose head is the sacred sun encircled by the solar serpent of fertility and life.

The God also holds an ansata cross, the symbol of life. On each side of the boat are two baboons squatting, the symbols of Thothian wisdom.

The two baboons are not of equal size, the one on the right of Horus is larger, indicating the male of the species and the one on the left is smaller, indicating the female. This scene corresponds with Utnapishtim and his wife flanking Enlil in the boat of the flood. The theme of the union of opposites is reinforced by the black and white squares under the female baboon.

The ansata cross held by the deity also signifies the union of opposites, the "temporal" that is the Latin cross, signifying finite time by its finite limbs which also correspond to the four temporal cardinal points, and the spiritual, by the "eternal" circle.

It is perhaps not surprising that the Hebrews who predominantly nurtured monotheism, the adversary of heliopianism, were also able to sustain, by an oral tradition only, the philosophy of the Qaballah, associated with heliopianism.

The Elysian Fields illustrates the extent to which emerging cultures relied upon the concepts, archetypes and rituals of earlier cultures. This implies that there is no such thing strictly as a new culture, and that culture is part of a continuously developing and mutating continuum.

There resides in the human psyche ancient cultural archetypes, the older, the more powerful. This accords with Jungian theory concerning archetypes and the collective unconscious and throws into relief the awesome depth of the archetypal memory.

As Jung's own dreams testify, such cultural evolvement infers those subsequent cultures always incorporate elements of past culture, often selectively as we shall see, to be presented as, in some cases, new. This is presumably for various motives, but primarily for survival.

This is reasonable for as the Qaballists of old were aware, the culture behaves as collective (macroscopic) man, hence the collective unconscious and archetypal memory etc., is driven by the same urges as the individual (microscopic) man. This is why individuals in myths represent quite validly, the culture as a whole.

Many archetypes were incorporated on seals, themselves the stamps of authority, to promote the cultural concepts of the culture. The archetypes were largely derived from myths. Before examining some scenes from ancient seals the final chapters of the epic shall be examined.

The Return and Death of Gilgamesh

It is evident that there is no reference in depictions of the Elysian Fields to the final chapters of the epic, which describe the ultimate death of the hero Gilgamesh. The reasons for this may be:

1) The scenes of the Elysian Fields are to propagate the concept of eternal life, and the concept of death has no place except as a starting point for the journey.

2) The epic, with Utnapishtim and his wife representing the whole of mankind, or macrocosmic man in the Qaballistic sense, can be regarded as true, that collectively, human life is eternal. On an individualistic level however, such universality is possibly not applicable, though the philosophy of Qaballism does allow the possibility of spiritual rebirth. The epic describes precisely this and links it with a necessary questing on the part of the individual, which is the reason for describing Gilgamesh's search.

Qaballistically related philosophies such as Gnosticism, Christianity and Philosophical Alchemy are also specific in this concept of rebirth.

The Ancients were undoubtedly aware of the esoteric nature of such a philosophy, but also recognised the universal need of the individual for a belief in eternal life, if for no other reason than the individual's awareness of death and its attendant dread.

The concept of eternal life therefore was given a universal dimension not at odds with the concept of diviocracy. The popularising of such an idea would result initially from its inherent attractiveness and the need to believe, which would be further propagated by the proclivity of people to receive myths literally and the herd behaviour of the populace.

Utnapishtim would become the prototype individual. A notable example of this imitative literalism arises from the final chapters of the epic that describes the entombing of the king and the leaving of offerings, a ritual that was prevalent in the funerary rituals of the Egyptian nobles and kings.

Given the cultural development of the human race at that time, few individuals, even presented with the opportunity of intellectual development, would possibly grasp the sophisticated concepts of the Qaballistic view of the universe. The promise of eternal life therefore arises quite naturally alongside the concept of judgement after death in the Egyptian culture, the whole designed to set the course of civilising and civilisation for the near barbarous but culturally developing beings.

This circumstance was reflected in the developing cycles of gods, from animal, animal-human to human.

The ultimate development was observed in the Greco-Roman cosmogony, with its liberalism and concept of the after-life. This was in contrast to the austerity of autocratic monotheism and its literal concept of the afterlife.

The ancient Sumerians appear to be more realistic regarding the fate of the individual. The power of Fate is recognised, albeit to a lesser extent than the Romans and Greeks, for like those, Fate was a deity, and it offered the possibility of the culture surviving.

In the epic however, as the laws of history and cultural development demand, the culture, as represented by Gilgamesh, was not to survive. Utnapishtim puts the question:

"As for you Gilgamesh (representing the culture) who will assemble the Gods for your sake so you may find that life for which you are searching? But if you may find wish, come put it to the test; only prevail against sleep for six days and seven nights."

Gilgamesh fails to do this for he is weary after his long journey. The culture, macroscopic Sumerian man, is ageing and to illustrate this, Utnapishtim admonishes Urshanabi and banishes him for embarking on a futile journey and subjecting Utnapishtim to the harrowing spectacle of Gilgamesh in his desuetude.

"But this man before whom you walked, bringing him here, whose body is covered with foulness and the grace of whose limbs has been spoiled by wild skins, take him to the washing place. There he shall wash his long hair clean as snow in the water, he shall throw off his skins and let the sea carry them away, and the beauty of his body shall be shown, the fillet on his forehead shall be renewed and he shall be given clothes to cover his nakedness…these clothes will show no sign of age, they will wear like a new garment."

With this restoration of dignity and authority in old age (as symbolised by the garment) which is a kind of renewal, Gilgamesh and Urshanabi launch the boat for the return journey to Uruk. It is at this point that the epic discloses the possibility of individual or cultural rebirth. Utnapishtim speaks to Gilgamesh:

"I shall reveal a secret thing, it is a mystery of the Gods that I am telling you. There is a plant that grows under the water, it has a prickle like a thorn, like a rose; it will wound your hands, but if you succeed in taking it, then your hands will hold that which restores his lost youth to a man."

The rose is the archetypal symbol of love and in the crown of thorns of the dying Christ, can be seen the application of the ancient archetype associated with the Sun (the crown) and rebirth.

Gilgamesh recovers the plant by tying heavy stones to his feet (a not fortuitous association of stone and water perhaps) and commendably resolves to give the "the old men are young again" plant to the elders of Uruk to eat. His elation is briefly lived however, for shortly after, whilst bathing in a cool well, the plant is snatched by a serpent in the depths, rising out of the pool. It immediately sloughs its skin and returns to the water.

It is appropriate that a serpent is the one who devours the only possibility of the culture surviving for it may represent the mythical equivalent of Apophis the serpent of the primeval waters, the foe of Ra and heliopianism. It is then symbol of the snake fertility culture of Cretan Atlantis that will vanquish the culture, the Ancient Sea God, deposed autocratic adversary of the younger heliopian cultures.

The serpent also represents the means whereby the species eternally reproduces itself (i.e., rebirth) symbolised by the sloughing of the skin.

Gilgamesh is naturally distraught and sat down and wept.

"O Urshanabi, was it for this that I toiled with my hands, is it for this I have wrung out my heart's blood…I found a sign and now I have lost it."

The hero is finally eulogised before the epic ends with the sacred seventh chapter:

"He was wise, he saw mysteries and knew secret things, he brought us a tale of days before the flood. He went on a long journey, was weary, worn out with his Labour, returning, engraved on a stone the whole story."

The recording is a tradition typical of heliopian cultures and consistent with the importance they placed on the lessons of (myth embodied) history. The final chapter of the epic, describing the death of the hero, opens with a prophetic tribute to the culture:

"The destiny was fulfilled which the father of the gods, Enlil of the mountain had decreed for Gilgamesh; In nether earth (future) the darkness will show him a light of mankind, all that are known, none will leave a monument for generations to come to compare with his. The heroes, the wise men, like the new moon, have their waxing and waning. Men will say, "Who has ever ruled with might and with power like him?" As in the dark month, the month of shadows, so without him there is no light. Oh Gilgamesh, this was the meaning of your dream, you were given the kingship, such was your destiny…he has given you power to bind and power to loose, to be the darkness and the light of mankind."

The latter has an echo in John's Gospel.

If Gilgamesh represents the culture, then there is a poignant pathos arising out of the demise of a culture that clearly regarded itself as Enlightener of Man.

"On the bed of fate he lies, he will not rise again

From the couch of many colours, he will not come again"

The couch of many colours alludes to Ishtar, who had a sanctuary in Uruk and also to kingship. "For Gilgamesh and all the Gods, Namtar (fate), Ninsun, Ningizzida, the serpent Lord of the Tree of Life, Ereshkigal, Dumuzi, Enki, Ninki, Endukugga, Nindukugga, Emmul, Ninmul, Shulpae, Samuquan, the forbears of Enlil and Mother Ninhursag, offerings are made; priest and priestess weighed out offerings of the dead. Gilgamesh, the son of Ninsun, lies in the tomb. At the place of offering, at the place of libation, he poured out the wine."

Sumerian and later Seals Depicting Mythological Culture

It is evident form seals discovered, that one of their primary purposes was to illustrate scenes from myths of the culture. Several show scenes from the great Epic of Gilgamesh. The hero is usually depicted with bow and arrow and distinguished by his headdress of a conical crown with tier folded horns, indicative of the Ishtar (or Inanna) bull cult. The distinctive conical shape is imitative of the Ziggurat and later Egyptian pyramid.

Such seals have been found as far north as Ebla (modern Tel Mardik) dating to the mid-third millennium BC[24] which show a half bull centaur-like figure grasping lions by their tails accompanied by a long-haired figure. A figure is shown holding a bull by the thigh.

These primitive and naive seals show Gilgamesh ("like a wild bull, two thirds god and one third man") and Enkidu, commemorating the episodes of the Bull of Heaven and Gilgamesh's defeat of the lions (Proto-Syrian Daganites) in the territory, the Northern Levant, that the epic describes.

The half man, half god figures correspond with the Ptah cycle of animal gods in Egypt. The Gods on the seals are mostly in human form, but the celestial aspect is conveyed by the addition of wings, symbolising spiritual creatures. A seal thought to be the "liberation of the Sun God", seems better to show Gilgamesh with bow and arrow passing through the Mashu Mountains wielding his sword, an allusion, presumably, to the defeat of the lions.

Waiting beyond the mountains is Utnapishtim with the raven of the flood in Dilmun between the two rivers. Winged Ishtar, the patroness of Uruk, pours water of eternal life onto the hero. The two-faced God of the Storm, Enlil, the patron of Utnapishtim, stands by him. The two-faced guardian god was prevalent in Anatolia and had a place in the Roman cosmogony as Janus.

Another instance of the widespread influence of the Sumerian culture can be traced via the centaur-like figure of Gilgamesh. As will become apparent, there was much cultural intercourse between the Anatolian Hittite and Mycenean Greek cultures.

The centaur, as one of the few bi-nature gods, was possibly a derivative of the Sumerian via the Mycenaeans, who invaded Crete around 1400 BC. The Minoans, who had ruled Crete for over 2000 years, were thought to have come to (or returned from possibly) Crete from Egypt circa 3000 BC[25] after the defeat of lower Egypt by the Upper Kingdom. (See the Palette of Narmar.)

Much mythological symbolism supports the assertion that the two kingdoms arose in Egypt because of a cultural invasion into the Delta in archaic times, probably from Crete, which was repeated several times throughout the following epochs. This will be illustrated at various points.

The symbol of the Lower Kingdom in the Delta of Egypt was the snake, an archetype commonly associated with Cretan fertility goddesses. Cretan mythology relates that Minos, who gave his name to the culture, was the son of Zeus, disguised as a bull, and Europa, daughter or sister of King Phoenix, from which Phoenicia, some claim, took its name.[26]

Europa, a fertility goddess, was imported from the southern shores of the Mediterranean. It is also related[27] that Europa was espoused in Crete to King Asterion "King of the Stars", the same title given to the Proto-Syrian and Pre-Egyptian god Dagan.

The Sea God Poseidon punished Minos over a matter of the sacrificing of a bull (the sacred bull of Atlantean fertility?). Pasyphae, his wife gave birth to the Minotaur, half bull and half man, similar characteristics to seal impressions of Gilgamesh.

In accordance with Sumerian cultural philosophy of heliopian diviocracy, heliopianism coexisted with an Ishtarian fertility cult, a situation that also plainly existed in Egypt, and probably in all the surrounding cultures. The allegory of Zeus as Cretan Bull and Europa aligns with this concept, in the bicultural marriage, symbolised by the issue, the Minotaur.

Another significant mythological link between Sumerian culture and Crete (cf Gilgamesh and Humbaba) is the myth surrounding Minos' son Glaukos, brought back to life by the soothsayer Polyido.[28]

The latter, incarcerated in a tomb with the corpse of the child, observed a serpent approaching the body. Polyido killed the serpent but another came, which, seeing the first serpent dead, fetched a plant and laid it on the dead serpent, which promptly came back to life.

Here is a remarkably similar event to that described in the epic of Gilgamesh, whose life-restoring plant is stolen by the serpent, the cultural adversary, now seen in possession of the Cretan Serpent after the demise of the Sumerian culture and clearly linked to it.

The serpent appears prolifically in archaic Near Eastern cultures, generally it symbolised the adversary of the heliopian cultures, as Apophis or Apep in the Egyptian, the enemy of the Sun God Ra, as the sea serpent Tiamat vanquished by Marduk, the Sun God in the Babylonian and as probably the "Prince of the Oceans", Yam, in the Canaanite. Its phallic symbolism signified fertility, most often indicating the ancient culture of Atlantean Crete.

In most heliopian cultures it was accommodated. The Egyptian culture depicted the uraeus, a serpent encircling the Sun and the Sumerian, as Ningizzida, the Lord of the (Sun crowned) Tree of Life, the fruitful fertile tree sometimes depicted as a phallus.

The Bible casts Ningizzida as the adversary of Yahweh, who replaces the Sun, for promoting partaking of the sacred fruit.

The Sumerians regarded the serpent as part of a concept of the marriage of the temporal and spiritual, signified by the tree.

In the Mesopotamian myth of Etana, the shepherd, the 13th king of Kish after the Flood[29] at the beginning of things, the eagle and the serpent had sworn a solemn oath of friendship. The eagle had its nest and young at the top of a tree, whilst the serpent and its young lived at the base. They undertook to protect and provide food for each other's young, which worked well for a time. The eagle broke its oath however and whilst the serpent was away hunting, devoured its young.

The serpent, on returning, appealed to Shamash for vengeance and to this end, Shamash showed the serpent how to snare the eagle, break his wings and imprison him in a pit. This is what befalls the eagle, which cries to Shamash for help. Directed by Shamash, Etana delivers the eagle, which promises to carry Etanna to the throne of Ishtar, from whom he may obtain the plant of rebirth, so Etana is told as he is ascending to the place of the gods.

The saga breaks off at this point, but here is another instance of the plant of rebirth associated with the serpent.

More striking is the parallel the myth has with the events in Egypt under Narmer, the late pre-dynastic period, circa 3000 BC.

Narmer of Upper Egypt is shown on the Pallet of Narmer defeating the ruler of Lower Egypt (the Delta, that is, Northern Egypt). The symbol of Upper Egypt was the eagle or hawk, and that of Lower Egypt, the serpent.

This division of the Egyptian culture is mirrored in the myth of Etana and indicates a similar bi-cultural state that also may also have existed in the Sumerian. This state of affairs probably arose as a result of the "cultural" flood and was transported into the Egyptian from Sumerian influences and also from the Cretan culture, the culture identified as the invading "flood" culture.

This bicultural mechanism can also be detected, as we shall see, in the Hebrew culture, which itself was derived from the Egyptian.

In the myth of Etana, the tree represents the culture, the upper part, the domain of the eagle representing Upper Egypt and the lower part, the domain of the (Cretan fertility) serpent. This geographically aligns with the seaboard invasions of Egypt by Crete in the form of the Hyksos and much earlier incursions.

In keeping with Sumerian Qaballism, the tree and the Egyptian culture also corresponded with the concept of macrocosmic man, at the top, the spiritual eagle and the base the temporal serpent.

The pallet shows Narmer in a characteristically pharaonic conquering pose in Sumerian related dress and crown. The eagle, symbolising heliopian Upper Egypt, stands atop reeds, symbolising the Delta, clutching a serpent in its claws, the symbol of Lower Egypt.

On the reverse side, the pharaoh of Lower Egypt is shown presumably, bringing tribute. His crown shows the lion's tail, seen in Hittite carvings, representing the authority of the Protosyrian Dagan, the foe of Gilgamesh, an early importation into Egypt.

The theme is continued in the middle panel where two lions, with serpentine necks, composite lion-serpent symbols of the Delta, are tethered by the victors.

The bottom panel shows the Gilgameshian wild bull crushing its adversary. The pallets, at the top have human faced oxen, probably meant to indicate male and female in keeping with Qaballistic opposites, but most certainly represent some Hathor cult, between which is the solar spirit.

All five symbols of the sun, serpent, eagle and the two crowns, were incorporated into a unified royal head-dress by later pharaohs who continually struggled to unify the opposing cultures which had come to settle in Egypt, but who were old enemies.

The widespread influence of Sumerian culture is not at odds with the notion that later cultures, like the Egyptian, were derived from it, as it spread westward.

This would indicate that the earliest myths were primarily Sumerian-Mesopotamian origin, developed by later cultures as a means of preserving heroic heliopian history, ensuring its survival. In particular, the epic of Gilgamesh, with its length and epic valour which infused all the great cultures of the Near East.

The epic may have served as a prototype for the Homeric sagas, for it is known, that the Greeks drew on the Egyptian culture when developing their mythology. This can be seen as a continuation of the process commenced by the Egyptians or more accurately, the Sumerians.

Such a cultural evolvement is natural in the philosophical universe of heliopianism. It was indeed left to the Greeks, with the arrival of the Alexandrian dynasties in Egypt, after a Dark Age of Amenite religious supremacy, to restore the ideal of cosmological diviocracy.

The Zodiac as Heliopian Cultural Commonwealth

It is under the Ptolemaic Greeks that we see evidence of pictorial representation of the heliopian Cultural Commonwealth. The idea that the stars, as celestial bodies, represented deities, was very old, as we have seen in the description of Dagan as "Lord of the Stars." It also appeared in the biblical description of the dreams of Joseph were.

"The stars (the gods of Egypt) made obeisance to him" and in the dreams of the Sumerian Gilgamesh, describing the god-like Enkidu as a "star from heaven."

With the almost universal dominion of Alexandrian heliopianism, the Greeks restated the heliopian cosmogony to include all the major heliopian pantheons, represented by respective gods as cosmic constellations.

This was a formidable attempt at cultural unification, a natural consequence of universal dominion. They however were not the innovators, but upholders of a more ancient heliopian tradition.

One of the earliest zodiacs which represents the celestial blue print for a temporal model, a commonwealth, a term the Romans used to describe their dominions, can be seen at Dendera in Egypt.

Appropriately, the Egyptians were something of mentors to the Greeks and it is significant that the fabled library was instituted in Alexandria.

The zodiac is in effect, a development of the Egyptian "Paut" of gods, itself no doubt derived from the Sumerian.

The word zodiac comes from the Greek, meaning "circle", the adjective, from the word meaning "little animal" and it is the name given by the ancients to an imaginary band extending around the celestial sphere having as its middle line, the elliptic, or approach path of the Sun.[30]

That the symbol of the Sun is central is appropriate to heliopian philosophy.

The Sumerians are known to have extensively studied the stars and the inception of the idea of linking the gods with the stars has been erroneously attributed to the Greeks, though the zodiac in its present form was probably a product of them and whose zodiac will be presented for reasons of comparison.

The Zodiac commences with Aries, which corresponds to one of two equinoctial points, Aries being the spring equinox, an important time of the year from the earliest times, for it signalled the season of rebirth and renewal, an important cultural survival concept.

The equinox represents the point at which the sun passes the celestial or equinoctial equator from south to north. In the Greek pantheon, scholars attribute the signs of the Zodiac thus[31]:

Aries – the ram, that which is central to the Golden Fleece myth of Jason and the Argonauts, or the ram that guided Alexander to water in the Libyan desert.

Taurus – the bull of Zeus and Europa myth. In this constellation are the seven Hyades and the Pleiades (doves)

Gemini – the twins, usually Castor and Polydeuces or Amphion and Zethus, Herakles and Apollon or Triptolemus and Iasion.

The saying "pi in the sky" is said to be a reference to this sign as the mathematical pi sign is often used to signify it.

Cancer – the crab, sent by Thera to assist the Hydra against Herakles. The Hydra, as we shall see, probably represents the island of Cyprus or Crete.

Leo – the lion, the Nemian Lion slain by Herakles.

Virgo – the virgin Astrea, the starry maid of Justice, or Demeter, Core, Isis or Atargatis.

Libra – there is no myth associated with this sign, originally, it was the claws of the Scorpion. It is usually depicted as a pair of scales, it is possible therefore that its origin was lost in antiquity and may, for example, refer to the Scorpion Men of the Gilgamesh epic, the guardians of the Mashu Mountain portal.

Scorpius – the scorpion which killed Orion. In Latin it was known as Nepa.

Sagittarius – the archer, has also no myth associated with it. It is generally represented as a centaur, sometimes as Chiron.

Capricornus – the goat. This has no myth associated with it and is sometimes represented as Pan.

Aquarius – the Water Bearer, is associated with Ganymede, Zeus' cup bearer. The sign is also the Egyptian hieroglyph for water.

Pisces – the fish, the sacred fish of the Syrian goddess Derceto. The Milky Way was said to be the milk spilt from the breasts of Hera or the path along which the horses of the Sun bolted when Phaethon, son of Helios, the Sun God, tried to drive his chariot.

This was possibly intended as an admonishment to any member cultures that harboured any thoughts of usurpation or alteration of the ancient authority of the Celestial Executive, the Sun God. Such admonishment would naturally not be heeded by the adversary of heliopianism which, in its Christian form, utilised the concept embodied by the myth to bring about an eclipse of heliopianism as it existed in its advanced form in Imperial Rome.

The image of the Milky Way may have its origin in the fact that many of the cultures represented by the signs can be associated with a goddess, principally, Ishtar or the Sumerian Inanna. The Mother Goddess was a primordial symbol that metamorphosed through the ages to the Queen of Heaven, patroness of life and fertility.

Phaethon, the son of the Sun God has echoes of Horus, the son of Osiris in the Egyptian, the same concept by a different name translated into the younger culture.

There is in the myth, a hint that darkness descends as a result of Phaethon's action. This is in no way a new theme. The attempted usurpation of the senior deities by their juniors, is a facet of the natural world and in the cultural sphere, is part of the cultural conflict continuum between diviocratic heliopianism and autocratic monotheism.

The Greco-Egyptian zodiac at Dendera shows representations of what must have been, all major cultures and cults, which comprised a universal heliopian pantheon, many more of which are to be seen than the twelve of the Greek zodiac which have survived to the present.

The Dendera Zodiac dating to the Ptolemaic period[32] is partly based on sky maps going back to the third millennium BC. The signs, representing cultures, sometimes take unusual forms and can be detected proceeding clockwise from the top inner figures. The following can be seen:

1) **Aries** – a ram with leonine body couchant on a quadrature line. This would be representative of the Egyptian cult of Amen and serve as archetype for

Sumerians and Babylonians as well as North-eastern Anatolians and Judaic Semites. It was also a cultural archetype of Crete and Semitic Armenia, being associated with the myth of the Golden Fleece. The ram is the archetypal link between father, son and sacrifice associated with Abraham and his son. This theme is preserved in the Christian tradition with the archetype retained.

Canaanite Baal was also referred to as "the ram that mounts the clouds" Canaan was known to be the cult territory of Dagan the lion god.

2) **Taurus** – a leaping bull associated with Sumerian Inanna and Babylonian Ishtar. In Egypt, the bull was associated with Hathor or Isis and the Saqqara bull cult. It is also associated with the Atlantean-Cretan sacred bull cult, the Minoan bull cult etc of Greek myth.

3) **Gemini** – a male and a female figure holding hands. This may have been the original representation since it appears elsewhere as male and female figures. The depiction may have alluded to Isis and Osiris as brother and sister or the ancient conjunction of Utnapishtim and his wife, but undoubtedly evokes aspects of Sumerian and Egyptian Qaballism. The sign would also have Cretan cultural connotations as the twin culture of Castor and Polydeuces, the constellations born of Leda and Zeus.

4) **Cancer** – an eight-legged crab like creature, with two pincers. This has Greek mythical connections and is probably indicative of some Mediterranean Island culture with its maritime associations.

5) **Leo** – a lion standing on a serpent-prow boat, being held by the tail by a human figure. A bird forms the stern of the boat.

This presentation of a lion standing on a serpent raft also appears in the zodiac on the coffin base board of Soter (second century AD) and is redolent of the boat of Urshanabi. The twin symbols of serpent and lion, are the symbols of the two kingdoms of Upper and Lower Egypt. The lion was represented in the Nemset headdress of the Egyptian pharaohs and it was a central archetype of the Dagan cults extant in Syria, Lebanon and Canaan etc. The lion was also a prolific symbol in the Mycenean culture and as the Nemian lion of Greek myth. The figure holding the tail is evocative of the Hittite pantheon shown at Yazilikaya where the gods are seen holding a lion's tail, probably as a symbol of sovereignty over what was Protosyrian Anatolian Dagan, "the Lord of the Stars" territory.

6) **Virgo** – a female holding a sceptre, accompanied by Horus.

The sceptre is probably a flower or seedpod of fertility associated with the tree of life. The figure is possibly an allusion to the fertility goddess and would have wide significance as Isis, Demeter, Ishtar, Core, Cleito, Anat, Inanna, Aphrodite etc. On the coffin of Soter, she is shown holding in one hand, a sheaf, probably of corn, the symbol of Demeter among others, and in the other, an Ankh, the symbol of life.

7) **Libra** – a pair of scales, at the pivot point of which, sits a god on a throne (of judgement?) in a sphere. This is an unequivocal allusion to the Egyptian Maati Hall of the Gods and the Judgement of Thoth and Horus before Osiris and the paut of Gods. On the coffin of Soter, instead of a god, a baboon headed human sits, the emblem of Thoth.

8) **Scorpius** – a scorpion, a related archetype to the previous, in so far as scorpion men of Sumerian myth were guardians of the Mashu mountain portals of Heaven and keepers of the entrance to Irkalla, the Underworld.

9) **Sagittarius** – a winged centaur, whose upper torso shows a dual faced god as an archer. This, in the main, is a Sumerian archetype though it does appear in the Greek and refers to the Gilgameshian "two thirds god and one third man." Man equating to animal and god to human is a concept common in early cultural cycles of gods. The Ptah cycle depicts the chief god as human and other as animal/man combinations. This accords with Darwinian man as being a development from the animal, a fact obviously appreciated by the ancients. The hero Gilgamesh is often represented on seals as, and is referred to as possessing skill of, an archer. It is also a Canaanite archetype appearing in the myth of Danel and Aqhat.

10) **Capricornus** – half goat (or cow) and half fish. This representation is also shown on the coffin base of Soter and has Sumerian, Phoenician and Canaanite connections, for goats are shown on artefacts, in the company of Ishtar and Ashera, her Canaanite counterpart. The goat may also have been meant to represent the ibex, an emblem of the Moon God and Athtar, the god manifest in the Venus star. The fish torso also suggests a coastal people with maritime connections and it is known that the Philistines were a settled Canaanite people originally known as Pulisati from Crete.

11) **Aquarius** – a pharaoh of Upper Egypt, pouring water from a jar in two streams. On the coffin of Soter, this is a female figure pouring two streams. The male on the Dendera Zodiac suggests the ascendancy of Upper (heliopian) Egypt over the fertility goddess.

It is not surprising to find male and female forms of this sign, for many pictures abound from all the major cultures (Egyptian, Sumerian, Babylonian and Assyrian, for example) which display the king as dispenser of the celestial waters of life or fertility, in accordance with the natural laws of selection. These demand that the strongest and fittest to survive proliferate their seed, the king being the divinely appointed temporal representative of the celestial executive. The water is seen as a product of the Gods. The two streams may allude to the two rivers of Dilmun, the home of eternal man and the Gods. The female form of Aquarius refers to fertility goddesses, primarily Ishtar, who is also often depicted dispensing the "living water" from the "never failing jar" an archetype dating back to at least the third millennium BC.[33]

12) **Pisces** – two fish attached at their tails by a v-line in between which is a symbol of water, possibly representing the sea. This is another maritime cultural symbol, probably Cretan. The artefacts of Crete often depict fish and are probable symbols for people.

Many other constellations are present in the Zodiac and the symmetry of the whole is maintained by the twin Horus figures at the equinoctial and mid-equinoctial points and by, appropriately, the figure of Nut, the Sky Goddess who wears the solar necklace. On the coffin of Soter, Nut appears in the style of the Cretan fertility goddess. At her head is the solar emblem and at her feet, the sacred scarab Khepera, the Sun at Night.

The Dendera Zodiac[34] appears as a mandala, combining circle and cross, a feature displayed in many cultures, for example, in the Indian, Tibetan, and Aztec. That the zodiac of the stars is arranged as a mandala is perhaps intriguing when one considers the occurrence of stars in dreams in ancient myths, and mandala[35] frequently occur in dreams of individuals.[36]

In the centre of the zodiac can be seen a Thothian figure with ape head which stands beside a thigh of a bull, thought to represent Ursa Major.

Around the outer rim can be seen a procession of gods and kings, including the ram of Amen, Horus, Anubis, Hathor, Thoth, Osiris and others predominantly male. Such a procession studded with stars possibly represents a calendar.

Inside this group, appear the female goddesses representing cults and cultures. Isis with a child, Demeter, wearing her characteristic Anatolian crown, Ishtar, with a bow and arrow, as she is often depicted on Sumerian seals and Hathor shown as a cow on a boat with a star between its horns, are all present.

The support points formed by the hands of the figures, are positioned at the junction, in most cases, of the twelve zodiac signs and may signify the twelve months of the Egyptian calendar which had existed from antiquity. The twelve positions may also correspond to the twelve mansions or the twelve positions of the sky divided by great circles through the north and south points of the horizon.[37].

The Greeks are credited with instigating the science of astronomy centred on Alexandria. It is unlikely however that a tradition of studying the heavens, extant for several millennia in the older cultures, had not yielded any astronomical knowledge prior to the Greeks. It was realised that the study of the heavens, from the earliest times, was important in order to formulate a calendar to predict major religious festivals. However, in the ethos of the time, studying celestial constellations was thought to be observing the domain of the Gods, and even the Gods themselves[38].

As the Gods determined the fate of mankind, such studies were clearly important to the point of sanctity. It was there that the influence and importance of astrologers and astronomers in society lay. With the Gods fixed in the firmament in a diviocratic pantheon, was the celestial reticulation that ensured no god, except possibly the Sun God, ever attained ascendancy over the rest.

References Chapter 6

[1] S. A. Handford, Julius Caesar, The Conquest of Gaul

[2] N. K. Sandars, The Epic of Gilgamesh, page 98

[3] Ibid, page 123

[4] Elisabeth Lansing, The Sumerians, page 39

[5] S. H. Hooke, Middle Eastern Mythology, page 61

[6] Chambers Encyclopaedia, Vol 7, page 451a

[7] Sir L. Wooley, Ur of the Chaldees, page 50

[8] Ibid, page 53

[9] N. K. Sandars, The Epic of Gilgamesh, page 110

[10] Ibid

[11] D. Fortune, The Mystical Qaballah, page 3

[12] N. K. Sandars, The Epic of Gilgamesh, page 110

[13] A. de Selincourt, The Histories Herodotus, page 85

[14] C. G. Jung, Memories, Dreams, Reflections, ed A. Jaffe, pages 119 and 204

[15] N. K. Sandars, The Epic of Gilgamesh, page 112

[16] Ibid, page 114

[17] D. Fortune, The Mystical Qaballah, page 307

[18] C. Burland, North American Indian Mythology, page 61

[19] J. Baines and J. Malek, The Atlas of Ancient Egypt, page 222

[20] J. Gray, Near Eastern Mythology, page 56

[21] N. K. Sandars, The Epic of Gilgamesh, page 110

[22] Sir A. E. Wallis, Budge Tutankhamen, pages 59 and 63

[23] D. M. Field, Greek and Roman Mythology, page 184

[24] P. Matthiae Ebla, An Empire Rediscovered, page 88

[25] D. M. Field, Greek and Roman Mythology, page 23

[26] C. Kerenyi, The Gods of the Greeks, page 96

[27] C. Kerenyi, The Gods of the Greeks, page 97

[28] Ibid, page 98

[29] S. H. Hooke, Near Eastern Mythology, page 59

[30] Chambers Encyclopaedia, Vol 14, page 809a

[31] Ibid, Vol 3, page 621b

[32] J Haddon *Zodiac of Dendera,* page 33

[33] J. Gray, Near Eastern Mythology, page 119

[34] J. Haddon Dendera Zodiac Multiple images

[35] C. G. Jung, *Psychology and Alchemy,* page 103

[36] Ibid, pages 95–101

[37] Chambers Encyclopaedia, Vol 2, page 768 B

[38] Ibid, page 66f

Chapter 7
Intercultural Influences Between Myceneans, Cretans and Hittites

It has been proposed that some pre-historical cultural links existed between the Sumerians and the Cretans from an examination of Sumerian myths. The sacred bull cult of Ishtar, represented by the archetype of the bull, and the fertility goddess seem to feature frequently in Cretan or Cretan associated mythology. These ancient archetypes together with others such as the Tree of Life, eagle and lion composites, can be found at Knossos, the capital of the great Minoan Empire.

It is possible, as has been suggested that the Sumerians themselves inherited them from India, from the centres of civilisation such as Mohenjo-Daro in the Indus Valley or Harappa in the Punjab.

It is known that artefacts, pottery, seals and beads etc reached the Mesopotamian cities from the Indus Valley in the time of Sargon of Akkad (circa 2350 BC).[1]

Seals from Mohenjo-Daro (circa 2350 BC.) depict sacred bulls, a Gilgameshian figure fighting a bull and the Tree of Life motif flanked by two bulls.

It would appear however that the Sumerians were more advanced than these civilisations, for they were familiar with cuneiform writing on clay tablets as early as 3400 BC.[2] which may indicate the Sumerians as the senior culture. Nonetheless some cultural difference enabled them to reach a more advanced stage of development earlier than the parent culture, perhaps because they were heliopian. A characteristic of heliopianism is the rapid development of the culture wherein it is propagated. This is due to its inherent pluralism of religious belief that promotes maximum creativity by the free interaction of ideas from different cultures. This is in contrast to autocratic monotheism which, by its very nature, sanctions new ideas and permits only rigid adherence to a standard dogma.

As in the Sumerian, where a fertility goddess is found associated with a bull cult, the same is found in the Cretan culture. Cretan myths are not very abundant, being largely integrated with Mycenae/Greek, however, it is possible to identify and deduce Cretan mythological influence from the adjacent Hittite and Mycenean/Greek cultures, especially the latter whose prolific myths provide many clues.

The double headed eagle motif found at Yasilikaya in Anatolia is a symbol that has been found on Cretan artefacts.

A gold Minoan brooch shows a goddess grasping two birds that are standing on dual serpents. The goddess stands on a boat with a triple wing motif. Suspended from the brooch are five discs. The figure wears a feathered headdress that was typical of Pulisati or Peleset warriors who became the biblical Philistines and who, the Bible states, originated from Kaphtor, that is, Crete.[3]

The Pulisati made up some of the contingents of the "Sea Peoples" who invaded the Southern Mediterranean circa 1200 BC. The dual serpent motif is again encountered with the figurine of a bare breasted fertility goddess found at Knossos, the capital of Minoan Crete.

The goddess is grasping two serpents, a pose that occurs frequently on Greek and Cretan pottery and her dress is very similar to the national folk dress to be found on Crete today.

(Folk dress is an interesting manifestation of the retention of archetypal symbolism by the collective unconscious).

The serpents are archaic fertility symbols and also represent the adversary of the Sun god. In the Cretan culture, it is a central archetype and is depicted on Greek artefacts as being associated with Thetis and Athena among others. Artefacts exist which also show Hekate, "the strong one" in the Cretan pose, supporting two birds.

Two Mycenean lions maintain the symmetry on the primitively drawn picture where also, a bull's head and thigh can also be seen.

The picture on a shard abounds with gamadians, which are characteristic of Cretan ware as also are the whorls made by the lion's tails. These whorls like lion tails are also to be observed at Yasililaya, the Hittite sanctuary. A fish forms the lower torso of the goddess that suggests a goddess of the sea. The arms of the goddess are shown as wings, such a winged goddess is also depicted as the Winged Artemis and Echidna, whose lower torso is a serpent.

Artemis, the Moon goddess, often associated with the Anatolian (Hittite) stag, is shown holding two birds. This may indicate a Hittite influence.

Hekate, who belongs to the earliest of the Greek myth cycles, was the daughter of Perseus and Leto, and was revered by Zeus above all others[4]. He let her have a share of the earth, sea and starry sky. Her name links her with Apollon and Artemis, also called Hekatos and Hekate. Hekate's grandfather was Krios, a titan whose consort was Eurybia.

The name Krios means "ram of heaven"[5]. A ram is the same found in Sumeria associated with the tree of life and is also the symbol of the Ancient Egyptian cult of Amen.

Cretan infusion into the Egyptian delta, of which the Hyksos were probably one wave, seems to be indicated by the shared archetype of the serpent, often seen held by the Cretan and Greek goddesses. The serpent was the symbol of the Lower (Delta) kingdom and the Bible describes Moses as wielding a "serpent rod."

Eurybia, traditionally was the daughter of the Sea (god) and Gaia, Mother Earth, both of which are of the oldest of archetypes. Her siblings were Nereus and Phorkys, known as "the old ones of the sea"[6].

Hekate therefore has much in her ancestry to associate her with the Sea gods (or the Flood god).

The Hittite myths relate how the celestial usurper, Kumarbi, married the Sea's daughter and produced the monstrous mountain Ullikumi, whom, it is asserted, was also the fierce mountain of Sumerian myth, Humbaba.

Teshub, the Hittite Storm god, and Ishtar were able to see Ullikumi from the Anatolian mainland, that is, to see the threatening culture, Crete, in the form of Ullikumi on the shoulders of Upelluri. Upelluri became the Greek Atlas, from which the name of Crete (the island of Atlas) was known in the legend of Atlantis. Ullikumi was on Upelluri's shoulders in the form of a diorite pillar. A sacred pillar is the central archetype in the legend of Atlantis.

Atlas, according to Homer, had a daughter on a remote western island and kept pillars "which hold the sky roundabout."[7]

The myth of Atlantis describes the Sea god mating with mortal woman to produce a daughter of the Sea, Cleito. Cleito gave birth to twelve kings and the sacred pillar culture was established.

Crete became in those archaic times, a powerful culture. Crete was known in the Ancient Egyptian as Keftiu. Keft has a root connected with Kaphtor, the biblical name for Crete and Caput meaning "the capital of a pillar."

The Hittite myth describes in mythological terms, the invasion of this powerful culture into Anatolia, for initially, the fight against Ullikumi did not go well for the Weather god.

Ullikumi reached the Weather god's city, Kummuya, forcing the god to abdicate. After appealing to Ea, the "all wise" God of the Nether Waters (i.e., cultural psychological sea), the Weather god defeats the invader by striking the pillar at its foot with a saw (or sickle) given to him by Ea taken from the ancient (celestial) storehouses. The storehouses translates in mythological terms to the collective unconscious repository of archetypal cultural symbols and concepts of the culture. Thus the balance of power between heliopianism and the ancient even primordial monotheistic Sea God of phallicism was maintained.

The saw, often depicted as being curved could have been a stone age flint sickle and probably had a potent phallic significance and representing the vitality of the Anatolian heliopianism and its claim to supremacy over the older darker fertility culture.

As we shall see, Polytheistic heliopianism existing with the Sumerian and derivative cultures, had to continually fight off challenges for celestial supremacy from the primordial fertility culture. Though evident in the Hittite mythology, the struggles are more extensively documented in the Greek myths. The claim for supremacy by the primordial culture was on the grounds of seniority, the Sea god being the oldest (and only) god prior to the inception of the heliopian family of gods, as embodied by Zeus, Hera and their celestial family. (On another 'macrocosmic' level it is the collective conscious struggling against the collective subconscious that is reflected in the microcosmic man's struggle of conscious against the subconscious or id.)

Zeus, also using a sickle, achieved a similar feat against the monster Typhon, from whose shoulders grew a "hundred heads of serpents."[8]

It is likely, as serpents are a common archetype of Cretan culture and associated with the goddess that the myth describes in mythological language, one of the many encounters between the Mycenean and Cretan cultures.

The Cretan fertility goddess is sometimes depicted as a gorgon, shown winged and clasping two birds. She was popularised as having serpents springing from her head who, when countenanced, turned the viewer into stone. This is a similar phenomenon to the Biblical Lot's wife who was admonished not to look back and was turned to stone.

Discounting the literal absurdity, in mythological terms, this probably meant that Lot's wife, looking back, i.e., went back to her old ways, that is probably, the worship of On, the pillar (or obelisk), the pillar being the same phallic symbol and derived from the sacred pillar of Cretan Atlantis.

Encountering the Gorgon had probably a similar intent of meaning that of being conquered by or converted by her culture, the culture probably of Crete.

It should also be remembered that Humbaba, the monstrous mountain and adversary of Gilgamesh, had a similar ability with his eye of death.

The reasons for the presence of Sumerian and Hittite or pre-Hittite influences in ancient Crete can be deduced from interpretation of their myths, which record both cultures vanquishing the "mountain and pillar culture of Atlantean Crete."

The throne room of Knossos, the ancient capital of Minoan Crete, shows the throne forming a tree between the two eagle headed lion guardians of the tree of life.

A fresco depicting a ritual, shows offerings being made mainly by women, probably priestesses, led by a priestess in a distinctive dress.

The oblations and offerings are being made to two pillars whose capitals are crux axes. On top of the pillars, between the axes are birds. Calves form part of the offerings and wine is being poured into a sacred cauldron between the pillars. This is the same ritual that is described by Plato, which took place in the sacred grove of the Sea god in Atlantis.

There were many gods of the sea in Greek mythology. The husband of the Earth Gaia was simply, the Sea, whose sons were the ancient Sea gods, Nereus and Phorkys. In later myth cycles, the god was Poseidon or Poteidan[9] whose name meant "Husband of Goddess Da." Da may have been, or evolved into Demeter, another manifestation of the fertility goddess, Ishtar.

Cults have existed throughout the ages that venerated the earth and its fertility and although the sea was accepted literally as the spouse of the earth, it also was the symbol, as water, for celestially bestowed human potency.

Poseidon's surname, Gaiaochos, means "Husband of the Earth"[10] and tales concerning him reveal a turbulent god. He could also be called simply "Pater", father, a term still applied to the contemporary monotheistic god.

The Greek myth concerning Poseidon's bride, is similar to the Atlantis legend, for Poseidon carried off Theophane (she who appears as a goddess) to an island, probably Crete, the name of which meant "the island of the ram."

Poseidon, as a child, was hidden by his mother Rhea, amongst a flock of sheep which were by a spring "Arne, the spring of the sheep."

Poseidon, in order to consummate his marriage, turned his bride and all the inhabitants of the island into sheep and himself, into a ram. From the union was born the ram with the Golden Fleece that Phrixos later carried to Colchis in the vicinity of present-day Semitic Armenia. Poseidon is here then clearly identified with fertility and a symbol that came to be associated with the Christian god.

Other symbols associated with the Sea god, together with the ram, are the trident, horse, ass or donkey. The latter are ancient symbols of religious power. The Judaic god was represented by the Romans as an ass. Christ rode into Jerusalem on an ass, which would have been widely recognised by the populace, as symbolising his authority and claim to kingship under Judaic law.

It is probable that the Egyptian Amenite "hidden god" whose symbol was the ram, found its way into Egyptian culture via a Cretan incursion, though there was also a sacred fertility, golden fleeced ram in the Sumerian culture.

The latter may have entered the Sumerian culture as a result of the Flood conquest.

There were many waves of Cretan cultural influx into the Egyptian Delta of which, the Hyksos were one wave and the Pulisati (latterly the Philistines or Palestinians), another. Examination of the Greek myths as we shall see, indicate much earlier invasions into the Egyptian Delta.

The Protosyrian Daganite lion was associated with the Cretan goddess in her many forms as Hekate, Thetis and Rhea etc. (The multiple identity of the fertility goddess has already been encountered as a central archetype in the surrounding cultures. To the Greeks, the Protosyrian Lion became the Mycenean Lion. This probably occurred before the rise of the Mycenean culture was at its peak and the symbol was probably imported from Anatolia or the Southern Mediterranean.

The lion's tail, is reflected in the crook of the Egyptian Pharaoh and can be seen on the Palette of Narmer that shows the conflict between the Upper and Lower kingdoms of Ancient Egypt. The symbols of the Lower Kingdom show many common to the Cretan Atlantean culture indicating that even at the time of Narmer, the land was inhabited by two cultures at odds with each other. One of the cultures was probably an influx from pre-historical and pre-Minoan Crete.

The crown of the Delta or Lower Kingdom shows the lion whorl, birds on top of the standards, dual serpents and spectacular lions with serpentine necks. On the reverse of the palette can be seen, the eagle of the Upper Egypt, holding a serpent in its beak. The symbol of the Lower Kingdom of the Delta became the cobra.

These archetypes indicate Cretan cultural infusion into the fertile Delta of Egypt and account for the bicultural nature of Ancient Egypt. This was later manifested in the two kingdoms, the unification of which, for internal stability, was the major task of succeeding pharaohs throughout the ages.

This was an enormously difficult task, as it amounted to attempting to unify cultural opposites and success was never totally achieved. One of the reasons was that there were several waves of the same alien culture invading the Delta, giving rise to internal instability, one celebrated documented case hitherto unrecognised is the biblical account of Moses which we shall examine later. This cultural situation was, paradoxically, in tune with Qaballistic philosophy one of whose central tenets is the reconciliation of opposites. Although thought of as the oral tradition of Judaism, it is thought to have originated in Sumeria and elements of it can be seen for example in tomb paintings of Seti I.

The symbolism of the Narmer palette is almost a fulfilment of the Sumerian myth of Etana and the Eagle, concerning a battle between an eagle and a serpent. The myth describes a heroic military event, one of many, which gave rise to the pre-history mechanism of recording of a nation or culture's history, that is, the telling of stories of valiant deeds, the myth.

Whether this obviously great battle was the inspiration of the Sumerian myth or some other event may never be known. The event probably was the cause of some sort of exodus, maybe the Mosaic Exodus.

The dualistic nature of the Egyptian culture was to give rise, throughout the ages, to many exoduses. The heliopian culture was always in the ascendancy and gave birth to the golden age of the second millennia BC.

There were periods when it was threatened and even temporarily eclipsed as with the cultural ascendancy of Amenism. When Amenism did eventually become the monotheistic religion of Egypt, the culture was in decline.

Because of the success of heliopianism, the exoduses would consist of adherents of the Delta culture, the followers of a Hidden God. Their leaders would have been familiar with the potency of serpent rods, and whose wish would have been to preserve their ancient monotheism as the senior and oldest culture. This would be reflected by the dominance of the cult and similar monotheistic cults by patriarchs. They would be implacably opposed to pluralistic heliopianism with its temporal, tolerant commonwealth.

The swan or goose symbol is often associated with the snake goddess, and these most likely arose with myths concerning Zeus, Nemesis and Leda.

Nemesis, whose name meant "righteous anger", was depicted in later portrayals as winged[11] like the snake goddess. Artemis, to whom Nemesis was very close, was also winged, even in the most ancient times. She is often associated with the Anatolian stag.

Zeus pursued Nemesis, an unwilling suitor, to the Black Sea where she turned herself into a fish, a symbol common on Cretan artefacts.

After turning herself into many creatures, she turned into a goose, and Zeus assumed the shape of a swan.

Nemesis bore an egg from which sprang Helen, the beautiful woman whose face launched a thousand ships and the war with Troy. The myth seems to be indicating an alliance between some Black Sea state and the Mycenaeans which threatened the Hittite Anatolian mainland and ultimately, lead to war.

Helen could also be seen as representing the island of Cyprus, an important strategic base in the Eastern Mediterranean. for both Mycenean and Hittite purposes of trade and copper mining for arms.

Cyprus was reputed to be the birthplace of Venus or Aphrodite, the archetype of beauty. It is probable therefore that the site of present-day Troy was not the scene of the Homeric epic, though was probably the scene of earlier skirmishes between the two young cultures. The scale of the epic suggests a catastrophic vanquishing of a major cultural empire such as the Hittite, which occurred around 1200 BC with the sacking and burning of Hattusas by a grand alliance of surrounding states.

The archaic cultural adversity between Greek and Turk can still be observed today on the island of Cyprus, an example of the immutability and impunity of culture to temporal time scales. Another example of the tenacity of culture is the signal lack of success the Christian Church had, despite centuries of savage repression, in suppressing the pre-Christian European Nature religion labelled by its enemies as Witchcraft.

The Cretan Snake Goddess of Minoan Crete
With Kind Acknowledgements to J.V. Luce and Granada Publishing Ltd

In the myth of Zeus and Leda, Zeus took the shape of a swan which coupled with Leda under the summit of Mount Taygetos and begat Kastor and Polydeukes, the celestial twins. Leda is not a Greek name, which, among the Anatolian Lycians, meant "woman."[12]

The myth can be interpreted as Zeus, the Greek-Mycenean culture, penetrating the Eastern Mediterranean mainland at some early date, probably not for the first time. It has been observed with for example the Cretans, who

175

preceded the Mycenaeans, that cultural penetration, when observed on the cultural continuum, is more like the flowing and ebbing of a tide. Flowing in youth and ebbing in old age for culture, as the ancients observed, had a life like a human, indeed was the macrocosm of the microcosmic man and could therefore be depicted as the hero in myth as we have seen with Gilgamesh, Herakles, Perseus et al.

This curious circumstance of cultural wave theory is apparent in the known history of Ancient Egypt which conquered southern and eastern territories then contracted, at the end of a particular epoch, to its natural boundaries. Subsequently, it expanded again in a later dynasty. Two notable epochs were under Tuthmosis III and Ramesses II. This characteristic of ebb and flow is universal to all cultures though not often obvious because of the temporal time scale involved. From knowledge of such mechanisms, conclusions and even predictions can be made. Remembering the while, to use the cultural time scale, knowing the approximate age of a culture can indicate whether it is expanding or contracting. Observations may indicate how it is mutating. The latter of course is a function of cultural interaction (in the form of war and trading) and communication which following the communications revolution of the twentieth century must have an accelerating effect on cultural mutation or globalisation of culture.

The birth of Kastor and Polydeukes (Castor and Pollux as they are latterly called) was possibly a device aimed at unifying the parent cultures. In the earliest zodiacs, the twins were male and female, which, in Qaballistic terms, signified the unity of opposites.

If the winged goddess of swan (or goose) and serpent was the Cretan fertility goddess, then many of the Greco-Mycenean myths make sense as early accounts of pre-history Mediterranean culture.

In her many forms the Cretan goddess also appeared as Thetis and Athena, both of whom are associated with the Sea god in relationships similar to that in the Legend of Atlantis.

One of the stories concerning the birth of Athena relates how Zeus took Metis, the daughter of Okeanos, the ancient Sea god and Tethys, to be his first wife. Metis, in one version, about to give birth to Athena, is tricked by Zeus with beguiling words and Zeus puts Athena in his own belly. Metis gave birth to her first born, the owl eyed maiden, Tritogeneia. The latter name was the surname of Athena.

Another story relates how it is Zeus himself who gives birth to Athena after having devoured Metis, for he feared Metis may have given birth to something stronger than lightning, the power of Zeus.

Athena was born beside a peak on the shore of the river Triton, hence her surname. Both the births of Athena and Leda are linked to the archetypal mountain.

Athena was known as "the terrible", "the awakener of the din of battle", "the chieftainess of armies."[13]

These myths of Zeus devouring Metis, his first wife, daughter of the Sea god, describe the conquest of the Cretan culture by the Greco-Mycenean at some early date. The robustness of the ancient Cretan culture as the description of Athena implies, is testified to by the numerous expeditions which Greek myths describe of the Northern Mediterranean shore culture's attempts to marry, annex or absorb the Cretan culture.

The Homeric myth of Peleus and Thetis, describes one such successful attempt. Thetis, whom for the Greeks, may have been synonymous with or identical to Tethys[14], was a granddaughter of Okeanos, the Sea god, whom Homer calls the "origin of the gods" and "the origin of everything."

Thetis was the daughter of Nereus, an ancient Sea god, an "old one of the seas" and both Zeus and Poseidon desired her.[15]

Themis, the mother of Prometheus, warned against either suit and advised the brothers to give Thetis to a mortal hero, Peleus from Pelion, the mountain of Chiron the centaur.

Dissatisfied with either prospect, Thetis employed similar tricks to those employed by Leda. She metamorphosed into fire, water, a lion, a serpent and various sea creatures, archetypes indicative of Crete.

Peleus, being an artful wrestler, eventually succeeded in capturing Thetis. Sea dwellers reported that finally, she assumed the shape of a cuttle fish, a predominantly Cretan symbol, when Peleus took her.[16]

The issue of Peleus and Thetis was the Hero Achilles, who commanded the Cretan forces at Troy. This myth then, describes cultural interaction between Crete and mainland Mycenae, from whose union, a mighty contingent fought in the Aachean expansion campaigns against mainland Anatolia culminating in the battle of Troy.

Such cultural intermixing instigated from military incursions from the earliest times between the Greek mainland culture and Cretan hegemony, lead to

Cretan ritual being absorbed into the Greco-Mycenean culture, ritual, similar, not surprisingly, to that described in the myth of Atlantis.

Cretan cultural influence was not the only one to find its way into the Greco-Mycenean, for it is apparent from the earliest cycles of Greek myths, that neighbouring Protosyrian, Hittite and Sumerian influences are to be found. This is not unreasonable from what has already been concluded from the myths of those cultures already examined and what is known of heliopian philosophy of cultural integration etc.

It is valid to propose that the copious nature of the Greek treasury of myth, like the Egyptian, is owed in part and is proportional to, the many and varied contributions to that culture from earlier and contemporary cultures. These were fashioned by the elder cultures, for such was the heliopian way of things, for the younger culture, containing, in symbolic form, exquisite accounts of pre-history military, and hence, cultural conquests of the civilisation.

In pre-history and before written records, it was considered necessary to record the exploits of a nation or culture. The means in those days was by the oral relation of myths, the more fabulous and fearful the imagery, the more memorable and ease of recollection.

It is natural to ask the question "why was it necessary to record the successful exploits of a tribe or nation or culture." Clearly the ancients learnt a long time ago that such recollections were, if not essential, certainly good and conducive to good morale in the perennial struggle for the nation's or tribe's survival.

The hero, as embodied by today's sporting and other heroes provide role models for the general populace. This is the reason why history is always written by the conquerors, not from vanity, though that may be the immediate motivation, but from a natural and probably subconscious drive embracing certain knowledge that such presentation of events facilitates survival.

Propaganda is still recognised as a potent weapon of war. A reputation for valour or ruthlessness also counts as a weapon. Myths were all of these things for the culture about whom they related, and they kept the concept of heroism alive.

The cultural tide of influence appears to have been from the civilised southern Mediterranean cultures up through Crete and Anatolia into the northern shores of the Mediterranean.

On the cultural continuum can be seen the Cretan 'flood' expansion with its ebb in the face of Sumerian expansion into Anatolia and probably Crete. This was taken up by Anatolian expansion into Crete and Mycenae. Then came the Mycenean expansion as depicted by the Labours of Herakles.

The Mycenaeans formed the boundary of the heliopian cultures of the Mediterranean and beyond them were the Saxon-Celts of Central Europe, culturally younger and less developed.

The superiority of the Near Eastern cultures, particularly in terms of artisan skills and military strategy and experience, was largely due to the openness of heliopian societies and their toleration of new cultures and ideas.

There does exist however, a natural cultural law which renders it impossible to wholly eradicate a culture once it has taken root. It again is to do with collective survival. There have been many instances of cultural expansion and shrinkage but few if any of cultural annihilation, for cultures in terminal decline tend to mutate like some extinct species into a new culture.

An example of a dead culture was the Sumerian, which was eventually eclipsed but only to be found as the source of fundamental influences and cultural traits in the later Egyptian and Babylonian cultures.

If we regard the Renaissance as obeying the cultural law and growing according to the cultural timescale, then with its conception in the 1100 AD, its childhood was realised in the 16th and 17th centuries then it is presently growing according to heliopian pluralism.

For some idea of the time span of cultural life one should examine the ancient cultures. Something in excess of a millennium would constitute a short cultural life.

One can observe cultural boundaries today in Europe which have been shaped by past circumstances. One of the most noticeable is the confines of the Celtic culture. At one time covering most of France, England and Ireland, it was driven into Northwest France by the Roman Conquest. Later in Britain, it was driven westwards into Wales and south into Cornwall (to preserve its contact with Brittany) by the invading Saxon tide filling the vacuum of the withdrawal of the Roman legions. A similar event happened in Spain with the (blue eyed) Visigoths in Spain driving the Roman remnant into what is now Portugal and they themselves later being driven into the north east corner of Basque Spain. The common Roman cultural content of Portugal and Britain may be a contributing factor to the unusual amity which exists between the two nations.)

Archetypes of the Protosyrian Daganite culture as symbolised by the lion, infused the Mycenean city states prior to their integration into a cohesive empire by trade and conquest as the Southern Mediterranean cultures had done before them.

Cretan/Atlantean rituals are described by Homer in the *Odyssey* and *Iliad*. Telemechus, the son of Odysseus finds at his first port of call, Pylos, in his search for his father:

"People on the sea beach sacrificing jet black bulls to Poseidon, Lord of the Earthquake, god of the sable rocks (and also the god of Atlantis); there were nine companies in session with five hundred men in each and every company had nine bulls to offer."[17]

Peisistratus, the son of Nestor, the Gerenian charioteer and king of Pylos, offers Athena a twin handled golden cup of wine, and the goddess prays to Poseidon.

The Sea god and his fertility goddess are present here, so is the Atlantean ritual of slaughtering the sacred bull (of strength and fertility) accompanied by the ritual drinking of the blood. This was an ancient form of magic that inferred that the qualities of the animal being sacrificed were transferred to the drinker. This is an ancient ritual to be found in many cultures notably in the Mayan for example.

Even at the time of the Iliad, the ritual had been civilised by the replacement of blood by wine. The immutability of such ritual is illustrated by the fact that the in the Reformed Church at the time of the Renaissance of Greco-Roman culture in Europe, it was felt necessary to remove even the replacement of blood by wine in the sacrifice in the Mass.

Poseidon is associated with the sea and earthquakes, the volcanic nature of Atlantis and in all probability was the god via Amen associated with the Judaic-Christian archetype of the rock.

A little later in the Odyssey, Nestor, recounting the return of the ships from Troy, describes a successful arrival at Geraestus after which:

"Many a bull's thighs we laid on Poseidon's altar after spanning that weary stretch of water."[18]

The thigh of the bull was a feature of the battle between Gilgamesh and Enkidu and the Bull of Heaven, and probably had a special significance.

In another part of the Odyssey, we read:

"They swiftly dismembered the carcass, cut slices off the thigh in ceremonial fashion."[19]

Another part of the ritual was the gilding of a calf's horns with gold, in preparation for sacrifice to Athena. The ritual also involved a "flowered bowl of lustral water, a basket of barley corns, an axe to cut the victim down and a dish to catch the victim's blood."[20]

These are ancient symbols of fertility and many statues exist in all of the Near Eastern cultures of a fertility goddess dispensing water of fertility.

The ritual began with the throwing of a lock of the gilded horned victim's head on the fire. Prayers were then said and barley corns scattered. The tendons of the heifer's neck were then cut with the axe, then its throat was cut and its blood collected. Ceremonial strips of thigh were then cut and burnt whilst the king sprinkled red wine over the flames.

Telemachus, in preparation for the meal, is bathed and then rubbed with olive oil by Nestor's youngest daughter.

The barley corns are a symbol associated with the Anatolian fertility goddess Ceres or Demeter.

The association of water and blood in ancient fertility ritual can be encountered in the New Testament account of the Marriage Feast of Canaan where Christ reputedly turns water into wine.

The bathing of Telemachus prior to the taking of the ritual wine, has its reflection in the Last Supper.

Whilst Nestor is reminiscing, he describes Peleus, consort of Thetis, the daughter of the Sea god and father of Achilles of Crete as:

"burning fat from an ox's thigh in honour of Zeus the Thunderer."[21]

When Nestor was wounded, he was served refreshment by Hecamede, the daughter of Arsinous from Tenedos, which consisted of:

"some yellow honey and sacred barley meal together with Pramian wine sprinkled with grated goat's milk cheese and white barley."

The drink was served in a "magnificent beaker adorned with golden studs which the old man had brought from home. It had four handles, each supported by two legs, and on top of each, facing one another, a pair of golden doves were feeding."[22]

Nestor also describes his father, Neleus, as having twelve sons, a similar number to Cleito, the queen of Atlantis.

The birds on the goblet are reminiscent of Cretan birds associated with the Cretan goddess. The axe for the ritual slaughter is evident at Knossos in Crete where the axes form the capitals of the pillars surrounding a cauldron of sacrifice.

A dove or bird is sited between the axes at the top of the pillars. Bearers are present on the fresco holding sacrificial heifers and are offering them to the goddess who is outside of her temple. Golden horned rhytons have also been found at Knossos. The ritual gilding of the horns is related in the Epic of Gilgamesh:

"Over the thigh of the Bull of Heaven, she (Ishtar) set up lamentation. But Gilgamesh called the smiths and armourers all of them together. They admired the immensity of the horns. They were plated with lapis lazuli two fingers thick."[23]

"Gilgamesh and Enkidu cleared the trees of the forest of Humbaba as far as the banks of the Euphrates" (i.e., cleared the land of enemy).

If, as has been proposed that the Flood was in fact a military campaign of a monotheistic culture, then one would expect to find evidence of cultural influence of the victor, that is Sumerian influence. (It is also probable that flood symbolism had the same meaning in other mythologies.)

In this respect this was part of normal cultural intermixing attained in a peaceful manner usually, by the heliopians. The monotheistic method was the opposite of this, the promotion of the monotheism by conquest and annihilation of opposing, usually heliopian, cultures according to the law of cultural opposites.

The myth of Proteus betrays Cretan influence in Ancient Egypt.

Proteus, an ancient sea god, one of the "old ones of the sea", had the ability like the fertility goddesses, to metamorphose. When Menelaus sets out to capture him, that is, conquer Crete, he changes into a lion, leopard, serpent, pig, water and a tree.[24]

Proteus was associated with Egypt, he was known as the "Sea greybeard of Egypt" and was a "subject of Poseidon." This seems to indicate that there was a sea god cult following in Egypt of the Ram god. It also suggests the presence of Amenites or Hyksos (from Crete) or both. It may indicate an even earlier Cretan infusion into Egypt. There is further Greek mythology to support this theory which we shall examine later.

Although it is claimed the story of the Flood, which came from the East, never gained acceptance in Greece as it did amongst the Eastern and Southern Mediterranean peoples[25] certain similarities exist surrounding at least three great floods in Greek mythology with the Sumerian Flood myth.

A great flood is offered as the reason why the Telchines, represented as a primitive people and famed as evil magicians, left Rodes.[26] The Telchines were nine in number and, it was told, they came to Crete with Rhea to rear the child Zeus. The Telchines were more widely known as the rearers of Poseidon, and they were helped in the task by another Sea god's daughter, Kapheira.

Here then is a link connecting a tale of flood with the Sea god Poseidon, the god of Plato's Atlantis. The root of Kapheira probably derives from the same root as that for Kaphto, biblical Crete. The ancient pre-Minoan culture of Creten Atlantis embraced the Anatolian and pre-Mycenean mainlands, and, according to Sumerian mythology, much of the Levant and Sumeria in pre-history archaic times.

It also penetrated Ancient Egypt and dominated the major islands of the Mediterranean according to Greek mythology, if one examines the progeny of Poseidon.

Poseidon the ram god, had six sons and a daughter, Rhodos, by Halia, a sister of the Telchines. Halia's name meant "the Sea goddess."[27]

In the Amenite priesthood of the ram god of Egypt can be seen shades of Telchine magi and their association with female goddesses and queens.

Rhodos was destined for Rhodes, but was prevented from landing by Poseidon's insolent sons. For this, the goddess punished them with madness, so they sought to lie with their own mother (possibly indicating alliance with Anatolia or Mycenae). Poseidon, as a consequence, punished them by causing them "to sink beneath the earth", a similar fate to Atlantis?

The cultural provenance of Halia is uncertain, but may have been protosyrian, pre-Hittite Anatolian. This small incident seems to translate as Rhodes wishing to remain as part of Anatolian or some such culture rather than becoming a vassal of the Cretan culture. This aligns with some military upheaval or flood causing some cultural sect, the Telchines having to leave Rhodes. (Similar cultural exoduses occurred in Egypt at various times.)

The invasion was possibly from the Anatolian mainland. The marriage of Poseidon to Halia is standard myth-speak for a strategic miliary or cultural alliance.

Rhodos or Rhode, was also said to have been the daughter of Aphrodite or Amphitrite, both of whom were sea goddesses. Aphrodite also known as Cythera was "born of the sea" near Cythera, the island of Cyprus. It is entirely natural that islands in the middle of the ocean should be deemed to have risen out of the (womb) of the sea but what is interesting is their cultural provenance.

The four names, Aphrodite, Halia, Amphitrite and Kapheira, "must have applied to one and the same Great Goddess"[28] The circumstance of an important deity having many different names reflecting multicultural communities, was a feature of the Sun god of Ancient Egypt which we have seen in an earlier chapter.

The custom was undoubtedly developed over the ages to assuage different groups and render recognisable important gods which had been incorporated into the heliopian pantheon.

The many different names of the Sea god in Greek mythology were probably used to similar effect. The multiplicity of names which increased through the ages, paradoxically serves to illustrate the immutability of the cultural philosophical dichotomy between the autocratic monotheism and pluralistic heliopianism.

As the ancient Qaballists were aware, these two cultural forces constituted a macrocosmic reflection of aspects of microcosmic man, the holon of macroscopic culture.

Another reference to a great flood occurs with Zeus being told that by means of a flood was how he "ought" to exterminate the terrible and mighty Race of Bronze. (This may be a reference to some race that had discovered bronze and its use as what would have been powerful weapons which threatened the survival of the pre-Greeks.)

In its simplest version[29] Deukalion, the son of Prometheus who ruled over Phthia and Thessaly, took a wife, Pyrrha, the "red blond."

When Zeus was about to destroy the Race of Bronze, Deukalion, on the advice of Prometheus, made a wooden box, stored in it all that was necessary, and climbed into it with Pyrrha. Zeus caused mighty rain to fall from heaven and flooded the greater part of Greece. All men perished except those who had fled to the nearest high mountains. The whole country, as far as the Isthmus and the Peloponnese, became a single sheet of water.

Deukalion floated for nine days and nights, finally landing on Mount Parnassus. In return for sacrificing to Zeus for his safe delivery, Zeus granted his request carried by Hermes, for more human beings to populate the earth.

Zeus bade Deukalion to take stones and throw them over his shoulder. The stones which Deukalion threw became men and those which Pyrrha threw, women, hence the word "laoi" for people and peoples in Greek, is similar to "laas" or "laos", meaning stone.

In another version, the couple threw behind them the bones of Mother Earth and new beings sprang up.

Similarities with the Sumerian Flood myth are evident in the Greek Flood myths. The box, redolent of the coffin of Osiris, is similar in purpose to the ark. Animals (i.e., composite animal deities) are not mentioned as the later Greek culture, more developed than its predecessors, did not require a predominance of bi-natured or animal deities and such hybrid deities were never, with the exception of Pan and the Centaurs, prominent in the pantheon.

The myths probably refer, like the Sumerian, to Cretan or some other cultural conquest, possibly Protosyrian, of the Mycenean mainland, and Zeus, later triumphant as Celestial Executive, is attributed as being the broker of celestial power. Zeus is cast as Enlil, the Sumerian Storm god who ordered the Flood of Sumerian myth. The archetypes of mountain, sacred stones and the presence of a fertility goddess, seem to indicate Cretan involvement.

The "cultural flood" extends from the Isthmus to all the Peloponnese. Deukalion and his wife land at Parnassus on the northern shore of the Gulf of Corinth, which forms a natural strategic barrier. This can be defended by holding a narrow stretch of valley, less than ten miles in length, between Loutraki and "Isthmia" which separates the Saronic and Corinthian Gulfs. It would appear that those "who had fled to the nearest mountains", fled northwards beyond this point.

Deukalion, in sacrificing to the god Zeus, is, like Utnapishtim, recognising the head of the diviocratic pantheon.

Sailing nine nights and days has echoes of the Telchines of Rhodes who, it is said, left Rhodes because they foresaw the coming of the "flood", the domination of Rhodes by Crete.[30]

The Sun god reigned supreme in Rhodes, which Zeus had given him as his portion. Prometheus, who espoused the cause of the human race against Zeus[31] is the counterpart of Ea in Sumerian mythology and Mount Nisir, the equivalent of Mount Parnassus in the Greek.

The Greek and Sumerian flood myths show that the heliopian pantheons are already established and their philosophies contain concern for the survival of the human race and pluralistic heliopianism. The birth of Greek heliopianism lies in the most ancient of myths of the culture.

In Greek mythology, we see similar themes to those in the Hittite, Babylonian and others, of attempts at usurping the heliopian celestial order.

In real terms, these are the attempts, often successful, of the idea of autocracy supplanting that of pluralistic democracy, with its temporal manifestations of mental and physical oppression of thought, and the general spread of the darkness of ignorance and tyranny.

Kronos is persuaded by his mother Gaia, the prototype fertility goddess, to castrate his father, Ouranus, the Sky God (who may be compared to the collective consciousness) by means of a saw-toothed sickle. The implement is easily equated to the phallic member and in some respects the action is entirely in accordance with the animal law of nature, the usurpation of age by youth, in order to ensure the future survival of the fittest.

In human terms, this is in the domain of the subconscious or animal part of the human condition.

The sickle is commonly found on Akkadian seals, was associated with the Sun god. Teshub, the king of the Hittite pantheon, amputated the monstrous Ullikumi with the copper knife of heaven. Seth, the brother of Osiris dismembered the body of the Sun god. Kronos in Greek mythology, is the equivalent of the Hittite Kumarbi who would usurp the power of Anu, the head of the pantheon.

Kronos severs his father's vitals and flings the severed parts to earth. The drops of blood issuing, cause the Furies to be born.

This event is similar to the myth of Seth and Osiris and in the Babylonian myth involving the celestial usurper Tiamat and his commander Kingu.

In human psychological terms, this common theme must in some respects reflect the gradual segregation of the consciousness from the all-pervading archetypal hitherto animal subconscious.

In the Egyptian myth, Seth dismembers Osiris, and flings his phallus into the Nile, associating the symbol of water with fertility.

Kronos endeavours to maintain an autocratic hegemony over the pantheon by devouring his children. In temporal or real terms this translates as extending domains and vassalage. Kumarbi in the Hittite, is made to spit out the (cultural) seeds or children which are to flourish into co-members of a subsequent heliopian pantheon.

These are symbolised naturally as great rivers, symbols of (celestial) fertile strength and life.

Zeus, the Greek Teshub, eventually defeats Kronos and proceeds to father the Greek heliopian pantheon, whose gods, like the Egyptian, reflected all religious shades of the cultural members.

Proteus is and archaic form of Protogonis, "the first born."[32] If at first the human condition manifested primarily only a primitive and therefore superstitious consciousness and the animal subconscious, then one would expect the earliest gods to be fertility gods associated with symbols which the subconscious recognised as fertility, that is, water.

Poseidon or Poteidan, the Sea god was the husband of the goddess Da, the ancient name for Gaia the Earth.[33]. He was also known as "Father."

There is therefore, an association of the Sea god with the earliest mythological gods, those prior to, and those subsequently involved with the emergence of heliopianism and the vanquishing of autocratic monotheism.

It would not be unreasonable to suppose that the ancients recognised this path of human development and encouraged enlightenment, the development of reason and attributes normally referred to as "divine" (or realistically non-animal). The dual nature of the human condition was almost certainly recognised and reflected in the wisdom of the ancient Qaballists with the concept of the Union of Opposites.

Needless to say, on the timescale of the cultural continuum, the development of the human condition is an eternally slow process as man the animal is refined to man the human.

Had Lucius of Samasoa realised the project of the ancients, possibly he would not have been so eager to challenge the validity of the existence of the gods.

The Greek pantheon, whose main incumbents were represented as fully human by comparison to contemporary and senior cultures, reflected the continuous process of humanising the gods, whose forms were a measure of the development of man's consciousness.

Each succeeding heliopian pantheon was a development of a previous one, as indeed it required to be if the eternal project was to reach fruition.

The Greek pantheon was a development in many respects of the Egyptian as the Egyptian was a development of the Sumerian.

Earlier cycles of gods had contained bi-natured deities commensurate with the development of the culture's collective psyche of the time and as such, represented a marker in man's psychological development.

The Greek culture was, as many would agree, something of a plateau in man's cultural development. The Greek pantheon served, with minor variations, as the pantheon of the Romans who, as we shall see, were ethnically and culturally from the same cradle as the Greeks and their achievements correlate with the human conceptual potential that the Roman culture embodied.

The Roman culture was far from being a Greek invention, for, by accident or design, each succeeding heliopian culture contained influences from the previous, arising from the inherent heliopian philosophy of assimilation etc., and also from cultural intercourse engendered by trade and conquest.

Ultimately, the Greek culture was to fuse with one of its parent cultures, that of Egypt subsequent to the Alexandrian conquest (circa 300 BC). This was to provide the great commonwealth of heliopian cultures with the common fabric that held together the Roman Empire.

One consequence of this was the great admiration that the Romans had for Alexander whose strategies were clearly, much studied by them.

The Sea god and his associated fertility goddess together, as adversaries, is the subject of many of the Greek myths which describe the struggle for Greco-Mycenean autonomy from the hegemony of Crete. Subsequently, Crete is overcome and absorbed into the culture, as a prelude to its expansion across the Eastern and to the Southern Mediterranean shores, many centuries before its expansion under Alexander.

This is another example of the wave nature of cultural expansion and contraction in the "sea" of culture. Generally such cultural ebbs and flows are not noticed because of the length of the time scales between contractions and expansions. This movement of culture should not be surprising, as much else in the universe is cyclical. It is also fitting that culture, which is after all a collection of human beings bound by established religion, rites, language etc should have a similar life cycle like the individual holon having a birth, a youth, a maturity, an ageing and a death, the only difference being that the life period is some 50 times longer.

It was clear to the manipulators of the darker forces of human kind (and advertisers throughout the ages) that there is a mesmerising effect of phallicism on the human psyche which can be used for control of human behaviour. It is a powerful motivator also and forms part of the mechanism of conflict which seems to be an essential feature in the struggle to survive.

Phorkys, an old sea god, had the ability to bring his daughter back to life.[34] This seems to be a mythological device to explain the ability of the (Cretan) culture to re-emerge after an epoch of subjugation. It is similar as an allegorical device to the serpent shedding its skin as appearing to live again.

In the myths of Herakles, we are probably not looking at an original Mycenean-Greek archetypal hero but a Protosyrian-Hittite importation signifying some extensive Anatolian influence in pre-Mycenean culture.

Herakles or Hercules, though human to the Greeks, has many attributes of the Hittite Storm God. This is marked by his inseparable club of olive, which was an associated archetype of Teshub, and as such, testifies to the archaic nature of the hero. Not surprisingly, Herakles is featured in one of the oldest myths of the Greeks, as assisting Zeus, probably representing the infant Mycenean culture, in his battle against the Giants.[35]

The Giants were possibly, the Central European Saxons and Celts, who were significantly taller on average, than the Middle Eastern populace or they may have been vassal states of Ouranos born of his spilt blood that is, military conflict.[36]

Herakles is often engaged in battles with sea creatures of a serpentine nature. He slew Skylla, the Sea Goddess of Hekate, for stealing his kine (territory and or inhabitants?) Phorkys, her father, restored her to life.

Herakles also "wrestles" with Phorkys, the "Old One of the Sea" under his alternative name of Nereus[37] in the process of which, Nereus metamorphoses into a lion, a buck and a serpent, thrusting their heads out of his fish-like body.

It would seem that Herakles is contending with surrounding cultures, the animal symbols representative of Cretan and Anatolian cultural factions. This becomes more clear when we examine the Labours.

Another episode tells of Herakles fighting with Archeloos, another water god, as well as with sea gods, Nereus and Triton.

Archeloos, according to Homer, is set above Okeanos, "the origin of everything." Okeanos, whose equivalent in the Hittite was Kumarbi, was portrayed as an old man with horns of a bull. Here is another association of the Sea God with strength and fertility symbolism.

Archeloos was the prototype of Okeanos with horns and a lower body consisting of a serpent-like fish. One of the horns was broken off by Herakles and from the blood that dripped, the Sirens were born.[38] This imagery again suggests Cretan cultural involvement.

In the ancient tongue, Seirenes (masculine) described bees or wasps. Bees were associated with the Anatolian goddess Demeter and known as "melissa."

Sirens could be either male or female, having a bird's body, a human head and women's breasts and body. The taloned feet often ended in a lion's paw. This imagery is an amalgam of Sumerian and Protosyrian archetypes with an unmistakable Cretan element of the bear breasted fertility goddess.

The Sirens had musical talents, not least, the ability to sing, and whose voices enchanted and awoken desire, presumably, one of the functions of a fertility goddess.

In the Garden of the Hesperides, the guardians were female who sang with bright songs. Mother Earth had produced in the garden, a miraculous tree bearing apples as a gift to Hera, who sent the serpent Ladon as guardian.

In attempting to obtain the apples, Herakles slew Ladon. The Hesperides were the daughters of Atlas the Giant[39] and stories tell how he obtained the apples without force.

Crete, as we have seen, with its serpent goddess was reputedly the island of Atlas and Atlantis. Poseidon the Sea God was its deity. Poseidon, as well as assuming the shape of a bull on occasions, changed himself into a stallion, in order to couple with Demeter, who had changed herself into a mare.[40] This seems to suggest the attempted formation of an alliance between Crete and Anatolia at some point.

The horse, as a cultural archetype, represents some new cultural epoch, for it was to revolutionise warfare as a powerful new introduction to military hardware. It is generally thought that the Hyksos introduced the horse into Egypt.

Herakles is almost invariably depicted as wearing a lion skin insinuating one who vanquishes lions in the heroic mould of Gilgamesh. He is shown on some Roman wall paintings as dark skinned, compared to the goddess with whom he is shown. This suggests that he was from some southern Mediterranean land as the Egyptians claimed.

His son Telephus, a name similar to Telepinus, the son of the Hittite Storm God, is shown being suckled by a hind. Telephus is also cast as an enemy of the invading Greeks in the war with Troy where he, as king of Mysia, resists the Greeks and is wounded by Achilles.[41]

The hind or stag was a Protosyrian archetype of ancient origin, which was held as Lord Protector by the Hittites. Gilded horned stags have been found at the ancient site of Catal Hoyuk, dating to early circa 2900 to 2700 BC, and at Ubaid near Ur, dating to the early second millennium BC.

The stag was sacred to Artemis, the Moon Goddess, who was prominent in the Hittite pantheon. It is possible that Herakles, in accordance with the northern drift of culture from the south, was an Anatolian importation into the Mycenean culture.

Herakles's exploits against the sea gods of Cretan hegemony could equally apply to conflicts between that culture and Protosyrian Anatolia, eventually culminating in penetration of the Greek mainland from a conquered Crete. Whether this was the case or not, the Labours of Herakles, when interpreted, give a distinct impression of consolidation of Cretan and mainland Mycenean states by the culture that Herakles represented.

Nor was it the only such occurrence, for the pattern is repeated with later heroes like Perseus and Theseus. The exploits of Herakles, were some of the earliest, due to his appearance in the earliest cycles of Greek myths.

We see also in the Labours, archetypes of several cultures based mainly on animals or other creatures. This aligns with the archaic epoch in which they are supposed to have taken place, for example, prior to, or contemporary with, the Ptah cycles of cultural gods in Egypt before circa, 2000 BC.

The Labours of Herakles

Herakles undertook the labours to free himself from service to Eurystheus, the king of Tiryns. They are:

1) The Nemean Lion

Herakles first labour was to slay the Nemean Lion, a beast that would not be killed by weapons of stone or metal. The Lion archetype could indicate some penetration of the Mycenean mainland by some Anatolian influence, evidenced by the supernatural nature of the beast.

Nemea is only a short distance from Mycenae where stone lions guarded the main gate forming a dual symmetry with a (sacred) pillar. Herakles, armed with only his club and bow given to him by Athena, the weapons of Teshub and Gilgamesh, strangles the lion, losing a finger in the process. This latter detail may be an indication of the small effort or number of casualties involved in the task.

Tiryns is just south of Mycenae and its triangular stone gate is similar in style to those found at Hattusa, the Hittite capital in Anatolia, modern Borgaz Koi.

2) The Hydra

This was the object of Herakles second labour. The Hydra was a sea monster with nine snake-like heads, one of which was immortal. It was reputedly to be found at Lerna, near the south of Mycenae. It was possibly the island of Hydra lying off the south coast of the Peloponnese.

The imagery is unmistakably associated with the Gorgon and the Cretan snake-headed goddess. The fact that one of the heads was immortal corresponds again with the archetype representing a culture. In this case it also reinforces the probability of a Cretan culture as the immortal head has shades of the Sea God's power of being able to restore his daughter to life.

Herakles is depicted on Roman frescoes as battling with a hydra. The Hydra, having a distinct flavour of Cretan symbolism, featured in the myth of Baal and his battle with the seven headed sea monster. This would seem reasonable as it is quite possible that in its ascendency, the Canaanite culture probably beat off a seaboard invasion from the northern islands of the Mediterranean or some large culture occupying adjacent territory. This is indicated also in the numbers seven and nine, both of which were sacred, though seven was more prevalent in the Southern Mediterranean cultures as nine was in the Northern Mediterranean especially, in the Greek.

Seven was clearly a sacred number in the Sumerian culture as can be discerned by its regularity of use in the Epic of Gilgamesh.

Nine had mystical associations for the Greeks and derived cultures, possibly as its being thrice the sacred number three, the number associated with the sacred tripod of Apollon and the tripod of the Sea God.

At Tiryns, which existed circa 1600-1100 BC, is next to Lerna (circa 3300-1500 BC) there was found a megaron with a large circular hearth surrounded by four pillars. In the porch of a megaron were found plaster floors painted with octopuses and dolphins and the walls portrayed a boar hunt, another event that occurs in the Labours.[42] Megarons were common to many Peloponnese ancient sites and may have served as temples.

The Hydra could also have been another version of Scylla, the daughter of Hekate and Phorkys, into whom Poseidon's jealous wife, Amphitrite, had thrown three herbs, which caused her to be changed into a monster with six dog's heads. Coastal communities would no doubt have temples where such monsters could be appeased.

Poseidon's wooing of Scylla, casts her as some potential island vassal of archaic Crete.

A (ritualistic) cauldron found at Salamis in Cyprus, thought to be Uratian-Hittite[43] has six serpent heads issuing from its rim. Each head is wearing a Shardarna helmet. In between two serpents is a fish-bodied winged figure which is the motif of the Cretan sea goddess and serpents. The cauldron sits on a tripod with a three leafed motif which is also found on the relief of the Hurrian equivalent of the Weather God, Tersheba at Adilievas Uratu.

The lightning of Zeus was often depicted as three bolts so we see the sacred triple was a feature of many Western Mediterranean cultures.

The Shardana have been identified as one of the contingents of the Sea Peoples of the Ramessean III conspiracy circa 1200 BC[44] who swept down from the Northern Mediterranean and overran the Levant and parts of Anatolia, up to the boundaries of Ancient Egypt. It is probable that these hordes were the forces that sacked Hattusa the capital of the Hittite Empire of Anatolia in 1200 BC, a battle which was the legendary Battle of Troy. The Sea Peoples probably were invaders from Mycenae, the Greek Islands, Crete and Cyprus.

Cyprus was culturally the same as Crete, according to the myths and was regarded as an attractive and enviable possession, not least for its copper, the metal associated with Aphrodite and the metal of weapons.

3) The Cerynean Hind

This was one of five bronze hooved, gold antlered hinds or stags, four of which drew the chariot of the Moon Goddess, Artemis. Herakles was commissioned to capture one of them which he succeeded in doing, by hunting it for half a year until it was exhausted. These celestial stags clearly had cult significance, which probably originated in the Protosyrian hinterland.

Hittite depictions show a god astride the creature who was known as the "Great Protector." The gilded horns of the stag formed part of the Nestorian ritual at Pylos, dedicated to the Sea God and his fertility goddess. Sources point out that such harnessing of four stags (or horses in the case of the Sun God) was inefficient for pulling as the inside horses tended to do all the work.[45]

This seems to underline the symbolic nature of the image, the four horses or stags being intended, like the Four Sons of Horus, to represent universality of the heliopian pantheon, by representing the four points of the compass.

The Romans showed Jupiter Dolichenus wearing a Phrygian cap, standing on top of a bull, in the same manner as the gods at Yasilikaya and the Great Protector. In one representation, he holds the rope and tiller of Fortuna and an eagle stands beneath the bull. A stag rhyton, a ritual cup found at Catal Huyuk, shows the god on the back of a stag, holding an eagle. He is dressed in early Sumerian fashion.

The Cerynean Hind labour holds therefore, the history of some Mycenean-Hittite or Protosyrian encounter, possibly a campaign lasting sometimes, six months in cultural time, and the stag represents some vassal state. This may have been and island under Anatolian mainland hegemony, eventually falling to the younger growing culture as it consolidated infant city states.

4) The Erymanthian Boar

This exploit of Herakles took place as the process of consolidation continued on the Mycenean mainland. Herakles drove the troublesome beast up into the snows of Mount Erymanthus where he was able to capture it and bind it in chains, which is probably myth speak for successful military encounter.

The myth has its echoes in the myth of the Grey Sow that Theseus slew, and also in the Caledonian Boar Hunt. Whoever the warriors were, symbolised by the boar, they were certainly formidable and not easily subdued.

The Vikings were symbolised in myths as boars and dragons and boar crests were carried on their helmets. As archetypal symbols long reside in a culture it is possible that the boar represented some early Central European strain of Saxons.

The boar can also be found on many helmets of classical Greek warriors, a tribute to their prowess.

The Erymanthus river is fed from the mountains of Achaia in the Northern Peloponnese Peninsula. The Greeks of the Iliad took their name from this region, the Achaians.

5) The Stymphalian Birds

This episode also takes place on the Peloponnese Peninsula, a few miles north of Nemea in the marshes near Mount Cyllene. The birds were often depicted as having human heads and bodies, indicative of the human cultural allegory embodied in the myth.

Winged human-animal composites as archetypal symbols were to be found in the Sumerian and Cretan cultures and later, in the Hittite and several other cultures.

The device used by Herakles to rid the land of the creatures was to take a bronze rattle up a mountain and create a mighty din. A similar ruse was used at Jericho by blowing rams horns to cause the "walls to fall."

The incident provides an archaic example of psychological warfare where the enemy takes flight at a mighty show of arms and a roar of war cries. This is economically encapsulated in the rattle of Herakles.

Two things are significant in this allegory, firstly, the myth describes mountain dwellers like the Nemean lions or Erymanthian Boars, suggesting guerrilla type of bands and have echoes of the Deukalion survivors.

Secondly, as Herakles was only able to frighten the birds, this seems an indication of the strength of the fighting forces.

We encountered the "din" made by the human race that was of such annoyance to Enlil in the Epic of Gilgamesh and also in the recorded Ancient Egypt tale concerning the king Sequenenre (circa 1600-1560) and the Hyksos king Apophis. The word seems to be a popular mythological term for describing war.

Apophis was the serpent enemy of Ra, the Sun God and is probably indicative of the major deity of the Egyptian Delta culture imported from the serpent culture of Crete via an earlier pre-Hyksos infusion. The cobra became the symbol of the Delta culture or Lower Kingdom and formed one half of the dual culture of the land, the eagle or vulture symbolising the other half.

Sequenenre complained to Apophis without success, that the hippopotami in his pool were keeping him awake at night "with their roaring." Water horses, symbolic of the Sea God, suggests some rebellious or warlike force threatening the peace of Sequenenre. Shortly thereafter, the Hyksos were expelled from Egypt (circa 1555-50).

The outcome of the Heraklion strategy in this labour was that the Stymphalian Birds flew east, to the Isle of Aries in the Black Sea, presumably to their parent culture outside of the sphere of Cretan-Mycenean hegemony.

6) The Cleaning of the Augian Stables

Eurystheus demanded that Herakles clean out the stables of King Augeias at Elis, which had accumulated dung over many years. Herakles accomplished the task in one day by diverting the course of the River Alpheus through the stables.

Elis is just south east of Mount Erymanthus and the myth suggests the clearing out of some troublesome religious cult as symbolised by the horse and stables, houses of religious power. The horse was sacred to the Sea God Poseidon and water the symbol of fertility, is apt for overcoming some cult power.

Alpheus, "the first" reflects the claim of predominance of the Sea God. The letter "aleph", the first letter of the Hebrew Alphabet was originally constructed as the horns of a bull, an ancient symbol of strength and fertility. The bull was also sacred to the Sea God and figured in the sacrifice of (Cretan) Atlantis.

In the Christian tradition, Christ refers to himself as the Alpha and Omega, and in the Gnostic Gospels, he refers to the apostle Thomas as having partaken of his "bubbling stream."[46]

The labour shows a continuation of the process of consolidation within the Greek mainland.

7) The Cretan Bull

In this labour, Herakles is sent to capture a fabulous fire breathing bull that was trampling the crops on the Island of Crete. Although King Minos was keen to assist Herakles, the hero captured the bull alone and brought it back to King Eurystheus, who set it free, an action which suggests that the bull represented a cultural ally.

The myth describes Herakles for the first time, leaving the Peloponnese Peninsula, signifying an offshore expansion of the culture represented by the Hero.

The fire breathing bull signals some sort of insurrection or marauding guerrilla type of activity on the island whose members seem to be followers of the Sea God. They or their representatives are transported to the mainland and consequently set free probably bound by some form of alliance, but recognised as a powerful force and with good reason.

King Minos was reputedly the son of Zeus and Europa, a Southern Mediterranean fertility goddess who was abducted by Zeus in the form of a bull. Zeus, as representing heliopian Mycenae is shown exerting hegemony over Crete by some marriage alliance and the progeny culture rebelling.

It is possible that the bull of the seventh labour represents some faction of the old Atlantean culture attempting to regain power in the island. The fire breathing bull trampling the crops suggests military activity with some dire consequences on the local populace. The episode has the flavour of insurrection against Mycenean domination or influence.

The myth may be related to the story involving Minos' wife Parsiphae, "the all illuminating" daughter of Helios and Perseus, the Sun God and Moon Goddess.[47]

Parsiphae gave birth to the Minotaurus, a human with a bull's head which was held prisoner in a labyrinth. Parsiphae had deceived Asterios, "the king of the stars." The "bull of Minos" with the help of Daidalos, constructed a cow in which the queen hid herself in order to be impregnated by the Bull.

The Bull of Minos would seem to represent the leader or king pretender of the ancient Atlantean cult and adversary of Minos, possibly the same faction as the Cretan Bull of the seventh Labour. The hybrid culture of the alliance, represented by the Minotaurus was clearly a threat to Mycenean hegemony and therefore confined or constrained or garrisoned, represented by the labyrinth.

The translation of the myth suggests intrigue by the Sea God culture to gain access to power via the succession in a similar manner to the Ancient Egyptian Amenites during the reign of Queen Hatshepsut. This mechanism is to be seen in operation, often effectively, through the ages by the monotheistic forces in order to gain access to power via the queen of a culture. The Atlantean-Cretan fertility culture would reach Ancient Egypt in the mists of pre-history as will be shown subsequently in the Tenth Labour.

8) The Mares of Thrace

Following the Seventh Labour, which saw the Heraklion culture extended beyond the mainland of Mycenae to Crete, the eighth Labour indicates a

197

continuation of the expansion of the culture to the north and east of the Peloponnese Peninsula.

In this exploit, Herakles sets off to subdue and capture four man-eating mares which were terrorising the countryside. The mares were the property of King Diomedes, probably the forerunner of the hero of the Iliad renown for his horses. He was a Thracian.

The horse played a major part in the culture of Thrace. The Thracians were akin to the tartars of the present day, mainly hunters of the plains.

In the Iliad, the Thracian contingent of the Greek forces were ferocious fighters, symbolised by Diomedes. They must have served as cavalry in much the same way as they supported Alexander. The Mares may indeed refer to Macedonians who, in Alexander's time, were renowned as an elite corps of foot and horse soldiers known as the Hetaeri.

Herakles is pursued by Diomedes and his followers. Herakles, by cutting a channel to allow the sea to rush in and flood the field of battle, ultimately fells Diomedes with his club and feeds his body to the fabulous mares which he then carries off. This suggests that Diomedes is defeated militarily, deposed by his army and hostages or prisoners are taken to Mycenae.

This Labour has similarities with the Sixth labour where water is used as an allegory of military might. The same allegory is used in the Biblical account of Exodus when it is used to describe a pincer movement during the Mosaic flight from Egypt. It is more widely known as the Parting of the Red Sea and we shall encounter it in a later chapter.

The mares of the labour suggest a cult associated with the Sun God or Moon Goddess, and again suggests Thrace as being under or influenced by Protosyrian Anatolia. In Alexandrian times, part of Thrace extended into Anatolia. The fact that the horses were mares, suggests the cult may have been associated with Demeter, the Anatolian fertility goddess who turned herself into a mare.[48]

There is a link also with the myth of the Stymphalian Birds who settled on the Isle of Aries in the Black Sea, which is bordered by Thrace. There seems to be a thrust eastwards by the culture represented by Herakles, which is continued in the next Labour.

Diomedes, devoured by his own mares, which are carried off, suggests Diomedes' deposition and the subjugation of the Thracian culture. The Iliad describes Diomedes, the son of Tydeus, as a Danaan, one of the "horse loving" Danaans, as Agamemnon describes Idomineus of Crete.[49]

198

9) The Amazons

The Amazons were reputedly a race of warrior women, known as the Children of Aries and they lived near the Black Sea. The girdle worn by Queen Hippolyte (or Hypolita), given to her by Aries as a sign of her superiority over other women, was desired by the daughter of Eurystheus (a vassal?). On the way to and from the country of the Amazons, Herakles took part in several wars, one boxing match, and two wrestling bouts. The latter encounters are probably to be interpreted as minor engagements.

The myth takes place in the environs of the last labour. The thrust eastwards, as indicated by this labour seems to be running out of steam, probably due to logistics and extended lines of communication, as the Amazons are not defeated. This can be divined from the fact that, initially, there is friendly accord between Herakles and Hippolyte, who had agreed to give Herakles her girdle. This seems to suggest some sort of alliance between the two cultures.

In one of the many versions of the myth, some violation of the accord takes place, for the Amazons are led to believe that Herakles is abducting the Queen and they attack his ship. Herakles, suspecting treachery, immediately kills Hippolyte and makes his escape with the girdle. Presumably, the Amazons remain unvanquished.

The central archetype of the myth is the girdle, and it is of interest to speculate on its significance. In reality, it is unlikely that a race of purely warrior women existed, but if one regards their femininity as representing a characteristic of a culture, probably a Celtic culture, then the symbolism begins to make sense.

The Celts fought naked except for a serpent girdle which was a central archetype of the culture. Such serpent like artefacts were to be found among later Celtic Orphites in Ireland up to the coming of Christianity. The Orphites were of course repressed by the Christian proselytisers but the archetypes remained and lived on in legends of serpents and "worms" etc. The legend of St Patrick ridding the land of snakes clearly translates as repressing Orphites.

The Saxon/Celts were known to, in later times, not be averse to royal female leadership. Bodicea in Britain is an example of such leadership and she probably represented a much older tradition. This collective femaleness of the culture seems to be a particularly Celtic characteristic and it is perhaps significant that France, who was predominantly Celtic before the Roman Occupation is still referred to as "La Belle France" and is symbolised by the Phrygian capped maid.

Britannia is also a female representative though with more male oriented characteristics.

The serpent girdle, appropriate to such a relatively undeveloped culture as the Celts would have a special significance to the Cretan-Mycenean culture, being associated with its fertility goddess, and may explain in part the initial amity between Herakles and Hippolyte.

The Celts, it is known, fought the Greeks in Anatolia around the fourth century BC, where, after their defeat, the Greeks erected a monument to them at Pergamon, testifying to their valour in battle.

According to the "wave theory" of culture, this was not the first time the Saxon/ Celts had penetrated the Mediterranean cultural sphere. It would appear that the descriptions "Sons of Aries" and "Children of Aries" are mythological terminology for military able or warlike cultures or states. The Saxons remained for the most part, as the Romans found to their cost, warlike and unvanquishable.

10) The Cattle of Geryon

This labour entailed Herakles stealing the gorgeous red cattle of Geryon, the strongest man alive, who lived in the West. The cattle were guarded by Eurytion, a son of Aries, and a two-headed dog, Orthus. Before reaching the land of Geryon, which was almost certainly Egypt (the strongest culture alive at that time), there are stories of Herakles setting up two pillars or rocks as a memorial of his journey. These are known as Gibralta and Centa.[50]

Ovid and other writers have Herakles travelling the length of Italy and discovering Sicily. The culture represented by Herakles displays accomplished maritime skills, expanding this time, westwards.

King Minos, one of the earliest rulers of Crete, possessed, according to Thucydides, a fleet. It is this tradition that probably gave rise to the titles "Sea Peoples" of the late second millennium.

It was during the second palatial period of the Minoan culture of Crete (circa 1700-1400 BC) that it spread to mainland Greece, though probably not for the first time, as the myths indicate, and according to the wave nature of culture. The ebb of this culture was to bring in its wake the Mycenaeans back as the dominant power again, not only in Crete, but ultimately in the whole of the Eastern and Southern Mediterranean coasts up to the gates of Egypt.

This labour depicts one such incursion or expedition to Geryon or Egypt. This is indicated by several coincidental symbols which have unique parallels with events in recorded Egyptian history which we shall see presently. Geryon is slain by an arrow and the cattle carried off.

The labour demonstrates the relative invincibility of some cultures. This expedition would not be the last cultural wave from the north for the tide would turn again and flow, manifested as the Sea Peoples, and later again the cultural wave would engulf Egypt and Hellenise it under Alexander.

It is possible that the Tenth Labour refers to the Hyksos or much earlier pre-Hyksos Mycenean /Cretan incursion into the Egyptian Delta, for Egypt was known to be split by opposing cultures in the time of the Pharaoh Narmer, some centuries before the Hyksos.

At the time of the Hyksos invasion, the Egyptian culture was comparatively advanced, having had hieroglyphic writing for several centuries and was already developing hieratic script, a more advanced and esoteric form of writing in some ways.

The Mycenaeans and Cretans it would appear, were less developed in this respect, which may explain the extensive mythological content of the Greek culture (of circa 800 BC and later) which arose from the greater necessity for mythological record in the absence of the means of more "permanent" historical records. The amount of mythology is also of course, related to the exploits of the culture in its development and also is indicative of the nature of the culture in times past. The content of the myths gives some indication of how warlike the culture is and has been in times past.

It is significant that the advanced Egyptian culture was vanquished by Alexander, only when the Greeks had possibly surpassed the cultural attainments of the Egyptians, who were, by that time, an aging culture.

One of the sacred emblems of the Sea God was reputedly, introduced into Egypt by the Hyksos, who provided a brief dynasty of Egyptian Pharaohs. The Tenth Labour may have been the source of a claim by the inhabitants of the Delta, under Tiberius, that others of comparable prowess to Herakles, took his name, but the original bearer of that name, according to Tacitus came from their country.

Arrian, in his "Life of Alexander" describes the latter's visit to the shrine of Ammon (Amen) in Libya. Alexander went to consult the oracle because it was reputedly, infallible. Perseus and Herakles were also reputed to have consulted it, Perseus, when he was sent by Polyducts' to slay the Gorgon, and Herakles, during his journeys in Libya and Egypt in search of Anaeus and Busiris.

In the Gorgon can be seen the same Cretan snake goddess archetype, but in the Delta of Egypt it could represent a Cretan cultural infusion into pre-history Egypt. It is likely that the Mosaic exodus occurred at the end of these Hyksos periods when the Hyksos were expelled from the Delta. The most likely exodus being the expulsion under Ahmose. The mythical red bulls of Geryon probably refer to the followers of the Delta bull cult of the pre-Narmer Red Kingdom of the Delta.

The description of the journey of Herakles, first to the West, as described by the myth, suggests a coastal progression around the Mediterranean, before deep sea techniques had been developed.

Reaching Gibralta, which linked the North to the South coasts of the Mediterranean, would indeed be regarded as a major maritime feat, warranting the erection of sacred pillars marking the boundary of the earth. In the face of the vast Atlantic, it would have appeared as such.

Progress along the North African coast would then be swift, to the unguarded flank of an, as yet, ununified Egypt, though, even at that time, Geryon represented, in mythological terms, "the strongest man alive."

The description of Geryon being a man who divided into three at the waist, with three heads and six arms is a mythological allegory, and vindication of the suggestion that Geryon refers to the epoch of Egyptian history when three kingdoms existed, prior to the unification of the country into two kingdoms of the North and South.

The three kingdoms were, the Red Kingdom of the Delta, the White Kingdom or Middle Kingdom and the Kingdom of the South or Upper Egypt. We see again here the myth using a human archetype to represent a nation or culture, as was the case in the Epic of Gilgamesh.

The same archetype is described in the dream of Babylonian King Nabuchadressa, monarch of a culture derived from the Sumerian. In the dream, a human figure represents the Babylonian culture. (See Chapter 9.) It is of interest to note that in many accounts of dreams in the Bible and elsewhere such as the Epic of Gilgamesh, it is the king, nature's selection by way of valour in battle, aggression, fertility of bloodline, etc., who is visited by dreams which usually have some portent regarding the survival of the culture.

Such dreams may be exclusively presented to cultural leaders by the collective unconscious or to those who can effect or contribute to a culture's survival.

The gorgeous red bulls of Geryon probably represent the populace of the Delta where bull cults existed from the earliest times, as Saqqara has demonstrated. It is known that red oxen sacrifices were made to the chief god of the earliest heliopian cycle of gods, Ptah, at Memphis, as part of the cult of the Apis Bull.

In the second millennium BC, King Suppiluliumas of the Hittites (circa 1380-1340 BC), in correspondence with the king of Kizzuwatna, wrote:

"Now the people of Kizzuwatna are Hittite cattle and have chosen their stable, they have deserted the Hurrian and gone over to my majesty."

This illustrates the contemporary allegory used in communications of the time, probably deriving from the oral tradition which preceded it.

The description of the red oxen may have been associated with the Red Kingdom, placing events in the myth somewhere between the late and middle third millennium BC. The bull cult was a very powerful cult, whose patroness was Hathor. It was extant in Sumeria allied to Ishtar and in Atlantean Crete under various fertility goddesses, but primarily Hekate.

Ptolemy I introduced the Zeus Serapis cult at Memphis in the fourth century BC, clearly to enamour the local populace to the Greek dynasty. By placing the ancient cult under the aegis of Zeus, he maintained continuity and placed it in the heliopian pantheon. This was in accord with the fundamental philosophy of pluralism, characteristic of heliopianism, producing extensive and liberal pantheons which harnessed creativity of many cultures.

Orthus, the fabulous guard dog which Herakles kills with his club, has associations with Anubis, the Egyptian canine god whose duty it was to protect the gods. This also seems to indicate Geryon as Egypt.

Orthus, as well as having two dog's heads, had seven serpent heads or a serpent's tail. The serpent tail seems to indicate the Delta, and the seven heads again points to the "Prince of the Oceans" of Canaanite myth, and indicating Cretan presence in the Delta.

Orthus also lay with his own mother Echidna, a Cretan serpent goddess, and begot the (Egyptian) Sphinx, another association with Egypt. Echidna was half maiden and half (Protosyrian or Mycenean) lioness. It is clear therefore, that some Cretan/Mycenean culture was influential in the formation of what was to become the Egyptian culture as represented by the Sphinx.

The Sphinx was part bull, part lion, part eagle and part man. As has been suggested earlier, the lion stylised by the Nemset headdress of the Pharoah, almost certainly indicates an Anatolian cultural influence, probably Dagon, the lord of the Stars, represented by a lion. This found its way at some point into the Greek mainland as a cultural symbol of Mycenae.

The other major influence was the Sumerian culture. probably as an emigration after the "Flood" and represented as Utnapishtim of the Epic of Gilgamesh.

The Sumerian myth of The Eagle and the Serpent amounts to a description of what was to become the two kingdoms of Ancient Egypt, the eagle representing the Upper Kingdom and the serpent, the Lower or Delta Kingdom.

Sumerian influence in the Egyptian culture was likely the first to be felt, as part of a general westerly migration which started in India or was a result of, or was stimulated by the "Flood", and was probably heliopian in nature. Subsequently, the Atlantean Cretan culture arrived, attempting to settle the Delta, though it is possible that some Cretan settlement had already taken place in the Delta. Eventually, these opposing cultures gave rise to the bi-cultural nature of the Egyptian culture, forcibly united under the later Pharaohs but always unsettled and threatening rupture.

Maintaining this unification was a perennial task of the Egyptian administrations and the Pharaoh as "King of the North and South" and not always without cost and internal strife. This can be witnessed in present day bicultural situations (Ireland and Cyprus etc).

It is likely that the many exoduses throughout the united kingdom period of Egypt were the end result of measures to maintain national unity.

This bi-culturalism can be seen in the Judaic culture subsequent to the Exodus.

The Israelites display bicultural characteristics of heliopianism and monotheism throughout much of their history, manifested also in the two kingdoms of Israel and Judea. (See Chapter 9)

Geryon is killed by a single arrow through his three torsos, this presumably indicating vanquishment of all three kingdoms in a single battle and also seems to indicate a triple alliance between the three kingdoms for the purposes of common defence.

The cattle, presumably the populace, are led away by Herakles. Subsequently Cretan/Mycenean colonisation of the Delta would have resulted, in this case an early pre-Hyksos tidal cultural invasion. It probably pre-dated the conquering of the Delta by Narmer and unification of the county circa 2000 BC.

The latter event is symbolised on the palette of Narmer by the Upper kingdom, as represented by the Eagle, capturing the Lower Kingdom represented by the Serpent.

With the rise of Cretan culture in the middle of the second millennium BC, the (Cretan) Hyksos would return to the Delta (in accordance with the wave theory of culture) to gain ascendency over the Heliopians for a time.

The device used by the heliopians to describe the eternal aspects to which the culture aspired was to have the hero of a saga, representing the culture, to descend to Hades and return, so demonstrating the culture's ability to defeat death. This device, which was adopted by subsequent cultures (for example Christ descending into Hell in the Christian culture) can be seen in the eleventh Labour.

The mechanism was different for the monotheists who used a more characteristically magical solution, which was to invest the ancient Sea God with the ability to bring his daughter, representing a renewed culture of fertility, back to life.

11) The Capture of Cerberus:

The Journey into Hades Some sources would place this labour as the last of Herakles' Labours and the quest for the Golden Apples of Hesperides, as the penultimate, which is probably how the myth was intended originally. This Labour and the twelfth are concerned not with temporal conquest, this having been accomplished over the then known world, but with the (eternal) life of the culture and its maintenance, represented by the hero's conquering of death.

This myth, coming at the end to the sequence of Labours, corresponds to the search for everlasting life by the Sumerian hero Gilgamesh, but the outcome is different. Herakles returns from Hades to become a god, for surely only gods can conquer death. In later cultures, such a feat became the necessary credential of a would-be divinity.

The main objective of this Labour is to capture the black, many headed hounds, that guards the gates of Hades.

There is a similarity between Cerberus and Skylla, the six dog-headed sea creature, daughter of Hekate. Skylla, like her mother, was not, significantly, a member of the Olympian pantheon.

It is related how Skylla stole the kine of Herakles in her mouth where she had death dealing teeth set in tridentine rows. Skylla is most probably an allegory for some warlike culture, probably the ancient Cretan or Egyptian if the tridentine jaws signify the three kingdoms of warriors. Teeth in myths translate as soldiers or warriors.

The allegorical teeth alluding to military attributes and soldiers, were found in the myth of the Golden Fleece and elsewhere.

Cerberus also, like Orthus of the last Labour, had a barbed serpent tail, which also probably alludes to some military characteristic. A similar device is to be found in the relatively modern medieval Dragon myths of Yorkshire. The vanquishers of the Lampton Worm and that of the dragon of Nunnington, both wore a type of spiked armour clearly representing a military force.

On his journey to Hades, Herakles is guided by Hermes, the messenger of the Gods. He is said to have encountered Meleager, one of the heroes of the Caledonian Boar Hunt. He also meets Theseus stuck to the Chair of Forgetfulness and wrenches him free.

Theseus, it would appear, belongs to a later cycle of Greco-Mycenean hero myths and is an embodiment of the culture. This incident may represent an admonishment by the ancients of the need for constant vigilance against cultural lethargy in old age. It is a reminder not to forget the heroic exploits of the culture's past should it become vulnerable and effete in old age. History is still substantially taught, for the most part and rightly so, as an account of the valour of its heroes in battles of times past, presumably so that future generations can emulate and learn from the cultures' history how to survive. Often, to the intelligent observer, this does not appear to be the case because wisdom, learning and leadership appears to be rare in modern statesmanship.

Herakles is the perennial hero, the representative of an eternal culture, an older hero still extant and so selected for godhood. It is little wonder that he was such a popular divinity with the Romans.

Herakles, like Gilgamesh, coerces Charon, the Greek equivalent of Urshanabi, to ferry him across the Styx, "the hateful", the waters of death.

On another level, the imagery of Cerberus and Hades as a place of death, suggests a later struggle between the Mycenean culture and the Cretan, many of such encounters took place.

Theseus, another Olympic hero, possibly represents the moratorium on Mycenean conquest during the second millennium BC when the resurgence of Cretan Minoan culture took place.

Mycenean conquest resumed in the latter half of the second millennium with the Doric ascendency, represented by Theseus, who repeated many of the exploits of Herakles.

Theseus is cast in the epoch of Minoan domination of Athens. He is rescued by Ariadne, King Minos' daughter, from the labyrinth where he had been taken with others to feed the Minotaurus. This suggests he was a hostage, an ancient means of ensuring treaties were kept and tribute paid.

Theseus later became King of Athens and was responsible for the formation of the union of Attic (Athenian) settlements as a federalised Athenian state, a process of consolidation that can be detected in the Heraklion Labours.

Theseus' first wife was Hippolyta, the Amazon queen. This represents an inter-state alliance and a more advanced culture than that depicted in the Labours. The alliance comes to grief with the help of Poseidon (Cretan culture) in the myth of Phaedra, which concerns Theseus' second wife and his son Hippolytus.

One may be tempted to assume that Theseus predates Herakles in so far that he married Hippolyta whom Herakles slew. This would be to fall into the trap of literalism. Hippolyta represents a culture (probably Saxon or Celt) and in that sense is eternal. This culture postdates the Hippolytan culture of Herakles.

Theseus marrying Hippolyta represents a cultural alliance between two cultures.

Ultimately, Herakles seized Cerberus by the throat, and, being protected by his lion skin against the barbed tail, forces the creature to submit. With Athena's help, he is able to recross the Styx back to the world of the living.

Athena, although she was associated at one time with Crete, is seen here as an ally of the hero and eventually became exclusive to the Olympian pantheon which, according to heliopian tradition, incorporated its old enemy, the Sea God, into the pantheon, an indication it seems of a solid consolidation of Crete as part of the Greek heliopian pantheon.

Athena in one myth, is in contest with Poseidon for dominion over Attica. The winner, it was agreed, would be the one who gave the Athenians the most valuable gift. Poseidon struck the Acropolis with his trident and a salt water spring issued from the rock (a feat similar to that performed by Moses in the Judaic tradition). Athena wins by raising an olive tree beside the spring.

It is interesting that the two archetypes involved, water and tree, are both ancient fertility symbols previously often encountered as the water from the never-failing jar, and the tree of life.

The club of Herakles symbolic of his power was made of the wood of the olive. The lion skin, it would appear, was used in ritual as indicated on Egyptian tomb paintings. It was evocative of Dagan, the "Lord of the Stars" and probably symbolised authority or under the protection of the deity in the same manner as the ephod or mantle of Samuel was given to David.

The Lord of the Stars as the head of the Protosyrian pantheon can be traced back to neolithic Anatolia (7100-6300 BC) where, at Catal Huyuk, evidence was found for ritual involving the lion skin.

The depiction on the chapel of the tomb of Seti I (or Sethos), shows the king giving audience to a youth, priest, deity or son, dressed in a leopard skin. Dagon was an early archetype to enter the culture of the Ancient Egyptians.

There are several instances in the Bible where divine authority was bestowed or assumed by the donning of a mantle as we shall see in a later chapter.

Twin headed anthropomorphic pots of the chalcolithic period (6300-4000 BC), reminiscent of the "heroic brothers", Gilgamesh and Enkidu, were found at Hacilar. These clues may support the contention that the Southern and Eastern Mediterranean cosmogonies were in competition with the monotheistic culture for possession of the new Northern Mediterranean territories, as seems to be indicated by the myths. This of course would be the normal pattern of things in the ancient cultural struggle.

12)   The Golden Apples of the Hesperides

It is probable that, as some sources claim, this Labour was the penultimate, for in its symbolism we see a brief period of Mycenean culture as upholder of the earthly universe. It was to be replaced, once again, by the Atlantean culture, represented by Atlas. Whilst the perennial fertility culture will once more regain supremacy as the Mycenean culture declines, the fruit of the Gods is secured.

This ancient symbol of knowledge and enlightenment will again bear effulgent fruit in renaissances of Hellenistic culture after dark eclipses. This would lead naturally to the final Labour in which the hero defeats death, symbolised by his journey to Hades and his return to become eternal in the company of the Gods. Unlike the Sumerian Gilgamesh, the Greek culture is reborn in a later great age of Mycenean expansion in the mid-second millennium BC, again in the first millennium BC and again in the mid-second millennium AD. This triple renaissance is unique in all the heliopian cosmogonies and is testament to what became the Classical Age (of Greece), but more so, to the Helipian philosophy of the ancients.

The garden of the Hesperides was a gift from the ancient Earth Goddess Gaia to Hera (Crete) on her marriage to Zeus (Mycenae). It was guarded by Ladon, the serpent son of Phorkys (the Sea God) and Keto.

The Hesperides were said by some to be the daughters of Atlas, which presents another link with Crete.

It is likely that Hera represented the unhappy or jealous Crete in the union of Mycenean and Cretan culture. Herakles, with the help of Nereus, another form of the old Sea God, slew the serpent and obtained the apples.

In an alternative version of the myth, Atlas volunteers to obtain the apples if Herakles will take over the holding up of the Heavens, to which, Herakles consents, having been warned by Nereus that Atlas may make some excuse not to resume his divine task. Herakles, when Atlas refuses to resume his burden, asks the Titan to hold the heavens whilst he dons his hat as protection. Atlas is fooled into taking back his burden and Herakles departs with the apples. This trick invests Herakles with an intelligence not hitherto displayed in the Hero, the emphasis being on physical prowess required for the survival of a young culture. This would be in keeping with an ageing culture forced to use guile in mature years. This attribute was put to great effect by Homer later, embodied by the great hero Ulysses.

Maybe this aspect of the myth is indicative of the fact that this labour should truly have been the penultimate, where the hero is invested with a human (i.e., divine) attribute in preparation for his being accepted into the company of the gods. This being achieved when he conquered death in what would seem fitting, the last labour.

One may recall that in Hittite myth, Upelluri, an Atlas figure, complains that a diorite pillar-god hurts his right shoulder. In the heavenly pantheon, it would seem, there is a troublesome Cretan pillar culture.

In a sense, this myth could be, fittingly, the final labour of the cycle, for it represents, again, following the last labour, Mycenean hegemony over Crete, though not an end to the struggle.

In the myth of Perseus and the Medusa, we see the hero as representative of Greco-Mycenean culture in a later epoch, since he is aided by Athena, now patroness of the Dorian-Mycenean Greeks.

It is significant that in this myth Perseus is told that he would find the Medusa in Africa. This substantiates the assertion that Cretan culture invaded the Egyptian Delta as Medusa is clearly a Cretan archetype. Her being in Africa suggests an earlier than Perseus occupation.

When Perseus arrives in the desert, he finds a colony of gorgons, all asleep, "surrounded by weatherworn images of petrified men", presumably, stone images of gods and pharaohs. It is easy to see, given the Ancient Egyptian proclivity for stone carving, that the myth is referring to an ancient Egyptian-Cretan culture that held the serpent sacred and literally turned men into stone. This state of advanced art would be held in awe by less developed cultures. The serpent of course was the symbol of the Delta and Lower Kingdom.

If Perseus represents a post-Heraklion epoch, though some say he founded Mycenae, then we again see the process of cultural tide in action.

The sleeping gorgons represent the Delta inhabitants in a state of military unpreparedness. Perseus, the Mycenean or Greek culture, with his shield given to him by Athena, who also guided him as he kept his back to the Medusa, cuts off the Gorgon's head with a sickle.

One may consider a sickle a strange weapon in the context, but it indicates a cultural struggle and has a fitting mythical effect, as it is an ancient archetype of celestial power, an instrument of the gods, instanced in the Hittite and Greek cycles of early myths concerning the usurpation of the heliopian pantheon. The sickle was also carried by some of the Sea Peoples.

Perseus, who was given winged sandals by Hermes, which may imply a fleet, and a helmet by Hades which made him invisible, has to don the helmet in order to escape the sister gorgons, awakened by the Medusa's children. On his return journey, his is forced to use the head of the Medusa to change various adversaries into stone, in his hunt for Andromeda.

The tone of this myth has the characteristics of a surprise expeditionary force. The fast fleet, the shield, a small protecting force, the not showing the face, and sleeping enemy suggest a short camouflaged or night campaign to take the king or pharaoh of the Delta.

The waking sisters suggest a large federalised union (in the same family) which is quickly mobilised, forcing a rapid retreat of the hero.

The myth has similarities with the Tenth Labour which saw Herakles "stealing" the bulls of Geryon, that is indicating a raid, rather than a major campaign. This fits with the known facts that Egypt was too large and mighty a power to suffer from a sea borne assault from a smaller adversary.

The twin cultures of Egypt were successful in repelling would be invaders and succumbed in later periods to later waves of the initial invading culture, the Hyksos. Eventually, these were also ejected from Ancient Egypt under Kamose and his son Ahmose, the latter, the likely pharaoh of the Judaic Exodus.

(Ka-mose has similar roots to Moses, as does probably 'mases' as in Ra-mases and is likely a common royal title. Ka was in Ancient Egyptian, part of the spirit. This points to the fact that Moses or Mases held some royal association and could have been a likely candidate for the throne. In his efforts to secure such an ambition, a civil war ensued followed by an exodus by the vanquished tribes. This is possibility is investigated in another chapter).

This chapter has endeavoured to show how the myths, as instruments to preserve pre-historical events of cultural development, were used to record, in characteristically bizarre images, early interactions of the Cretan, Mycenean and Southern Mediterranean cultures from which the Mycenean-Dorian state emerged and consolidated.

The great achievement of the ancients was to discover and utilise, in the event of the absence of the written word, the archetypal memory of the individual and hence the collective unconscious of the culture. This indicates a stunning knowledge of human psychology in those far off days.

Many myths have been omitted which would throw light on several similar and other aspects of the emergent culture. A study of the myths together with the latest archaeological knowledge could also help in unravelling the true sequence of the myths which are not tied, for various reasons, to a real time scale.

The next chapter investigates how the young northern culture expanded east and south, providing the cultural tide line for the next swell under Alexander.

References Chapter 7

[1] 'The first world survey of human cultures in early times', Dawn of Civilisation, ed. S. Piggot et al, page 230

[2] J. Gray, Near Eastern Mythology, page 141

[3] M. Wood, In Search of the Trojan War, page 218

[4] C. Kerenyi, The Gods of the Greeks, page 31

[5] ibid, page 30

[6] ibid, page 29

[7] J. V. Luce, The End of Atlantis, page 42

[8] C. Kerenyi, The Gods of the Greeks, page 23

[9] ibid, page 161

[10] ibid, page 161

[11] ibid, page 93

[12] ibid, page 94

[13] ibid, page 105

[14] ibid, page 14

[15] ibid, page 198

[16] ibid, page 199

[17] Homer, The Odyssey, Trans E. V. Rieu, pages 50, 52 and 61

[18] Ibid, page 55

[19] ibid, page 70

[20] ibid, page 62

[21] Homer, The Iliad, Trans E. V. Rieu, page 218

[22] Ibid, page 214 and 215

[23] N. K. Sandars, The Epic of Gilgamesh, page 88

[24] C. Kerenyi, The Gods of the Greeks, pages 38 and 39

[25] Ibid, page 199

[26] Ibid, page 175

[27] Ibid, page 162

[28] Ibid, page 163

[29] Ibid, page 201

[30] Ibid, page 77

[31] Ibid, page 26

[32] Ibid, page 38

[33] Ibid, page 163

[34] Ibid, page 36

[35] Ibid, page 26

[36] Ibid, page 24

[37] Ibid, page 37

[38] Ibid, page 49

[39] Ibid, page 56

[40] Ibid, page 163

[41] D. M. Field, Greek and Roman Mythology, page 124

[42] Atlas of Ancient Archaeology, Ed. J. Hawkes, page 122

[43] J. Mellaart, The Archaeology of Ancient Turkey

[44] N. K. Sandars, The Sea Peoples

[45] D. M. Field, Greek and Roman Mythology, page 140

[46] E. Pagel, The Gnostic Gospels, page XX

[47] C. Kerenyi, The Gods of the Greeks, page 97

[48] ibid, page 163

[49] Homer, The Iliad, Trans. E. V. Rieu, page 83

[50] E. Hamilton, Mythology, page 165

Chapter 8
The Cultural Symmetry of Opposites

The myth of the Golden Fleece is possibly a story of the earliest Dorian-Mycenean expansion, for it portrays an organised sea-going military force, not, as yet, with the capability for deep sea going, but developed enough to undertake long coastal voyages. Mycenean maritime skills would have existed in the form of voyager explorers, as can be seen in the Tenth Labour of Herakles and the Perseus myths.

A similar pattern of naval development can be seen in the medieval navies of Spain and Britain. It is clear though, that the Cretan Atlanteans of archaic times were capable of maritime exploitation of the Mediterranean.

Herakles appears in the myth as a contemporary of Jason, as he did with Theseus. This was probably done for psychological reasons, as Herakles was in fact a much older archetype. The myth probably describes events much earlier than circa 1300 BC when an Attica federation was likely to exist[1] and which, the Argonauts possibly represent.

The saga relates how the heroes set out to find the fabled golden fleece which hung in a grove in Colchis on the present-day Georgian/Armenian shore of the Black Sea, guarded by a serpent.

The ram and serpent are both archetypes of the Cretan monotheistic Sea God fertility culture, and the golden fleece is also a feature of the ancient fertility ram of Ur, which provides a cultural link between the cultures of the Flood.

The ram had carried Phrixus and Helle, the children of Athamas and Nephele, a cloud spirit, out of harm's way to Colchis, but Helle, unfortunately, fell off at the Dardanelles or the Hellespont.

Ino, the second wife of Athamas, had plotted to kill the children by bribing messengers from the Delphinian Oracle, to claim that the children be sacrificed to save the land from famine, brought about by Ino herself.

The mythical allegory of famine and drought of military subjugation is evident. The threatening invading force represented by Ino and her allies is possibly Thracian, for she was the nurse of Dionysus and at Lemnos, the first port of call, the Argonauts were at first thought to be enemies from Thrace, which clearly was at that time, a regional force.

It would appear that the intrigue by Ino accomplished something, for Pelias, Jason's uncle, usurps his father, the son of Athamas, the rightful heir. Jason himself would have been killed, but was put under the protection of Chiron, the wise centaur, half man and half horse, a Cretan archetype, who was also the protector of Achilles the Cretan.

The myth refers to an epoch approaching the Trojan War, for a state of animosity existed between the Greeks and Trojans the latter, of whom it has been assumed, were Hittites.

The heroes have to pass the Hellespont guarded at night by the Trojans. The quest is undertaken because Pelias claims the country is afflicted with curse which will not be lifted, nor his rule ended, until the golden fleece is returned.

This is a similar circumstance which arose in Rome with the Sibyline Books. In the latter, the cult of Demeter, the fertility goddess, had to be brought to Rome in order to deliver the city from Hannibal, the Carthaginian.

The golden fleece and its associated serpent are archetypes common to the Cretan monotheism, and the myth of the fleece relates how, with foreign assistance, a culturally allied race in present day Amenia, the Greek usurper is despatched.

Following such a strategic alliance with Colchis, a probable adversary of the Trojans, the scene would be set for a battle for supremacy between the two major powers of the North and Eastern Mediterranean, the Trojans and the Greeks.

The golden fleece, hanging on a tree in the sacred grove, guarded by a serpent, has unmistakable Sumerian cultural symbolism and aligns closely with the so called "ram in the thicket" found at Ur by Wooley. It was in fact, a ram erectus associated with, or guarding, the golden Tree of Life.

The serpent would be Ningizzida, the Lord of the Tree of Life, an archetype which found its way into Greek culture associated with the gods of healing, Askelepios and Hygeia, often shown next to a tree on which a serpent is entwined.

The quest for the golden fleece appears therefore like the events of the Sibyline Books, an appeal to the return of ancient cultural beliefs.

By the late 17th century BC, any amity between Babylon and Hattusa had evaporated and in 1600 BC, Mursili I, the Hittite king, sacked Babylon, after the previous Hittite kings, Labarna I and II had united the Hittite city states between 1680 and 1620 BC[2] in a process which must have been similar and contemporary with that which occurred on the Mycenean mainland. From thence, the Hittite Empire was expanding until Suppiluliuma I (circa 1388-1348 BC), with an almost Aztec sounding name, controlled most of Asia Minor and would likely be looking north and west for further expansion. Mursili I inexplicably withdrew from Babylon, an event similar to the sudden withdrawal from Rome by the Carthaginian Hannibal in the Sibyline Books affair.

The Carthaginian culture, according to mythology, was derived from the Anatolian-Levantine culture. Phrixus and Helle have a duality that matches Mycenean and Dorian Greece, and may have been the archetypal Gemini twins who were, in early times, depicted as a boy and a girl. Their fleeing to Colchis may have signalled some sort of Thracian ascendancy represented by Ino the nurse of Dionysus, who possibly signified the Thracian culture, a culture renowned for its equine prowess.

Dionysus was later to become a powerful god in the Greek pantheon and was often associated with lion skin clad satyrs, symbols which displayed at the same time the relatively primitive Thracians and their fertility prone culture.

A similar figure called Bes was to be found in Egypt, suggesting the figure may have been imported via Crete, or some allied culture.

The lion skins are redolent of a Heraklion aspect and may allude to Mycenean or Anatolian links with Thracian culture, in the case of the latter, passing the Hellespont would have been doubly hazardous for the Argonauts.

On his return to Greece, Jason has only one sandal, much to the alarm of Pelias, for he lost one helping an old woman, who turned out to be Hera, to cross a river. Hera, Zeus' powerful consort, probably representing an alliance with Crete, was like Demeter or Sibyl and Ishtar, a fertility goddess, of similar beauty to Athena and Aphrodite according to the myth of the Judgement of Paris.

The clue as to why a missing sandal should so alarm Pelias may lie in the ancient Hittite myth of the Missing God, who put his sandals on "the wrong feet" for it portended mythical famine and drought, that is, military vanquishment, a suitable cause for Pelias' concern.

A sculpture commissioned by a Syrian merchant depicts Aphrodite holding a slipper or sandal, assisted by Eros, warding off the advances of a satyr. The sandal has clearly some powerful significance.

In Qaballistic philosophy, the sandal is the symbol of the lowest sphere of the celestial spheres, and represents the earth, the sphere of the sub-human satyrs.

The fact that the hedonistic Dionysus ultimately joined the Hellenistic pantheon indicates that Thrace became part of the Dorian Greek hegemony, a powerful force in what was becoming a strategic encirclement of the Hittite Empire.

The exploits of the Argonauts are in the heroic Greek heliopian tradition of Herakles, Theseus and Perseus.

After successfully negotiating the Hellespont, the heroes arrived at the land of the Dolonians in time to take part in the wedding feast of King Cyzicus, a son of Aeneas, a Hittite vassal possibly. The argonauts are attacked by six-handed giants and on returning to the shore, after driving them off, are again attacked, this time by the Dolonians, who do not recognise them or more likely, recognise them as enemy Greeks, and Cyzicus is killed.

Following this, an incident occurs which describes the rivalries that exist, for Herakles proposes a rowing race against Jason which he wins and which, must have undermined the leader's authority.

Putting in for repairs to Herakles's broken oar, Jason is persuaded to leave without him, for Herakles is searching for Hylas, his youthful companion. Hylas however, is drawn under water by a nymph, who saw the rosy flush of his beauty and wished to kiss him.

On the island of Bebryos, the heroes are obliged to enter boxing matches with King Amycus, who Pollux fells. The heroes next encounter the blind King Phineus, plagued by the Harpies whom Calais and Zetes, the sons of the North Wind, put to flight.

These representatives of some northern culture are killed by Herakles for urging Jason to depart without him. Next, on the advice of Phineus, a dove is sent through the Symplegades, dangerous clashing rocks which crushed boats, and which represent some powerful enemy territory.

Following the dove, which lost only a tail feather, presages a successful passage with only minor damage, the heroes eventually reach the Island of Ares where the Stymphalian Birds had taken refuge.

The dove and the Stymphalian Birds appearing in sequence, suggest some subterfuge of disguise or scouting party, to gain access to the territory of the Stymphalian Birds.

In a similar manner to the Heraklion Labour, the birds are driven off. This is done by creating a din by the beating of shields. This show of strength, was a standard form of psychological warfare instanced in the Bible, and was employed by Caesar on occasions in Gaul.

From the Island of Ares, the argonauts recruit two new members, the sons of Phrixus, shipwrecked there on their way back to Greece.

Finally, the heroes reach Colchis where King Aietes, the son of Helios, the Sun God, though mostly identified with the opposite and counterpart of Helios[3], requires Jason to yoke fire-breathing bulls to plough the fields. The fire-breathing bulls is a mythological allegory of some army which Jason has to subdue, they may even allude to the Tauri or Shardana one of the contingents of the "Sea Peoples" who wore battle helmets with bull's horns, indicative of some Istarian fertility cult.

Jason has to sow the fields with serpent's teeth which immediately spring up into armed warriors. Jason defeats them by hurling a (sacred) stone into their midst.

This part of the myth has similar symbolism to the myth of Kadnus, the legendary founder of the Greek Thebes. Kadnus was the brother of Europa and the son of Harmonia and Ares suggesting southern Mediterranean origin, or possibly Hurrian. He too defeats the Serpent of Ares (Crete?) which guarded a sacred stream and sowed its teeth which became warriors into whose internecine fighting, he flung a rock.

Such symbolism, as we have seen, appears in the Mesopotamian myth of Marduk the Sun God defeating Tiamat, the Sea Serpent (Crete).

Cadmus was also a descendant of Io, an early paramour of Zeus, who has been identified with Isis.[4]

Mythologically, there are cultural links between Crete, Egypt and Caucasian Colchis, semitic Armenia. It is perhaps worth noting, that part of the Islamic Hag ritual, the pilgrimage to Mecca, the faithful have to run seven times past two mountains and cast stones against pillars to ward off the powers of evil. Perhaps this is a remnant of the Sumerian culture, where the two mountains represent the Mashu mountains, portals of the Sumerian heaven.

The pillars would correspond to the "flood" forces of the Sacred Pillar Culture of Crete.

In any event, it instances the Archetypal Memory in action. Islam and Judaism were never the best of friends and it is argued later that the inception of Islam was a direct result of the ascendency of the ancient monotheistic forces, particularly, the filial culture of Judaism, Christianity.

Jason, with the help of Medea, the king's daughter, who ensures the serpent guardian is asleep, steals the golden fleece.

In another version of the myth, Athena has to rescue Jason who is devoured by the serpent, that is, the heroes have to be liberated from some southern military cultural forces.

In essence, both versions are the same, as Medea, like the biblical Delilah and Athena, is the key to the removal of the Golden Ram locks.

Medea, whose reputation as a sorceress proves useful to Jason, after many encounters, on the return journey in Crete, Talos, a troublesome bronze giant is dispatched. Talos probably represents rebels or alien invaders (an archetype previously encountered) and is creating havoc thrice daily on the island by burning and throwing stones.

Apparently, like Achilles, Talos' weakness is his vulnerable ankle, which proves his undoing.

Finally, the Argonauts arrive back at Iolcus and an unwilling Pelias. Medea, pretending to be Artemis, is allowed to enter the city, where she persuades Pelias' daughters to cut their father into pieces. and boil him in a cauldron which would return his youth. This seems like a palace coup and a division of the kingdom. This incident comes immediately after the intervention of Apollon, who saves the Argonauts from a storm, an allegory for battle possibly.

Even in this early age, it is no surprise to find the cauldron associated with the return of youth or rebirth. The struggled between Apollon and Herakles for possession of the sacred tripod, the symbol of the power to be reborn or eternal life, is an allegory for the cultural struggle for survival or ascendency between the Anatolian and Greek cultures.

The cauldron was a common Gnostic archetype.

Herakles makes the journey to Hades and returns with the cauldron, the vessel of the Sun. He is reborn by demonstrating power over death, and eventually therefore, is made a god.

This allegorical defeat of death by the hero as representing the culture, became the hallmark of godhood and was a feature of many heroic Greek heliopian sagas.

Under Roman heliopianism it became a necessary part of the mythology of Christ for the religion to be acceptable.

By inference, the gods, representing the culture, by their longevity, had achieved immortality in the face of repeated assaults by the usurping autocratic monotheistic forces.]

The cauldron was a symbol of the Philosophy of Alchemy, among whose earliest writers were Zosimos (3rd century AD) and Democritus (1st century BC), though references are made to archaic figures.[5]

In the Golden Fleece saga, with its strong veins of intrigue, Pelias is deposed. The death of the unfortunate Jason, who did not become king, hints at intrigue, for in a Sophoclean situation, he contemplates suicide in the shadow of his old boat, the Argo, and is killed when the (serpent?) prow falls on him.

He is romantically, in a sense, a captain going down with his ship.

Such times of intrigue form the background to the next phase of Mycenean-Dorian Greek expansion across the Eastern and Southern Mediterranean, culminating in the cataclysmic Trojan War, the vanquishing of the great Anatolian power, the Hittite Empire with the destruction of Hatussas.

Rameses III wrote in 1194 BC:

"The foreign countries made a conspiracy in their islands (or the lands of the north were agitated). No land could stand before their arms, from Hatti (the Hittites), Allepo, Carchemish, Arzawa and Alasiya (Cyprus) on being cut off at one time (cut off one at a time)"[6].

Assuming Ahhiyawa, that is, Thrace and Caucasian Colchis, were now allies of Greece, then the Greek forces represent almost total encirclement, a classic pincer movement of mainland Anatolia and the Hittite kingdom.

It is known that the last Hittite king, Suppiluliuma II (circa 1255-1195 BC), had engaged in action with the (pre-) Assyrians, and Cyprus had either revolted or been taken by the Sea Peoples.[7]

With the Assyrians hostile to Hatussas, the circle would be complete.

The encirclement would not be simply a union of disparate states, but a unified culture, deriving for the most part, from the Dorian-Mycenean, itself, an amalgam of Cretan, Hittite and Mesopotamian.

By 1200 BC, Mycenean settlements were already established on the Canaanite coast. The stealing of the golden fleece, which must have had the same cultural effect as Trajan's looting of the Temple of Jerusalem, would not have improved relations between Hurrian Hittites and Mycenae. The manner of stealing is oddly reflected in a strange symmetry by the legendary immediate cause of the Trojan War, that was, the stealing in Greek eyes of Menelaus' wife Helen by Trojan son of Priam, Paris. Paris possibly represented a Hittite vassal. He was described by Lucian as a mountain dweller from Phrygia, i.e., Anatolia.[8]

It would seem, though possible, the abduction of Helen, would hardly have provoked and international war if Homer's account is taken literally.

A further clue as the real cause of the war may lie in the "Judgement of Paris", a popular theme with artists and symbol smiths throughout the ages, itself thought to be the original cause of the Trojan war.[9]

At a banquet on Mount Olympus, Eris or Strife (appropriately), threw a golden apple among the company of Gods which was "for the fairest." There were three claimants, Hera, Athena and Aphrodite. Zeus summoned Paris, to award the apple.

Aphrodite had promised to obtain for Paris, the most beautiful woman alive and, as a consequence, was given the apple. Subsequently, with Aphrodite's help, Helen of Argos was abducted to Troy by Paris.

Accordingly, when this is translated from the literal, it is plain that the outbreak of hostilities between the two cultures was about a territorial seizure or annexation, a common cause of conflict.

Helen represents some prize possession or ally under Mycenean hegemony, and, as Venus was awarded the apple of strife, this was probably the island of Cyprus of which she was patroness and which was one of the first to fall to the invaders.

Cyprus was rich in copper, a valuable commodity in those days and was traditionally, part of the Cretan (Sea God's) heritage.

Possession of Cyprus was disputed under Suppiluliuma II, who had regained possession after the rebellion or occupation, in a sea battle, according to a tablet found at Hatussas.[10]

Cyprus, even today, is a chestnut of contention between Greek and Turk and provides another example of an archaic cultural dispute and the relative immutability of cultures.

The Iliad and Aeneid are characteristically more detailed in the narrative as the language of the poet approaches the recorded history of the observer, leaving the glades of pure mythology of the storyteller and seer, the formulators of the symbolism.

Another reason for the voluminous nature of the epic poems was the enormity of the events they describe. They are the records of some momentous shifting of cultural power, events as important in those days and that sphere of the known world as the Great War was to contemporary geo-politics.

This then is a reason for discounting the fact that the whole Mycenean-Greek might would be focussed on a small Anatolian coastal town designated by Schliemann as Troy.

The length of the conflict, ten years, though the action of the Iliad covers only fifty days[11], whether in temporal or cultural time, represents a considerable period, and, if one assumes that the Trojans, as the Iliad describes, were equal in valour and guile to the Mycenaeans (which is usually the case in similarly advanced cultures), then another meaning must to be sought for the explanation of the battle being won by a simple ploy of a "Wooden Horse."

The horse, as we have seen, was a Cretan-Mycenean archetype associated with the Sea God and the Wooden Horse in poetic terms represents a cultural penetration of the Anatolian mainland culture.

This was shown to be the case by interpretations of ancient Sumerian and Hurrian-Hittite myths. A sixth century BC Greek vase painting depicts this, the Trojan (Mycenean) Horse followed by the Cretan Swan confronting and penetrating the Protosyrian (Anatolian) lion, a scene that speaks volumes of the necessary contemporary form of communication as well as the effectiveness of the medium.

A major Greek penetration of the Hittite culture is illustrated by the striking resemblance of parts of the Nesian (Hittite) language with the Greek[12], indicative of some past commerce and/or occupation of the country.

Hittite hieroglyphs read uniquely, alternately left to right and right to left in a similar manner to early Greek inscriptions from the Ionian coast.

It is known that the Achaians, the Homeric Greeks, wrote their diplomatic letters in Hittite cuneiform.[13]

There is also a close relationship among case endings between Hittite, Greek and Roman[14] all of which, as the myths infer, indicate Hittite influences in the Greek and Roman.

This may not be surprising, if we are to believe the mythology of the Aeneid, which narrates the exodus of the defeated Trojans, culminating in the founding of the Roman culture.

Another epic wandering is embodied in the Odyssey of Homer which could be interpreted as the spreading by exploration of the post war Mycenean culture.

In historical terms, the league of peoples comprising Homer's Achaians, the invading Greeks, were probably what have become known as the Sea Peoples. This was the name given by the Ancient Egyptians to the invaders who had threatened Egypt on at least three occasions[15] during the reigns of Rameses II (circa 1280 BC) Merenptah (circa 1210 BC) and Rameses III (circa 1180 BC).

They were a league of peoples called by the Egyptians, Sherden, Weshesh, Shekelesh, Aqaiwasha, Tjekeryn, Turska, Lukka, Danuna and Pulisati. The latter have been identified with the Biblical Philistines, natives of Crete, whose distinctive headdress was an imitation of the feathered headdress of the fertility goddess of Crete.

Pulisati pottery has similarities with Mycenean pottery, as one would expect, and Mycenean settlements existed on the coast of Canaan, Philistine country, at that time. (circa 1280 BC)

The Aqaiwasha practised circumcision like the Israelites, the practice served two functions, as a fertility rite, rendering the male member more like a serpent a Cretan archetype and also as a shibboleth, a means of identification against alien infiltration.

The Pulisati joined the Sea Peoples against the Egyptians. Rameses III makes mention of a "Tursha of the Sea" which may be a reference to the legendary Teucer of the Aeneid and Iliad.

It was on Teucer's recommendation that Dido of Carthage befriended the Trojan refugees.[16]

"Well do I mind me how in days gone by there came to Sidon, one, Teucer, who having been banished from his country, sought help from Belus, that he might find a kingdom for himself. And it chanced that in those days, Belus my father, had newly conquered the land of Cyprus. From that day did I know the tale of Troy and thy name also (Aeneus) and the chiefs of Greece. Also I remember that Teucer spake honourably of the men of Troy saying that he was himself sprung of the old Teucerian stock."

It would seem that Belus, whose name indicates the Canaanite culture, was part of the Sea Peoples who had seized Cyprus. Teucer of the Iliad, after the war, returned to Salamis then migrated to Cyprus[17], presumably to a kingdom.

Teucer, according to Virgil, was from the Caucasus[18], which may explain his empathy for the Trojans.

The main thrust of the Sea Peoples seems to have begun about the time when relationships between the two great Mediterranean powers, the Hittites and Egyptians, were at their worst, contemporary with, or just after, the epic battle of Kadesh. This of course would make strategic sense.

According to Rameses III's inscription at Medinet Habu, the invasions were the work of an organised alliance which proved to be a formidable force against which, few, including the Hittites, could stand and testifies to a necessary cultural unity.

The inscription continues:

"A camp was set up in one place in Amurru or Amor. They devastated its people and its land was like that which has never come into being. They were advancing on Egypt (after burning Hattusa) whilst the flame was being prepared for them. Their league was the Puliset, Tjeker, Shekelesh, Denyen and Weshesh united lands. They laid their hands upon the lands to the very circuit of the earth (to the eastern and western boarders of Egypt (a similar pincer movement to the encirclement of the Hittite empire), their hearts confident and trusting…I organised my frontier in Djahi…I caused the river mouth (the Delta) to be prepared like a strong wall with war ships, transports and merchantmen."

The ruthless and destructive nature of the invaders laying waste to lands was clearly abhorrent to the civilised Egyptians and against the accepted conventions of warfare.

A naval battle took place in the Nile Delta as well as a battle on land. The naval battle was a decisive victory for the Egyptians.

Is this where the mythological truth of the Odyssey meets historical fact?

In the episode of Odysseus' encounter with the Egyptians, suggested by some sources[19] and evident in mythological interpretation, it seems so.

According to the Odyssey[20]:

"On the fifth day we (Odysseus and crew) reached the great river of Egypt, and there in the Nile, I brought my curved ships to. And now I ordered my good men to stay by the ships on guard while I sent out some scouts to reconnoitre from the heights. But these ran amok and in a trice, carried away by their own violence, they plundered some of the fine Egyptian farms, borne off the women and children and killed the men. The hue and cry soon reached the city and the townsfolk roused by the alarm, turned out at dawn. The whole place was filled with infantry and chariots and the glint of arms.

Zeus the "thunderer" struck abject panic into my party. Not a man had the spirit to stand up to the "enemy" for we were threatened on all sides. They ended by cutting down a large part of my force and carrying off the survivors to work for them as slaves."

This scene or similar is shown on the walls at Medinet Habu.

The narration continues:

"I quickly doffed my fine helmet, let the shield drop from my shoulder and threw away my spear, then I ran to the king's chariot and embraced his knees, moved to pity, he spared my life…I passed seven years in the country and made a fortune out of the Egyptians who were liberal with me, one and all. But in the eighth, I fell in with a rascally Phoenician who had already done a great deal of mischief in the world…he put me on board a ship bound for Libya…in order that he might sell me for a handsome sum."

As well as the Aeneid, cultural evidence exists for links between Anatolia and Libya. Similar steles of a god holding a child (which appear as Zeus and Ganymede or Hermes and Dionysus in the Roman culture) depicted at Hittite Yazilikaya, can also be found at Tanis in Libya. It is interesting to note that the trait of Royal Hospitality afforded to the Biblical Abraham by the Egyptians, can be seen centuries later with Odysseus.

One of the last tablets composed at Ugarit on coastal Northern Syria, describes the King desperately seeking information as to the situation in and around Cyprus from his father the King of Alashia (Cyprus). Enemy ships had been sited off the Lycian (Anatolian) coast between Ugarit and Cyprus. He describes towns in his kingdom burnt whilst his troops are deployed in Hittite territory, presumably helping the Hittites who are also under attack. Shortly thereafter, before the tablet could be fired, the city was burnt. The signs of internal dissent inside Anatolia had been present for some time and the confederacy of states had recently suffered a civil war in 1286 BC[21]. Under Amuanda III (circa 1235-25 BC), Egypt, under Merneptah, in 1235 BC had sent grain ships "to keep alive the land of Hatti" as the Hittite Empire was known.

All of this indicates a ripeness for conspiracy and the possibility of a coup from a young burgeoning northern confederacy.

Although it would appear that temporal causes instigated the Trojan War, the underlying cause was cultural as the Wooden Horse of Troy indicates. A closer examination shows the underlying cause was the old cultural enmity between the primordial pillar (serpent) culture and the heliopian cosmogeny. This aligns with the cultural pincer movement that evolved around Hattusa.

Although the Greeks ultimately were a heliopian culture, it was initially under the influence of Crete and Sea God monotheism. Anatolian and Sumerian influences and a process of cultural absorption eventually led them to become diviocratic.

In the myth of Prometheus, the bringer of fire to the human race (war? cf Rameses III "preparing of fire") Zeus is, naturally, outraged at his disclosing the secret of fire to mankind, and punishes him by suspending him in bonds at the highest point of the Caucasus, nailed there by Hephaistos. It was told that Zeus bound the cunning Titan with special chains and drove a "pillar" through him in the middle.

An eagle tore at his immortal liver during the day, which grew again at night. Herakles killed the eagle and he was released after 30,000 years, and was bound to keep the secret.[22]

There was a clear delineation of the Cretan-Atlantean Empires stretching to the Caucasus in the east, the scene of the myth of the golden fleece and other places, one of which was the Delta of Egypt with its infusion of serpent culture. Herakles, as we have seen, played a major part in the formation of the heliopian Mycenean culture, defeating (like Teshub, Baal, Gilgamesh, Marduk and Ra), the serpent, the cultural adversary, the Apophis of Cretan domination.

He was an extremely popular deity among the Trojan derived culture, the Romans.

As a child Herakles strangled two serpents that entered his cradle.

The Mycenean heliopian culture was none the less imbued with the Atlantean fertility culture, always a powerful influence represented in the classical Greek cosmogony as Poseidon the Sea God.

In Roman mosaics, the Sea God as Neptune can be seen holding a cornucopia of fruitfulness in the presence of a stole-arched goddess, a classic pose of his associated fertility goddess, with phallic allusions. On other occasions, he is represented by his six-horsed sea chariot which is bearing his associated goddess and consort.

The horse is a potent religious symbol of power with sexual connotations. The horse at that time, was revered as a powerful extension of armoury.

The sacred pillar of Poseidon in the Atlantean myth was clearly phallic, and often such sacred pillars were shaped as such. It was probably also the prototype of the obelisk. It was anointed with newly slaughtered bull's blood, a ritual which echoed primitive fertility beliefs.

In the Mycenean and Roman myths however, the use of actual blood seems to have been replaced with the symbolic wine. (A refinement later added to early Christian ritual no doubt to satisfy the sensibilities of the civilised Romans.)

In the Homeric texts on the death of Patrocolus, ritual wine is referred to as "flaming wine", the same reference that can be found in Hittite literature.[23]

In the Aeneid, Virgil refers to the same ritual[24] linking Rome with ancient Anatolia.

The use of real blood is therefore not generally characteristic of the advanced heliopian tradition, though some cults in Rome involved the actual slaughter of bulls and ritual use of their blood, but these were mainly cults, as one would expect, devoted to some fertility goddess such as Demeter.

Early Judaic tradition shows the same ritual use of blood of a slaughtered animal, if one considers for example, the Passover ritual of daubing blood, significantly, on the door pillars of the Israelites in Egypt. It seems also to be confirmed by the Greek myths of the house of Atreus to whom Agamemnon, instrumental in bringing about the exodus from Troy, belonged.

Agamemnon was a descendant of Tantalus, a king of Lydia on mainland Anatolia, and according to some accounts, a son of Zeus.[25] Here again is mythological indication of Anatolian cultural influence in the Greek.

Tantalus offended the Gods by inviting them to dinner and, not having enough food, served them his own son Pelops. All but the Anatolian goddess Demeter, in her grief, noticed, and were horrified. Demeter ate Pelop's shoulder causing Tantalus to be punished by the gods. He was suspended over a lake with celestial fruit above him. When he wished to eat or drink, the sustenance receded.

It is clear that the myth is concerned, as is usually the case, with territorial claims. Pelops probably represents the Mycenean mainland to which he gave his name. The archetypal shoulder, as we have seen, appeared in the Hittite myth of Upelluri, Atlas, who bore on his shoulder, the diorite pillar. The pillar represented the Atlantean culture of Crete. Demeter, who possibly represents the culture of Anatolia or the fertility culture of Crete, in eating the shoulder of

Pelops, has annexed some part of the Peloponnese, upsetting the celestial cultural order. This was probably on the instigation of Tantalus, who may represent some Anatolian aspect.

This myth has similarities with the Egyptian Seth-Osiris myth which also features a celestial banquet at which Seth kills the Sun God. Later, he dismembers the body of Osiris, scatters it about the land and ultimately throws the penis of Osiris into the Nile.

Seth, the Greek Typhon, the serpent, is an evolved form of Apophis the serpent adversary of Ra, the ancient form of the Sun God. Seth is the brother, that is co-culture of Osiris and clearly represents the fertility culture of the Delta derived in archaic times from Cretan infusion.

The animal which was sacred to the god Seth, an evolved Sea creature god was the ass, a form of horse, a symbol of the Sea God Poseidon.

Isis had the onerous task of reassembling the body of her husband Osiris, that is, re-establishing the heliopian culture. Naturally, Isis according to Apuleius, found the ass most hateful of all the beasts, which as Robert Graves realised, represented Seth, her enemy.[26]

It is perhaps not surprising that the ox and ass are present in the Christmas tableau depicting the Madonna and child, which celebrates childbirth or fertility and renewal.

Tantalus had a daughter Niobe who claimed to be superior to Leto, the mother of Apollon and Artemis, on the grounds that she had more children (vassals?). She was punished for this by Artemis, the Moon Goddess for all her children died. Niobe, weeping in grief, eventually, appropriately turned to a pillar of stone, the fertility culture she represented. The pillar continued to issue water, the symbol of fertility.

A similar fate befell Lot's wife as related in Genesis and according to Exodus, Moses'(serpent) rod could strike a rock from which water issued. These symbols suggest a cultural link between the Cretan fertility culture and Ancient Egypt (via the Egyptian Delta and Sumerian cultural intercourse with Crete).

Joseph, the father of the Egyptian Israelites, married into the Pillar culture when he took the daughter of a priest of On or Anu, for a bride. The symbol of On was a pillar or obelisk.

Pelops, had sons Atreus and Thyestes, rivals for the throne of Mycenae. Thyestes was willing to surrender his claim if the Sun should go backwards, that is, that the Anatolian heliopian ascendency be reversed. Zeus urged Atreus to extract the promise, and made the Sun go backwards, signifying a recession of Anatolian influence and the rise of the (Greek) house of Atreus or Mycenae.

"Three times did Patrocolus scale the walls (of Troy) but three times Apollo drove him back."

The headdresses of cultural groups often emulated the central archetype or archetypes of the culture to which the group belongs. (cf chapter 2) This is further illustrated by the archetypal Herakles whose head bore the Protosyrian lion god Dagan in the form of a lion skin.

Contingents of the Sea Peoples can be identified culturally, for example, the feathered headdress of the Pulisati is seen to be emulating the feathered headdress of the Cretan fertility goddess.

The Shardana also had a distinctive headdress embodying the Atlantean archetypes of bull's horns and a central pillar. Shardana appear on the walls of Medinet Habu in Egypt as members of Egyptian forces together with Pulisati and Shekellesh who fought against Libyan incursion[27] three years before the battle against the Sea Peoples. The same contingents later are shown as the enemy, possible justification of Ramesses III's complaint of a conspiracy.

The same Shardana motif can be seen on the Uratian Salamis cauldron which depicts serpents with Shardana helmets together with the twin bird helmeted winged goddess, typical Cretan archetypes.

The Shardana, if as some sources believe, who may have represented Cyprus, were culturally aligned to the Cretan Minoan culture whose pottery depicts them. Cyprus in any event, was mythically, a daughter of the Sea God and hence was part of the same culture.

If the fall of Troy was due to a "wooden horse" that is, with the assistance of allies within, then such assistance may have already been planned for the Egyptian Delta, vindicating Ramesses' assertion, for it was a region culturally imbued with waves of Cretan-Atlantean culture though over many centuries.

This situation may have been the cause of the Judaic (Cretan-Atlantean) Exodus that would have taken place in Egypt when the Sea Peoples and their internal allies were defeated.

This may have been the case according to the law of Cultural Action and Reaction which is a feature of the duality of macrocosmic culture. According to this law, any major cultural growth breeds its opposite movement (arising from the necessity of conflict). This results in consolidation of cultural boundaries, often along older cultural boundaries. The cultural realignment resulting from the demise of the heliopian Hittites was probably not the first and certainly not the last. For example, the Judaic-Christian culture was to bring a semitic southern cultural reaction in the form of Islam, as well as an eastern Greek Orthodox reaction to the Roman Latin. From the all-conquering monotheism, ultimately would spring, in the course of cultural time (measured in millennia), the adversary of orthodox Roman Christianity and Islam.

All these monotheisms however, were simply factionalising of the ancient opponent of heliopianism, autocratic monotheism, these opposites representing the primordial duality of the Cultural Law.

The exodus of the Anead as heliopian, as opposed to the Mosaic as monotheistic will be examined later, together with a short examination of Roman cultural heliopianism. The exodus of the Israelites can be viewed as the complement of that of the Aeneid. Indeed it may have been somewhat contemporary, taking place as a result of the successful repulsion of the Sea Peoples by Egypt, for the Israelites were, it is proposed, cultural allies of the invaders.

The Judaic Exodus of Moses seems also to have been a similar cultural cataclysm as that of the Aeneid, which would align with the law of Cultural Action and Reaction.

The Exodus of the Israelites from Egypt, of which there were many, is often attributed to solely ethical causes, but it is clear that it was also a result of cultural causes and was part of the situation in Ancient Egypt at that time, there being two distinct cultures. This was reflected in the centuries of effort to unite the two kingdoms, which represented the dichotomous cultural situation.

This dichotomous cultural situation was carried by the Judaic culture into the eastern territory where they settled and is manifested in its history, which will be examined later.

It is still apparent today, not surprisingly, when viewed from the stand point of the apparent immutability of culture.

The Exodus of the Israelites

There were several exoduses throughout Egyptian history by Kabiru or Hebrews, as the former became known. For example, there was almost certainly one following the unification of the country by Narmer, when the eagle (Upper Egypt) defeated the serpent (Lower Egypt or the Delta).

Although we are not told of the reasons for Abraham's migration from Ur in Sumeria, other than by command of the "Lord", they may have lain in dynastic dispute, for there are indications that Abraham was of royal blood.

He was certainly a wealthy and powerful man judging by the size of his possessions and lineage (Gen X1V-14). He was powerful enough to rescue his brother Lot and restore the possessions of the King of Sodom (Gen X1V-27).

Melchizadech, the King of Salemand "priest of the most High God" pays homage to Abraham as "possessor of Heaven and Earth", and although Abraham is never referred to as king, he possessed concubines.

He is described as "blessed of the Most High God" (Gen X1V-19) and as a "mighty Prince" by children of Heth (Gen XX111-6). Abraham passed off Sarai, his wife, as his sister in order to gain entry to the Egyptian court, there being a famine in the land.

The discovery of the deception is cultural anathema to the Egyptians, and results in the expulsion of Abraham and his people from the land.

From the earliest times of recorded Judaic tradition, therefore, there is the association with, or aspiration to kingship and subsequent migration.

This is reflected in events surrounding Moses and Christ, figures central to major turning points in the fortunes of the Israelites. Examining the account of the Exodus of the Old Testament in the context of its symbolic and mythological style, characteristic of the period, it would seem reasonable to assume that, through Joseph, the tribe of Abraham, or at least part of it, enjoyed access to the highest strata of Egyptian society.

Moses was only one step removed from the royal bloodline, having enjoyed a regal upbringing. A man in such a position, had he been even the son of a royal concubine, may have legitimately lain claim to the succession, for it was not unknown in Egypt (or in other heliopian cultures, for example, the Hittites) for the son of a royal concubine, to accede to the throne.

This was certainly the case with Tuthmosis III, an event that led to a civil and religious crisis in the wake of Hatshepsut's accession.

At that period in Egyptian history, as was the tradition, though this was to change during the Ptolemaic period, the king had to be a male, for he was the embodiment of Osiris the celestial executive and king of the celestial cosmogony.

This was the case in all contemporary heliopian cultures, a Qaballistic concept of "as above, so below." If the royal bloodline was left without a male heir, then the male issue of a royal concubine would be considered in preference to royal female siblings. The accession of a woman would therefore constitute a threat to the whole concept of the divinity of kings and the order arising from it.

One consequence would be that the priests would become the arbiters of the celestial Will instead of the king, in effect, shifting power from the secular to the religious. This may have been the reason why only female progeny of Akhenaton were ever depicted in royal pictures, implying an urgency possibly, to protect any male heir from adverse magic from disenfranchised Amentites.

The young age and confused lineage of Tutankhamen testifies to this.

The cultural importance of maleness, took precedence over blood on occasions, but not in the Greek or Roman cultures, perhaps because the powerful Sea God formed a triumvirate at the pinnacle of the cosmogony with Zeus and Hades. A similar state of affairs existed in the Hittite culture which, together with the Egyptian, was derived from or largely influenced by the Sumerian solar cosmogony.

King Telipinus (circa 1525-1500 BC), a contemporary of Tuthmosis III (circa 1479-1425 BC) decreed:

"Let a prince, the son of a wife of the first rank, let one who is a son of the second rank become king"[28].

This law was enacted to end the recurrent crisis arising from disputes regarding accession. When King Muwatallis died without an heir two hundred years later, Urhi Teshub (after the celestial executive), the son of a concubine, acceded to the Hittite throne.

This also illustrates important common cultural concepts coincident in application, but transcending natural boundaries, implying a common celestial (cultural) source.

The question of the Hebrew in Exodus "who made thee (Moses) a prince and a judge over us" (Exodus II-14) may not have been therefore, purely rhetorical.

The title of judge in the contemporary culture held eschatological associations with the Maati Hall of Judgement, implying some divine arbitration in matters of the after-life. Osiris was the chief presiding deity, the patron of kings, hence the association of prince and judge implied total authority.

The accession of a female pharaoh would have resulted in deep religious conflict between the heliopian and the Amenite priesthood, who after all, were associated by their Cretan cultural connections, with a much more exulted status of the female in the form of the fertility goddess, the consort of the sole god, the Sea God.

The Amenite priesthood tried to validate Hatshepsut's right to the throne of Egypt by propagating her dream, wherein the god Amen became her father by marrying her earthly mother[29] a similar situation to the parentage of Jesus.

The myth or story of her divine birth was invented. Paintings in her mortuary chapel depict a sacred wedding between the god Amen and a human woman, who later became the mother of Hatshepsut.

Hatshepsut, like Cleopatra at Dendera, is shown with cow's ears, associating her with the fertility goddess Hathor. Why would the Amenite priesthood persist with her claim to the throne when, having married her half-brother, the son of a concubine, she was legitimately queen, consort to the king?

In her appropriation of the memorial site of Mentuhotep III, "it would seem that Hatshepsut was expressing an ambition to be credited with the restoration of traditional authority in that part of Egypt that had been dominated by the Hyksos."[30]

It has been asserted that the Hyksos were derived from Crete and represented only one of several waves of settlement in the Delta of Egypt, giving rise to the dual adversarial cultures, the heliopian of Upper Egypt, and the Cretan fertility culture of the Delta or Lower Egypt.

It is interesting to note that Upper Egypt was in fact the south of the country and Lower Egypt, in the north. The designations of Upper and Lower, are psychological and cultural, and align with the myth of Etana where the eagle (Upper Egypt) resided at the top of the mythical tree and the serpent (Lower Egypt) at the bottom.

One may encounter a similar effect now when people refer to "going up to London" despite the fact they reside in the north of the country. They are of course going up to the head (capital) of the cultural body.

It is known that the Hyksos also occupied Palestine around 1700 to 1550 BC contemporary with their occupation of the Delta, from finds made at Tell Beit Mirsin.[31] Scarabs found there bear Cretan motifs, such as the Cretan whorl, fish, the Protosyrian lion and dual serpents (see chapter 7).

Many of these appear on a Hyksos scarab belonging to the reign of Khian, fourth ruler of the fifteenth dynasty (circa 1585-1542 BC)[32] a cartouche of whom was found at Knossos in Crete. At the same site, a stele found shows a serpent goddess wearing the distinctive feathered headdress of the Cretan fertility goddess and which was the headdress of the Pulisati, a later wave of settlers in the same area from Crete.

In propagating the myth of Hatshepsut being the daughter of Amen and mortal woman, the Amenite priesthood was presenting itself as representative of the Sea God of ancient Cretan-Atlantean myth, who also married mortal woman, whose daughter became the Queen of Atlantis from whom the ten kings issued.

The God Amen therefore became the ancient and powerful Sea God of the Hyksos culture and in relation to Hatshepsut, would represent the source of her authority and sovereignty, effectively becoming the sole source of power.

This situation of course was strenuously opposed by the heliopians, mainly of Upper Egypt and eventually Tuthmosis III was restored, with the obliteration of all traces of Hatshepsut who represented anathema.

The symbol of Amen was the ram, which was also the symbol of the Sea God Poseidon, the Lord of Atlantis. It is known from Wooley's finds, that a golden fleeced fertility ram was extant at Ur the city from which Abraham emigrated. The ram cult was probably the result of the cultural "flood" which is recorded in Sumerian mythology and may have been imported into Egypt by Abraham, from which period, the appearance of the god Amen is noticed as a cult (circa 2000 BC).

It would be natural for an emigrant prince to make for a culturally sympathetic state. This is even more the pre-requisite for a mass exodus. The Cretan fertility culture would with the god Amen, have come full circle, to meet in the Egyptian Delta, the nome (province) emblems of which, show a predominance of bovine forms and the Nestorian bull's thigh.

Hatshepsut, with her cow's ears, identifies her with the Hyksos fertility goddess and also the Isis-Hathor cult at Saqqara, which may have originated in Crete (a culture which may have itself been the result of some off shore migration from surrounding heliopianism).

Hatshepsut did become Pharaoh, though she was obliged to adopt the compromise title of "His Majesty herself." Such circumstances must have greatly disturbed the heliopians, for the power of Amen became paramount.

It was at the accession of Hatshepsut's successor, Tuthmosis, that the power of the god is evident, for it is the god's image that is instrumental in the appointment of the successor.

The priesthood of Amen had become the intermediaries of the gods and not the king. However, from Tuthmosis' account, it would appear that the heliopians arranged for the god to appoint their candidate, Tuthmosis. His account is repeated here for convenience:

"The God (seated in the Sekhet Boat, the vessel necessary to sail across the waters of death) made the circuit of the hall on both sides of it, searching for my majesty in every place, though the hearts of those in front did not comprehend his action. On recognising me, he halted. I threw myself on the pavement, I prostrated myself in his presence."[33]

It is clear that the supporters of the god were not in on the plot to restore a king to the throne. It is of note that the process of thought or awareness, was associated with the heart and not the head, as if such faculties were instinctive, as would be the case with a relatively undeveloped common populace and priesthood that presided over the subconscious.

It is probable that it was believed that the effigy of the god actually contained the spirit of the god, entirely in keeping with what is known of Egyptian magic at that time, and indeed such belief manifests itself in modern times.

Tuthmosis III became Pharaoh and, many consider, History's first great general, significantly, subjugating Crete. Initially however, he inherited a divided nation, his claim to the throne likely, in dispute.

In Exodus Chapter IV, Moses' rod is turned into a serpent:

"That they may believe that the Lord God of their fathers, the God of Abraham, the God of Isaac and the God of Jacob hath appeared to thee."

The serpent as we have seen, was a Cretan cultural archetype associated with the Sea God and his fertility goddess. It was also the symbol of Lower Egypt, the Delta, and as such, represented royal authority.

Moses is informed by the Lord "See I have made thee a God to Pharaoh" (Exodus VII-1). This was tantamount to claiming kingship, for the only divine person in the culture was the king.

It is also recorded that Moses is admonished to seek a meeting with the Pharaoh and to cast Aaron's rod to the ground with the result that:

"For they cast down every man his rod, and they became serpents but Aaron's rod swallowed up their rods" (Exodus VII-12).

The rods, being symbols of power, in this case possibly, military might, insinuates the threat of military confrontation. Exodus, written many centuries after the actual event, paints a picture of a successful objective achieved, namely, to evacuate the Israelites from Egypt. It is understandable that recorded histories of conflict tend to salvage desirable aspects of a culture. This is apparent in the translations of myths, and is probably necessary for the survival and morale of the culture.

This is a feature common today in conflict situation reporting, as it has been throughout history.

The original circumstances of the causes of the Exodus, have already been hinted at, arising from the dichotomous culture of Egypt. The more immediate causes may have been the result of a civil war arising from a disputed claim to the throne, a common occurrence in any era.

The whole picture painted by Exodus shows civil strife on a large scale often veiled in the contemporary allegorical style, for it is written:

"For in this self-same day have I brought you and your armies out of the land of Egypt" (Exodus XII-17).

The Pharaoh is not intimidated or impressed by the rod of Aaron, and events move into a more violent theatre, characterised by sabotage and guerrilla tactics, the first of which, is the destruction of water supplies.

Moses, using his rod or baton of authority, turns "the rivers to blood."

"Rivers running with blood" is the ancient allegory for a violent military battle. The water or rivers may also be an allegory for fighting manpower of whom the king was the primary source (of celestial water) and begetter in heliopian cultures.

The fertility goddess in her many forms, was also represented as a source. If the "rivers" are to be taken at face value, then there is a mythological precedent for Moses' action in the Egyptian culture, which would be classed as psychological warfare. It would not be the first appropriation of a myth for a cultures' own benefit, as the Amenites, of whom Moses was probably party to, or allied to, demonstrated.

The precedent concerns an Ancient Egyptian myth known as the "Old Age of Ra"[34] which is clearly related to the Canaanite myth of Anat and the Sumerian Flood myth.

Ra (the Sun God), growing old, felt his authority over gods and men was failing, whereupon, he summoned the gods and told them that men were plotting against him. Nun, the eldest of the gods, advised that the eye of Ra, in the form of Hathor, should be sent to punish mankind. This she did, wading like Anat, in blood.

Ra, not desiring the complete destruction of mankind, devised a plan, which involved making several thousand jars of barley beer, dyed with red ochre, to resemble blood. This was poured into the fields to a depth of nine inches. When the goddess saw the flood shining in the dawn, reflecting her beauty, she was allured and (presumably mistaking the red beer for blood) became drunk, forgetting her rage, so mankind was saved.

Such a ploy on Moses' part, who it would appear was well versed in the culture, by invoking primordial fears by association with "rivers of blood", would for the local populace, be interpreted as, anger of the Gods, thus devaluing the Pharaoh's cause.

Another Egyptian text concerning the slaying of the enemy of Ra, the serpent Apophis (the Cretan derived Delta culture) by the Sun God, the Pharaoh states: "for they were ordered to annihilate my enemies by the effective charms of their speech and I sent out those who came into being from my own body, to overthrow that evil enemy" (Apophis).[35]

The turning of the rivers to blood either literally or metaphorically, implies in the one case, military threat and on the other, a psychological threat, the violent punishment of the contemporary childlike collective psyche by a voracious mother (fertility goddess) figure.

The application of the same primordial blood archetype was again invoked in the dubbing of the door pillars of the loyal Israelites with blood (Exodus XII-22) a ritual at the heart of the Atlantis myth.

If the poisoning of the rivers is to be taken literally, then many of the so-called plagues called down by Moses, become simply the natural consequences of such an action, though it was more likely allegorical. Either way, fish would die, allegorically, men would die, and frogs would proliferate, allegorically, the serpent followers would triumph, the frog being the same, symbolically, as the snake.

Bodily hygiene, about which heliopians were meticulous, recognising early its efficacy in the fight against disease (cf the Romans) would naturally be impeded, giving rise to the propagation of fleas, head lice and disease.

The carcasses of the dead frogs which, "they gathered them together upon heaps and the land stank" (Exodus VIII-14), would be a breeding ground for flies, resulting in epidemics among men and animals ("plagues of boils, blains and murrains" (Exodus IX)) common today in drought ridden areas of Africa.

The Delta, where much of the population lived, would be the worst affected, creating much civil unrest. It is well documented that the Ancient Egyptians were familiar with some aspects of basic chemistry, as demonstrated by their mummification procedures, which required the production of natron. It is possible and probable that they could refine oils and pitch, the residues of which contain toxic substances.

When they "took ashes from the furnace…and sprinkled it towards heaven", was this simply part of the strategy of sabotage, for a scorched earth policy is clearly evident when Moses purports to bring down hail and fire, allegorically, warfare upon the land, except in Gosham where the Israelites resided.

The Ancient Egyptian year was divided into three seasons of four months[36], the "Akhet" season of inundation and period of sowing, the "Pert" growing season or Spring, and the "Semut" season of harvest and beginning of inundation. According to Exodus IX-24:

"There was hail and fire mingled with hail, very grievous such as there was none like it in all the land of Egypt since it became a nation…and the barley was smitten, for the barley was in ear and the flax was bolled but that the wheat and rye were not smitten for they were not grown up."

Taking the literal meaning, after the dry season, which seems to be indicated by the pollution of the rivers, hail storms would not be unknown, however, crops still green and young, would not burn as would fields of mature flax and barley, indeed, during dry spells, spontaneous bush fires would be common.

The military strategy begins to emerge, first the water supplies are attacked, then the food supplies. The plague of locusts, "there were no such locusts as they, neither after them shall be such" (Exodus X-14) provides a clue as to the real nature of the "locusts."

They were "brought into thy coast…and they shall cover the face of the earth and shall eat the residue of that which is escaped" (the hail and fire).

The hail and fire evocative of Ramesses III "fire was prepared", like the locusts, are allegorical in this context. The hail and fire, like the flood, is a military allegory for battle, the locusts were probably imported mercenaries or allies but, as a result of "a strong west wind" (Exodus X-19), another allegory for military might as we saw in the Epic of Gilgamesh, the locusts are cast into the Red Sea and:

"There remained not one locust in all the coasts of Egypt."

In contemporary symbolism we see the strong west wind as a mythological description of military forces, presumably, the Pharaoh's, driving the invaders "into the Red Sea" that is, into the territory of the Mosaic forces, the ancient Red

Kingdom of the Delta. The Sea of the Sea God being used again as a collective for people or culture.

Presently we shall see the use of the metaphor again as the Mosaic armies are finally routed. The locust episode therefore translates as a substantial victory for the Pharaonic forces and resulting gloom for the defeated for "there was a thick darkness which may be felt" (Exodus X-21,22).

These days of gloom, when the war was being lost by the Israelites, culminate in the banishment of Moses; "get thee from me, take heed to thyself, see my face no more, for in that day, thou seest my face, thou shalt die" (Exodus X-29).

That Moses was spared was probably due to his royal associations and upbringing, a customary tradition often, with royalty. In the allegory of slaying of the Egyptian first born we see a retreating army resorting to genocidal slaughter of the indigenous population who support the Pharaonic forces.

The first born of the Egyptians not already in the army would represent a threat to the retreating forces and so are put to the sword.

The urgency of the retreating forces is indicated in Exodus XII-31, when Moses and Aaron are summoned at night by the Pharaoh and ordered to leave the country. This ultimatum was issued with the threat that if they did not implement the order with "haste", then they would "be all dead men" (Exodus XII-33).

This may have been a strategic ploy by the royal forces to attack the retreating armies as later events show.

The forces of Moses were camped "between Migdol and the sea over against Baal Zephon, before it ye shall camp by the sea" (Exodus XIV-2), which was strategically questionable, unless means of escaping by sea existed.

The sea may have been meant allegorically, as the Red Sea, that is, the population of the Delta supporters, for Exodus describes how the Israelites perform a rear-guard pincer movement in order to secure a retreat.

"And the angel of God, which went before the camp of Israel, removed and went behind them and the "pillar" of the cloud went from before their face and stood behind them. And it came between the camp of the Egyptians and the camp of Israel, and it was a cloud of darkness to them but it gave light by night to these, so that the one came not near the other all the night. And Moses stretched out his hand (the order to attack) over the sea and the Lord caused the sea to go back by a strong "east" wind all that night and made the sea dry land and the waters were divided" (Exodus XIV-19-21).

These passages describe in allegorical terms, a redeployment of Mosaic forces as the opposing armies are camped. It will be noted that the Mosaic forces are referred to as a strong "east" wind, in contrast to the strong "west" wind of the Royal forces.

The Mosaic forces, signified by the Red Sea "waters", in fertility culture terms, have been split into two, forming an ambush into which the Royal forces will ride, the middle "dry ground" in pursuit of the Mosaic forces.

"And the Children of Israel went into the midst of the sea upon dry ground" (Exodus XIV-26-28), then "Moses stretched forth his hand over the sea, and the sea returned to its strength when the morning appeared…and covered the chariots and the horsemen and all the host of Pharaoh that came into the sea after them" (Exodus XIV-24-28).

We know in fact, that it was not a Mosaic victory of any import for the retreating forces were expelled. Those initial chapters of Exodus therefore look like a cultural and dynastic struggle centred on the cultural division of the country which, from the earliest times, successive Pharaohs had striven to unify.

Ever since Narmer I, the uniter of the Kingdom in which the heliopian Upper Egypt had defeated the fertility culture dominated Delta, there was an undercurrent of secessionism in the Delta which was the richest part of the kingdom economically, and whose fertile lands originally induced Cretan infusion and settlement.

Amenism had risen in strength to such a level, that Aknaten was forced to introduce a form of autocratic heliopianism as a focus for anti Amenism sentiment, in a symbolic gesture, relocating the capital from Amenite dominated Thebes, to Aketaten, the mid-kingdom capital during his reign. The temple carvings were, as always, made for cultural and or religious purposes, for the populace. Like the mediaeval populace, the Ancient Egyptian populace readily understood the symbolism of hieroglyphics, though they were otherwise illiterate.

The carvings of Ramesses II and Ramesses III on the great temples, depict scenes of the Kings ostensibly hunting bulls with their armies. These are not frivolous depictions of the King at leisure, but as we have seen, represent great events in the survival of the culture.

The giant bulls being pursued into the reeds (of the Delta), would be an allegory of defeat and rout of secessionist Delta fertility forces, represented by the hieratically presented Saqqara Bulls. Just such an event is described in Exodus. Frequent reference is made to the Pharaoh throughout Egyptian history as "Lord of the South and North", that is, King of the Upper and Lower kingdoms, to emphasise unity.

Tuthmosis III consolidated the Kingdom and extended its borders to Syria in the east and Lebanon in the north. He ruled for over forty years, the length of the banishment of Moses "in the wilderness."

We know that Tuthmosis found it necessary to subjugate the Keftiuans or Cretans. If the Mosaic forces were aided by their parent culture Crete, then Tuthmosis would have good reason to regard them as a threat, and this would explain why the Mosaic forces camped by the sea, for the Cretans were along established maritime race, enabling them to colonise the Delta in antiquity.

There was also an urgent need for Cretans at that time to emigrate to a land where they could survive, for a cataclysmic eruption on the island of Thera (now it is thought to be Santorini) destroyed a major part of the Minoan palaces, with the exception of Knossos, rendering the land uncultivatable.

This gave rise to a Cretan exodus (circa 1475 BC)[37] and some sources have attempted to link the Hebrew Exodus chronologically with the Thera eruption.[38]

Attempts have been made to equate the "dust from the furnace" and the three-day darkness which could be felt as a Biblical record of volcanic activity to explain the ten plagues of Moses. It is certainly plausible as a psychological warfare ploy, to alarm the populace of impending catastrophe, signified by the sprinkling of ash from a furnace, and would indicate a Cretan-Delta communication.

According to the wave theory of culture, such emigration from Crete would be to the Southern Mediterranean coast which had often, in times past, been colonised by the Cretans in the form of Pulisati, Philistines and Hyksos as well as many previous unnamed settlements.

It is possible, the "strong east wind" described in Exodus was a union of culturally descended peoples from Canaan and Palestine, enlisted to assist the Hyksos Delta forces, a pattern which was to be repeated with the invasion of Egypt by the Sea Peoples.

It is known that the Hyksos also occupied Palestine from about1550 BC to 1200 BC and it would have been necessary for a retreating army to either return to its own territory or to a territorial ally (cf present day Palestinians).

The Hyksos, recent occupiers of the Delta and Palestine, indicate that Palestine would be the culturally receptive area and explains why Palestine became the "Promised Land", for it was ethnically and culturally the same as the land from which the Israelites were being expelled, the land of the Hyksos which had briefly provided dynastic kings of Egypt.

Equally, the "land of milk and honey" would apply to the Delta, the land promised to the Israelites in the Book of Joshua.

"From the wilderness and this Lebanon, even unto the great river, the river Euphrates, all the land of the Hittites and unto the great sea toward the going down of the Sun shall be your coast", an area which corresponds largely with the sphere of influence won by Tuthmosis III. The initial years of Tuthmosis III's reign would have been concentrated on securing his borders before pursuing his enemies. This would have provided a respite for the retreating Mosaic armies to establish themselves in allied territory. This is accompanied by a cultural purge and the institution of a religious and cultural code embodying a code of law, as the first steps in welding together a culturally similar but now nationless group of allied tribes.

Instructions are given about the sacrificing of a bullock and a ram, whose blood is used, like in the Atlantean ritual, to anoint an altar (Exodus XXIX-10-16).

Moses is commanded to go up Mount Sinai from which the populace is barred, where he obtains sacred stones. Both the stones, encountered in the epic of Gilgamesh, and the mountain, are central archetypes of the Sumerian and Cretan cultures, the parent cultures of the Delta Hebrews.

The esoteric access of Moses indicates his role as religious intermediary, priest-king or priest. The stones on which are inscribed the Ten Commandments, traditionally are identical in shape to the headdress of Amen and are evocative of the altar of the Moon God at Ur. This may appear to be trivial, but the presentation of central archetypes of the culture as constituting the headdress of the king was the practice at that time (and indeed is still practised today). (See Chapter 2.)

Reinforcing cultural archetypes in the collective unconscious, especially at occasions of ceremony, was clearly helpful to unity and hence survival of the culture.

Apparently, whilst Moses is engaged on the sacred mount, Aaron gives instructions for the fabrication of a golden calf:

"After he had made it, a molten calf, and they said these be thy Gods O Israel which brought thee out of the land of Egypt" (Exodus XXXII-4).

Exodus makes it clear that these words are spoken by the Egyptians "for mischief" (Exodus XXXII-12). It would appear that among the retreating forces of the Israelites, are devotees of the Hathor bull cult from the Delta.

Subsequently, three thousand such followers are slain for threatening the autocracy of the Lord. This, to a certain extent, signifies the termination of recognition of a fertility goddess in the religion and the relegation of women to a non-status.

The story of Exodus may therefore have been the consequence of an unsuccessful invasion of, or attempted secession of the Delta Kingdom.

The Cretan culture was, in any event, in rapid decline and sometime in the fifteenth century BC, ceased to exist in that form.

References to Keftiu after the reign of Amenopsis II (circa1411-1412 BC) are no longer found and Mycenean-Egyptian relations begin.

The ancient archetypes of the culture however, were retained by its migrants in the Judaic tradition who, as we shall see, were not initially wholly monotheistic. This is not entirely surprising, for much of Palestine after Tuthmosis III, was subject to heliopian cultural domination or influence for many centuries.

It would seem that the similarity between Amenism in Egypt and the Judaic monotheistic god, differed only in the means whereby supremacy in the celestial realm would be achieved.

For the Amenites, this was determined by the strong heliopian environment in which it existed. Nonetheless, its relentless drive for primacy continued.

The victory stele of Tuthmosis III is dedicated to Amen-Ra, a composite name to satisfy both of the cultures in the land.

"I have come that I may cause thee to trample down the Western Land (Libya?). Keftiu and Isy are under awe of thee. I have come that I may cause thee to trample down those who are in the Islands, those who are in the midst of the Great Green (the Delta?) are under thy battle cry."

Similar tributes are made by subsequent Pharaohs. By the end of the Twentieth Dynasty (circa 1196-1070 BC), heliopian influence had almost vanished in Egypt. During the Twentieth Dynasty, the most important far-reaching change was that a high proportion of the land passed to temples, in particular, to those of Amen at Karnak.[39]

The temple of Amen eventually acquired virtual control of Upper Egypt, probably the reason for siting the temple there in the beginning. Priestly offices became hereditary and thus, virtually independent of the King forming, eventually, a dynasty to rival the King.

Naturalised Libyan prisoners retained their cultural identity, which together with dissipated royal power, and its rival religious power, were forces which were splitting the country into an almost feudal society by comparison to its former state of civilisation.

By 1070 BC, the Kings at Tanis ruled only the Delta. Upper Egypt was ruled by the Amenite priesthood. Amen appears on royal cartouches of Shoshenq I (circa 945 BC) who attempted to unite the country by installing his son in Thebes, the centre of Amenite power in Upper Egypt. He fought a campaign in Palestine, restored and extended some ancient monuments and a hundred years of peace followed his reign.

Civil war resulted when Takelot II (circa 860-835 BC) appointed his son Osorkon as high priest of Amen, an office he combined with military functions[40]. Clearly, this was an attempt to curb the influence of the Amenites, provoking a powerful demonstration of their power. Osorkon was usurped probably with the help of the Amenites, by Shoshenq III and the crown divided amongst several claimants.

By the end of the eighth century BC, there were numerous kings with the Twenty Second and Twenty Fifth Dynasties ruling contemporaneously. With the advent of the Nubians (circa 717 BC), the Twenty-Fourth Dynasty was founded which eliminated the other kings.

It is at this point, that the god Amen disappears from royal cartouches corresponding with the infusion into the culture of several heliopian cultures, starting with Esarhaddon the Assyrian, whose culture produced the great library of Ansurbanipal (circa 660 BC), signifying the return of enlightenment

Egyptian-Greek cultural exchanges began again to take place from 600 BC with Solon ushering in the age of science and the Greek renaissance.

From 525 to 332 BC, the Persian culture dominated Egypt followed by Alexandrian heliopianism which would be carried into the heliopian Roman culture.

The legacy of the ascendancy of Amenite religious power, was a decent into a dark age and feudalism, for a once great culture. This was not the first time a culture reaped the wages of monotheism (the celestial equivalent of temporal dictatorship) for the Sumerian Flood myths have presented a similar story.

Nor was it to be the last, the same autocratic celestial forces would decree the same fate for the great Roman civilisation.

A certain cultural symmetry is maintained with the Sea Peoples of predominantly Cretan cultural sway, defeating the Hittite heliopian culture, precipitating an exodus described in the Aeneid, whilst the Egyptians repulse a cultural invasion or secession, resulting in the Judaic exodus.

It is probable that the former was (in cultural time) a reaction to the latter. In any event, such events were simply encounters in the eternal conflict between Ra and Apophis.

References Chapter 8

[1] D. M. Field, Greek and Roman Mythology, page 118

[2] The Empire Builders Time-Life, page 20

[3] C. Kerenyi, The Gods of the Greeks, page 171

[4] D. M. Field, Greek and Roman Mythology, page 102

[5] C. G. Jung, Psychology and Alchemy, page 295

[6] J. Mellaart, The Archaeology of Ancient Turkey, page 71

[7] ibid, page 70

[8] Lucian Satirical Sketches, trans P. Turner, page 56

[9] C. Kerenyi, The Gods of the Greeks, page 199

[10] J. Mellaart, The Archaeology of Ancient Turkey, page 70

[11] Homer, The Iliad, trans E. V. Rieu, page X

[12] O. R. Gurney, The Hittites, page 124

[13] M. Wood, In Search of the Trojan War, page 185

[14] O. R. Gurney, The Hittites, page 120

[15] M. Wood, In Search of the Trojan War, page 217

[16] A. J. Church, Stories from Virgil, page 73

[17] The Aeneid

[18] Homer, The Iliad, trans E. V. Rieu, page 463

[19] A. J. Church, Stories from Virgil, page 87

[20] The Aeneid

[21] M. Wood, In Search of the Trojan War, page 223

[22] Homer, The Odyssey, trans E. V. Rieu, page 222

[23] J. Mellaart, The Archaeology of Ancient Turkey, page 70

[24] C. Kerenyi, The Gods of the Greeks, page 197

[25] A. J. Church, Stories from Virgil, page 130

[26] The Aeneid

[27] O. R. Gurney, The Hittites, page 16

[28] N. K. Sandars, The Sea Peoples, page 119

[29] C. Kerenyi, The Gods of the Greeks, page 197

[30] Apuleius, The Golden Ass, trans R. Graves, page 13

[31] O. R. Gurney, The Hittites, page 66

[32] C. Barocas, Monuments and Civilisation of Egypt, page 81

[33] ibid, page 171

[34] W. F. Albright, Archaeology of Palestine, page 84

[35] J. Baines and J. Malek, Atlas of Ancient Egypt, page 42

[36] E. Payne, All about the Pharaohs, page 75

[37] S. H. Hooke, Middle Eastern Mythology, page 73

[38] ibid, page 74

[39] Sir A. E. Wallis, Budge Egyptian Language, page 135

[40] J. Baines and J. Malek, Atlas of Ancient Egypt, page 48F

Chapter 9
Archetypes of Hebrew Monotheism

A culture or its derivative, can be identified by the archetypal symbols employed in the literature and art of the culture, for they reside in the cultural archetypal memory. Jung has demonstrated that ancient archetypal symbols can be manifested by individuals in dreams and art.[1]

There are certain archetypal symbols which are characteristic of the ancient Atlantean-Cretan culture, referred to in myths and displayed in art, such as the mountain (Ullikumi and Humbaba) the sacred triple (as trident), the pillar, the serpent, the horse or ass and the ram etc. These are all associated with the primacy and exclusivity of one deity, the ancient Sea God.

Other archetypal symbols originated with concepts in the Sumerian culture, such as the sacred stones, the tree of life and the bull. Many of the Cretan archetypes are to be found in the literature of the Bible, and to a lesser extent, are associated with the Philistine culture that originated in Crete.

The serpent rods of Moses and Aaron are a striking example of a shared archetype with the Cretan fertility goddess. Specific instructions are given to the Israelites regarding the construction of the Tabernacle, calling for twenty pillars at the north and south, ten on the west and three, each side of the gate, maintaining a triple symmetry.

It is not surprising to find the emigrant Israelis sharing the land of the Philistines and Hyksos forebears who earlier, had welcomed Abraham and his tribe.

By 1100 BC, the Philistines had set up five city-states on the Canaanite coast and had absorbed much of the Canaanite heliopianism. They had introduced iron implements, a powerful new strategic material, which they naturally withheld from the Hebrews:

"Now there was no smith to be found throughout the land of Israel, for the Philistines said, 'lest the Hebrews make themselves swords and spears.'" (I Samuel XIII-19-21)

The Book of Samuel makes clear that the Hebrews were vassals of the Philistines, a consequence of which, they absorbed some of their culture:

"Yawed remained amid all assimilation of Canaanite worships, such as high places, groves, or sacred pillars, the God of his chosen people."[2]

These archetypes reflect the cultural origins of the Philistines, that is Crete, the home of the Sea God culture and testify to the long residence in the collective archetypal memory. One may also at this point recall the pillar set up by Jacob as an altar. The Biblical quotation above was only true after considerable cultural dissension within Israel.

Sacred groves occur in myths regarding Atlantis and the Golden Fleece of the Northern Mediterranean cultures. "High places" was a feature of Sumerian ritual with Ziggurats, man-made mountains, with a sanctuary of the god on the top. This architectural feature may have been inherited as a result of the "Flood", from Crete, and Sumerian influence probably carried it into the Egyptian culture as the Pyramid.

Long flights of steps characterised such edifices and their influence on Egyptian eschatology is apparent. They were probably also the prototype of Jacob's Ladder.

The Pulisati or Philistines were known to have been the allies of Tuthmosis III, which would have been necessary for him to extend the empire. They were also the allies of Ramesses II at the battle of Kadesh, though by the time of the invasion by the Sea Peoples, they had joined the enemy, their cultural forebears. Much of their culture had been heliopianised and in the Book of Judges, they are described as worshippers of the originally ancient Protosyrian god Dagan or Dagon (Judges VI-23) The Lord of the Stars, who was also an integral part of the Egyptian culture at one time.

It is in their temple, gathered to sacrifice to Dagon, that Samson, placed between the two "pillars upon which the house stood", caused the temple to collapse. (Judges VI-29)

Such an image, where the pillars represented the virility of the culture, would constitute considerable propaganda value to a culture that also held the pillar as a sacred totem. A similar invocation of an ancient sea god symbol appears in the account of Samson's slaying of a thousand Philistines with the jawbone of an ass. (The archtype of the ass we have come across before.)

The anecdote is probably intended for its psychological efficacy, rather than its dubious literal meaning, as with the destruction of the Philistine temple "for at that time the Philistines had dominion over Israel" (Judges XIV-4).

It would seem much of the story of Samson is written in poetical symbolism, adjusted on occasion to obscure the allegory.

Samson desired a wife who was a Philistine, a desire that naturally, horrifies his parents. At Timnath, "a young lion roars against him" which he kills with his bare hands.

On returning sometime later to collect his bride, he discovers a swarm of bees in the carcass of the lion from which he takes honey. Samson, as was the custom, prepares a feast "for so used the young men to do" (Judges XIV-10) at which he issues a riddle; "out of the eater came forth meat, and out of the strong came forth sweetness."

The guests are obliged to provide the answer within seven days or forfeit thirty sheets, and thirty changes of garments. The answer is obtained from Samson by the Philistines pressing Samson's wife, which is symbolically expressed as "If ye had not ploughed with my heifer, ye had not found out my riddle."

The story, taken literally, proves entertaining though a little facetious and meaningless in parts. The Philistines are shown to be unscrupulous. If however, the tale is translated from the allegory, a different and more realistic meaning emerges. The myth technique of using animal archetypes allegorically is present. The "young lion" is clearly a young Dagonite or Philistine, slain for no apparent reason, though it can be assumed that it was the result of a quarrel, possibly deriving from the proposed mixed marriage.

Samson's wife, cast as a heifer, was possibly a temple virgin, a representative of the fertility goddess Astarte, the equivalent of the Sumerian Ishtar, one of whose symbols was the cow. The riddle then translates "out of the strong, the lion Dagon, the Philistine culture, came forth sweetness" that is, Samson's bride, the object of his journey. Such a translation, of course, would not be appropriate for the chroniclers, for it accredits the Philistine god with power, possibly greater than that of Yahweh, and the culture as possessing a certain beauty.

Any issue of such a union "out of the eater came forth meat", that is, out of the Dagon culture came his bride, would endanger the exclusivity of the

Israelites, dilute the culture and, as a consequence, would weaken the power of Yahweh, the priesthood, or the prophets.

Not surprisingly, for reasons that are not stated, Samson's Philistine wife, is given to his friend, who was probably a Philistine.

The incident of the wedding feast, for that is what is indicated, has similarities with the Wedding Feast at Canaan of the New Testament, in so far as it is Jesus the Nazarene or Nazorite who is attending, some would maintain, his own wedding in the Palestinian or Philistine territory of Canaan.

"Jesus of Nazareth" it is maintained was a mistranslation from the original Greek.[3] The Nazorites were a sect that forbade the cutting of the hair of the head:

"And no razor shall come on his head." (Judges XIII-5)

Such a fetish explains the allegorical meaning of Samson's losing his strength when his head is shaved, whose hair style apparently, is arranged in the Sumerian sacred seven locks (Judges XVI-19) the mystical number of arms on the Hebrew candlestick.

Such an action as unwittingly having one's head shaven, in religious and psychological terms would be traumatic, welcoming sectarian and social opprobrium and ostracization, redeemable, in all probability, only by sacrificing one's life for the culture.

"Samson was reduced in status from his position of influence in the society to 'lose his strength' and be like any other man."

Part of the Nazorite initiation involved a period of "separation" (Numbers VI) when the initiate was forbidden to eat or drink any

"Liquor of the grapes nor eat moist grapes or dried."

Grapes, being an ancient symbol of fruitfulness, seems to imply that the ritual was to do with male fertility, indicated by a period of abstinence and avoidance of death:

"He shall not make himself unclean for his father, or for his mother, for his brother or for his sister when they die." (Numbers VI-7)

After a sacrifice of two lambs and a ram (symbols of the Sea God and Amen) the acolyte's head was shaved in the entrance to the Tabernacle, and he was covered with unguents of the sacrifice, reminiscent of the sacred bull ritual of Atlantis.

The symbolism of such a ritual of admonishment would not be lost on the populace. Christ's fasting in the wilderness may have echoed the same ritual for John the Baptist was also regarded as a Nazorite[4] and, according to some, one of the duties of a Nazorite, was the defence of Israel against aliens, hence the double infamy of Samson the Nazorite, turning from his excelling in duty of defence, slaying the Philistines, to his sacrilegiously wishing to marry an alien, resulting in his ignominious shriven shame. The cultural pressures on the Israelites from surrounding cultures were considerable. Joshua, who was king in all but name, still found it necessary to admonish his people.

"Choose you this day whom ye will serve; whether the gods which your fathers served that were on the other side of flood, or the gods of the Amorites, in whose land ye dwell; but as for me and my house, we will serve the Lord."

The inherent tendency by some to adhere to the heliopian pantheon is clearly still present. The flood referred to here may be a reference to the Red Sea incident of Exodus when they, the Israelites lived in heliopian Egypt or it may be an allusion to the Sumerian Flood prior to which, the forebears of the Hebrews lived under heliopianism.

The cultural dichotomy, inherited from Egypt (and to some extent from Sumeria) and instanced in Joshua and Judges surrounding Samson, is to be found throughout Judaic Biblical history (according to the cultural law of relative immutability), especially associated with the Kings.

By the end of the second millennium, the pressure to appoint a king over the Hebrews, testament to external cultural pressures, where the norm was king, not prophet, as head of state, was mounting among the Hebrews. This was, naturally, resisted by the priesthood for concomitant with it, was the divinity of kings as the source of divine authority.

Outside of Israel this was not the priesthood, as sole arbiters of Yahweh's will, but the monarch as representative on earth of the chief executive of the celestial heliopian pantheon. The influence of the heliopian Philistines of Canaan is already evident in Judges.

Gideon, considered a Judge of Israel, is also called "Jerubaal" (Judges VIII-35), a name clearly linked to the Canaanite Sun deity. One of Gideon's sons to a concubine is named Abimelech, the name of the Philistine king in Genesis. Abimelech is elected king by the men of Shechem "by the plain of the pillar that was in Shechem." (Judges IX-6)

In the event, Abimelech dies by his own hand and it is not until the time of Saul, that the cry arose from the Hebrews that they should be the same as the surrounding nations.

"Now appoint for us a King to govern us like all nations." (I Samuel VIII-5, 6)

Naturally, the priest caste resists such a demand as an assault on their authority. Samuel warned the Hebrews that a king would oppress and exploit them, their sons taken as soldiers and their daughters as servants.

This sentiment possibly became the basis of the tradition in the Roman epoch whence Hebrews, being a priest-oriented culture, were ultimately exempted from military service in the legions. After the fall of heliopianism, the monotheistic empire replaced military conquest with cultural conquest.

Samuel grimly warned the people that their paramount duty remained obedience to the Lord's commandments, and by implication, to Samuel as the Lord's intermediary.[5]

In his consultation with Yahweh, as a result of popular demand, and despite efforts of dissuasion, he is "informed":

"Hearken to the voice of the people in all that they say to you, for they have not rejected you but have rejected me from being King over them."

Saul was elected the first King of the Hebrews, a choice manifestly to Samuel's and the prophet's distaste, for it is clear from the outset that Saul meant to exercise his kingship as primary authority.

Subsequent to a general mobilisation of the Hebrews, Saul was instructed to wait seven days for the arrival of Samuel to perform the ritual sacrifices to Yahweh, prior to battle. In the event, the prophet failed to turn up for reasons not disclosed.

Saul, on his own authority, performed the necessary sacrifices and engaged in battle, despite inferior armoury Philistines countered and the Hebrews were dispersed. The prophet eventually appeared and rebuked Saul furiously one can imagine, because Saul had, as first King, set a dangerous precedent. He had appeared in the role of priest-king aligning himself with the practice in surrounding contemporary cultures and had thus undermined the authority of the prophet.

Fortunately for Samuel, the battle went badly for Saul. The narrative of Saul's election has two versions in Samuel. The second alludes to an earlier course of events than the first[6] whence Saul is elected following a successful attack on a marauding Amorite ruler.

The first indicates selection by the prophet accompanied by divine revelation.

Saul, after a private meeting and appointment by Samuel, undergoes a profound spiritual experience involving a band of musical prophets (I Samuel X-5) "coming down from a high place", the traditional Sumerian-Cretan Atlantean residence of the Sea God.

It would seem therefore, that Saul, king by popular choice, is made to appear as the choice of the prophets and therefore, Yahweh.

The Philistine influence is again evident entering the Hebrew tradition at the highest level, for Saul's youngest son was named Eshbaal, after the Canaanite Sun deity, Baal, meaning "man of God" (Baal).

The later Hebrew editions of the Scriptures renamed him, understandingly, Ishboshet meaning, "man of disgrace."

Whether this was because he was particularly villainous, or purely because his name was anathema, is not stated.

The lineage of Saul was not to be allowed to survive. In the reign of David, who was adopted by Samuel as a young rival candidate, and groomed, whilst Saul was still king, annihilated the Sauline bloodline.[7]

After several successful campaigns against the surrounding kingdoms of Ammon, Moab and Edom, Saul, of which the scriptures say little compared to more favoured leaders, is ordered by Samuel to declare a holy war on the Malekites, and to spare none, human or animal.

Saul, being a man of honour, disobeyed the command whereupon Samuel himself hacks the captive Amalekite King to pieces. Amid such tension and, after several condemnations of Saul by Samuel, the latter invokes the archetypal symbol of the EPHOD.

This was a mantle symbolising priestly authority. A similar garment, called the "pallium"[8] was given to bishops of the early Christian Church by the Roman Pontiff. This empowered them to consecrate other bishops, and was a symbol of their authority. The practice, it was believed, was adopted from a (later) Imperial tradition.

Saul tried to restrain Samuel by clutching at his clothing. The Ephod tears and Samuel seizes the opportunity to condemn Saul:

"The Lord has torn the Kingdom of Israel from you this day and has given it to a neighbour."

A later editor, according to some sources, added the references to a successor. The symbolic renting of a mantel and its psychological impact, especially if the mantel was sacred, is repeated on several occasions in the scriptures. The ritual donning of a mantel is symbolic of investing or passing of authority. The renting of the Temple Veil in the New Testament, is an instance of this, symbolising, in a similar manner, the destruction of the old Hebrew order in its acquiescence to Roman heliopianism.

In this respect, it is possible that the ram's skin worn by Jacob, was part of a ritual surrounding the golden fleeced fertility ram of Ur, indicating his authority to obtain Isaac's legacy. If this was the case, then the ritual held the respect of antiquity and was therefore, a very potent archetype.

In the Hebrew archetypal memory, Christ "the Lamb of God" would invoke archaic associations of authority, as well as invocations to be childlike.

As far as Saul is concerned, Samuel sets out forthwith, to destroy him, by secretly anointing David, then a shepherd boy.

The choice of a shepherd boy is, possibly, not coincidental for there existed in the tradition of the Sumerian, Egyptian and Hyksos kings, to be known as "Shepherd Kings", casting the populace as sheep, to be cared for by the shepherd, appropriate also for the god whose symbol was a ram.

David's reputation is promoted from the outset, as a warrior contender for the kingship, with his slaying of the Philistine giant, Goliath. Significantly, this is achieved with a stone, a central archetype with sacred connotations.

In the context of known warfare of those days, the incident, like many in the scriptures, was probably intended to be understood allegorically. Goliath was probably meant to represent collective Philistine might.

The Cretan serpent archetype, which was evident in Exodus, is still extant in the Hebrew tradition in the allusion to the sacred serpent rock[9]. This was where Adonijah, David's eldest son sacrificed sheep and oxen on his declaration of successor to David.

Another Cretan archetype is alluded to during the battle to take Jerusalem. David is reputed to have said to his warriors:

"Whoever would smite the Jebusites (the occupants of Jerusalem, thought to be Canaanites), let him get up the water shaft to attack…" There is a textual problem in the translation of water shaft. In Hebrew, the word is "tsinnor", though meaning a water pipe is thought to be, by scholars, technically unsatisfactory. One suggestion is that the word means a weapon shaped like a trident, the symbol of the Cretan Sea God and was possibly (or probably), also used by the Philistines.

In order to legitimise his claim to the throne, David needed to marry into the royal family and despite fierce opposition from Saul, he married Saul's daughter Michah. After Saul's death, David was in a position, with the support of the army and the clergy, to take the crown. This David did, becoming the first King of Judah.

After the assassination of Saul's heir, Ishboshet, and the defection of Saul's commander, Abner, he also became King of Israel. David then set about uniting the country and driving the Philistines into the sea by attacking the coastal plain. However, in the face of such a formidable force as the Philistines, the Hebrews were forced to resort to guerrilla warfare, narrated in terms very similar to those describing the Mosaic campaign in Egypt.

The Ark (the bark of Amen?) had been captured by the Philistines some decades before and was housed in the temple of Dagon. This was in keeping with the heliopian tradition of cultural accommodation, symbolising the unification of the two cultures. The statue of Dagon, "the Lord of the Stars", is caused to fall to the ground, an event of some cultural and psychological significance. Coincident with this, and redolent of the warfare of Exodus, a plague of boils breaks out in the town and the fields are infested with mice, with the consequence that the Philistines return the Ark to the Israelites, symbolising their independence.

David, in a celebratory ritual, wearing the Ephod, is seen as God's appointed King of Israel. This is reflected in the Psalms, many of which are thought to have been written or commissioned by David.

"The spirit of the Lord speaks to me, his word is upon my tongue. The God of Israel has spoken, The Rock of Israel has said to me…"

(II Samuel XXIII-2-4)

Here again is the ancient Atlantean/Sumerian sacred mountain or rock archetype.

As David came to ending his reign, the traditional laws of blood succession were again abrogated. Adonijah, David's eldest surviving son, whose name meant My Lord[10], though supported by the loyal commander Joab, was not the prophet's choice. Solomon, the son of a concubine, was anointed king, further removing the crown from the house of Saul. Shortly after, Adonijah and Joab are assassinated. Few rank with Joab in ancient narrative, as an example of enduring loyalty.

Solomon's reign saw great prosperity from controlling the Mediterranean and the Red Sea, the tollgate through which much of international eastern and western trade passed. Solomon's prestige was greatly enhanced by his marriage to the Egyptian Pharaoh Siamun's daughter, thought to have come about as a result of Solomon's conquest of the coastal plain towns, including Canaanite Gezer, which formed the princess's dowry.

Siamun (or Siamen) was the penultimate pharaoh of the Libyan dynasty, corresponding to the epoch of almost total supremacy of the Amenite priesthood. The following dynasty saw a brief period of Egyptian conquest in Palestine under Shoshenq I, reputedly, an ally of Solomon[11]. It may have been this however, that occasioned Solomon's cultural and diplomatic links with Arabia Felix, the land of Sheba.

Sheba, in a "marriage" alliance, bore Solomon a son who founded a dynasty of Ethiopian rulers, resulting in cultural links between the two countries that are still evident today.

David, in his liaison with Bathsheba (the house of Sheba), may have had a strategic alliance in mind, for Bathsheba was married to Uriah, a Hittite.

Solomon therefore, with his alliance with Hiram of Lebanon, and the House of Sheba, would be power broker between the Assyrian neo-Hittite north and east, and Egypt on the west.

David, with the marriage to his third son Absalom to the daughter of Talmai, King of Geshur, an Aramean state on the Golan Heights, was probably part of David's northern defence's strategy against the nascent empire of the Assyrians.

Solomon's reign saw the resurgence of Sumerian Qaballism, which in the Hebrew, was an aural tradition, and almost certainly met with the disapproval of the prophets.

Towards the end of Solomon's reign, Jeroboam revolted, aided by the prophet Ahijah. This was because of the pagan, that is, heliopian practices, typical of surrounding cultures, were being practised at Solomon's court.[12]

Ahijah, imitating Samuel, ritually tore his new garment to pieces, to impress upon Solomon his prophecy that the kingdom would be split. The rebellion was suppressed and Jeroboam was given sanctuary in Egypt, an indication possibly, that old cultural rivalries remained.

It is significant in this respect that the reigns of Solomon and Shishak (Sheshonq) were typified by prosperity and concomitant building programmes.

Both kingdoms were an amalgamation of two kingdoms, a reflection in the Judaic culture, of the Egyptian culture, from which the Exodus took place.

With the end of Solomon's reign, the power of the prophets increased, leading to the Deuteronic Code and thence the rise of Rabbinical rule, reflecting the similar state of affairs in Egypt.

Solomon's death quickly brought a split between the Northern Kingdom of Israel and the southern kingdom of Judah. The North seceded under Jeroboam, returned from exile in Egypt, whilst Rehoboam retained Judah, including Jerusalem.

Jeroboam, possibly influenced by his sojourn in Egypt, prudently did nothing to prevent the diviocratisation of the Northern Kingdom's pantheon, being surrounded as he was by similar cosmogonies as the Canaanites, Phoenicians and Philistines.

He revived two ancient sanctuaries of Bethel and Dan, in the extreme north east, as rival cult centres to Jerusalem. In these he placed a golden calf, the symbol of Hathor and the Delta Saqqara bull cult.

Clearly then, two strains of Delta culture, the bull cult and the Cretan snake-pillar cult evident in the Exodus, were still cultural veins in the Hebrew culture at this time and again testifies to the longevity of cultural traits residing in the archetypal memory.

The dual culture of the Hebrews reflected in the two kingdoms, transported in the Exodus from Egypt heliopian north and monotheistic south, still persisted in the nations of Israel and Judah. The symmetry of opposites (predominantly heliopian Egypt and predominantly monotheistic Israel) was maintained as southern (upper heliopian) and northern (lower monotheistic) kingdoms in Egypt and complemented as northern (heliopian) and southern (monotheistic) kingdoms in Israel.

The bull cult was associated with the Sumerian Ishtar, who was in the Canaanite, Astarte or Asherat, hence, Jeroboam was instituting a measure of cultural harmony with surrounding cultures, lessening the threat of aggression.

Judah remained the stronghold of the orthodoxy under Asa and Jehosophat. The "pagan" practices perpetrated by Maacah, Rehoboam's widow and regent during Asa's minority, were stamped out and idols destroyed.

Between 876 and 850 BC, when Omri and his son Ahab reigned in the Northern Kingdom, some measure of prosperity was regained, in alliance with the Phoenicians.

Omri built in Samaria as a counter attraction to Jerusalem and that he fostered Phoenician-Israeli relations is evidenced by the marriage of his son Ahab to the Sidonic Princess Jezebel, named after the Canaanite Sun deity.

The Bible states that he "did more evil than all who were before him." (I Kings XVI-25)

Ahab is similarly condemned for legitimising the worship of the Canaanite Sun God Baal.[13]

The heliopianisation of the Hebrews was fiercely resisted by the orthodox prophets of monotheism, the leading exponents at that time being Elijah and his protege, Elisha, who were the arbiters of the potent magic of Yahweh.

A notable instance involving the sacrifice of an ox by the priests of Baal, is used to demonstrate Yahweh's power.

Elijah calls for two bullocks and challenges the priests of Baal to choose one and lay the pieces on a pyre, but not to light it. He would also do the same and then they were to call on "their Gods" to initiate the burning. (I Kings XVIII-23-42).

The priests of Baal accept the challenge but are unable to provide, by their intercession, spontaneous ignition of the pyre. Some hours later, after midday and much mocking by Elijah, the prophet orders twelve stones to be placed around the pyre and the sacrifice is drenched three times with "water".

In the evening, at the time of sacrifice and feasting, the "fire of the Lord fell and consumed the burnt sacrifice, and the wood and the stones and the dust and licked up the water that was in the trench."

Clearly, the bull cult, which was anathema to Moses, is still prevalent in the kingdom of Israel and also the description has similarities with the Cretan-Nestorian sacrifice of the Odyssey.

Elijah is familiar the flaming wine ritual not surprisingly, since the culture was derived from the Cretan infused Delta of Egypt, the history of which, the prophets would be aware, being the scholars of the tribe.

The distillation of alcohol described as flaming wine had been known for some centuries. Ethyl alcohol is, in appearance, indistinguishable from water. The magic of Yahweh then begins to look like the appliance of scientific knowledge, often appearing as magic to the unlearned.

A strategically aimed burning arrow perhaps was the spectacular "fire of God." Fire, which held archaic associations with Moses, was an archetype symbolising the presence of God.

It was used in the New Testament to symbolise the Pentecostal presence of the Deity. The ancient and potent archetype of the stone is also invoked and numbering twelve, the number associated with the twelve apostles led by Peter, the rock.

Elijah is versed in the priestly tradition of the Hebrews and is deft in the use of archetypes for he evokes the "Ephod" ritual of Samuel on his meeting with Elisha. Elijah throws his mantle over the young man who at the time is ploughing with "twelve yoke of oxen" (I Kings XIX-19) as a symbolic gesture of appointed authority.

Again, the mantle of Elijah, when he is being borne to heaven in a fiery chariot, falls upon the shoulders of Elisha as a spectacular conferring of authority and a sign of succession.

The event takes place at a gathering of the populace "and when the sons of the prophets which were to view at Jericho, saw him they said the spirit of Elijah doth rest on Elisha." (II Kings II-8)

The power of the Ephod ritual is made manifest at the gathering, for like Elijah, Elisha:

"Took the mantle of Elijah that fell from him and smote the waters and said, 'where is the Lord God of Elijah' and when he also had smitten the waters, they parted hither and thither and Elisha went over."

In the same allegorical sense as Moses parting the waters of the Red (kingdom) Sea, Elisha, smiting the waters which moved hither and thither, is walking among the gathering waving his mantle and reinforcing his claim to religious authority in the wake of the great Elijah.

This is in the great Mosaic tradition, a tradition that was nurtured and associated with Jesus.

The priestly power of appointment is still extant in modern Christian coronation ritual deriving from the Holy Roman Empire and the wearing of a cloak or mantle is still central symbol of authority in primitive cultures.

Another ploy of Moses is used by Elisha to deter invading Moabites. He has the valley dug with ditches that fill up with water. When the Moabites see the water in the sunlight, it appears to them as "red as blood" (II Kings III-22) which they believe to be the blood of slain, and take flight.

The incident has much in common with Moses making the rivers run "red with blood" (Exodus VII-20). To the Moabites, this signalled the anger of Astarte or Anat, the goddess whose symbol was a cow.

Like Hathor in the myth of "the old age of Ra", Anat waded in the blood of the slain.

Another Cretan archetype appears in the reign of Ahab, giving rise to an accommodation of the Sun God and the fertility culture, similar to that in Egypt with Osiris and the pillar of Anu. In the Northern Kingdom of Israel, Ahab had erected a pillar of Baal symbolising the unity of the two cultural undercurrents of the Exodus culture, the Egyptian heliopian and the Cretan derived Delta fertility. Ahab's action was to provoke a bloody coup, instigated by Elisha, with the purpose of liquidating the royal line of the Northern Kingdom. Such was the hatred of the Sun God by the orthodoxy, that his name came to mean Satan, Baal Zebub, "the God of the flies" which is a corruption of Baal Zebul, "God of the lofty place", the Mashu Mountains, the portals of Heaven.

In an act of treachery, Jehu slays Ahaziah, the son of Ahab, and Jehoram, the king of Judah, and proceeded to annihilate the royal line, consisting of some seventy persons, starting with Jezebel. He smashed the pillar of Baal and oversaw the decline of the two kingdoms, culminating in the dissolution of the monarchy and the institution of the Deuteronomic Code, laws devised and administered by the priest caste, a religious autocracy under Yahweh.

With the death of Athaliah (842-837 BC) of the house of Omri, the only woman to occupy the throne of the Hebrew kingdoms (like Hatshepsut until the Ptolemys), the religious heliopian pluralism's struggle with monotheism was virtually over. Israel, within three generations, would disappear under the might of the Assyrians, and the southern kingdom, a century later, would be absorbed by the Babylonians under Nebuchadnezzar.

As long as the possibility of kingship existed, then the practice of Baalism would persist as occurred with Ahaz[14], indeed, it would be said that kingship offered some guarantee of national identity and survival, if only by marriage alliances.

At the end of the eighth century BC, Assyrians under Sargon conquered Israel (circa 727 BC) whence it remained the Assyrian province of Samaria.

The prophets, led by Isiah, endeavoured to consolidate monotheism in Judah under Hezekiah, who, with his religious reforms, that is, the eradication of Baalism, was recorded favourably for doing "what was right and faithful before the Lord his God" (II Chronicles XXXI-20).

With Assyrian might still in the ascendancy and burgeoning westward, it was inevitable that strategically and culturally, Judah presented an obstacle.

Senacherib, Sargon's successor, attempted to take Jerusalem and almost succeeded.

It was possible that Hezekiah's alliance with Egypt, the Pharaoh of which was referred to by Ezekiel as "a whale in the seas" (Ezekiel XXXII-2), provoked the Assyrian attack. Manasseh saw things differently and was an obedient vassal to Senacherib's successor Esarhaddon, who invaded and conquered Egypt. Heliopian practices were restored in the kingdoms under the Assyrians.

It is during the Assyrian period that the mission of Jonah occurred. Jonah reputedly spent three days in the body of a "whale" however, if the whale is taken to be Nineveh of the Assyrian ruler's court, in the same sense as Ezekiel describes the Pharaoh, then Jonah becomes some sort of emissary, spending some time in the invader's camp negotiating terms.

This was possibly at the inception of Manasseh's reign. The myth serves, like all myths, to illustrate the need to disguise history (of the prevailing culture) in mythological form, necessary for its survival.

Explicit history would, no doubt perishes in unfavourable climates and this explains why myths, ostensibly absurd stories, taken literally, were allowed to survive, providing the cultural heritage and adhesion necessary for the culture to survive.

The Judaic culture was aware of this and it was quick to suppress pagan culture on the ascendancy of Judaic Christianity in the Roman culture.

Religious pluralism began to re-emerge with the Renaissance and the rediscovery of the Greco-Roman cultural tradition.

With the decline of the Assyrian Empire, Judah regained some independence under Josiah and the prophets instituted the Deuteronomic Code, similar to the Islamic Sharia today, that is, the laws of God as enunciated by the prophets.

Josiah was defeated at Meggido in a disastrous encounter with the Egyptian Pharaoh Neco (circa 607 BC), who in turn was vanquished by Nebuchadnezzar and the Babylonians at Karchemish. Judah was absorbed into the Chaldean Empire (circa 586 BC). The tribe of Abraham was once more part of their original culture in more senses than one.

Many of the Hebrews were forcibly relocated to Babylon where, for forty-eight years, they were exiled. Without a king, their monotheism, administered by the prophets, preserved their cultural identity amidst the surrounding pluralistic cultures representing, as it did the ancient polar opposite and adversary of the ancient heliopian Sumerians.

Ultimately, as the Book of Daniel reveals, an alliance between the exiles and Persia would culminate with the defeat of Babylon and a return of the Hebrews to Judah.

Daniel, we are told in the Bible, was "understanding in all visions and dreams" (Daniel I-17) and together with Hananiah, Misheal and Azariah, was a royal prince of Judah, the issue of Jehoiakim, the last king of Judah.

The princes were taken to the court of Nebuchadnezzar by Ashpenaz, the Master of Eunuchs with whom, Daniel was "in favour and tender love" (Daniel I-9).

At the Chaldean court, the four were given Chaldean names of Belteshazzar, Shadrach, Meshach and Abed-nego respectively. Daniel's name is almost identical with Nebuchadnezzar's successor Belshazzar, which seems to indicate some sort of royal elevation of Daniel and which, seems supported by the status of Daniel as court adviser and magus or vizier. Both names also contain the royal prefix of the Sun God Bel or Baal accorded as in Egypt only to royals.

Daniel finds favour with Nebuchadnezzar by first, determining what the dream was that the king had forgotten, and secondly, by interpreting it to the king's satisfaction. All that is said in the Bible as to how Daniel was able to determine what the dream was, is in the statement "Then was the secret revealed to Daniel in a night vision" (Daniel II-9), in other words, in a dream. The dream that Daniel presents as the king's is, or could equally have been Daniel's own as it expresses, from Daniel's point of view, a large measure of wish fulfilment of one held hostage by an enemy.

The dream, which the other magi were unable to ascertain, and which Daniel presents, is recounted in Daniel II-31 and following:

"Thou, O King, sawest and behold a great image. This great image, whose brightness was excellent, stood before thee, and the form thereof was terrible. This image's head was of fine gold, his breast and arms of silver, his belly and thighs of brass, his legs of iron, his feet, part of iron and part of clay. Thou sawest till that a stone was cut out without hands, which smote the image upon his feet that were of iron and clay and brake them to pieces. Then was the iron, the clay, the brass, the silver and the gold broken to pieces together and become like the chaff of the summer threshing floors; and the wind carried them away, that no place was found for them, and the stone that smote the image became a great mountain and filled the whole earth."

Clearly evident in the dream are Sumerian and Cretan archetypes. The great image of a man, whose members progress from base clay for the feet through iron (which by the 6th century BC, had become more common than brass), brass and silver to gold at the head is Sumerian Qaballistic Macroscopic Man, representing the Babylonian Empire culture.

A similar symbolism appertained in Egypt with the members of the body of Osiris making up the Egyptian heliopian culture that Seth, the brother of Osiris (i.e., the Cretan Delta culture) scattered over the land and which, Isis laboriously reassembled (i.e., re-established heliopianism).

The personification of the culture was often made under the image of the king, as Pharaoh meaning Egypt or Caesar, meaning Rome or Jacob, meaning Israel. The increasing nobility of the metals incorporated in the figure of the dream from the feet, represent the social groupings in the culture and also the various gods who together, make up the celestial body of gods, gold, the Sun, silver, the Moon etc.

The (Cretan) archetypal stone (also the "sacred stones" of the Sumerians) represents the twin veins of the Hebrew culture. The stone "that was cut out without hands" is evocative of the tablets of Moses wrought on the instructions of Yahweh, and is the stone that will eventually destroy Babylon, Daniel's and the Israelite's captor.

It is a tribute to Daniel's guile that he sells the king the idea that Babylon is the empire that is represented by the stone:

"And in the days of these kings shall the God of Heaven set up a kingdom which shall never be destroyed…and it shall stand forever, for as much as thou sawest that the stone was cut out of the mountain without hands, and that it break in pieces together…and the stone that smote the image became a great mountain and filled the whole earth." (Daniel II-44, 45)

The archetypal mountain, often invoked in the Bible for example, "They shall not hurt or destroy in all my holy mountain" (Isaiah II-6-9) had great religious significance. It was associated with the divine law of Mount Sinai and Moses. It had archaic origins, appearing in the Hittite myth of Ullikumi, the Cretan "Monstrous Mountain" adversary of the Weather God and as the foe of Sumerian heliopianism, Humbaba, in the Epic of Gilgamesh.

It is also linked to the Cretan-Atlantean legend. The temple of the Sea God, the god from water, the symbol of fertility, was situated on an acropolis in a country "said by him (Solon) to be very lofty and precipitous on the side of the sea, the country immediately about and surrounding the city was a level plain itself surrounded by mountains which descended towards the sea."[15]

The mountain represented perhaps, the ultimate in security and constancy and its symbolism is still used in latter day hymns. It was the symbol that Jesus chose to establish the claim to eternality of his church.

Daniel is promoting monotheism with the clever use of potent archetypes in a traditional prophetic way which, on observation, seems to suggest a psychological mechanism not withstanding precognition, that if something is suggested often enough, it will come to pass where the group is concerned.

It is similar to the mechanism of imagination that must contain some element of precognition, often eventually comes to pass. The idea is parent to the reality.

The Babylonian Empire, shortly after the prophecies of Daniel, was destroyed by an alliance of the Hebrews and Medes (the wind of the threshing floor). The great mountain would fill the whole earth in the form of Christianity, the filial culture of the Hebrews.

We are told that Nebuchadnezzar "fell upon his face and worshipped Daniel" and made him "ruler over the whole province of Babylon", which seems a little strange in the context, for Nebuchadnezzar, yielding to fashion of the time, had erected a great image of gold, 90 feet high. This image, one can assume, was of himself as a god.

Mishach, Shadrach and Abednego, but not Daniel, were arrayed for not worshipping the statue.

In one of Nebuchadnezzar's own dreams, we see the appearance of the Babylonian/Sumerian archetype of the tree of life (Daniel IV-10 and following) which serves to distinguish between the two cultural heritages of the two "dramatis personae" Nebuchadnezzar and Daniel.

The former, was purely Sumerian in antecedent and the latter derived from a heritage containing Sumerian, Cretan and Egyptian influences.

In his dream, Nebuchadnezzar "beheld a tree in the midst of the earth and the height thereof was great. The tree grew and was strong and the height thereof reached unto heaven and the sight thereof to the end of all the earth. The leaves thereof were fair and the fruit thereof much, and in it was meat for all, the beasts of the field had shadow under it and the fowls of heaven dwelt in the boughs thereof and all flesh was fed off it. I saw, in visions of my head upon my bed, and, behold a watcher and a holy one came down from heaven. He cried aloud and said thus, Hew down the tree, and cut off the branches, shake off his leaves and scatter his fruit, let the beasts get away from under it and the fowls from its branches. Nevertheless leave the stump of his roots in the earth even with a band of iron and brass in the tender grass of the field and let it be wet with the dew of heaven and let his portion be with the beasts in the grass of the earth. Let his heart be changed from man's and let a beast's heart be given unto him and let seven times pass over him. This matter is by the decree of the watchers and the demand of the holy ones; to the intent that the living may know that the most high ruleth in the kingdom of men and giveth it to whomsoever he will and setteth up over it the basest of men."

The archetype is the ancient Sumerian fertility tree of life "feeding all flesh" and with "meat for all." The fowls of the air, are symbols for spirits.

Often in seal depictions and stone carvings, the king is shown as dispenser of the celestial waters of fertility on to the tree of life. The tree in the dream represents the king as proxy for the culture.

Nebuchadnezzar is given a vision of his own destruction indicated by the personalisation of the description. The destruction is urged by a celestial watcher or shaman who can be no other than Daniel or some cultural ally. It is small wonder that Daniel was "astonied" for one hour and that his thoughts "troubled him" (Daniel IV-19) for the dream, to the skilled interpreter, represents the King's subconscious awareness of what would amount to a conspiracy to destroy the culture, legislating in favour of the "most high" that is, Yahweh.

Daniel confirms that the King is represented by the tree; "The tree thou sawest...it is thou O King" and proceeds to forecast the King's downfall as an inevitable consequence of the watchers urging "that they shall drive thee from men and thy dwelling shall be with the beasts of the field, and they shall make thee to eat grass as oxen and they shall wet thee with the dew of heaven." (Daniel IV-24-25)

Daniel is careful not to offend the King for he assures Nebuchadnezzar that his kingdom will be secure. "And whereas they commanded thee to leave the stump of the tree roots; thy kingdom shall be secure unto thee...if it may be a lengthening of thy tranquillity." (Daniel IV-26, 27)

It is clear however, that Daniel is capitalising on the dream for propaganda purposes, for the dream, in the light of subsequent events, is presaging the King's death. "All this came upon King Nebuchadnezzar. At the end of twelve months, he walked into the palace of the kingdom of Babylon...the same hour was the thing fulfilled upon Nebuchadnezzar and he was driven from men and did eat grass as oxen and his body was wet with the dew of heaven till his hairs were grown like and eagles feathers and his nails like bird's claws." (Daniel IV-28-34)

In symbolic terms, the passage could be translated:

"He was driven from (the world) of men" and "did eat grass as oxen", was buried where his body would be "wet with the dew of heaven."

"His hairs were grown like an eagle's feathers and his nails like bird's claws", is the ancient symbolism for the spirit guardians of the tree of life, often seen flanking the tree of life as eagle men. The stump of the tree has the same symbolism as "being cut down in the prime of life." The remaining verses in the Book of Daniel, revert to the first person in which Nebuchadnezzar eulogises Yahweh, a circumstance at odds with historical evidence which describes Nebuchadnezzar and his son Nabonidus spending most of their reigns restoring ancient Sumerian temples of the Sun God and the Moon God.

The verses may therefore have been added to give the impression that Babylon adhered to the cult of Yahweh.

The Bible infers that Belshazzar is the son of Nebuchadnezzar (Daniel V-11-23) but other sources[16] refer to Nabonidus (circa 556-539) as succeeding Nebuchadnezzar.

Belshazzar his son ruled Babylon when the Nabonidus retired to Arabia. It is in the reign of Belshazzar, whose name reflects the prevailing heliopian culture, that the destruction of Babylon and the restoration of the Hebrews to their land occurs. This uncharacteristic act of generosity on the part of the Medes infers that the restoration of Israel to the Hebrews was in fact the result of a military alliance between the Hebrews and the Medes.

A close examination of the Biblical passages concerning the "writing on the wall" support this assertion.

The Book of Daniel recounts that during a great feast to a "thousand of his lords", the king had brought the gold and silver vessels which "his father Nebuchadnezzar had taken out of the temple which was in Jerusalem. They drank wine and praised the gods of gold, silver and brass, of iron, of wood and of stone."

The passage indicates that the sacred vessels of the Hebrews were among the sacred vessels of the Babylonian heliopian cosmogeny. This is consistent with heliopian diviocratic philosophy, all the gods united in a family pantheon.

This policy was clearly evident in Ancient Egypt and later in heliopian Greece and Rome, where the Sea God, Poseidon was united in the pantheon with almost equal authority as Zeus, as was Seth with Osiris in later Egyptian heliopian periods. Only Delta (Cretan) and Amenite factions opposed this policy requiring absolute ascendancy for their god.

This policy also aligns with the original policy of the Babylonians in attempting to ameliorate the Hebrew's recalcitrant monotheism by culturally absorbing them, unsuccessfully as it turned out, into the Babylonian culture.

The passage also confirms the role of dream symbolism. In the first dream that Daniel is called upon to interpret, that is, the image of gold, silver, brass etc., represented the culture and the gods of the Babylonian cosmogony, which Daniel, wistfully, as with the dream of the tree, uses to convince the Babylonians of the destruction of their culture.

The narration of the feast continues:

"In the same hour came forth the fingers of a man's hand and wrote over against the (sacred) candlestick upon the plaster of the wall of the King's palace and the King saw part of the hand that wrote. Then the King's countenance was changed and his thoughts troubled him so that the joints of his loins were loosed and his knees smote one against the other." (Daniel V, 1-6)

The influence of Daniel at the court has apparently waned, for the King has to be informed by the Queen that he can interpret the writing. (Daniel V-11)

The association of prophet and Queen occurs frequently throughout history. It was instanced in Egypt with Hatshepsut and often, in early Christian times, the King is converted subsequent to influential pressure from the Queen.

According to the Bible, the words written on the wall were: "Mene, mene, tekel upharsin."

"Mene, God has numbered thy kingdom and finished it; Tekel, Thou art weighed in the balances and found wanting; Peres, Thy kingdom is divided and given to the Medes and Persians." (Daniel V-25-28)

Biblical scholars give the meaning of the words mina, mina, as a shekel and a half shekel, being weights or units of money.[17] The sixteenth century "Heraica Biblia" which translates the Hebrew into Latin, has the translation of the words as "Numera, Numera appende and (sint) dividentes."[18]

Numera or Numerati, were irregular infantry, mercenaries or partisans.[19]

This translation suggests that some sort of military threat is imminent. The country is divided (into Babylonians and Hebrews) possibly due to an uprising in which foreign mercenaries are involved.

In this situation, which is not dissimilar to the situation which arose in Mosaic Egypt when that country was also divided between heliopian and Mosaic fertility forces, many of the incarcerated Hebrews would be sympathetic to an allied invasion force and possibly actively supported it by sabotage and guerrilla tactics.

The language on the wall is foreign to the Babylonian court but not to Daniel. This is not surprising for the writing, taken literally, is a reference to the ancient Egyptian ritual of Judgement in the Maati Hall of the Gods. This involved weighing the heart of the deceased in a balance against truth. The ritual, or knowledge of it, seems still to be extant in the Delta expatriate Hebrew culture at the time of Daniel.

It is testament again to the longevity of cultural archetypes and accounts for the concept of the "Last Judgement" being carried into the Christian tradition from the Judaic.

Foreign words mysteriously appearing on the wall of the court evocative of the God Thoth or the Babylonian equivalent would, in that era, prove unnerving to the Babylonians and it instances again the use of archetypes as a means of psychological warfare.

"Peres", added in the Biblical text, shows a distinct similarity to the Egyptian word "Pero" meaning "the house" or "the house of", from which the word Pharaoh is derived, hence the Biblical translation "thy kingdom (or house) is divided."

That the writing on the wall was manifestly foreign to the Babylonian court suggests that it may have had some connection with the Egyptian language familiar to Daniel, after all, the sacred stones or tablets of Moses were probably inscribed with the language familiar to Moses, that being Egyptian hieroglyphs or hieratics, which suggests Hebraic involvement.

The writing was, in the light of subsequent events, a cipher. The cause of Belshazzar's terror is clear, for in essence the message was, "your kingdom is split (or broken, or finished), the enemy forces are at the gates" and his deposition is imminent for the narrative continues:

"In that night was Belshazzar, the King of the Chaldeans slain and Darius the Mede took the kingdom about three score and two years old." (Daniel V, 30,31)

Darius I has been identified as Hystaspes[20] and since sources identify Cyrus as the instigator of the decree allowing the Hebrews to return to Judah[21] it seems the Hebrew chronicler is exercising poetic licence as Hystaspes reigned after the first return of the Hebrews lead by Zerubbabel.

The natural tendency of the Hebrews to align themselves with the enemy of their captors was not the only grounds for the alliance, for there were also cultural reasons in the nascent creed of Zoroaster.

The latter was an Iranian prophet who lived between 630 and 553 BC, the era embracing the Hebrew exile. He converted Wishtaspa, king of a kingdom in Eastern Iran when he was forty-two years old. (circa 588 BC) He has also been connected with western Iran by Western Iranian magi who claimed he had been a magus, after accepting his doctrine in the second half of the fifth century BC Zoroaster's religion, differing from later Zoroastrianism, appears as monotheistic but also containing the ethical dualism of two opposing principles, truth and falsehood.

God, known as Ahura Mazda, acts through seven emanations with one emanation on the side of falsehood. The phrase "and let seven times pass over him" (Daniel IV-16) in connection with Nebuchadnezzar's death, although an ancient Sumerian mystical number, may have had some Zoroastrian significance to the Biblical chronicler.

The almost pure monotheism of the Zoroastrian creed, which rejected images and temples of idolatry, provided the perfect cultural ally to the interned Hebrews surrounded as they were, by their heliopian foes.

Seen in this light, it is quite possible that Cyrus allowed the re-colonisation of Judah in return for services rendered and presumably as a strategic buffer state between the heliopian west and his own sphere of influence. Such a cultural alliance throws into perspective the visit of the Eastern Magi at the birth of Christ. Indeed, Christianity, the cultural child of Hebrew monotheism, it could be said, was pre-empted in its cultural inception by Mithraism, the refined cultural child of Zoroastrianism.

This was to become one of the main adversaries of Christianity, from which, the latter would borrow much ritual and mysteries. Much Mithraic symbolism is evident in Ezekiel's vision, Ezekiel being a contemporary of Daniel, was in exile in Babylon during the rise of Zoroastrianism in Persia.

Daniel, like Ezekiel, also had "prophetic" visions which, in the light of inaccurate chronology, seem to be the application of either wish fulfilment or accounts written after the event as prophecy, as a method of influencing future events. Nonetheless, the visions are interesting because of their archetypal content.

Daniel is recounted as seeing in his vision, "The four winds of heaven strove upon the great sea, and four great beasts came up from the sea one another. The first was like a lion and had eagles wings. I beheld till the wings thereof were plucked and it was lifted up from the earth and made to stand upon feet as a man and a man's heart was given to it. And behold, another beast, a second like a bear and it raised up itself on one side and it had three ribs in the mouth of it between the teeth of it…After this, another like a leopard, which had upon the back of it four wings of a fowl and the beast had also four heads…and behold, a fourth beast…and strong exceedingly and it had great iron teeth…and it was diverse from all other beasts before it and it had ten horns…and the ten horns out of this kingdom are ten kings." (Daniel VII)

The imagery is classically mythical in form, the representing of cultures as fabulous beasts one of which is transformed into a man.

Here is another example of a man representing the culture. We see also the cultures arising from the sea or the ancient mythical "nether waters", the allegorical waters of the collective subconscious.

The first beast is reminiscent of Assyrian or Persian imagery similar to what can be still seen at Persepolis, city of the empire that was to rise after the exile of the Hebrews. The four animals are reputed to represent respectively, Babylonia, Greece, Macedonia and Asia Minor[22] but it is clear that much of the symbolism is Cretan, Mycenean and Anatolian in the form of the Protosyrian Daganic lion and leopard.

The Assyrian and Babylonian eagle with four wings depicted on Northern Palestinian and Phoenician ivories. The "great sea" is, in visionary terms, is a reference to the "psychological sea", the sea of the collective subconscious. The phallic horn imagery that became the ten kings, the most fertile of the tribe, evoke the sons of the Sea God's consort Cleito.

The vision is most likely a contemporary account in the genre of the time, of the cultural tides of the Persian Empire preceding that of the Greeks under Alexander in the fourth century BC.

The heliopian cultural tide under Alexander was to sweep over most of the known world and more, including the great Persian Empire of Darius who is mentioned as a contemporary of Belshazzar in the sixth century BC.

The vision of Ezekiel, though similar to that of Daniel, contains more specific Mithraic (Persian) symbolism. Ezekiel's vision of the four cherubim that is, winged sphinxes, shows a mixture of Egyptian and Zoroastrian archetypes:

"Everyone had four faces and everyone four wings…the sole of the feet was like the sole of a calf's foot. As for the likeness of their faces, they four had the face of a man, and the face of a lion on the right side, the face of an ox on the left side, the four also had the face of an eagle…their appearance was like the burning coals of fire and like the appearance of lamps…and out of the fire went forth lightning…behold one wheel upon the earth…as their rings were full of eyes." (Ezekiel I-5-16)

The faces of man, lion, ox and eagle are classical Egyptian archetypes of the major cults of the culture, the eagle of Upper Egypt, the ox of the Delta and the universal Daganic lion. The face of the man is the pharaoh, the representative of the celestial executive. These archetypes betray the persistence in the Hebrew culture and archetypal memory of the archetypes of their ancestors.

Up to the Middle Ages do we see their promotion as Christian images purported to represent the four evangelists, the chroniclers of the sacred words, an archaic link to the ancient chronicler of the Maati Hall of Judgement, the god of words and magic, Thoth.

Fire has long been regarded by Zoroastrians as sacred. Light or lamps were symbolic of truth, goodness and enlightenment in Mithraic dualism. Lightning later became part of Mithraic symbolism and associated with Zeus in the Roman Pantheon, derived from the Anatolian Weather God Teshub.

The wheels, though evocative of the Sun and therefore the Sun God, associated with eyes, reinforces the imagery of the Sun God which in the Egyptian was often represented as the "Eye of Ra" or the "Eye of Horus", the son of the Sun God.

This imagery would hold Mithraic associations with the eyes as the gods of the heavens. These were represented in Mithraic symbolism as the Zodiac, sometimes depicted as a wheel.

In heliopian Rome, the wheel was also a symbol of Tyche, the Goddess of Fortune. In the vision therefore can be seen Persian cultural influences entering the Egyptian derived Hebrew tradition, stirring ancient heliopian archetypes in the Hebrew psyche. This cultural infusion produced a cultural affinity between the Persians and the Hebrews, as symbolised by the visit of the Magi of Christian tradition, and was to lead ultimately to a bitter conflict between the new, in cultural terms, nascent cultures of Mithraism and Christianity, one derived from the Persian, the other from the Hebrew.

After the defeat of Darius by Alexander and the Hellenization to some extent of the Persian culture, Mithraism was ameliorated to become a powerful cult in the Greco-Roman culture, particularly among the military.

The Hebrew tradition remained the monotheistic repository of opposition to heliopianism now embraced by its former ally Mithraism, and Christian symbolism eschewed many central Mithraic archetypes, though not ritual.

Many of the Ancient Egyptian archetypes remained naturally, such as the sphinx composite of man, eagle, ox and lion, associated with the sacred texts. Mithraic "tongues of flame" are referred to in the New Testament. In the course of time, according to the law of cultural action and reaction, the two cultures became adversaries for cultural ascendancy in a heliopian world. Mithraism in the van of the heliopian cultural forces was ultimately defeated by monotheistic Christianism and once more the Ancient Sea God had ascendancy.

It is clear that the Bible contains much poetic symbolism, despite the admonition to believe its stories literally. It is probable that such veiled symbolism was a necessary concomitant for its survival as a national history of the Hebrews.

References Chapter 9

[1] C. G. Jung, Archetypes and the Collective Unconscious

[2] W. G. De Burgh, The Legacy of the Ancient World, Vol 1, page 51

[3] M. Baigent, R. Leigh and H. Lincoln, The Holy Blood and the Holy Grail, page 286

[4] A. Cruden, Cruden's Compete Concordance, page 238

[5] J. Comay, The Hebrew Kings, page 14

[6] Ibid, page 13

[7] Ibid, page 36

[8] Bede, A History of the English Church and People, trans L. S. Price, page 334

[9] J. Comay, The Hebrew Kings, page 57

[10] W. G. De Burgh, The Legacy of the Ancient World, Vol 1, page 51

[11] Ibid, page 20

[12] J. Comay, The Hebrew Kings, page 70

[13] W. G. De Burgh, The Legacy of the Ancient World, Vol 1, page 51

[14] J. Comay, The Hebrew Kings, page 120

[15] J. V. Luce, The End of Atlantis (from Plato's Timaeus and Critias), page 167

[16] M. Baigent, R. Leigh and H. Lincoln, The Holy Blood and the Holy Grail

[17] D. and P. Alexander Lion, Concise Bible Handbook, page 230

[18] Hebraica Biblia Vol 3 (1546), page 1391

[19] J. F. Johnson, Hadrian's Wall, page 27

[20] Chamber's Encyclopaedia, Vol 14, page 826a

[21] W. G. De Burgh, The Legacy of the Ancient World, Vol 1, Page 49

[22] D. and P. Alexander Lion, Concise Bible Handbook, page 231

Chapter 10
The Romans

The starting point for examining the Roman culture in relation to other heliopian cultures is the Aeneid. This is a story rich in symbolism, as are all myths. It is a story of an exodus or migration of peoples ostensibly from several Eastern Mediterranean heliopian cultures.

As with all heliopian cultures, the Roman culture's uniqueness was not that it was a new culture, but paradoxically, that it was a development of preceding heliopian cultures. This involved incorporating and developing older concepts and philosophy, which was the tradition of heliopianism. It was just this heliopian traditionalism which essentially was cultural pluralism, that enabled the Roman culture to encompass such a large area of the then known world. This expansion was itself not unique, as each great heliopian culture before it, from the Sumerian through the Egyptian to the Greek, had increased the boundaries of cultured civilisation. This was not noticeably so in ancient times for cultural propagation is not in itself linear but follows more, an exponential, a natural curve, being a living entity.

In the Aeneid are mentioned various leaders and their races, Dardanus, Orontes and his Lycians [1] for example, Teucer from the "rocks of the Caucasus"[2] which indicates Anatolian or near Anatolian origin. Dido, the Queen of Carthage, refers to her Libyans as "Ye men of Tyre."[3] The latter is an allusion to her kinsman Teucer, King Peleus of Tyre and the old alliance between Phoenician Levant and Carthage. These are shown in the Odyssey as trading partners when Odysseus, after his sojourn in Egypt, encounters the rascally Phoenician.

Dido in offering Aeneas regency of Libya, displays some cultural affinity with the refugees and Aeneas. Rejection by Aeneas presages later Carthaginian animosity to Rome, manifested in the Punic Wars and Hannibal's invasion.

It was the Libyans that provided pharaonic dynasties during the Armenite ascendancy in Egypt. Cretan/ Mycenean influences were present on the Southern Mediterranean shores from an early date, as the Heraklion cycle of myths indicates.

Herakles (Mycenean/Cretan culture) travelled around the Northern and Southern shores of the Mediterranean, so it is possible that the Libyan culture contained Northern Mediterranean cultural traces as well as Anatolian. Herakles, as has been suggested, also represented Anatolian cultural influences.

The tradition that Herakles discovered Sicily and Italy seems to be corroborated by the Aeneid when the Trojans find Greeks already settled in Italy.[4] It is a partly for this reason that the Greek culture played such a dominant role in the Roman culture.

The Greek culture, as we have seen, was a development and distillation of Cretan, Hittite, Egyptian and Sumerian influence. Anatolian Hittite (Trojan) had strong Sumerian and Cretan influences. Cretan influence in Carthage may also be indicated by the presence of a queen in those ancient times, a tradition existing in Atlantis.

The Aeneid leaves little doubt that the exodus is primarily and culturally, Cretan /Anatolian in nature. Anchises, the father of the hero, is described as "pondering in his heart the things which he had learnt from men of old time, spake thus:

'There lieth in mid-ocean a certain island of Crete wherein is a mountain Ida. There was the first beginning of our nation. Thence came Teucer, our first father to the land of Troy.'"[5]

It is probable that Mount Ida was the sacred mountain of the Sea God of Atlantian Legend, for Venus the patroness of the Trojans was associated with Cleito and Crete. She was one of the daughters of Poseidon, the patron of the island.

Venus, "born of the sea foam", "brought from Mount Ida the herb dittany…The wild goats (Cretan warriors?) know it well if so that they have been wounded by arrows."

Venus was also associated with Cyprus, the subject of dispute between the Hittites and invaders, probably the Sea Peoples, Mycenaeans/Cretans.

A stone carving of a fertility goddess flanked by two goats has been found on the Canaanite seaboard. The same figure appears on Cretan vases, thought to be Astarte or Ishtar, another form of Venus.

In the story of Laocoon can be seen evidence of the Atlantian ritual in Troy. This supports Anchises postulation "For while Laocoon, the priest of Neptune (the Sea god) was slaying a bull at the altar of his god, there came two serpents across the sea from Tenedos whose heads and necks whereon were thick manes of hair."

Laocoon, among the few but influential, doubts the claim that bringing the Trojan Horse into the city will render it invisible, is crushed by the serpents that have fatally embroiled his twin sons. This story is rich in symbolism, for in the climate of intrigue and debate, the serpents with hairy heads are clearly enemy agents who appear to have won over the sons of Laocoon. The serpents suggest a mixture of Cretan serpent archetype and Mycenean /Protosyrian lion, the probable cultural mix of the invading (Greek) forces.

The horse, the symbol of the Sea god signifies the fall of the city by internal cultural allies of the Greeks. The employment of the Wooden Horse seems a similar strategy to that employed in the story of the Sibylline Books in later Rome. It appears as an attempt at adopting the invading culture in the hope that the Trojans will be seen as enemies.

This would have been a valid strategy when viewed in the context of cultural time. The traditional length of the war, ten years, in mythological time, represents a very long period of cultural hostility. In the historical context of the time, ten years was an inordinately long time to conduct a battle and seems to indicate the period, like the rest of the epic, was meant as an allegory.

Such bull slaying rituals as associated with Laocoon, are performed by the migrant Trojans[6] and are also found in the Odyssey. Such rituals also formed part of Hittite religious burial rites:

"There they brought four black oxen, and the priestess poured wine upon their heads and cut hairs from between the horns. And when they had burnt these they slew the oxen, holding dishes for their blood…Then they burnt the entrails with fire pouring oil upon them."

These rituals seem to be Cretan in origin and being extant in Anatolia indicate the extent to which the culture permeated in the archaic "Flood" era and subsequently, in accordance with the tidal cultural law.

Protosyrian influences are also present in the Aeneid. Acestes, King of Sicily, is described as having "the skin of a lion on his shoulders", presumably in the tradition of his country's discoverer, Herakles.

Among the funeral games of Anchises, the Trojans engage in a boxing tournament, a sport prominently displayed in frescoes at Knossos in Crete. From Anchises' tomb emerges a great snake which had seven coils, an ancient Cretan archetype and probably meant to symbolise the continuation of the Trojan culture after the death of the king.

Aeneas, representing the nascent Roman culture, being of divine birth, and in the tradition of the Anatolian Storm God derivative, Herakles, has to demonstrate the immortality of the culture. In the myth that demonstrates the heliopian philosophical tradition, this is achieved by the hero defeating death, illustrated by undertaking a journey to Hades and returning.

Anchises shows Aeneas what becomes of the spirits of the dead:

"Then Aeneas looked and beheld a river, and a great company of souls, thick as bees on a calm summers' day in a garden of lilies."

Here are archetypes associated with the Cretan snake fertility goddess and the Anatolian Cybele or Demeter who later appears associated with Roman mythology in the story of the Sibylline books. Water, souls as thick as bees and lilies, the ageless symbol of life. The devotees of Cybele, the great fertility goddess of Asia Minor, were known as "melissae" or bees, the agents of fertilisation.

In the Christian tradition, there is echoed the relationship of a demigod, Christ the son of a Madonna, representing fertility, as that between Aeneas and Venus. Christ's decent into Hades and return also echoes the founder of Roman culture. Christ cast as the second Moses the legendary founder of the Hebrew tradition, therefore unifies his claim to cultural acceptance in the Roman culture. Both cultures were derived from the Cretan, the Roman via the Greek (and Hittite) and the Hebrew via the Egyptian.

The Aeneid continues:

"And when he would know the meaning of the concourse, Anchises said, 'these are mortal souls which have yet to live again in mortal body and they are constrained to drink of the water of forgetfulness.' And Aeneas said, 'Nay my father, can any desire to take upon them the body of death.' Then Anchises made reply:

'Listen my son, and I will tell thee all, there is one soul in heaven and earth and the stars and the shining orb of the Moon and the great Sun himself, from which soul also cometh the life of man and of beast, and the birds of the air and the fishes of the sea. And this soul is of a divine nature, but the mortal body maketh it slow and dull. Hence came fear and desire and grief and joy so that, being as it were shut in a prison, the spirit beholdeth not any more the light that is without. And when mortal life is ended yet are not men quit of all the evils of the body seeing that these must needs be put away in many marvellous ways. For some are hung up to the winds, and some with their wickedness are washed out by water or burnt out with fire. But a ghostly pain we all endure. Then we that are found worthy are sent into Elysium and the plains of the blest. And when after many days, the soul is wholly pure, it is called to the river of forgetfulness, that it may drink thereof and so return to the world that is above.'"[7]

In this description which has some concepts in common with Buddhism, can be seen the heliopian concept of celestial unity, but in a way which incorporates the Cretan primacy of a single (Sea) god or life spirit. The Egyptian concept of Elysium is present and the planetary deities acknowledge that they are all unified in a universal spirit, the giver of all life. This has clearly shades of what was to become the widespread philosophy of Stoicism in Rome.

The concepts of punishment, purification and thence to the plains of Elysium after death are, in essence, from the Egyptian Judgement Before the Gods and the subsequent working in the Elysian Fields, before being taken to the company of the gods, the world that is above. The concept of a world above is hinted at in Mithraic imagery where the god Mithras holds two torches, one inverted. The upright torch, its fire symbolising the spirit and that which above and the inverted torch, that which is below, in the world.

The four archetypal elements of Earth, Air, Fire and Water are evident as elements in the process of purification. These symbols, found in Qaballism also emerge in the Philosophical Alchemism of the Renaissance.

It is clear that this eschatology was not far removed from the Judaic/Christian concept of Purgatory, so prior to the Christian ascendancy, there was in the Roman culture, concepts which could be refashioned to suit the cultural proclivities of the Roman populace. Indeed, later it can be seen how little of Christianity's, ritual and archetypes did not already reside in heliopian facets of the Roman culture. This is not surprising in view of the relative immutability of culture and that the mechanism of cultural ascendancy involved the appropriation, incorporation or adoption of existing cultural archetypes etc., as we have seen with the expansion of heliopianism.

Heliopianism and autocratic monotheism were macrocosmic manifestations of the duality of the nature of man the individual, culture being a living entity made up of the collective beliefs, customs, etc of individuals of a particular (ethnic, regional, national, or international) group.

The main difference between heliopianism and autocratic monotheism was a matter of philosophy, the former being pluralistic and divergent and the latter, autocratic and convergent in so far as when aspects of the Roman culture were selected primarily to find support, and to be philosophically acceptable, all else was suppressed with the intention of destroying it. Because culture is a living group entity, this is almost impossible to do or do quickly, for several reasons. Possibly the main reason being that it would be impossible to eradicate one of the major adversaries entirely as this would abrogate the fundamental law of survival that requires two adversaries (or more) to provide the necessary conflict, the fuel of striving which ensures the survival of man.

Although with the Christian ascendancy, there appeared to be the demise of heliopianism, the cultural archetypes still resided in the collective human psyche, which, after a dormant period, re-emerged with the Greco-Roman traditions of the Renaissance.

The concept of cultural rebirth was central to heliopianism, which resulted in its literalistic form as in many of the mystery religions of the Roman culture, particularly in the widespread cult of Isis and Osiris.

One would expect to see the Sumerian archetype of the Tree of Life, arising from Sumerian and Hurrian influences in Hittite Anatolia. Several instances occur in the Aeneid alluding to sacred trees and groves.[8] King Latinus, the son of Faunus the god, had a "great Bay tree" dedicated to Phoebus, the Sun God:

"On this there lighted a great swarm of bees, and hung like unto a cluster of grapes from a bough thereof. And the seers beholding the thing cried, 'There cometh a stranger who shall be husband to Lavinia and a strange people who shall bear rule in this place.'"

Here we see the bees, a symbol of Demeter or Cybele, the Anatolian earth goddess who is often seen accompanied by two lions.[9] She was another form of Isis, Ishtar, Artemis and Aphrodite. Her disciples were referred to as 'Melissa' or bees and they performed the Taurobolium, the ritual sacrificing of bulls. The bees appearing as grapes symbolised fruitfulness of the earth mother goddess. The imagery of the scene is easy to see, as did the seers, that the followers of the fertility goddess (Venus in the Aeneid) would colonise the culture (the Bay tree).

It is known that the pre-Christian Celts of Britain, a priest caste culture, maintained sacred groves where the Oak and Rowan were held to be sacred.

Strabo tells of an island near Britain where sacrifices were offered to Demeter and Kore, her daughter[10] and some claim Stonehenge shows Mycenean influences.

In the Merovingian king Childric's tomb, in what had become Romanised Gaul, were found three hundred miniature gold bees.[11] Napoleon, who literally crowned himself emperor, dispensing with previous Christian coronation ritual, presumably as a gesture of ancient regal supremacy, had the Merovingian bees attached to the coronation robes. This was an example maybe of the manifestation of a residual Roman archetype in the archetypal memory of Napoleon and the French psyche harking back to Imperial Rome or a deliberate gesture by Napoleon to re-establish the pre-Christian tradition of Augustus who was Emperor in all but name and also pontiff. Certainly this would accord with the extraordinary military expertise of Napoleon.

According to the Aeneid then, the initial Roman culture consisted mainly of Atlantean/Cretan and Anatolian elements, some traces of which still exist today due to the longevity of cultural archetypes.

It is possible that present day Venice was originally settled by immigrant Cretans taking their skills as canal and boat builders to a group of islands in a lagoon, a replica almost of the island of Atlantis with its canals and bridges, described by Solon and Plato. The association of Venice with a queen of the Sea God is described by Shelley:

"Sun girt City, thou has been

Ocean's child and then his Queen"

The Venetians were renown during centuries of known history, for their navy and seamanship. In the sixth century AD, the Byzantine Empire built a church for the Venetians in recognition for the ships they provided to transport the Byzantine army to Ravenna, a prelude to the ascendancy of the Venetian Mediterranean Empire.

This was based on their sea power, which by the tenth century AD under the republic, controlled the Adriatic and the Syrian coastal ports. At its height, the empire held most of coastal Eastern Mediterranean, including Crete, Cyprus, Morea and Corfu. The Venetians returned to their ancient cultural sphere on a flowing cultural tide after the ancient ebbing.

At a spot two miles north-west of Phaestos, an ancient 1600 BC site containing a sarcophagus which depicts the bull ritual with the double headed axe and horns of consecration, was found. The ancient name of the site in Minoan

Crete is not known, but it is now called Hagia Triada (Holy Trinity), from a Venetian church there.[12] Here then is the sacred triple of the Sea God.

Such cultural tides have been encountered in the Delta of Egypt with successive waves of Cretan infusion over several epochs.

The Mongol invasion of the Eastern Mediterranean in the twelfth century AD may have been such a return to a former cultural sphere, when one examines Hittite artefacts that show distinct Sino cultural characteristics.

The Mongols were halted by the ancient Hittite adversary, the Sultan of Egypt at what was, possibly, their ancient cultural frontier of the Levant. It is possibly no accident that St Mark's Cathedral in Venice is surmounted by four golden horses, one of the symbols of the ancient Cretan (monotheistic) Sea God often seen pulling the deity's sea chariot. The horse is also a symbol of religious power.

The fifteenth century architecture of such buildings as the Ca d'Oro display the builder's preference for the (sacred) three terraced arrangement of arched windows. Possibly the most striking remnant of the culture is the long surviving ritual of "Sposalizio del Mare" extant until the fall of the Republic. This ritual, which re-enacted a marriage of the Doge to the Sea, may have had its origins in the Cretan-Atlantean marriage of the Sea God to Cleito. The Sea clearly had some ancient religious significance related to fertility, virility and survival of the culture.

Aspects of the Roman Cosmogony

It is not possible to cover every deity in the Roman pantheon, of which there were many. Ancient heliopian cultural policy was to incorporate new deities encountered in new territories into the pantheon as was the custom in parent heliopian cultures. By the time and because of the ultimate expansion of the Roman Empire, deities representing all major cultures were represented in the pantheon. Often, the same god was known by several cultural or regional names, as was the case in Ancient Egypt. The attempt at cultural unity represented by a universally recognised diviocratic pantheon was no doubt intended from the earliest times to promote peaceful government and to curb man's propensity for mutual destruction. It is interesting to note that the movement of syncretism that came to exist in the culture which involved combining beliefs and practices, possibly arising from the perception that the pantheon was becoming too unwieldy, was derived from the Greek word for a confederation of Cretan states.

Holy wars and their attendant barbarism, characteristic of later monotheistic cultures, were virtually precluded. The exception to any accommodation was the cultural repository of ancient Cretan /Atlantean monotheism which jealously resisted any attempts at its incorporation. Little or no mention of religion or religious conflict can be found in Caesar's or Tacitus' accounts of military campaigns, nor indeed in any of the Greek or Egyptian accounts. It would seem that military campaigns as a result were much more honourable and civilised by comparison to History's accounts of the barbarities and atrocities of wars conducted in the name of Religion.

With the Greek heliopian culture being a development of the Cretan, Hittite and Sumerian, with later Egyptian influences, and its pre-Aeneid occupation of Italy, the Roman culture became a development of the Hellenic insofar as it existed as a separate culture.

Jupiter was originally the Greek Zeus, the father of the gods but also called Tonaus the Thunderer, Fulgur, lightning[13] indicating aspects of his cultural forebears, the Hittite Teshub and Sumerian Enlil, the king, the chief executive of the pantheon, the Weather God.

He was widely known as Jupiter Heliopolitanus and Jupiter Dolichenus, indicating his status as the Sun God and a development of Osiris, Shamash, Marduk and Baal. The latter, Philo of Byblus explicitly identifies with Jupiter Dolichenus, found throughout Phoenicia and Syria. Jupiter Dolichenus was highly popular among, and his following spread by, the soldiers. In its Mithraic form, the symbolism of the Sun God was by far the most popular in the second and third centuries AD[14] especially at frontiers of the Empire where many monuments to "Sol Invictus" the "Invincible Sun" have been found. Mithras could be separately identified by the Zoroastrian eastern cultures whilst reflecting the Greek filial relationship to Zeus.

What has not survived the process of cultural eradication by later monotheistic cultures are any of the Mithraic liturgies or other writings[15] or much of any other cultures' literary output, for example, that of the Celtic or Saxon, following the ascendancy of Christianity.

With the advent of the infusion of Greek Alexandrian culture into the Egyptian under the Ptolemies, Zeus was given the title of Zeus Serapis, originating at Memphis, the centre of the ancient Apis Bull cult.

This was not an example of an artificially produced god as some sources hold, but simply an example of the heliopian policy of cultural assimilation. Not unnaturally, Zeus Serapis was very popular in the Greek world because of its affinity with and derivation from in all probability, via the Egyptian, the Cretan Bull cult that formed and influenced early pre-Greek, Mycenean culture.

The cult survived into the Roman era, but the cult of Hathor-Isis was more popular, where Alexandrian deities were worshipped. This is perhaps not surprising, for Hathor-Isis and her equivalents, Hera, Artemis, Aphrodite, Demeter, Ishtar etc., had from the earliest times, been associated with the powerful bull fertility cult.

The Amenite priesthood had attempted to harness its popular appeal, to legitimise the pharaohship of Hatshepsut, by propagating the story that she was the progeny of a marriage between Amen and Hathor-Isis.

Central symbolism of Mithraic mythology depicts the god slaughtering a fertile bull that places the god in sympathy with the heliopians.

Herakles was an embodiment of the Hittite Teshub and as a demi-god hero was in the tradition of Gilgamesh. He also commanded wide devotion that was indicative of Anatolian and Protosyrian elements existing in the Roman culture.

Juno

The consort of Jupiter or Zeus was the Greek Hera and represented the elder fertility goddess. The Romans identified her with Artemis, Aphrodite and Isis.[16]

She probably entered the Greek culture after the Mycenean ascendancy over the Cretan Atlantean Empire. She was associated with a bull cult and was a mother or Madonna figure, as was Isis. As such, Juno represented, like Isis, a very potent archetype to the individual and collective adherents as modern psychology has demonstrated, providing a role analogous to the queen in a swarm of bees. Mary the mother of Christ filled this essential role in Christianity with some modification. The cult of Demeter was promoted on this basis literally.

The fertility Madonna was always like Isis, the devoted adherent and protector of the Sun God, whose sister she was. With the absence of the Sun God in Christianity, the fertility Madonna necessarily had a modified status. In the form of Mariolatry, the archetype was used to marshal devotion and adherence to the faith.

There was a slight shift of direction of her traditional constancy and subservience from the sibling Sun God or father figure, to her son.

This was an acceptable substitute as Isis was also acknowledged to be devoted to her son Horus, the son of the Sun God.

In her form as Cybele, a variant of Demeter, can be seen echoes of her origin in Crete. Like Venus, Cybele was associated with the sacred Cretan Mountain of Ida.

One myth of many that personifies Mycenean/Cretan cultural interplay describes how Sybille was sleeping as a rock when Zeus tried to rape her. Zeus' seed falling on the ground spawned the monster Agdistis, who was castrated indirectly by Dionysus. From the blood of Agdistis sprang an almond tree. This was the instrument by which Dionysus affected the castration of Agdistis, by tying his genitals to it whilst he slept.

From this tree, Sangarius, the daughter of the river god plucked fruit and placed it in her lap, resulting in the birth of Attis, with whom Cybele fell in love.

The myth contains many archetypes associated with Crete, for example, the rock and monster featured in the Hittite myth of Kumarbi and Ullikumi, and the Sea God and his daughter of the Atlantis legend. The fruit of the fabulous tree is reminiscent of the garden of the Hesperides and the tree of life.

Myriad forms of the fertility goddess witness the claim of the Sea God to be able to bring his daughter back to life and insinuates a common and widespread religious concept derived from an ancient common source. This invention was clearly introduced in order to harness a naturally occurring universal subconscious need, more strong in primitive and emotionally underdeveloped humans.

Cybele was introduced formally into the Roman culture around 205 BC when Hannibal the Carthaginian was invading Rome during the Second Punic War.

The principal instruments of senatorial policy were the so-called Sibylline Books. The purpose of the policy was, according to some, the destruction of the Commons and its procedure, the introduction of deities and practices from Greece and the East.[17] The Senate, it is said, when the tide of war was turning against Rome, proclaimed a prophecy that an alien invader would be driven from Italy if the Great Mother from Ida, Cybele was brought to Rome.

A commission was sent to bring the black stone sacred to the Goddess. Games celebrating the event were instituted; the next year, Hannibal left Italy.

From a cultural point of view, it is probably this event which portended the ascendancy of monotheistic cultures of Judaic Christianism and Islamism, a central archetype of which is the Rock, manifested as for example in the Caba at Mecca.

Cybele is often to be seen flanked by, or in, a chariot drawn by lions, indicative of her influence in Protosyrian Anatolia probably arising in the archaic past from Cretan hegemony there. Athene was also associated with the Cretan goddess, often depicted with her symbols of owl and snakes.

In Britain, a temple at Chichester was dedicated to the Sea God Neptune and Minerva, the Roman form of Athena.[18]

It is possible, if not probable, that the stone of Cybele was in fact a pillar having a phallic significance.

The myths of the cults of Cybele taken literally, led to primitive practices of castration and orgiastic violence which were quickly barred by the Senate. The male counterpart of Cybele by his mythical association, was Dionysus, another eastern deity. The bacchanalian ritual spread alarmingly, naturally among the young and resulted in strict legal controls. In the context of what was a ritual fertility cult, Dionysus was often to be seen with a dwarf erectus, a Pan-like figure, a human animal composite, who in Egypt as Bes, was a phallic icon.

Sacrifices to Dionysus usually involved goats, creatures associated with Venus and Mount Ida.

Other Roman state gods widely acknowledged or worshipped, included Apollon, the Sun and his sister the Moon, Artemis or Diana the Huntress.

The ancient Qaballistic concept of the unity of opposites embodied in Osiris and Isis, was maintained with Zeus and Hera and Apollon and Artemis, all representing the solar deity and his consort the Lunar Goddess. Mars or Aries, Minerva Athena and Herakles were also popular.

As the Empire expanded into Celtic and Saxon cultures of Central and Northern Europe, the cosmogony expanded in accord with ancient heliopian cultural policy.

Many Celtic and Saxon gods were incorporated, often under combined Roman and native titles such as Jupiter Tanarus, the German God of Thunder, Sulis Minerva, patroness of the hot springs at Bath, as was Apollo Graunos, the patron of healing waters in Germany. Maponus (young hero) was a Celtic Apollo and later, the Mabon of Welsh Arthurian Legend (cf The Mabinogen).

Other native deities were Brigantia, Veten Tamus, Mogon, Liud, Matunus Ancaster, Harimella and many more.[19]

Of the various cults, Mithraism, which incorporated the cult of the Invincible Sun, was by far the most popular, especially among the frontier military. Its strong rivals were the worship of the Great Mother of Phrygia (Cybele/Demeter of Anatolia) and Isis and Serapis of Egypt.[20] There is a balance (according to the law of cultural action and reaction) between Mithraism, a heliopian cult, and the rest, with the exception of the Isis cult. Mithraism was a solar heliopian cult in the classical male hero tradition, the others being fertility cults associated with bull sacrifice and a fertility goddess.

The central symbolism of Mithraism depicted the destruction of the bull of fertility, which, in Mithraism, was associated with the forces of darkness, represented on some reliefs as a pillar entwined by a serpent.

The Roman culture, as was the classical Greek, was secularised in essence, being centred on heroic military conquest according to heliopian cultural integration. Initially, the state was a monarchy then becoming a secular republic, the military being largely heliopian Mithraists. This was in contrast to the monotheism which, originating in early Cretan culture, manifested in Judaic monotheism derived from the Cretan via the Egyptian was priest led. The next cultural upheaval would originate with the ancient monotheistic foe of heliopianism arising from the Judaic culture to eclipse the Roman culture. This would not be for half a millennia from the meeting of the two cultures.

It ought not be surprising to view such cultural conflict as ostensibly, unchanging, for cultural change to be perceived requires viewing over millennia, unlike recorded history, which is chronicled over a few generations or centuries highlighted by detectable changes.

On the macrocosmic level, culture is as unchanging as the human unconscious with which it is inextricably entwined. Culture changes as a very slow-moving tide. Prior to the eclipse of Roman heliopianism and the rise of monotheism, the previous perceivable change in cultural high tide as it were, was the Sumerian "Flood" circa four millennia BC which was an allegory for a sea change in culture, the previous ascendancy of monotheism. The last cultural change or return of the tide, started in Europe with the Renaissance and so it will continue but on a millennia unit time scale. After the "Flood", heliopianism returned for several millennia, ending with the Roman culture. With the rise of Christianism the "Flood" tide turned, monotheism again rose and a Dark Age returned.

The cult of the Sun God in Roman culture was very strong and traces of its existence in the young culture have been found on third century BC coins of the Republican period.[21]

The Sun God's titles were Sol Indigis, Sol Invicto and others, presumably arising from the longevity of his rule against the forces that would depose him. Similar claims of eternality of the Church were made by the early Christians that would have served in part, to counter such heliopian claims.

The identity of the Sun God mainly centred on Zeus and Apollon, but he had other names that were the Roman equivalents of the deity's names in other cultures, in accordance with heliopian accommodation of alien gods.

This was of course not a new tradition in Rome for the god had many names in other heliopian cultures due to the same ancient tradition. In Egypt he was known as Osiris, Khepera, Temu and other names and in the surrounding heliopian cultures, as Marduk, Shamash and Baal, all of which were synonymous with kingship.

It is perhaps at first glance, remarkable that the pantheon was preserved under the Roman Republic when kingship had been abolished, but the heliopian concept of "diviocracy" was in fact a celestial model of terrestrial egalitarian republicanism such that the heliopian cultural concept found a harmony with the republican ideal. The Greeks however were the first to establish temporal democracy from the celestial (spiritual) diviocracy.

Another Roman deity that became widely popular was the goddess Tyche. She represented to some extent, the role of the Gods who had always been sole arbiters of Man's fate within a modest matrix of freedom of action and responsibility, for such was the basis of accountability under Greco-Roman Law. This was an ancient heliopian concept going back to the earliest times with the Egyptian eschatological Judgement after Death.

An innovation which became evident in Roman culture and which is still the modus operandi of Eastern European states was the practice of accusation before the law. This placed the burden of guilt on the accused, having to prove innocence, in contrast to what became the basis of European Law, which assumes innocence before guilt that has to be proved. This would seem to originate in the waters of strict conformity where deviation was regarded as anti-social. Little evidence can be found for its existence in pre-dynastic Rome and is characteristic of the mechanisms for retaining absolute power under the ascendancy of the Emperors.

The concept of Emperor or king above kings was the step on the road, it could be argued, to celestial autocracy being in accord with the concept of celestial kingship but at odds with heliopian diviocracy. This could have led to the relegation of all sibling cultures to vassalhood.

The disintegration of the Republic was hastened by the immense concentration of power in certain families and the presence of overweening personal ambition. The same forces probably propagated the argument for the need for strong centralised government to avoid the disintegration of the Empire. This would legislate for the ambitions of individuals who could see greater power and fame than the legendary Alexander. Caesar, according to Shakespeare, let the concept of kingship be mooted and ostensibly did nothing to encourage it. He was assassinated because of that. Augustus possibly gauging the republican feeling and aware of Caesar's fate was careful not to assume the title of king or Emperor. Subsequent decadence allowed despotism to arise under Tiberius and the Julians. This was a reaction to the still strong republican sentiments that were still harboured by the more noble of the Roman aristocracy.

Caesar, the brilliant military strategist, in encouraging the ambitions of the Julian House possibly unwittingly set a course for the culture which would render it prey to autocratic forces of not only a temporal nature, but of a celestial nature. The culture became a model which entertained autocracy, a temporal move in the direction of celestial autocracy, which, when the time arrived (a short period on the cultural time scale) the adversary of heliopianism would assume like a prepared mantel.

As Chance and Fortune, Tyche was the Saviour Goddess, daughter of Zeus and responsible for a large part of Man's destiny. She was referred to as Agathe Tyche[22] Good Fortune. She was represented as the consort of Zeus and sometimes as a Madonna with Zeus as the child, and as such, she embodies aspects of the female mother goddesses. The chief symbols of Tyche were the rudder and the wheel of Chance or Fortune.

The central archetype of the fertility cult was the rock, representing secure ground in stormy seas of the god of life waters a tacit implication of non-searching or seeking and stationary permanence.

The rudder on the other hand implied exploration, questing, communication and necessarily, valour. This aligned with heliopian heroic tradition and evoked the central archetype of ancient heliopianism, the barc of the Sun. Tyche represented protection by, rather than protection from a deity.

Other symbols of Tyche were a ship's prow, wings, a fruit measure and a corn ear, reflecting her mother goddess aspect. From Palestine has survived a winged griffin seated with one paw on an upright wheel and is dedicated by Mercurius. The symbolism clearly combines the eagle, the favourite of Zeus[23] the Protosyrian lion and Tyche the mother goddess, all ancient archetypes of Near Eastern cultures, indicating possibly, her use as a cultural unifier or rationalisation.

Tyche would appear to have no historical links with the Near East, but in fact there is one.

Chance or Fortune was also represented as the seven Tychai or planets of the Sky[24] according to a magical papyrus "Eine Mithras Liturgie" preserved in Paris. Two of the planets are the Sun and the Moon, and it is a fair guess that the others are Venus, Mercury, Mars, Jupiter and either Saturn or Earth.

These planets and the Wheel of Fortune form part of Taro symbolism and Ancient Sumerian Qaballism as well as Mithraism.

Tyche, known to have been extant since before the third century BC, was honoured by Nero and was still popular under Julian in the mid-fourth century AD.

The Tyche of Antioch shows the goddess seated on a rock, Mount Siliphon, evocative of Demeter or Venus and Mount Ida. This is also effected by her emblems of fruit measure and corn ear and her status as mother.

Tyche may have represented an attempt at cultural rationalisation in her being symbolic of both the power of fate and also a mother goddess. She was not to be preferred to the more humanly envisioned goddesses like Isis, Cybele and Demeter et al whose "personalities" were born out of copious mythology and were deeply embedded in the collective cultural psyches of the Near Eastern cultures.

The concept embodied by Tyche legislated against the Judaic/Christian concept of Free Will. Early formulations of the concept are to be found in the writings attributed to the prophet Ezekiel at the time of the Hebrew captivity in Babylon. It is known to have been tacitly implied in, and therefore derived from, Egyptian eschatology, much of which the Hebrews retained. In any event, there would have been a reaction to the concept that the gods were masters of man's fate by the Judaic culture as that was attributed, for the most part, to Yahweh.

Sources state "Ezekiel was uncompromising in his assertion of individual responsibility and retribution…Each man stands or falls in Yahweh's sight by his own acts."[25]

Ezekiel was co-contemporary with seminal Zoroastrianism in Persia, the ally of the Hebrews, and his vision of the cherubim, wheels and fire shows the same archetypes as the Persian/Phrygian Tyche of Antioch. This is possibly an allusion to the cultural links of Persia with the Hebrews.

Tyche, associated with Mithras by the Zodiac symbolism, provides the cultural link between the Phrygians (Persians) and the Hebrews apparent in the Hebrew exilic tradition.

The vision (Ezekiel X-6-16) describes four cherubim, beside each of which is a wheel, and between them is fire. The cherubim have wings and four faces, one a cherub, on a man, one an eagle and one a lion. The symbols are associated with Tyche or Mithras. The latter cult was derived from Zoroastrianism, often incorporated aspects of Fortune in the Roman culture. It was from the schools of Hebrew monotheism and Zoroastrianism which represented heliopianism, that the two major cultural adversaries who were to occupy the Roman stage, were derived. It was an ancient contest involving the same combatants under slightly different cultural guises, autocratic monotheism and diviocratic heliopianism. The former represented by Judaic Christianism and the latter, by the Mithraists with their pluralistic planetary and star cosmogony.

The powerful cult of the fertility goddess was incorporated on the side of the old Sea God in the form of Mariolatry, the (great) Mother of the God-King. This was an image where the son of Yahweh has replaced the heliopian King and Sun King of Heaven, Zeus and Apollon his son. It was a battle the ancient heliopians were to lose, happily, not for the first time.

Mithraism and Christianity

Possibly, because of the cultural meeting of the waters during the Babylonian Captivity of the Hebrews, Mithraism and Christianity arrived in Rome at about the same time, that is, in the first century AD.

It is known that in 71 AD, there were Mithraists in the XVth Legion at Carnutum in Britain.[26]

Some sources maintain that Mithraism originated in India at about the same time as Buddhism to which it is related. Some scholars have suggested that Buddhism may have influenced the Gnostics[27] early Christians, who were

291

declared heretics by the orthodox Christians. This put them in the same boat as the Mithraists, as enemies of Christianity.

Both Gnostics and Mithraists believed in the esotericism of sacred knowledge[28] like many of the major religions of the time, including that of the Cult of Isis. Indeed it is this tradition that probably engendered such mysteries that exist in the present Christian Church.

Buddhists were in contact with Thomasian Christian in Southern India. India, as probably the mother of Near Eastern heliopianism, is alone in retaining the ancient polytheistic pantheon of gods.

There was a danger of a cultural situation arising in Rome similar to that which arose in Aknaten Egypt. This involved the neo-monotheistic Amenites which had accumulated unprecedented power were arrested by the institution of an ostensibly monotheistic culture centred on the Sun, though it was clearly an emphasised aspect of heliopianism.

This was a natural cultural reaction at the time (and could be predicted by the law of cultural action and reaction) to the burgeoning usurping power of the Armenites. Like the myth of Cain and Abel or Osiris and Seth, Mithraism and Christianity were cultural brothers struggling for existence and power, by no means a new phenomenon.

At the height of its popularity in Rome, Mithraism had been modified and assimilated into the Roman culture according to the ancient heliopian tradition. No more is this apparent than from the archaeological evidence in Britain which shows Mithraic temples alongside temples of traditional Roman gods and those of Romanised Celtic and Saxon gods.[29]

Mithras in the Vedas is a divinity of light, subordinate to Ahura or Varuna. Mythologically, he is a heroic figure who, from his actions, is easily identified with the heliopian Greco-Roman and other heroic traditions beginning with Gilgamesh of the Sumerian myths and with whom, he has a lot in common as the adversary of the (fertility) Bull of Heaven.

In Sanskrit, Mithras means "friend", friendship being a prevalent theme in the Epic of Gilgamesh. Mithras, originally could be regarded as a celestial soldier[30] at Ahura's side, hence his appeal to the Roman military forces.

Similar imagery is to be found today in the story of Arjuna and Krishna in the Bhagavad-Gita, the Indian "Song of God."

Mithraism of the Romans was not an almost new religion as claimed by some, and later myth describes Mithras as being born from a rock. The advantages of such a myth to the heliopians was clear, for it associated the heroic Sun God with the central archetype of their adversary. It is also associated with the Mother Goddess Demeter, popular in Anatolian Phrygia, a troublesome and powerful province, imbued the archaic Cretan fertility culture.

Ahura Mazda's first creation had been a wild bull, a concept in accord with heliopian theology, aligning with the actual state of affairs concerning early man of which, the heliopians were no doubt aware.

The earliest gods arising in the course of man's emergence from animal nature were gods of fertility or more accurately, the god of fertility personified by the Ancient Sea God. This god whose symbol of water it had long been appreciated, represented man's creative sexual drive. It is natural that at emerging man's level of survival, his conscious awareness should dimly perceive that the driving force of all nature in pursuit of survival was something outside himself and therefore had to be divine.

In a manner similar to that described in the episode of the Bull of Heaven in the Epic of Gilgamesh, Mithras seized the Bull by the horns, eventually subduing it, dragged it to a cave. The cave in Mother Earth may have been intended to represent the vagina where the chaotic destruction of the rampaging bull was put to constructive purpose.[31]

Modern Hindu symbolism of the cave has it representing the heart. In this context the Mithraic deed still can be interpreted as the power of love vanquishes the chaotic forces of unbridled fertility. This would also accord with heliopian theology.

According to the myth, the bull escapes and the Sun sent his messenger, the raven, the symbol of the Sun God Apollon, to track it. Mithras, with his faithful hound (which may correspond with Anubis, the guardian dog of the Gods in Egyptian mythology) captures the bull and slaughters it. From the blood of the bull sprang corn, and ancient symbol of fertility, and other life.

Ahriman, the power of darkness, sent his servants, the scorpion, ant and serpent, to drink the life-giving blood, to prevent it spreading life.

The scorpion man, it will be remembered was the guardian of the portals of Hades in the Epic of Gilgamesh.

Ahriman's strategy fails and the blood spread over the earth. This image is evocative of the ancient ritual of Anat in Egyptian mythology.

At a higher level, the bull represents man's chaotic animal nature driven by fertility forces and Mithras, the divine part of man's dual nature, the apotheosis of man's development.

The fact that Mithras shown entwined by a serpent and surrounded by the symbols of the celestial bodies supports this concept. Divine nature coiled in human fertility (animal) nature.

The spilling of the blood on the earth as a symbol of renewing animal fertility and survival powers, applies in Nature. The kill of an animal, the lion for example, reinforces the animal's status though presumably the animal is only dimly aware of this, if at all.

A similar pageant to the Mithraic tableau is presented in the Epic of Gilgamesh, the demi-god who destroys the Ishtarian Bull of Heaven responsible for death.

The ancient belief that the blood of the slaughtered ox had life-giving properties was instanced in Homeric Mycenean Nestorian ritual and Cretan Atlantean myth. This is testament to the archaic religion and low level of cultural development of the populace. The ostensible disregard for life is at home in the survival context of the man as near animal and it is only with the development of consciousness that valid reasons for holding life sacred evolved.

As a cultural state, it was reinforced over aeons, in pace with the imperceptible development of man's consciousness wherewith came the development of gods reaching the company of gods. With these, refined concepts of universal order, tolerance through plurality and justice were born and developed.

The powers of darkness represented in Ahriman are those of the unconscious which would destroy life and enlightenment. This may seem a strange position that the survival driven subconsciousness is destructive. It can be so in the individual, for unlike the individual consciousness, the subconscious that an individual shares as part of the collective subconsciousness is eternal, as is the collective consciousness and the purpose of the collective subconscious is to ensure collective survival. If this arising in the animal nature of man, requires blood rituals of rivalry in the form of war to strengthen the fabric of collective survival as regards territory, food resources etc., then the individual is expendable.

Ironically it is the young bucks who represent the strength and future of the group who in such times are the most eager and willing to hazard death as a proving ground of virility, and so it is in the rest of Nature.

The serpent, an archetype of fertility, is associated with Ahriman, along with other lower forms of life. We would expect to see Ahriman associated in some way with water, the symbol of the Ancient Sea God, the adversary of the heliopian pantheon.

In another myth, Ahriman is described as attempting to destroy the earth by a flood and mankind is rescued by Mithras. The similarities with the Sumerian Flood Myth are clear, by which it was probably influenced. Another myth describes Mithras again as the saviour of mankind, saving it from drought. He fires an arrow into a rock from which a spring issues. Here, the ancient rock archetype representing bareness is pierced by the arrow of the Sun god to save mankind and restore fertility represented by the (celestial) water.

The Bible describes Moses performing a similar feat but striking the rock with his (serpent) rod.

The Sun rewards Mithras by investing him with a crown, the symbol of the Sun, which identifies him with the celestial executive of the Pantheon. This is in keeping with the heliopian tradition and typical of all the heliopian Middle Eastern cultures.

Mithras, as "the saviour of mankind" was possibly the prototype and source of the term and ideology that later became associated with Christ. The title "King of Heaven" was an ancient heliopian concept common to all the Near Eastern cultures that became part of the Christian mythology, as did the concept of the "Son of God." The latter as far as it is known, originated with the ancient Egyptian deities Osiris and his son Horus. The cultural cobbling by the fathers of the early Christian Church was to widen the appeal of the new cult and make it more palatable to the Roman populace already familiar with such mythical images and concepts.

Mithraism was at its peak in the second and third centuries AD when the Empire was expanding following the re-introduction of the concept of divine kingship after the collapse of the Republic.

Symbols often depicted on Mithraic tableaux are the raven, Athena, the scorpion. The raven like Khepera, the black scarab of Egyptian culture represented the Qaballistic opposite of the daylight sun, the sun at night and the spirit. Athena who rescued Jason from the serpent's mouth is represented as an owl, symbolising the patroness of wisdom. The scorpion, often also to be seen, may be derived from the Sumerian scorpion man of the Gilgamesh Epic, but also appeared in Mithraic myth. He guarded the entrance to the underworld and may be an allusion to death.

Very little remains of the religion of Mithraism or for that matter of the Saxon or Celtic religions following the ascendancy of Christianity in the Roman Empire. This is often attributed to the hordes of invading barbarians, but is more probable to the monotheistic intolerance of other religions, the opposite as one might expect to the tolerance of heliopianism.

It is now known that the invading Saxons and Vikings in Britain had a finely developed culture of their own and though contested Roman power, were not known to be partisan about religion.

The Mithraic reliefs that survive probably owe their survival, at least in part, to the fact those Mithraic temples or Mithreums were often in underground caves. The importance of the cave in the religion may have eschatological connotations and may have formed the environment for the ritual of rebirth, in a similar manner to the sepulchre which was the place of death from which Christ re-emerged, resurrected.

It is known that much of Mithraic ritual, including sacramental ritual, was borrowed by the early Christians from its cultural sibling.

In Mithraism, the process of rebirth, unlike Christian tradition, took place before, and not after death, as was the case with the cult of Isis and others.

Central to Mithraic reliefs is the slaying of the Bull of Chaos by Mithras dressed in Phrygian attire. Phrygians occupied Central and Western Anatolia after the demise of the Hittite culture and adopted Anatolian customs and beliefs, including the worship of Cybele[32] one of whose variants was the Moon Goddess. They shared therefore a cultural affinity with the Roman heritage of the Aeneid.

In the third century BC, Celtic Galatians occupied the western coastal regions of Anatolia. This was not an original incursion if one regards the Heraklion myths surrounding Hippolyta as referring to some early Mycenean/ Celtic encounter.

The Orphic serpent torcs (Hippolyta's girdle), and the caduceus of Hermes are prevalent in Celtic and Saxon symbolism. Other Celtic iron and Bronze Age artefacts show pre-Roman Anatolian influences, all of which assisted the Romans to successfully assimilate these cultures into the Roman cosmogony.

The snake, representing Ahriman, is at the bottom of the relief. At the top, the chariot of the Sun God is pulled by four horses. The horses probably represent the four points of the compass.

The chariot of the Moon Goddess is opposite; her billowing stole representing the crescent moon. Guiding both chariots are the cherubs symbolising rebirth. One is holding a torch of enlightenment and the spirit before the Sun's chariot. The other holds a torch pointing downwards, indicating enlightenment from above being passed down to the temporal plane. Between the chariots are three trees, the sacred triple, evocative of the Sun's sacred cauldron (which symbolised the vessel of the spirit), the sacred grove and the tree of life.

One branch shows prominently, three oak leaves, a feature to be found on Anatolian twelfth century BC reliefs.

Beneath the Sun's chariot is Athena's symbol of wisdom, the owl. The life-giving blood of the bull is being lapped by Mithras' dog which, in the context of "man's best friend" evokes an alliance akin to that of Gilgamesh and Enkidu the heroic demigod Bull slayers of Sumerian mythology.

The snake is not partaking of the blood, though on other reliefs it does.

Flanking Mithras are two other figures of the god, one on the right holding a torch pointing upwards and one on the left holding a torch pointing downwards. The god is thus depicted as intermediary of the knowledge and enlightenment of rebirth, a role also adopted by the early Christians, ascribed to Christ.

Some sources interpret this latter symbolism as light and darkness, summer and winter or good and evil. There is undoubtedly veins of duality in the symbolism as demonstrated by the presence of the two deities and the symmetry of the tableau.

Among cult followers of Isis and others was the belief that two types of magic were possible, right-hand magic, which was good and left-hand magic that was bad. Waite no doubt adopted such symbolism from the Masonic tradition for his design of his tarot cards. (See the Ryder-Wait tarot for example, the Devil and the Magician.)

Similar concepts regarding the source and means of enlightenment and rebirth are to be found in pre-renaissance Philosophical Alchemy.

The Mithraic figure on the left of the relief holds a bunch of grapes, signifying fruitfulness and bounty. The whole composition of the relief with the three major figures of the god form a unifying triple symmetry evocative of the sacred number of the Sun God and the symmetry of the Qaballistic tree of life.

On other Mithraic reliefs, the same themes exist though the symbolism is slightly different. Cybele's ear of corn for example replaces the grapes though the upright and inverted torches are always present. It is of note that Lucian of Samosata, the second century satirist, describes Paris, Priam's son, as being Phrygian[33] though he places Mount Ida in Phrygia, a further clue possibly to the fact that the Romans were expatriate Anatolians.

The windblown cloak of Mithras is generally present in reliefs and probably signifies the mantle of authority, often employed by Hebrew prophets and which, would hold a special significance for adherents of the religion in the Roman Legions.

On some bas-reliefs, the sun is represented by a raven or salamander. The latter is to be found in Philosophical Alchemy and is associated with the sun, fire of the spirit and renewal.

One should not be surprised to see the re-emergence of ancient cultural tradition and symbols centuries after their apparent demise, in view of the almost timelessness of cultural processes as we have seen. The ascendancy of Christian and Islamic cultural monotheism were certainly not the first manifestations of cultural autocracy and will probably not be the last.

On one relief, the torches are replaced by pillars with lotus capitals, one side upright, on the other, inverted. The lotus in Near Eastern cultures symbolised life.

Sometimes, the inverted torch is replaced by the caduceus of Hermes or Mercury, the messenger of the gods, symbol of wholeness, dual nature, male and female and redolent of the sun and moon. Sometimes it is aimed at the pillar of the serpent.

The principle of the marriage of opposites, often represented as man's dual psychological nature described by Jung is thus present, often depicted in Philosophical Alchemy as a man and a woman, or the sun and the moon, or Hermes.

The inscription "Deo Soli Invictor", the invincible Sun, is often seen on Mithraic reliefs, a title often adopted by Roman Emperors as early as Nero in the first century AD This demonstrates the essential heliopian nature of Mithraism, the emperor representing the ancient tradition of the king being the temporal reflection of the executive of the celestial pantheon.

As one authority states:

"The worshipper of Mithras felt no contradiction between his belief and the other faiths surrounding him." This was a characteristic manifestly absent from contemporary Christians.[34]

The Roman Taurobolium, of which Spanish bull fighting is related, arose from the myths of Gilgamesh and the Bull of Heaven, the myth of Mithras and the ancient Atlantis myth ritual. It was an archetypal ritual common to many Near Eastern cultures and as such, was a culturally unifying ritual in multicultural Rome.

The major religions of Cybele, Dionysus, Isis, Mithras, Aescelepius etc shared also common fundamental beliefs, most notably that of spiritual rebirth being possible during temporal existence. This was in contrast to the Christian belief. Most religions also, including the Christians, had initiation rites whose enactment provided the bonds of spiritual communion.

The serpent featured in fertility cults for example, that of Dionysus who was associated with Cybele.

Pre-Christian Orphites in Ireland venerated the serpent.

On certain Mithraic reliefs, the god is depicted with a serpent coiled around his body as he stands surrounded by the zodiac cosmogony. In this context, the serpent is presented as the imprisoning force, the foe of the sun God, to be overcome before the secrets of the god can be revealed.

A similar theme is described in "The Golden Ass" by Apuleius who is eventually admitted to the initiation of Isis after renouncing his debauched life style.

The Mithraic initiation rites for admission involved initially, entry to grades or "miles" called by the old legal term, Sacramentum[35] which in the Christian tradition became the Sacraments. This link with the law is relevant later, for the stirrings of the Renaissance were set in motion by an order of monks with distinct Mithraic ritual traits and who subsequently were intimately associated with the law and its reformation and devolution from ecclesiastical into secular code, at least in England and Scotland in the centuries beginning with the Crusades and subsequently. Evidence seems to suggest that the ancient order of Free and Accepted Masons was derived from them.

There were seven grades or sacramentum associated with the seven planets, which, it should be remembered, were symbolic of the heliopian cosmogony.

The fact that there were seven and seven Christian sacraments suggests that the Christians adopted the ritual or plagiarised the Mithraists.

The seven planets were Mercury, Venus, Mars, Jupiter, Sun, Moon and Saturn,[36] the same planets central to Qaballistic philosophy and those associated with the Goddess of Fate, Tyche.

The lower grades in ascending order were:[37]

Raven, Bridegroom, Soldier, Lion, Persian, Courier of the Sun, and Father. The Persian is a likely acknowledgement of the nation which founded the religion or the nation of Mithras' birth. It is probable that ritual and initiation were held in secret in the underground temples, which affords privacy. It is probable that the Templars had secret ritual, a tradition inherited by the Masons.

In the Bridegroom, we see the precursor of the "Alchemical Marriage."

The initiation ritual, like that of the Isis and other cults, involved tests of fasting and endurance. The soldier was offered a crown across a sword, symbols that appear on the Waite tarot Ace of Swords. The lion initiate had his tongue and hands purified with honey. This may have been an allusion to the goddess Cybele or Demeter. Honey was according to a myth concerning Demeter food of the gods. Devotees of Demeter were melissae or bees.

In a dispute about fasting, concerning Christ and the Pharisees, Christ invokes symbols of a Bridegroom, wine, garments and ears of corn (Mark 11, 18-23) in an allegorical theme concerning old and new and clearly directed against the existing Hebrew establishment. Such symbols formed part of Mithraic cultural vocabulary that, like Christianity, was relatively new at that time. Since both the religions shared a common cultural source, this may account for much of their early common ritual and symbolism. Part of Mithraic ritual involved a communion service that comprised of the drinking of communion wine and also a banquet in memory and celebration of the ascension of Mithras to union with the Sun God. In the Last Supper can be seen similar ritual.

After the ascension of Christ to heaven, tongues of flame are alluded to and disciples are foretold as "taking up serpents" (Mark XVI, 18), a symbol which always appears on Mithraic bas-reliefs.

The crown across a sword offered to the Mithraic initiate in the soldier grade has its parallel in Christian symbolism as the Crown of Thorns. It is perhaps not so much of a surprise and a curious irony that orthodox hegemony would be challenged from the ranks of warrior monks, the "Militi Christi" or the Templars. Their twelfth century temples show two figures flanking the altar, one on the left which holds a long scroll vertically and one on the right holding a scroll pointing downwards. The Mithraic arrangement is unmistakable.

The initiate to the lion grade was given a cloak embroidered with animals presumably representing the zodiac, similar to the Cloak of Olympus worn by initiates of the cult of Isis which no doubt symbolised the authority of the god conferred on the adept.

In Mithraism Sunday was naturally, observed as a holy day. December the 25th was celebrated as the festival of rebirth of Mithras. The Christians adopted both of these traditions. Mithras was particularly held to be worshipped by shepherds. Mithreums were generally caves below ground. The cave probably symbolised the heart or possibly, the subconscious.

In modern Hinduism the cave represents the heart which, in the context of "thinking with the heart" is not far from the subconscious.

In an understandable attempt at defending the significant amount of Mithraic ritual and symbolism plagiarised by Christianism, one eminent source, a theologian, believed that many such affinities were probably borrowed by the Mithraists from Christianism.

Considering that Mithraic symbolism and ritual held much in common with contemporary religions and that being of a very ancient nature, such a claim is manifestly unfounded. Indeed, if one examines concepts claimed as original in the Christian tradition, it is clear that Christianity borrowed not only from Mithraism, but also from much older cultures.

The concept of judgement after death had its inception in Ancient Egyptian eschatology. The concept of Hell being an eternal fire is to be found in the Hymn to Amen Ra in which the god is cited "casting down his enemy into the flame."[38] The concept of the Son of God again predates Christianity in the myth of Osiris and Horus, a relationship not attributed to Mithras.

The ritual of Lenten ashes found its inception in biblical prophet times that signified subjugation of kingship to Yahweh's representatives, the prophets.

There are many other instances of ritual and archetypes inherited and incorporated by the Christian tradition from the Ancient Egyptian via the Judaic tradition.

Another claim made is that a "religion (Mithraism) that appealed to the heart to the exclusion of the head could not conquer the world", is probably untrue considering that at the height of the Roman Empire, Mithraism was the major religion. The claim also betrays the emotional blindness of the critic whose beliefs are supposedly centred on the creed of love[39] and which, did conquer the western world not by any free acceptance, but by admonition of the very young usually following conversion of the king or group leader. This was often achieved by first converting the female consort.

Mithras with the Zodiac
With Kind Acknowledgements to John Ferguson and Thames and Hudson

The ancient mechanism of cultural action and reaction arising from the nature of man, dictates that a new religion would engender its opposite.

If both Mithraism and Christianity had their roots from the time of the Babylonian Exile, then the traditions surrounding the birth of Christ seem to underline some mutual affinity. The birth was attended, according to tradition, by eastern Persian/Babylonian magi as indicated by their names; Caspar, Melchior and Balthazar. The latter name is from the same source as Belshazzar, son of Nebuchadnezzar and containing the name of the Sun god Baal. These magi were eastern potentates coming to honour one of their cultural kin.

The Christian cult spread among and was characteristic of the poorer classes within Roman society. The proclivity of such people superstition, imitative ritual and literalism when interpreting myths, led to accusations of cannibalism. As late as the fifth century AD, legends exist of early Christians being sacrificed voluntarily by their brethren in order to sanctify the site of a new church.[40]

Although such accusations were possibly largely unfounded, such practices were considered abhorrent to the more enlightened populace, none the less, the Christians, according to the precepts of diviocratic cultural pluralism, were tolerated and were required only to recognise the primacy of the Roman constitution. This they refused to do. Such refusals engendered suspicion in the authorities as to the real motives of the adherents, appearing as they did, seditious. The early Christians regarded their cult as superior and esoteric, placing the authorities in an intractable position regarding civil obedience.

In such matters as military conscription, the Christians refused to do military service, refuting the whole concept of cultural pluralism and equality under the law. This aligned with the autocracy of monotheism.

Pliny, Tacitus and others describe the extreme reasonableness and tolerance with which the early Christians were treated and the dilemma in which the authorities found themselves. Such confrontation ultimately led to the use of force by the authorities to eradicate such socially divisive tendencies and preserve military cohesion vital to the Roman cultural commonwealth. The Christians were therefore not outlawed but rather they were prosecuted under powers held by the Roman government for the enforcement of public order, as one source maintains:

"When innocence was discovered as by Plyny, the Christians proved uncooperative...This laid them open to the charge of high treason, but obstinacy, contumacy and this charge can be amply substantiated, was regarded with great gravity."[41]

To the observer, the events surrounding early Christianity show many similarities with the circumstances surrounding present day monolithic ideologies. Ultimately however it was due to economic privation that the greatest gains in political power were made by the Christians in the early fourth century when the inflation rate was running at around 2000% in the time of Constantius.

Mithraism did not, as one source would claim, die peacefully of inanition, but in fact much of its symbolism and some ritual other than that which was adopted by the Christians was preserved. This was preserved covertly for many centuries. It would not be easy if not impossible to erase the symbols from the archetypal memory of a culture one millennium old and older by association. Despite the fact that the practice of heliopian cultural pluralism was suppressed, it could not be totally eradicated, locked as it were in the Roman commonwealth psyche as the Renaissance demonstrated. In the course of time the culture would re-emerge as a necessary part of human spiritual existence from which it originally arose. The pendulum would have to swing as it had done throughout previous millennia.

Great efforts of course would be made by its adversary to prevent any such rebirth of heliopianism happening. This would be attempted by selective and intense monotheistic cultural inculcation of the collective human psyche within its compass, the establishment of Christendom and the severe restriction of the dissemination of knowledge over a protracted period. This gave rise to the not new occurrence of another Dark Age, a characteristic complementary period that follows a period of enlightenment. This phenomenon is a direct result of the cultural protagonists involved.

By a process of extrapolation it is possible to speculate on the intensity and periodicity of such eras of lightness and darkness. Originally, the period of darkness must have been formidably long as the early myths and knowledge of Stone Age and pre-stone age man suggest. Periods of light dawned with the development of man's consciousness. Conscious development seems to have been slow and probably followed, unsurprisingly, a natural, exponential curve. Heights assailed were modest, judging by man's present-day achievements.

In the Roman theatre of conflict between heliopian diviocracy and autocratic monotheism, the emphasis has been on the interplay of cultural influences, arising from the ancient Near Eastern cultures.

Two other significant influences were also present, that of the Saxon/Celtic culture of archaic European origin and that of the Gnostics.

The Gnostics, who in the early days of Christianity flourished as the major branch of Christian culture, propagated a philosophy based on.

"Gnosis" (literally "knowledge"). Gnosis was secret knowledge known only to initiates and, in this respect, the Gnostics held much in common with other mystery sects of the time, such as the Isis or Mithras cults.

Gnostics claimed that to know oneself is to know human nature and human destiny, not unlike central Buddhist belief. According to Theodotus, a gnostic teacher (140-160 AD), a Gnostic was defined as one who understands:

"Who we were, and what we have become; where we were; whither we are hastening; from what we are being released; what birth is and what is rebirth."[42]

Gnosticism shares much in common with Buddhism and like many of the contemporary religions, propagated the concept of spiritual rebirth. In the Gnostic religion, men and women were equal, reflecting the dual nature of the harmonious union of opposites in the original created being. The original creative force being feminine with the attribute of wisdom, the god of the orthodox Christians being her creation. In the rather abstract concepts of Gnosticism can be seen the ancient Sumerian threads of Qaballism and the ancient Cretan fertility mother goddess transported through the centuries by the Judaic tradition. The latter formed part of the dual culture of Ancient Egypt.

The Gnostics were attacked by the orthodox Christians for creating elaborate cosmologies with "room piled upon room, and assigned to each god."[43]

This placed the Gnostics in the camp of the enemies of the orthodoxy, the heliopians. Accordingly, it is not surprising that scholars have traced Gnosticism to roots in Persia and Babylonian Zoroastrianism, the same places and cultures that have been postulated, that were influences on Christianity.

By the middle of the second century AD, the Gnostic Christians were being denounced as heretics by the orthodoxy and probably, by the evidence at Nag Hammadi where several Gnostic gospels were recently found, were subject to persecution at some time in the fourth century AD when Christianity became the state religion of the Roman Empire.

The gospels of Nag Hammadi in Egypt have been dated to between 350 and 450 AD[44], the same period that saw the disappearance of Mithraism and contemporary religions. Gnostic concepts were not eradicated but were nurtured covertly, like Mithraism, to re-emerge as part of the Philosophy of Alchemism, contributing a Judaic dimension. Nag Hammadi scholars assert that the texts "unmistakably" relate to a Jewish heritage.

The Saxon/Celtic Cultural Influence

The Saxon and Celtic cultures surrounded the northern borders of the Roman Empire. The task of assimilation into the Roman Commonwealth of those ethnic groups that lay outside the Mediterranean ancient Near Eastern cultural sphere of influence, especially in the west, was never fully accomplished. This was principally due to the fact that the cultural intercourse between the ancient soup of Mediterranean cultures and the Saxon/Celts had been relatively tangential and recent, with possible Mycenean and Hittite contact in any way ancient time. Nonetheless, the Saxons and Celts were polytheistic and shared a common human if not historical heritage with the Near Eastern cosmogonies. Many of their deities found their equivalents in the Roman cosmogony, the distillation of earlier cosmogonies.

This together with the fact that the Roman civilisation, because of its cultural mix, was it could be argued, more advanced, enabled Roman colonisation of the Celtic and some of the German Saxon tribes. This was, at its most stable and peaceful, at least in Britain and Gaul, during the third century AD when by inference, heliopian diviocracy was at its zenith, a period of which remains, little historical record.

The ascendancy of monotheism coincided with the beginning of not only the disintegration of the Empire, but of the ostensible demise of the Greco-Roman culture.

The turning point of the ascendancy occurred under Emperor Constantius I (reigned 306-337 AD) who, though remained until his death bed, an adherent of heliopianism,[45] it is claimed, issued an edict in 323 AD declaring Christianity the state religion. This measure, it has often been argued, was an attempt to unify the Empire by the adoption of a single religion. History has shown however that such a measure destroyed the philosophical foundations (heliopian diviocracy) on which the cultural cohesion on which the Roman Commonwealth depended.

This action ignored all the lessons of previous ancient cultures, a trend apparent much earlier it could be argued, with Cicero and others in the events surrounding Caesar and the destruction of the Republic.

Even at the onset of Constantius I's reign, the monotheistic overlay of the constituent cultures was proving insufficiently cohesive and the Empire was beginning to break up into old cultural alignments. (This seems to indicate a relative immutability of cultures.)

The Christian Donatists of North Africa were signalling the cultural embarkation of the ancient Libyan (Carthaginian/Egyptian) alignment.

In the East, Mycenean/Greek/Anatolian alignment was drifting from the Roman (Cretan/Anatolian) seat. This process would continue until there was, not one, but three forms of monotheism based on Roman, Greek and Egyptian /Judaic forms.

The latter emerged in a flood from the North African dissidents at the same time as the Roman/Byzantine split, and would pincer the two other monotheisms on the east and west in a huge Southern Mediterranean crescent.

Under Emperor Julianus (reigned 361-363 AD), an attempt was made to stem the tide of monotheism by his re-instituting the heliopian cosmogony. He may also have had in mind the weakening of the Christian movement, a not inconsistent strategy, by encouraging its factionalisation and restoring dispossessed Donatists[46].

These were later forcefully suppressed with Augustine's consent who, like Paul, had been a former heliopian.

Darkness Falls – The Cultural Sun is Eclipsed

It is significant that Donatism and Arianism, variants of Christian orthodoxy, both emanated from North African Libya, for both movements sprang from the traditional cultural divide that separated Rome and Carthage, having its mythological roots in the Aeneid.

Though on the surface, both movements differed from Rome on doctrinal grounds, there existed an undercurrent of struggle for factional ascendancy, a primeval divisive characteristic of monotheism arising from its autocratic nature. This characteristic had its cultural opposite in the pluralistic heliopian concept of cultural unification by toleration and incorporation.

This divisive characteristic of monotheism would be manifest throughout the ages in the form of the cultural or religious (holy) war, a phenomenon unknown in the pre-monotheistic heliopian era.

The Donatists ventured with their brand of doctrinal purity and unofficial links with the "circumcelliones", a sort of religious warrior band not unlike the religious warriors of Islam which they were to become, to establish the epicentre of Christian religious power in North Africa.

In this they almost succeeded but they were condemned by Augustine who maintained that a sect confined to Africa could not form exclusively the Christian

Church.[47] Had the Donatists succeeded, the ramifications of subsequent cultural alignments may have been immense.

Augustine's condemnation served only to delay the split in the orthodoxy and the evolution of the Southern Mediterranean brand of monotheism.

Contemporary with the Donatists were the Arians who also were, in essence, monotheistic Christians but with a singular difference.

The Arians grew out of the teachings of Arius (died 335 AD), an Anatolian educated Libyan who taught that the Son of God was different in status from the father.

At a public examination, when asked whether the Son was morally mutable and could have fallen like Lucifer, Arius replied in the affirmative[48]. It is said that Arius began his teachings out of abhorrence for Sabellianism, itself a form of Monarchianism[49] a modalism which was a Christian theological view that excluded plurality from the divine being, either by making Christ a human individual invested with divine power, or by having a unipersonal godhead with three aspects[50].

It had been centred significantly, in Alexandria and at one time in the middle of the century, Libya was completely modalistic. Modalism was the precursor of Islam with its modalistic deity.

Arianism, in denying the same status to the Son as the Father, was not far removed from Modalism and like the Modalists, was repudiated by Rome and declared a heresy. The Donatists were likewise finally condemned at a congress in Carthage in 411 AD by the Roman orthodoxy.

The exclusion of such movements, which found widespread support on the southern shores of the Mediterranean and Anatolia (Bithynia), set the cultural scene for the rise of Islam in the next century in precisely those areas.

It is perhaps not surprising that the northern enemies of Rome, the Germanic Saxon tribes counted many supporters of Arianism among their ranks[51] even after it was proscribed by the Orthodoxy in 381 and 388 ADS.

The Germanic tribes overran Rome in the fifth century AD Faced with hostile monotheistic factions in the Southern Mediterranean and the secession of the Greeks of the Eastern Church, Rome embarked on urgent cultural colonisation of the territory to the north, relying primarily on support of the Gallic Celts who had been most successfully colonised by the Romans and whose priest-oriented culture formed the basis of a religious cultural affinity.

Consequently, France became the religious springboard and surrogate of Rome for the religious conversion of Britain and later, Germany as described in Bede.

Britain, being a cultural mix of Saxon and Celt with a large Roman element as a result of the conquest, would be the natural territory to be converted before attempting Saxon Germany and Central Europe up to the sphere of influence of the Eastern Orthodox Church.

By the eleventh century, this would be accomplished, opening the way for the cultural confrontation between old monotheistic enemies of Christian schism, the Roman Orthodoxy and Islam, now burgeoning in pursuit of temporal power, a far cry from the schisms of their infancies.

The forces of Islam had already tried and almost succeeded in preventing Roman orthodox consolidation when, like Hannibal, the Islamic culture with its irresistible tide, flooded into the former Punic colony of Spain in 718 AD The tide line reached Tour in France, to be stemmed by Charles Martel, the Frankish king, at the battle of Poitiers (732 AD) and to be expelled by Charlemagne 150 years later.

As with Pope Gregory, Constantius I and Alfred, Charlemagne was afforded the title "The Great" for services rendered to Rome.

The years during which these megalithic monotheistic cultures were consolidating have become known as the "Dark Ages" characterised by the absence of cultural toleration and enlightenment. Nonetheless, throughout that era, which must stand as tribute to the human spirit, the lamps of some heliopians were kept flickering as they kept their counsel.

The filial monotheistic culture was heading for a showdown with the patriarchal though younger monotheistic culture. Jews, reflections of this tradition would become victims of the confrontation and would be in the sphere of Christendom, and not for the last time, persona non grata bearing collective guilt for the death of the Saviour.

In a similar manner, they were held by Islam to be the cultural progenitors of their cultural adversary. They were resented for being ethnic esotericists, apropos the Southern Mediterranean ethnic grouping which became known as the Arabs and were generally unwelcome in the Islamic sphere.

These circumstances found the Jewish culture as bedfellow of the heliopian and allied cultural remnants that were to bring about the flowering of Greco-Roman concepts and a semblance of nascent cultural plurality of the

Renaissance. This was a process that took several centuries on a temporal time scale though a mere breath in Culture's eternity.

References Chapter 10

[1] Rev A. J. Church Aeneid, Stories from Virgil, pages 28, 34 and 33

[2] Ibid, page 87

[3] ibid, page 92

[4] ibid, page 92

[5] ibid, pages 7, 33 and 255

[6] ibid, page 130

[7] ibid, page 144

[8] ibid, page 150, 263

[9] J. Ferguson, The Religions of the Roman Empire, page 30

[10] ibid, page 15

[11] M. Baigent, R. Leigh and H. Lincoln, The Holy Blood and the Holy Grail

[12] R. Higgins, The Archaeology of Minoan Crete, page 59

[13] J. Ferguson, The Religions of the Roman Empire, page 33

[14] S. E. Winbolt, Britain Under the Romans, page 105

[15] W. G. De Burgh, The Legacy of the Ancient World, page 341

[16] Apuleus, The Golden Ass, Trans: R. Graves, page 270

[17] J. Ferguson, The Religions of the Roman Empire, page 32

[18] S. E. Winbolt, Britain Under the Romans, page 105

[19] Ibid, pages 104-106

[20] Ibid, page 105

[21] J. Ferguson, The Religions of the Roman Empire, page 45

[22] ibid, page 82

[23] Lucian Satirical Sketches, Trans: P. Turner

[24] J. Ferguson, The Religions of the Roman Empire, page 81

[25] W. G. De Burgh, The Legacy of the Ancient World, page 71

[26] J. Ferguson, The Religions of the Roman Empire, page 45

[27] E. Pagels, The Gnostic Gospels, page XXI

[28] S. E. Winbolt, Britain Under the Romans, page 109

[29] Ibid, page 110

[30] J. Hadfield, Dreams and Nightmares, pages 160-166

[31] Chambers Encyclopaedia, Vol 10, Page 712b

[32] Lucian Satirical Sketches, Trans: P. Turner, page 56

[33] 'W. G. De Burgh, The Legacy of the Ancient World, Vol 1, page 51'

[34] J. Ferguson, The Religions of the Roman Empire, page 233

[35] ibid, page 340

[36] ibid, page 112

[37] ibid, page 112

[38] Sir A. E. Wallis, Budge Tutankhamen, page 44

[39] J. Ferguson The Religions of the Roman Empire page 125

[40] Elaine Pagels, The Gnostic Gospels, page 18

[41] ibid, page XX1X

[42] ibid, page 16

[43] M. Baigent, R. Leigh and H. Lincoln, The Holy Blood and the Holy Grail, page 326

[44] Chamber's Encyclopaedia, Vol 4, page 601b

[45] The Holy Blood and the Holy Grail M.Baigent, R. Leigh, H. Lincoln, page 326

[46] ibid, 12, page 144b, 9, 476

[47] M. Grant, The Fall of the Roman Empire, A Reappraisal, page 321

[48] ibid, 1, 608a

[49] ibid, 12, 144b

[50] ibid, 9, 476

[51] M. Grant, The Fall of the Roman Empire, A Reappraisal, page 321

Epilogue

This epilogue has been added to further explain certain topics that were raised in the text. The more percipient readers will have realised that even though the struggles between Heliopianism and Autocratic Monotheism are described as eternal due to their ling cultural time scales, there will in fact be an end point to these battles when perhaps human consciousness reaches its apotheosis and maybe unites with the subconscious. The latter cannot be regarded in any way as being evil for C.G. Jung has demonstrated in his 'Psychology and Alchemy' that the anima in the male of the human species can, though initially opposed by the consciousness can ultimately cure the psychosis of a patient by influencing and creating the patient's dream symbolism. The same presumably applies to the female of the species where the animus and animas are correspondingly exchanged.

In the biblical tale of the defeat of the angels of light by the angels loyal to Yahweh we see, possibly, an early form of the forces of Autocratic Monotheism defeating Heliopianism. Though the biblical texts are thought to have been written around 300 BC it is clear that there is an often used mechanism, as we have seen, of cultural appropriation, the concept of 'Angels' had their inception in the Zoroastrian religion of Persia circa 500 BC. This is another case where a culture, having its inception at the same time as the Babylonian exile of the Jewish culture has interacted.

In the biblical story of the Garden of Eden, Adam and Eve are admonished for eating the fruit of the (sacred) Tree of Knowledge. The tree is almost certainly the ancient architype of the Tree of Life the giver of all life and the extant in all the Ancient Mediterranean Cultures. It embodies the myth of Etana, concerning the eagle (the symbol of upper ancient Egypt) and the serpent (the symbol of lower Egypt or the Delta). The serpent is cast as the tempter and the eagle does not appear for obvious reasons. The eating of the forbidden fruit of knowledge (a characteristic of Autocratic Monotheism) could be interpreted as the early stirrings in the human species in its evolvement from animal to human of human consciousness. Some would even go as far as to suggest that the Story represented some sort of interference in the species that started the whole process of macrocosmic man's path to consciousness. The battles between Heliopianism and Autocratic Monotheism have seen Man's consciousness increase over the millennia. The end of the battles maybe when the Gilgamesian description of his being two third human and one third god is part of a progression of the divine aspect of macrocosmic man. By that time, Man, as we have seen, will have left Mother Earth to explore the Stars, the Home of the Gods.